The Jews of Vienna, 1867–1914: Assimilation and Identity

SUNY Series in Modern Jewish History
Paula E. Hyman and Deborah Dash Moore, Editors

The Jews of Vienna, 1867–1914: Assimilation and Identity

Marsha L. Rozenblit

State University of New York Press
Albany

Published by
State University of New York Press, Albany

© 1983 State University of New York

All rights reserved

Printed in the United States of America

No part of this book may be used or reproduced in any manner whatsoever without written permission except in the case of brief quotations embodied in critical articles and reviews.

For information, address State University of New York Press, State University Plaza, Albany, N.Y., 12246

Library of Congress Cataloging in Publication Data

Rozenblit, Marsha L., 1950–
The Jews of Vienna, 1867–1914.

Bibliography: p. 251
Includes index.
1. Jews—Austria—Vienna—Social conditions.
2. Jews—Austria—Vienna—Cultural assimilation.
3. Vienna (Austria)—Social conditions. 4. Vienna (Austria)—Ethnic relations. I. Title.
DS135.A92V559 1984 305.8′924′043613 83–17885
ISBN 0–87395–844–6
ISBN 0–87395–845–4 (pbk.)
10 9 8 7 6 5 4 3 2 1

For My Mother
Reba Deener Rozenblit

Contents

Acknowledgments

My interest in the Jews of Vienna began in the summer of 1975 when I was searching for a dissertation topic and Deborah Dash Moore suggested that I work on the problem of Jewish assimilation in Vienna. In all the years of work on the dissertation and subsequent book, the Jews of Vienna have provided me with a constant source of intellectual stimulation, pleasure, and excitement. My teachers at Columbia University—Zvi Ankori, Ismar Schorsch, Naomi Cohen—taught me how to apply the standards of critical scholarship to the study of the Jewish past, and I hope that this book lives up to their expectations. Despite his initial skepticism of quantified methods, my dissertation sponsor Istvan Deak always supported and encouraged my work. His sensitive understanding of Jewish assimilation, his thorough knowledge of Habsburg Vienna, and his gracious wit saved me from many errors and prodded me to conceptualize masses of data. Above all, Paula Hyman has been a crucial mentor and friend. I thank her for our lively discussions of Jewish social mobility and Jewish social history, for her model of fine scholarship, for her continuous scholarly advice and support, and most of all, for her warm friendship.

Many archives and archivists extended their hospitality and assistance. Daniel Cohen, Aryeh Segall, and Hadassah Assouline of the Central Archives for the History of the Jewish People in Jerusalem made the beautifully catalogued Viennese Jewish Community collection readily available to me and made my time in Jerusalem so pleasurable. Yaakov Zabach carted truckloads of material from the warehouse to the archives for me with a great deal of humor and warmth. In Vienna, Herr Jabloner and Frau Elisabeth Weiss graciously allowed me to use the birth, marriage, and conversion records of the *Israelitische Kultusgemeinde.* I would also like to thank Dr. Oskar Schneider and Dr. Gehrholdt of the *Stadtschulrat der Stadt Wien* for allowing me to use the *Gymnasium* and *Mädchen-Lyzeum* registration records from the late nineteenth century, and Dr. Fenzl of the Catholic Archdiocese of Vienna for allowing me to use the baptismal records of nine parishes in the city. Grants and fellowships from the Whiting Foundation in 1976–77, from the National Foundation for Jewish Culture and the Memorial Foundation for Jewish Culture in 1976–77 and 1977–78, and the University of Maryland General Research Board in the summer of 1981 enabled me to make two research trips to Jerusalem and Vienna.

My colleagues in the History Department at the University of Maryland, College Park, provided an especially conducive environment for my scholarship. I thank my chairman Emory Evans for his faith in me and for his generous support of my work, and my colleagues Ira Berlin and Gabrielle Spiegel for reading the manuscript and offering suggestions for improving the organization and style of the book. I have had the pleasure of using the scholarly facilities of the Library of Congress since 1978. My friends on "D Deck" encouraged me during the difficult process of converting a dissertation into a book. Aileen Arnold typed the manuscript with accuracy and enthusiasm. Susan Suarez and Peggy Gifford of SUNY Press have been extremely gracious and helpful. The Cartographic Services Laboratory of the University of Maryland prepared the maps for this volume.

Finally, I would like to thank my family. My husband Kenneth Holum has been my strictest and most important critic. A historian of Late Antiquity, he took time out from his own busy schedule to read my manuscript, force me to clarify my thoughts, avoid logical inconsistencies, and vastly improve my prose. At the same time, his pride in my work sustained me through the difficulties of writing and revising. Words can never adequately express my gratitude for all he has done for me. His daughter Katy Holum has also encouraged me warmly. My parents were the ones responsible for instilling in me a love for the Jewish people and a passionate interest in understanding the Jewish past. My father, a survivor of Auschwitz who died when I was ten, enabled me to feel the pain of the Holocaust and the power of the Jewish will to survive. My mother, an ethnic Jew from Brooklyn, taught me about the nature of Jewishness. Her enormous pride in my accomplishments has always enabled me to go further. With her plucky spirit, her courage, and her love in the face of a difficult life, she has always been the most important model in my life. Because she has made everything possible, it is to her that I dedicate this book.

M.L.R.
Silver Spring, Md.

June 1983

List of Abbreviations

CAHJP	Central Archives for the History of the Jewish People, Jerusalem
CZA	Central Zionist Archives, Jerusalem
JV	*Jüdisches Volksblatt*
JZ	*Jüdische Zeitung*
LBIYB	*Leo Baeck Institute Yearbook*
MITOIU	*Mittheilungen der Oesterreichisch-Israelitischen Union*
MONOIU	*Monatsschrift der Oesterreichisch-Israelitischen Union*
NZ	*National-Zeitung*
NNZ	*Neue National-Zeitung*
Öst. Stat.	*Oesterreichische Statistik*
OW	*Oesterreichische Wochenschrift*
SE	*Selbstemancipation*
SJSW	*Statistisches Jahrbuch der Stadt Wien*
ZDSJ	*Zeitschrift für Demographie und Statistik der Juden*

List of Tables

List of Maps

List of Maps

1. *Introduction*

TO MENTION VIENNA in the waning decades of the Habsburg Monarchy is to evoke images of hedonistic gaiety, of the dethroning of the traditional values of Western culture, and of the birth of modernism. The aging Emperor Franz Joseph seemed to rule forever, a symbol of the apparent permanence of the old order. In the same city, meanwhile, Sigmund Freud probed the dark undersides of the human psyche, and Arthur Schnitzler's plays exposed the sexual framework of human relations. Karl Kraus satirized savagely the frivolities of bourgeois life, and Arnold Schoenberg revolutionized music by inventing a twelve-tone scale.[1] In the "Gay Apocalypse" of fin-de-siècle Vienna, the bourgeoisie loved waltzes and whipped cream while the members of the *Jung Wien* (Young Vienna) literary circle concerned themselves with literary aesthetics and symbolic meaning, describing, in the words of the historian Carl Schorske, "the social matrix in which so much of twentieth-century subjectivism took form."[2] Late nineteenth-century Vienna gave birth as well to rowdy, irrational, mass movements which would typify life in the twentieth century. The scene of violent antisemitism, repressed class conflict, and hysterical, chauvinistic nationalism, Vienna was the city in which the young Adolf Hitler learned important political lessons.[3]

Vienna has also become a symbol of the ability of Jews to participate in German culture, and to play a leading role in its avant-garde.[4] Perhaps even more than in the dizzy atmosphere of Weimar Berlin, Jews participated beyond their numbers in Viennese German culture, especially in its modernist development. In Vienna, Jews were both the producers and consumers of culture. The German Jewish novelist Jakob Wassermann, visiting Vienna for the first time in 1898, remarked that "all with whom I came into intellectual or friendly contact were Jews."[5] Jews provided an educated audience for the new literature and music.[6] Moreover, most of the members of the *Jung Wien* literary circle, including Arthur Schnitzler, Stefan Zweig, Karl Kraus, Peter Altenberg, Hermann Bahr, and Richard Beer-Hofmann, were Jews. Gustav Mahler and Arnold Schoenberg, both Jewish converts to

Christianity, composed works critical for the development of modern music. Non-Jewish writers, artists, and musicians were likewise plentiful, but the prominence of Jews in Viennese cultural life has prompted many historians to credit Viennese creativity to the presence of Jews. Hans Kohn, for example, argues that "Vienna at the turn of the century owes its intellectual character for the most part to men of Jewish origin."[7]

The profusion of Jewish literary and musical talent in late imperial Vienna is difficult to explain,[8] but it certainly depended on the fact that these writers and musicians and their Jewish audience had achieved a high level of assimilation into Viennese culture and society. The achievements of Freud, Schnitzler, Mahler, and other cultural giants have led scholarly and non-scholarly observers alike to conclude that indeed virtually the entire Viennese Jewish community had successfully and almost totally assimilated.[9] Jewish cultural luminaries thus represent the triumph of assimilation, the process by which Jews shed their traditional values and particularist modes of behavior, and embraced the modern secular world. The experiences of a few famous men have become paradigmatic for all Jews.

Extrapolating from the experiences of famous Jews in order to evaluate the assimilation of all Viennese Jews is one-sided and inadequate. Such methods place too much emphasis on the social patterns of only one group of Jews, and do not focus sufficient attention on how all Jews—the non-elite, the inarticulate, ordinary men and women—assimilated into European society and culture in the nineteenth century. Certainly many individuals of Jewish origin participated in German culture, but one must not judge Jewish assimilation into European society on the basis of these intellectuals alone. Instead, an analysis of the social and economic factors which led to the integration, but not necessarily the total assimilation, of the broad spectrum of Jews into European society at the end of the nineteenth century is in order.

Such an analysis for Viennese Jewry will produce some interesting conclusions. This book, a quantitative study of ordinary Jews who only appear in birth, marriage, and tax records, will reveal the diverse composition of Viennese Jewry and the limits which these Jews imposed on assimilation in order to remain Jews. The Jews of Vienna were immigrants or the offspring of immigrants who had arrived in the second half of the nineteenth century. The urban environment facilitated their rapid transformation, and for the most part they became typical Viennese burghers, but by no means did the urban setting lead to total assimilation and the end of Jewish group identity. On the contrary, in Vienna, Jews created patterns of economic and social behavior which continued to mark them as Jews both to themselves and to the outside world. Jews experienced assimilation in the company of other Jews. By living in predominantly Jewish neighborhoods, for example, and associating mostly with each other, Jews in Vienna prevented the kind of assimilation which might have led to the dissolution of the Jewish group. Jews did assimilate, but they also devised new ways of asserting Jewish identity, including Zionism and diaspora Jewish nationalism, which both perpetuated and justified Jewish distinctiveness.

The term "assimilation" with which this book deals is, to be sure, a problematic one. The word has tended to have negative connotations. The Zionists used it as a term of contempt, implying traitorous behavior toward the Jewish people, and cowardly subservience to gentile culture. In this book, however, the word assimilation will appear in a neutral sense, as American sociologists have used it. The most satisfactory definition is the one offered by Milton Gordon, who argued in his book *Assimilation in American Life* (1964) that assimilation is really a continuum. The first step in the process is acculturation, or cultural assimilation, the adoption of the cultural mores of the general society by the minority group. An ethnic group acculturates by adopting the dress, recreational tastes, economic patterns, language, cultural baggage, and political views of the general society without necessarily losing its sense of group identity. Acculturation, he emphasizes, does not *ipso facto* lead to total assimilation and group disappearance. One can adopt the economic, political, and cultural patterns of the general society and yet still maintain primary contacts—friendships, associations, and marriage and family ties—primarily with one's own group, thereby assuring the continued existence of that group.[10]

Total assimilation occurs, in Gordon's view, when the minority group fuses with the majority. This fusion takes place only if the host society is receptive to the ethnic group and relatively free from prejudice against it, and if there is considerable intermarriage between the two groups. Thus "marital assimilation" is the final stage in the assimilation continuum. According to Gordon, the key intermediary stage between acculturation and marital assimilation is "structural assimilation," that is, the establishment of extensive networks of primary relationships, friendships, and other social contacts between majority and minority groups. Through structural assimilation, "the keystone of the arch of assimilation," and intermarriage, a minority group loses its ethnic coherence and tends to become indistinguishable from the larger society. Structural assimilation leads to the disappearance of the ethnic group and its culture.[11]

Gordon's terminology seems appropriately flexible and precise, and it will therefore appear in this book. The term assimilation will refer loosely to the entire continuum from acculturation through intermarriage and disappearance. The more technical expressions "acculturation" and "structural assimilation" will also be applied in Gordon's sense.

The course of Jewish assimilation in nineteenth-century Europe from acculturation to group disappearance has usually been linked with urbanization, with the movement of Jews from the small towns of Eastern or Central Europe into cities and metropolitan areas. Freed from traditional restrictions on economic activity and domicile, late nineteenth-century Jews sought the greater social, economic, and educational opportunities which only the city could offer. In the cities, released from the restraints on personal life-style imposed by a small-town environment, Jews abandoned traditional economic, social, and religious patterns and assimilated into bourgeois society. Jews entered new professions, pursued secular education, and achieved a higher level of social intercourse with gentiles than ever before. The opportunities of urban life made Jewish assimilation theoretically open-ended.

The noted early twentieth-century Jewish sociologist Arthur Ruppin argued that "large towns are one of the great factors of assimilation—veritable hotbeds of the process—which goes on more actively and more rapidly there than in any other part of the country." [12] Ruppin feared that intermarriage and conversion, both more common in the city than elsewhere, would cause the disappearance of the Jewish people. Large cities were particularly dangerous, he insisted, because of the greater social interaction of Jews with non-Jews precipitated by the urban economy and common educational opportunities, as well as weaker church control than in towns and countryside, and the urban tolerance for diversity. In the cities, the bonds of the Jewish community were loosened and the Jews were susceptible to outside influence, with assimilation and communal dissolution the consequence. Ruppin recognized that antisemitism served to stem Jewish assimilation, but he nevertheless feared that Jews would only convert to Christianity in order to enjoy the benefits which the dominant culture could bestow.[13] Thus he declared: "Between the two millstones of anti-Semitism and assimilation, Judaism is in danger of being destroyed." [14]

Ruppin's pessimistic assessment of the impact of urbanization on Jewish identity makes the study of Jewish assimilation in Vienna particularly exciting and important. Vienna affords the historian an excellent opportunity to test Ruppin's theories and to analyze the collective nature of Jewish assimilation. The large size of Vienna and her Jewish community, the diverse origins of that Jewish community, and the heat of the antisemitic oratory in the city make Vienna a perfect case study of Jewish assimilation. Moreover, in Vienna it is possible to study the impact of the urban environment on the assimilation of all Jews, not just the prominent elite. The ready availability of sources which lend themselves to statistical analysis enables the historian to analyze the transformations which occurred in Jewish social and economic behavior and the mechanisms which the average Jew devised to ensure Jewish group survival. The understanding which such analysis provides for Vienna could easily be applied to Berlin, Budapest, Prague, and other Central European cities.

Vienna certainly exemplifies the kind of *Grossstadt* (metropolis) Ruppin had in mind when he spoke of the dangers for Jews of metropolitan life. In the second half of the nineteenth century, Vienna was one of the most cosmopolitan cities of Europe as well as one of the largest, with a population of almost two million. As the actual capital of large, polyglot, and multinational Austria-Hungary (even though Budapest counted legally as the second capital), Vienna was the center of political power and wealth in the Austro-Hungarian Monarchy. Its intellectual preeminence and economic opportunities made it an exciting place to live in, both for its native population and for the immigrants—Jews and non-Jews alike—who streamed into it.[15] Certainly it abounded in opportunities for Jewish assimilation.

In contrast to the situation in other Central European *Grossstädte,* however, the large Viennese Jewish community was composed of immigrants or their children who came from a wide range of linguistic, cultural, and religious backgrounds and who consequently coped with the enticements of Vienna in diverse ways. Numbering almost 200,000 by World War I, the Jewish community of Vienna had become the largest Jewish community in Western or Central Europe. Jews from the Austrian provinces of Bohemia, Moravia, and Galicia, and from Hungary, began flocking to Vienna when the Austrian government lifted Jewish residential restrictions after the Revolution of 1848.[16] These immigrants were both rich and poor, urban and rural, traditional and already assimilated, German- or Yiddish-speaking. Many sought total assimilation; others were committed to the preservation of Jewishness in its religious or national guise. Their different expectations and goals made for a rich and varied response to Vienna.

Finally, the strength of antisemitic politics in turn-of-the-century Vienna[17] underscores both the substantial obstacles as well as the potential goads to Jewish assimilation over which Ruppin anguished. The Christian Social Party, which dominated the City Council after 1895, demanded the elimination of the Jews from public life and successfully used aggressive antisemitic oratory to attract middle-class voters, angry with economic modernization or political Liberalism, into its camp. Christian Social Mayor Karl Lueger (1897–1910) never fulfilled his antisemitic promises, but the vitality of the antisemitic movement persuaded some Jews to convert to Christianity, and at the same time made total assimilation virtually impossible, even for those who devoutly desired it. Antisemites continued to remind the Jews, including the already baptized, of their Jewishness.

Certainly the Jews who migrated to Vienna from traditional or even nontraditional homes in Bohemia, Moravia, Galicia, and Hungary eagerly acculturated. Most ceased to dress, talk, and behave like small-town "shtetl" Jews and became European burghers; they abandoned Yiddish for German, traditional Jewish names for proper German ones, Jewish costumes for the styles of nineteenth-century Europe. They exchanged traditional Jewish economic functions for modern urban roles, sometimes becoming highly successful businessmen, industrialists, and professionals. They identified with Habsburg Austria, with the German Liberal Party that had brought them emancipation (even after the party abandoned them in the antisemitic fin-de-siècle), and especially with German culture. They attended the *Gymnasium* and university in record numbers, imbibed Western cultural values there, and participated well beyond their numbers in the Viennese population as producers and consumers of German culture.

Some Viennese Jews went beyond acculturation. For some, especially in the upper classes, Jewish identity was often attenuated, and apart from constant antisemitic reminders the only tie to it was, in the words of the writer Vicki Baum, a "little, Jewish" grandfather.[18] Most Viennese Jews who wrote memoirs came from assimilated backgrounds. The journalist Arnold Höllriegel noted, "I considered myself a German, my Judaism meant little to me." [19]

In particular, many of these well-to-do, articulate Jews abandoned Jewish religious practice. Gertrude Berliner, for example, noted in her memoirs that she grew up in an assimilated environment replete with Christmas tree, Easter eggs, and visits to the Catholic church with the maid.[20] Describing her childhood in Vienna, Toni Cassirer, the wife of philosopher Ernst Cassirer, remarked that "we were raised without religion. Father's family hadn't observed the rituals for three generations. . . ." [21] The playwright Arthur Schnitzler, despite his avowed Jewish self-consciousness, recalled the almost total absence of Jewish observance in his family, which barely observed Yom Kippur, the Day of Atonement and holiest day of the Jewish year. Although his grandmother fasted and prayed, the others celebrated the day "mainly for her sake, and after her death solely out of a feeling of reverence for her." Her generation fasted on Yom Kippur and ate Matzah on Passover, but "the generation which followed . . . tended to display indifference to the spirit of Jewish religion and opposition, sometimes even a sarcastic attitude to its formalities." [22] On Schnitzler's thirteenth birthday, his family deliberately avoided any Jewish rituals, but did give him important presents: a set of German classics, a gold watch, and a few ducats.[23] Despite his affirmation of Jewishness, Sigmund Freud held a negative attitude toward all observances of Jewish religious life, and no Jewish rituals were practiced in the Freud household.[24]

Some of Vienna's most assimilated Jews took the final steps to total assimilation. Vienna had the highest conversion rate in Europe. Gustav Mahler, Arnold Schoenberg, Otto Weininger, and Karl Kraus only represent the most famous examples of the attempt to break all ties with the Jewish past through conversion to Christianity. Many ordinary Jews converted in order to further their careers or marry gentiles and disappear into Viennese society. Of course the final ingredient in total assimilation—unprejudiced acceptance—was never widely available to the Jews in Vienna.

Along with the apparent success with which Viennese Jews outwardly acculturated, and with which some of their numbers almost totally assimilated, the Jews of Vienna continued to exist as a self-consciously distinct group on the urban scene. Arthur Ruppin's position was overly pessimistic. The following pages will demonstrate that if the urban environment facilitated cultural assimilation, it also provided the necessary demographic foundation for continued Jewish identity and the assertion of Jewish pride. In the city, Jews may have abandoned many of the traditional forms which had typified their communal life for centuries in Central and Eastern Europe. But they did not necessarily assimilate fully into the urban society into which they had moved. On the contrary, in Vienna, and presumably elsewhere as well, Jews created new patterns of Jewish behavior which differed from traditional ones but were nonetheless distinctively Jewish.

One interesting example of new, but identifiably Jewish behavior patterns can be found in the realm of occupation. Traditionally, Jews had engaged in independent trade and commerce, vocations which were regarded as typically Jewish. The Jews in Vienna, given greater economic opportunities, abandoned the old Jewish professions. Instead of assimilating into the economic mainstream, however, they chose a new role as salaried employees in business and industry. Since few non-Jewish Viennese worked as non-governmental clerks, salesmen, or managers, and since many Jews were thus employed, a new identifiably Jewish occupation had been created.

Moreover, not all Jews abandoned Jewish religious practice. Unfortunately, quantifiable data on Jewish religious observance is unavailable. But the memoir literature indicates that although many Jews modified their religious observances, they continued to celebrate certain important Jewish rites. Ernst Waldinger, for example, whose grandparents had been extremely Orthodox Galician Jews, remembered that his father had worked on Saturday when he was a boy. Nevertheless, the family celebrated Jewish holidays, went to the synagogue on Friday night after his mother lit candles, and saw to it that the boy received a good Jewish education. When Waldinger was a teenager, his father returned to a traditional synagogue, but the youth felt uncomfortable there.[25] The Nobel-Prize-winning writer Elias Canetti also recalled how he was sent to Hebrew school to learn the prayers "so that the fathers or grandfathers could reap honors with us in temple." [26] The Canettis were not particularly religious Sephardim from Bulgaria who lived in Vienna from 1913 to 1916, but they concerned themselves, to some extent at least, with instilling the Jewish tradition in the young Elias.

Most importantly, Jews erected barriers to structural assimilation and attendant group disappearance by associating primarily with other Jews. Even the assimilated intellectuals discussed above traveled in almost exclusively Jewish circles. The writer Stefan Zweig, for example, noted that nine-tenths of his friends were other bourgeois Jews.[27] Arthur Schnitzler moved "in the solid Jewish bourgeois circles," [28] and Sigmund Freud also associated almost entirely with other Jews. Only a few of Freud's disciples were not Jewish. Freud's son Martin recalled that all the Freuds had Jewish friends and business associates, and consulted Jewish doctors and lawyers.[29] Freud felt most at ease in the company of other Jews. With them he shared "the clear consciousness of an inner identity, the familiarity of the same psychological structure." [30] And Theodor Herzl, the founder of political Zionism, generalizing from his own experience as an assimilated Viennese Jew, wrote in *The Jewish State* (1896):

> We know that, with the exception of the wealthiest, Jews have almost no social relations with Gentiles. In some countries those Jews who do not support a few dinner-table parasites, spongers and flunkeys have no Gentile acquaintances whatever. The ghetto continues to exist within.[31]

Although Herzl may have exaggerated for dramatic effect, assimilated Jews did associate with other assimilated Jews. By the same token, all Viennese Jews, whatever their level of acculturation or assimilation, experienced a primarily Jewish social life. The Jews of Vienna lived largely in Jewish neighborhoods. When they attended

Gymnasium and university, which they did in numbers far exceeding their proportion in the population, they did so largely in the company of other Jews. Moreover, alarmists notwithstanding, intermarriage and conversion rates were not particularly high. And, finally, the Jews established an extensive network of Jewish organizations which permitted them to engage in philanthropic or political activity, proclaim a wide range of Jewish identities from assimilationism to Zionism and Jewish nationalism, and come into contact primarily with other Jews of similar social backgrounds. In this way, Jews institutionalized their separateness and created forums for publicizing Jewish identity in Vienna.

One might argue that the hostile environment of Vienna rendered Jews incapable of assimilating fully, in effect that antisemitism prevented the complete disappearance of a separate Jewish identity. Antisemitism could easily hinder the formation of Jewish-gentile friendships and consequent structural assimilation. Certainly many Jews were aware of the importance of antisemitism to their own rising Jewish consciousness. Schnitzler opened his memoirs by insisting that

> It was not possible, especially not for a Jew in public life, to ignore the fact that he was a Jew; nobody else was doing so, not the Gentiles and even less the Jews. You had the choice of being counted as insensitive, obtrusive and fresh; or of being oversensitive, shy and suffering from feelings of persecution. And even if you managed somehow to conduct yourself so that nothing showed, it was impossible to remain completely untouched.[32]

Of his year in military service in the army medical corps he wrote:

> Among the army medical students, as in almost every unit of those serving for one year only—and where not?—there was a . . . clear-cut division between Gentiles and Jews, or, since the national factor was being stressed more and more, between the Aryan and Semitic elements, and any private socializing was very narrowly circumscribed.[33]

Protesting (in the 1880s) that "not that any of us took it very much to heart," he did assert that his family persisted in its "stubborn emphasis on [Jewish] racial solidarity."[34] Stefan Zweig, preferring poetry to politics, professed to be oblivious to the antisemitism of Vienna,[35] but others felt a need to defend their Jewish origins in the face of antisemitic attack. Freud's biographer Ernest Jones argued that Freud's Jewish identity consisted of "the inherited capacity of Jews to stand their ground and maintain their position in life in the face of surrounding opposition or hostility."[36] Freud himself disingenuously remarked on the occasion of being honored by B'nai B'rith that "my service to the Jewish cause is confined to the single point that I have never disowned my Jewishness." [37]

Antisemitism may have accentuated the Jewish consciousness of many, but it did not create Jewish identity. A positive Jewish will to survive was also manifest in fin-de-siècle Vienna. Sigmund Freud, more than any other famous Viennese Jew, exemplified this proud assertion of Jewishness. Freud rejected Judaism as a religion, but he felt deep emotional bonds with the Jewish people and pride in his Jewish identity and heritage.[38] He was a member of B'nai B'rith from 1897, honorary president of the Vienna branch of YIVO (Yiddish Research Institute) from 1919, a collector of Jewish jokes and anecdotes, and a staunch defender of Jewish honor.[39] In 1939 he told the London branch of YIVO: "You no doubt know that I gladly and proudly acknowledge my Jewishness though my attitude toward any religion, including ours, is critically negative." [40]

Thus, in contrast to Ruppin's dire warnings, while urbanization certainly facilitated greater integration of Jews into European society, it also created a situation in which Jews could redefine themselves as a group within European society. The process of urbanization itself provided the impetus for forming new types of Jewish group identity and caused Jews to retreat partially from the push for assimilation at work since the beginning of the nineteenth century.

The following pages will focus on key elements in the process of assimilation and on the conscious and unconscious mechanisms by which Jews preserved their group identity and ensured their collective continuity. Discussion of Jewish migration to Vienna provides the necessary demographic framework for this study. The divergent backgrounds and expectations of Jewish and non-Jewish immigrants to Vienna can partially explain the distinctive Jewish modes of accommodation to urban life. In order to understand the ways in which Jews made use of urban opportunities, this book will analyze the transformation of Jewish economic preference, the role of the *Gymnasium* in ensuring social mobility and acculturation, and such attempts at total assimilation as intermarriage and conversion to Christianity. Lastly, this book will explore the brakes which the Jews placed on their assimilation, including the establishment of Jewish neighborhoods, and the creation of a vast network of political, social, religious, and cultural organizations in which Jews could meet each other and assert new forms of Jewish identity.

This study of Viennese Jewry commences in 1867 and terminates in 1914. In 1867, the same year as the Compromise Agreement creating Austria-Hungary, the Austrian government emancipated the Jews, that is, it granted them equal civil, political, and religious rights with all other Austrian citizens. In one stroke the Liberal government removed any remaining medieval disabilities on Jewish occupation, residence, or political and civil rights.[41] Jews now possessed the opportunity to assimilate and indeed the government encouraged them to do so. The encouragement was unnecessary as Austrian and similarly emancipated Hungarian Jews rushed to take advantage of the new opportunities. The beginning of World War I provides a natural terminal date for this study. The war resulted in the dissolution of the Dual Monarchy and the creation of a rump Austrian state in its former German-speaking territories. Moreover, during the war, large numbers of Galician Jews fled to Vienna to escape the onslaught of Russian troops who unleased waves of pogroms against them.[42] The influx of these Galician Jews, combined with the new problems of the Austrian Republic, created a Jewish community which differed markedly from its prewar predecessor.

The analysis of Jewish assimilation between 1867 and 1914 is based primarily on several quantifiable sources: Jewish birth, marriage, and conversion records, the registration records of several *Gymnasien* in the city, and the tax records of the organized Jewish community of Vienna, the *Israelitische Kultusgemeinde,* commonly called the *Gemeinde* or the IKG.[43] Of these, the birth and marriage records are valuable, despite their bias toward the more youthful members of the population, because they provide information on geographical origins, occupation, and residential preference of a cross section of Viennese Jewry. The tax records, on the other hand, contain similar data only on the older and more affluent members of the community. Austrian law required all Jews to belong to the *Gemeinde,* but only those prosperous enough to pay an annual tax of at least 20 Kronen, approximately one-third of Viennese Jewry, were entered in the IKG tax rolls. Samples of birth, marriage, and tax records, the first two cross-sectional and young, the third reflecting the middle and upper classes, provide insight into the origins and social composition of the Viennese Jewish community in a significant period of growth. The *Gymnasium* and conversion records offer specific information on education as a vehicle for social mobility and assimilation, and the extent of total assimilation into Viennese society.

Records such as those studied here appear to contain only bare-bones facts about Viennese Jewry. Nevertheless, close analysis of them reveals a good deal about how assimilation affected all Viennese Jews, not just the articulate elite who wrote memoirs of their own experiences. Memoirs, novels, and newspaper stories, although intimate and lively, permit an understanding of only a thin stratum of Viennese Jews, while the quantitative data enable the historian to understand social forces that affected the entire Jewish community.

On the other hand, mentality, mood, intention, the personal element are difficult to extract from computer printouts but abound in memoirs, novels, and newspaper articles. Neither a close reading of such literature nor a quantitative study offers a comprehensive picture of social change among Viennese Jews; taken together, however, they provide a deeper understanding of Jewish accommodation to modern life.

2. *The Creation of Viennese Jewry: Jewish Migration to Vienna, 1867–1914*

MORE THAN IN MOST European cities, the process of Jewish assimilation in Vienna was intimately connected to the larger phenomena of Jewish migration and urbanization in the nineteenth century. Almost all of the Jewish residents in the Austrian capital were immigrants or the children of immigrants who arrived in the city only after the Austrian government lifted the traditional restrictions on Jewish residence during the Revolution of 1848, and confirmed Jewish residential freedom in the Emancipation of 1867. Eagerly rushing from the small towns and cities of Austria-Hungary to take advantage of the economic and cultural opportunities of the *Grossstadt,* Viennese Jews arrived in the capital with a wide range of prior experiences and expectations of urban life. These Jewish immigrants were very different from gentile immigrants to the city. Moreover, Jews from different provinces of the Dual Monarchy diverged from each other in terms of their wealth, previous urban experience, level of already achieved assimilation, and attitude toward further assimilation. As a result, Jews from Bohemia, Moravia, Galicia, and Hungary experienced Vienna differently. Their backgrounds strongly influenced both their further assimilation and their allegiance to some sort of continued Jewish identity in the Habsburg capital.

Jewish migration from the provinces to Vienna was of course part of two larger population movements of the nineteenth century, the urbanization of Austrians and Europeans generally, and the movement of Central and Eastern European Jews from small towns into the cities and overseas to the United States. In the nineteenth century European cities grew enormously.[1] Men and women left their home communities and moved from villages to towns, from provincial cities to major metropolitan centers. Poor peasants abandoned the land to work in the newly established factories. The middle classes sought

Map 2:1

the greater economic opportunities that only the large cities could offer. Their migration contributed to the transformation of Europe from a largely agricultural society to a commercial, industrial, and urban one.

In Austria in particular, more and more people left the communities in which they enjoyed legal residence rights (*Heimatrecht* or *Zuständigkeit* in Austrian legal parlance),[2] which included the right to receive communal charity and vote in communal elections, in order to move elsewhere, especially to the cities. To clarify this process, a definition of the term "Austria" is in order (see map 2:1). After the Compromise Agreement of 1867, the Habsburg Monarchy became Austria-Hungary, with "Austria" and "Hungary" each managing its own internal affairs, and united only in a common foreign policy and foreign trade, a common army, and in the person of the Emperor Franz Joseph. "Austria" refers to all those provinces which were represented in the Austrian imperial parliament, the *Reichsrat*, in Vienna. Stretching in a large semi-circle around the Hungarian crown lands, "Austria" included the largely German-speaking Alpine provinces of Tirol, Vorarlberg, Salzburg, as well as Upper and Lower Austria, and the Slovene- and German-speaking provinces of Styria and Carinthia. It also included Slovene-speaking Carniola, and other provinces along the Adriatic sea: Gorizia-Gradisca, Istria, Triest, and Dalmatia. Included in Austria were also the Czech- and German-speaking provinces of Bohemia and Moravia, Czech and Polish Silesia, Polish- and Ruthenian-speaking Galicia, and multi-lingual Bukovina. Hungary, a territory much larger than the present people's republic, included the historical lands of the Crown of St. Stephen (including Transylvania), the South Slav areas of Croatia and Slavonia, and the port city of Fiume. Because of the Compromise Agreement, Austria considered Hungarians foreigners.

In contrast to the mid-nineteenth century, when most Austrians resided in the communities in which they had *Heimatrecht*, in 1890 only 64% of all Austrians possessed legal residence rights in the communities in which they lived.[3] In Lower Austria, the province in which Vienna was located, only 41.5% of the 1890 population possessed *Heimatrecht* in the towns and cities in which they resided.[4] Moreover, in the second half of the nineteenth century an ever larger percentage of all Austrians chose to live in cities.[5] In 1843, only 4% of all Austrians lived in cities with over 20,000 inhabitants, but in 1890, 12% did so. In the same period the number of communities with more than 20,000 inhabitants quintupled from seven to thirty-two.[6]

Population growth was particularly vigorous in those cities with over 100,000 residents. In the period between 1869, the first census to count actual and not just legal residents,[7] and 1910, the population of the seven largest cities of Austria—Vienna, Prague, Triest, Lemberg, Graz, Brünn, and Cracow—grew from 7 to 11% of the total Austrian population.[8] Moreover, these cities grew at an extremely rapid rate. Some of this growth was artificially generated by increasingly accurate enumeration and by the annexation of suburbs into the city limits. Even so, most of the major Austrian and Hungarian cities more than doubled their populations in this period. Lemberg, for example, grew from 87,109 in 1869 to 206,113 in 1910.[9] The two Galician cities, Lemberg and Cracow, were the fastest growing cities in Austria. In the forty-one years between 1869 and 1910, the population of Lemberg and Cracow expanded 137% and 205% respectively, or between 3% and 6% a year.[10] Vienna grew 234% in this period, from 607,514 in 1869 to 2,031,498 in 1910,[11] although much of this growth reflects the 1890 incorporation of the suburbs. In Hungary, Budapest's population nearly doubled between 1880 and 1900, growing from 360,551 to 716,376, a rate of nearly 5% a year.[12]

Nineteenth-century Jews were also on the move in Europe generally and in Austria in particular. Escaping poverty and persecution, masses of Jews emigrated from Russia, Rumania, and the Austrian province of Galicia to the United States.[13] Central and Eastern European Jews also flocked to the cities.[14] Traditionally excluded from agricultural occupations, European Jews had always been an urban, rather than a rural group. Nevertheless, living in small towns and acting as middlemen between the urban and rural markets, the Jews had been an integral part of the rural economy. In the course of the nineteenth century, Jews in increasing numbers left the countryside for the larger towns and cities. In Russia, this phenomenon was partly the result of governmental policy to eliminate the Jews from the rural economy and end their supposedly malevolent influence on the peasants.[15] In Austria-Hungary or Germany, the urbanization of the Jews was not caused by any governmental anti-Jewish pressure, but was a spontaneous response to the changes introduced by legal and civil emancipation. Freed from traditional restrictions, and attracted by the greater economic, social, and cultural opportunities elsewhere, Jews successfully created a new life whether in America or in the cities of Germany, Austria-Hungary, and Russia.

Urbanization was the most salient feature of Jewish demographic change in Austria-Hungary in the late nineteenth century. As a result, Jews concentrated more heavily in cities than any other Austrians or Hungarians. Only 10.6% of all Austrians—including the Jews—lived in the ten largest cities of Austria in 1900, but 23.3% of Austrian Jews lived there. Similarly, in Hungary only 6.4% of all Christians lived in the eleven largest cities, but 26.1% of the Jews in 1900 did so.[16] In Galicia in particular Jews much more than non-Jews concentrated in cities. In 1900, only 7.3% of all Galicians (including Jews) lived in the forty cities with over 10,000 inhabitants, but over one-third of all Jews did.[17] Moreover, within most Austrian and Hungarian cities Jews formed a noticeable minority. In western Austrian cities like Vienna, Prague, and Brünn, Jews composed only about 8–9% of the city population, but eastern Austrian cities like Lemberg, Cracow, and Czernowitz were between one-quarter and one-third Jewish, and many county seats in Galicia and Bukovina contained a Jewish majority.[18] The same was true in Hungary, where the county seats had very large Jewish populations, and Budapest, with one-quarter of its population Jews, was often pejoratively called Judapest.[19]

Urban Jewish population growth was most spectacular in Vienna. In 1857, only about 1% of all Austrian Jews lived in the capital; by 1900, 13% of all Austrian Jews were Viennese. Almost no Jews resided in the *Residenzstadt* in 1850, but the community grew at such a rapid rate that by World War I there were almost 200,000 Jews in the city (Table 2:1).[20]

Table 2:1. Jewish Population in Vienna, 1787–1910

Year	Number of Jews	Number of Viennese	Jewish % of Total Population
1787	532 or 230 (1784)	207,405	
1800	903 or 310	231,049	
1830	975 or 1,270	317,768	
1847	1,588 or 4,000*	402,501	
1857	6,217**	284,999** 476,222***	2.2%
1869	40,230[t]	607,514[t]	6.6%[t]
1880	73,222	726,105	10.1%
1890	118,495	1,364,548[tt]	8.7%
1900	146,926	1,674,957	8.8%
1910	175,318	2,031,498	8.6%

* See discussion below.

** The 1857 census counted only the *einheimisch* residents, i.e., those who had Viennese *Heimatrecht.* This number represents only those who had legal domiciliary rights in Vienna.

*** The 1857 census estimate of the number of actual residents in Vienna.

[t] Beginning in 1869 all Austrian censuses enumerated the actual resident population.

[tt] Viennese increase so large over 1880 because of the 1890 incorporation of the suburbs as Districts XI-XIX of the city. Few Jews lived in the outer districts.

Sources: Bevölkerung und Viehstand, 1857, "Nieder-Oesterreich," pp. 2–3; *Bevölkerung und Viehstand,* 1869, Vol. 11 (Nieder-Oesterreich), pp. 2–13; *Öst. Stat.,* 1:2, pp. 2–3; 32:1, pp. 46–47; 63:1, pp. 48–49; N.F. 2:1, p. 33*; *SJSW* (1885), p. 14; *SJSW* (1910), p. 25; Jeiteles, pp. 40–42; Löw, pp. 161–63.

Before the Revolution of 1848 the Imperial Government permitted few Jews to live in Vienna. Certain wealthy Jewish individuals, such as the court factor Samuel Oppenheimer, were "tolerated," that is, given special royal privileges to live in the *Hauptstadt* (capital city), along with members of their families, their servants, and employees.[21] Estimates vary as to the real number of Jews in Vienna during this *Toleranzperiode,* and the two which exist are both probably short of the actual number. Israel Jeiteles, calculating total population from the number of tolerated Jewish families, argued that there were about 1,600 Jews in Vienna in 1847.[22] Akos Löw, however, made a case for double that number. He compared the percentage of recorded Jewish births, deaths, and marriages to those for Viennese generally, and thus derived the percentage and number of Jews in the population at large. He reported that there were about 230 Jews in Vienna in 1784, 310 in 1800, 1,270 in 1830, and approximately 4,000 Jews in the capital in 1848.[23] Since the Jewish birth, death, and marriage rates differed from the general Viennese rates in the later decades of the nineteenth century, in all likelihood they also differed earlier in the century, especially since the pre-1848 community was a wealthy one. It is impossible, however, to arrive at any better estimate of the Jewish population.

In the decades which followed the 1848 lifting of restrictions on Jewish residence in Vienna, and especially after the 1867 emancipation of the Jews, the Jewish population of Vienna grew extremely rapidly (Table 2:2). In the 1860s, the community grew 46% *each year.* The growth rate calculated for the period 1857–1869 is, however, artificially high, since the 1857 census did not count all residents, but only native *(einheimisch)* Jews, always a small percentage of the total Jewish population of the city. During the 1880s, the Viennese Jewish community experienced its largest absolute growth. As the community grew larger, despite a constant influx of newcomers, the relative growth diminished. Even so, until the 1890s, Jewish population grew at a higher rate than that of the general population of Vienna (Table 2:2).[24]

The expansion of the Jewish community was, of course, not the result of natural increase, but of the massive influx of Jews from other parts of the Dual Monarchy.[25] Non-Jews also migrated to Vienna at this time, but immigration provided a much larger proportion of Viennese Jewish population growth than it did in the population at large. At the end of the century, about 45% of all Viennese were native born, but only about 20% of the Jews had been born in the capital.[26]

Jewish immigrants to Vienna may have participated in a larger Austrian population movement, but when they arrived in the city—as indeed after they had lived in the city for decades—they were a unique group, profoundly different from non-Jewish immigrants. Jews migrated for uniquely Jewish reasons, and they came from different areas of Austria-Hungary than did non-Jewish immigrants. Moreover, they moved as families, a common occurrence in Jewish migration, but not nearly so widespread in non-Jewish circles. Finally, unlike most immigrants, Jews were not peasants unaccustomed to city life.

Table 2:2. Growth Rate, Jewish and General Population of Vienna, 1857–1910

Year	Jewish Growth	% Jewish Growth	% Per Year	% General Growth	% Per Year
1857–69	34,013	547%	45.6%	27.6%*	2.3%*
1869–80	32,992	82%	7.5%	19.5%	1.8%
1880–90	45,273	61.8%	6.2%	87.9%**	8.8%**
				12.6%***	1.2%***
1890–1900	28,431	24.0%	2.4%	22.7%	2.3%
1900–1910	24,392	19.3%	1.9%	21.3%	2.1%

* Calculated from estimate of actual population for 1857 and actual population for 1869.

** Growth rate including newly incorporated suburbs.

*** Growth rate in Districts I–X, which had been the entire city of Vienna in the previous census in 1880.

On the contrary, Jews had lived in towns and cities and thus were able to make the necessary adjustments to life in the metropolis more easily than non-Jews. The unique situation of Jewish immigrants was an important factor in their continued distinctiveness in Vienna.

Unlike most cities which only attracted immigrants from their immediate provincial hinterlands, Vienna did draw a diverse immigrant population.[27] But Jewish and gentile immigrants to Vienna came from different areas of the Dual Monarchy. Unfortunately, official statistics did not differentiate between Jews and non-Jews, and thus it is impossible to ascertain the origins of gentiles as distinct from all Viennese. The typical immigrant to Vienna came either from Lower Austria, the province in which Vienna was located, or from Bohemia and Moravia, the Czech lands to the north and northwest of the city (Table 2:3). In 1890, for example, 45% of all Viennese—including the Jews—were native born, and 11% were Lower Austrian. Fully 30% of all Viennese, and 50% of all the immigrants came from Bohemia and Moravia. Virtually no men and women left their homes in the Alpine or coastal provinces, or in Galicia and Bukovina to live in Vienna. Hungarians sometimes moved to the Austrian capital of the Dual Monarchy, and between 7% and 9% of all Viennese had legal residence rights in Hungary.[28]

In order to determine the geographical origins of the entire Jewish community, and thus correct for the youthful bias of the two cross-sectional Jewish populations studied here (grooms and fathers),[29] it was necessary to combine the data from all five sample years and generate some average statistics. According to this 1870–1910 composite (Table 2:4), in contrast to typical Viennese, Jews divided fairly evenly into groups born in Vienna, Bohemia and Moravia, Galicia, and Hungary. On the average, the major difference between the general and the Jewish migration to Vienna lay in the importance of Galicia and Hungary as provinces of origin. Hungary, of secondary significance as the birthplace of all Viennese men and women, was the original home of almost one-quarter of the Jews in the city. Moreover, only 2% of all Viennese—including the Jews—were Galician, but one-fifth of all Viennese Jews were born in that Polish-Ruthene province. Because one-quarter of the Viennese Jewish community had been born in Bohemia and Moravia, it would appear as if these two provinces enjoyed equal significance as recruiting grounds for Jewish and non-Jewish immigrants. In fact, however, half of all immigrants to Vienna but only one-third of the Jewish immigrants (i.e., those not born in Vienna) came from these two provinces. Unlike typical Viennese, the Jews in Vienna almost never were born in Lower Austria, a province in which few Jews had ever lived. Due to the immigrant origins of the Jewish community, half as many

Table 2:3. Place of Birth and Heimatland of Viennese Population, 1880–1910

	1880 N = 726,105		1890 N = 1,364,548		1900 N = 1,674,957		1910 N = 2,031,498	
	Birth	*Heimat*	Birth	*Heimat*	Birth	*Heimat*	Birth	*Heimat*
Vienna	37.4%	35.2%	44.7%	34.9%	46.4%	38.0%	48.8%	55.2%
Other Lower Austria	14.6	13.1	11.4	12.1	11.4	11.4	11.1	8.2
Alpine and Coastal Provinces[t]	7.2	4.3	4.3	4.5	4.3	4.6	4.2	3.2
Bohemia	15.4	18.7	15.7	20.9	14.1	18.4	12.6	11.1
Moravia and Silesia	12.4	14.0	12.0	14.4	12.1	14.5	12.0	10.3
Galicia and Bukovina	1.8	2.1	1.8	2.1	2.2	2.7	2.3	2.4
Hungary		9.2				8.4		7.7
	11.2*		10.1*	11.0**	9.7*		9.0*	
Other Foreign		3.8				2.2		2.0
	100.0%***	100.0%	100.0%	100.0%	100.0%	100.0%	100.0%	100.0%

* Hungarians and Other Foreigners lumped together in statistics on Place of Birth.
** Hungarians and Other Foreigners lumped together in that census.
*** Figures in this and all other tables do not add up to 100 exactly because of rounding error.
[t] Alpine and Coastal Provinces: Upper Austria, Salzburg, Styria, Carinthia, Carniola, Triest, Gorz and Gradisca, Istria, Tirol, Vorarlberg, and Dalmatia.

Sources: Öst. Stat., 1:1, pp. 2–3; 32:2, pp. xxxvi-xxxvii, 1x-1xiii; 64:1, pp. 2–25; N.F. 2:1, pp. 33*, 2–27; *SJSW* (1901), pp. 34–41; (1910) endpaper; (1912), pp. 891–98; Sedlaczek, *Wien,* 1880, Part II, pp. 104–7; Rauchberg, "Der Zug nach der Stadt," p. 162.

Jews as Viennese generally were native-born Viennese. The pattern of Jewish migration to Vienna described here reflected, to some extent, the residential concentration of Austro-Hungarian Jewry generally. In 1857, at the beginning of the migration, 40% of all Jews in the Habsburg Monarchy lived in Hungary, 46% in Galicia and Bukovina, and 13% in Bohemia, Moravia, and Silesia.[30]

Looking at the average picture created here obscures the fact that indeed the Viennese Jewish community was created by three overlapping waves of migration from these different areas of the Dual Monarchy. The youthful bias of the cross-sectional samples provides especially good insight into the changing patterns of Viennese Jewish immigration (Table 2:5). The first Jews in the city, those who possessed imperial patents of toleration, were overwhelmingly Bohemian and Moravian. When residential restrictions were lifted in the 1850s and 1860s, Czech Jews migrated to Vienna in large numbers. They were quickly overtaken, however, by the second wave of migrants, those from Hungary. The Hungarian influx continued through the 1880s but began to taper off due to Magyarization in Hungary in the 1890s and afterwards. The third wave of migration consisted of Jews from Galicia who arrived only in the final decades before the First World War.[31]

Information on the geographical origins of the pre-1848 Jewish community is spotty at best. In the period between 1784, when Emperor Joseph II ordered Jews to begin recording their births, marriages, and deaths,[32] and 1848, the percentage of Czech Jews in the Jewish community of Vienna declined as the percentage of Hungarian Jews increased. In his study of the social structure of

Table 2:4. Place of Birth of Jewish Grooms, Composite, 1870–1910

Land	Number of Grooms	Percent
Vienna	178	20.3
Other Lower Austria	21	2.4
Bohemia	104	11.9
Moravia	129	14.7
Silesia	14	1.6
Galicia	167	19.0
Bukovina	14	1.6
Other Austria	3	0.3
Hungary	204	23.3
Other Foreign*	43	4.9
	N = 877**	100.0%

* "Other Foreign" includes 13 grooms from Germany, 13 from Russia, 5 from Rumania, 8 from the Balkans, and 4 from other areas.

** Differences in Ns and Total Sample Size in this and all subsequent tables caused by missing information.

Table 2:5. Place of Birth of Jewish Fathers, 1869–1910

	Overall* N = 1060	1869 N = 324	1880 N = 146	1890** N = 179	1900 N = 241	1910 N = 170
Vienna	17.6%	21.3%	11.6%	16.8%	16.2%	18.2%
Other Lower Austria	1.2	0.6	—	3.4	0.4	2.9
Bohemia	8.2	8.6	11.0	8.4	7.1	6.5
Moravia	12.5	13.0	15.1	14.0	12.9	7.6
Silesia	0.8	0.3	0.7	1.1	1.7	—
Galicia	18.0	10.5	13.7	15.6	20.7	34.7
Bukovina	1.0	—	1.4	1.1	0.8	2.9
Other Austria	0.4	0.3	—	1.1	—	0.6
Hungary	35.8	42.3	44.5	35.8	33.6	19.4
Other Foreign	4.3	3.1	2.1	2.8	6.6	7.1
	100.0%	100.0%	100.0%	100.0%	100.0%	100.0%

* Overall statistics are based on birthland for 1869, 1880, 1900, and 1910, and on *Heimatland* for 1890, the year in which land of birth was not indicated in the birth records.

** *Heimatland* figures.

Viennese Jews in this period, Akos Löw discovered that, between 1784 and 1806, 20% of the Jews in Vienna were Bohemian or Moravian, 21.3% were Hungarian, 17.8% were native, and 24.7% were of unknown origin. In the twenty years preceding the Revolution of 1848 only 19.7% were Czech, but 33.5% were Hungarians, 22.9% were native-born, and 11.7% were of unknown origins. At this time virtually no Galician Jews lived in Vienna.[33]

By the end of the 1850s, the majority of Jews in Vienna were Hungarian. According to a recent study of the manuscript census for 1857, only about 15% of the Jews in that year came from Moravia, and 4% from Bohemia. Twenty percent of the Jews were native-born, and Galicians accounted for about 10% of the population.[34]

After the Emancipation of the Jews in 1867, Jews streamed into Vienna from Bohemia, Moravia, Hungary, and Galicia, with the Hungarians at the fore. In 1880 (Table 2:5) 26% of Jewish fathers were Bohemian and Moravian, 14% were Galician, and 45%, or almost half, were Hungarian. Hungarian migration accelerated rapidly through the 1880s, then began to taper off in the 1890s and drop considerably by 1910. In 1869, 42% of all Jewish fathers were Hungarian, but in 1910, only 19% were Hungarian.[35] Immigration from Czech lands also continued to decline, and in 1910 half as many fathers were from Bohemia, Moravia, and Silesia as in 1880. Only at the very end of the nineteenth century did Galician Jews begin to move to Vienna in large numbers. By so doing they gradually transformed a Hungarian and Czech community into a Galician one. Only 11% of the Jewish fathers in 1869 were Galician, but by 1910 fully 35% of the fathers were born in Galicia. At the same time, the percentage of native-born Jews, which had declined between 1869 and 1880 because of the influx of immigrants after emancipation, also grew slowly but steadily from 12% in 1880 to 18% in 1910.

These Jewish immigrants came to Vienna to stay. Unlike gentile immigrants, Jews generally migrated with the hope, at least, of finding permanent residence in the city. Most nineteenth-century immigrants moved to towns and cities, and then, more often than not, quickly departed to seek their fortunes elsewhere. Transiency, not permanence, was the hallmark of urban life.[36] Jews, however, rarely possessing the luxury of returning to their former homes, remained in their new locations and made great efforts to adjust to their new life.[37]

Without the manuscript census it is impossible to determine the exact extent of Jewish transiency and persistence. The birth and marriage records do not lend themselves to this kind of analysis. The tax rolls of the *Israelitische Kultusgemeinde* do permit an inquiry into the stability of the Jewish community, but only for the middle and upper classes, the group which was the most likely to remain in the city.[38] Poorer Jews were probably more willing to leave Vienna than the affluent, and thus judging Jewish transiency on the basis of taxpayers alone is somewhat unfair. Unfortunately, there is no way of rectifying the problems with the sources.

The Jews who paid taxes to the *Gemeinde* tended to remain in Vienna a long time. Fully 53.8% of all *Gemeinde* members retained their membership for over ten years, and most of these, or 30.6%, were members for over twenty years.[39] Only 29.5% were members for five years or less. Figures for long-term membership would be higher if statistics were included from beyond 1914, the terminal date of this study. The richest *Gemeinde* members were the most likely to remain in the city. Of those who after an initial tax assessment were reassessed and paid between 100 and 499 Kronen each year to the IKG (N = 114), 78.9% remained *Gemeinde* members more than ten years, and very few (7%) less than five years. Of those whose first assessment was in this bracket, 63.7% remained in the *Gemeinde* more than ten years, and 21% more than 31 years. Death, not transiency, was the primary reason for ending affiliation with the *Gemeinde.*

Unlike many non-Jewish immigrants, most Jews migrated with their families,[40] and not as single individuals. Consequently, Jewish women in Vienna came from the same areas of the Dual Monarchy as Jewish men. Jewish women ignored the "rules" of female migration, and like men, moved long distances from the provinces to Vienna. Gentile women, moving mostly for the purposes of marriage or to work as domestic servants, followed the "rules" and crossed provincial borders much less frequently than men.[41] But Jewish women left their homes and migrated in more or less equal proportion to Jewish men from Bohemia, Moravia, Hungary, and even more distant Galicia (Table 2:6a). Given the general female trend to move shorter distances than men, one might have expected a large contingent of Jewish women from nearby Hungarian territory. In fact, Jewish women migrated from Hungary slightly less often than did Jewish men. On the other hand, Jewish women were just as likely as Jewish men to move to Vienna from Galicia, a trip of much greater length and discomfort than the trip from western Slovakia or Transdanubia in Hungary.

Of course not all Jewish immigrants arrived in Vienna with their families. Fewer Jewish women than men were willing to forego their homes to move to the metropolis. Thus, for example, for every 1,000 Jewish men in Vienna in 1900 there were 996 Jewish women, compared to 1,059 women for every 1,000 men in the population at large in that year.[42] Moreover, because of greater male migration—both into and out of the city—Jewish women (brides and mothers) were twice as likely as Jewish men to be native-born Viennese (Table 2:6b). Nevertheless, given the distance of Jewish migration, the large number of Jewish women who migrated to Vienna attests to the fact that they responded to the same impetus to migration as did Jewish men.

Because Jews and gentiles migrated for different reasons, Jewish men and women migrated from different regions[43] of the various provinces than did non-Jews from the same provinces. The differences were most substantial between Bohemian Jewish and non-Jewish immigrants. Almost none of the Czechs in Vienna were born in

*Table 2:6a. Comparison of Geographical Origins of Mothers and Fathers, 1900 and 1910**
(excluding the Viennese-born)

	1900		1910	
	Fathers N = 202	Mothers N = 75	Fathers N = 139	Mothers N = 117
Other Lower Austria	0.5%	5.3%	3.6%	4.3%
Bohemia	8.4	9.3	7.9	10.3
Moravia & Silesia	17.3	20.0	9.4	9.4
Galicia & Bukovina	25.7	21.3	46.0	47.9
Other Austria	—	2.7	0.7	1.7
Hungary	40.1	38.7	23.7	17.1
Other Foreign	7.9	2.7	8.6	9.4
	100.0%	100.0%	100.0%	100.0%

* The only years in which mothers' place of birth was recorded.

Table 2:6b. Place of Birth of Jewish Brides, Composite, 1870–1910

	Number	Percent
Vienna	339	39.3
Other Lower Austria	24	2.8
Bohemia	65	7.5
Moravia	110	12.8
Silesia	7	0.8
Galicia	123	14.3
Bukovina	13	1.5
Other Austria	2	0.2
Hungary	147	17.1
Other Foreign*	32	3.7
	862	100.0%

* "Other Foreign" includes 12 Germans, 15 Russians, 4 Rumanians, and 1 French woman.

central Bohemia, including Prague,[44] but between one-fifth and one-third of Viennese Jews from Bohemia were born in central Bohemia, and in Prague itself (Table 2:7). Moreover, while 70% of all Bohemians in Vienna—including the Jews—came from the two southern regions of the province,[45] only between one-third and one-half of all Bohemian Jews in Vienna (average of grooms, brides, and IKG taxpayers) between 1870 and 1910 came from southeast or southwest Bohemia. Since Jews migrated from all five regions of Bohemia, the forces which motivated Jews to move to Vienna from that province were fairly uniform throughout. Non-Jewish Czechs left southern Bohemia because of low wages,[46] but this economic factor did not influence the Jews, who were not day laborers. On the other hand, like typical Moravian immigrants, Moravian Jews who migrated to Vienna overwhelmingly left the southern half of that province.[47]

Different impetuses to gentile and Jewish migration from Galicia also meant that Jews were born in different regions of the province (Table 2:7) than the entire population of Galicians in Vienna, including the Jews. Two-fifths of all Galicians in Vienna came from western Galicia, and two-fifths from the northeast.[48] Among the Jews, however, only one-fifth to one-quarter were born in western Galicia, 12% in central Galicia, and two-thirds in eastern Galicia, with most of these, over half of all Galician Jews, born in northeast Galicia. Between 1870 and 1910 the number of northeasterners among Galician Jews in Vienna increased. While 45% came from the populous northeast of the province in 1880, 60% were from this area near the Russian border in 1910. Unfortunately, no information is available on the origins of Hungarian gentile immigrants to Vienna, and thus no comparisons between them and the Jews can be made.

Table 2:7. Region of Origin of Jewish Grooms, Brides, and IKG Taxpayers, Composite, 1870–1910

	Grooms*		Brides*		IKG Taxpayers (1855–1914)**	
	#	%	#	%	#	%
Lower Austria						
Vienna	178	89.4	339	93.4	809	99.1
Near Vienna	9	4.5	11	3.0	2	0.2
Not Near Vienna	8	4.0	12	3.3	5	0.6
Unspec.	4	2.0	1	0.3	0	0.0
Total	199		363		816	
Bohemia						
Central	23	22.1	12	18.5	66	29.7
Northwest	14	13.5	6	9.2	34	15.3
Northeast	22	21.2	11	16.9	28	12.6
Southeast	20	19.2	23	35.4	58	26.1
Southwest	18	17.3	10	15.4	27	12.2
Unspec.	7	6.7	3	4.6	9	4.1
Total	104		65		222	
Moravia						
South	103	79.8	80	72.7	138	65.4
North	24	18.6	26	23.6	71	33.6
Unspec.	2	1.6	4	3.6	2	0.9
Total	129		110		211	
Galicia						
West	35	21.0	34	27.6	38	24.1
Central	24	14.4	14	11.4	15	9.5
Northeast	79	47.3	57	46.3	85	53.8
Southeast	28	16.8	15	12.2	13	8.2
Unspec.	1	0.6	3	2.4	7	4.4
Total	167		123		158	
Hungary						
Left Danube	89	43.6	62	42.2	203	40.5
Right Danube	52	25.5	42	28.6	98	19.6
Danube/Tisza	30	14.7	19	12.9	99	19.8
Right Tisza	4	2.0	—	—	18	3.6
Left Tisza	5	2.5	3	2.0	9	1.8
Tisza/Maros	6	2.9	6	4.1	14	2.8
Transylvania	0	—	2	1.4	1	0.2
Fiume	0	—	—	—	4	0.8
Croatia/Slavonia	4	2.0	5	3.4	17	3.4
Unspec.	14	6.9	8	5.4	38	7.6
Total	204		147		501	

* Based on place of birth.
** Based on *Heimatland.*

Probably because there was little regional variation in the cause for their migration, Bohemian and Moravian Jews moved to Vienna more or less in proportion to their regional distribution at home. Most Moravian Jews lived in the southern part of the province,[49] and three-quarters of Moravian Jews in Vienna were born in southern Moravia. Minor regional variations in the causes for migration from Galicia did lead to differences between the regional origins of Galician Jews in Vienna and the regional distribution of Galician Jews at home. In particular, although 25% of all Galician Jews lived in southeast Galicia near the Hungarian border,[50] only 12% of Galician Jews in Vienna (average of grooms, brides, and IKG taxpayers) came from the southeastern region of the province. Jews from western, central, and northeast Galicia, however, eagerly migrated to Vienna (Table 2:7).

In Hungary, however, there was great regional variation in the causes for Jewish migration. Thus Hungarian Jews did not migrate to Vienna in proportion to their dispersion at home. Almost all Hungarian Jews in Vienna, about 70% of men and women alike, left western Slovakia and western Hungary, the regions on both sides of the Danube River relatively close to Vienna itself (Table 2:7). The bulk of the remainder of Hungarian Jews in Vienna came from the district between the Danube and Tisza Rivers, the region which included the city of Budapest. Only a scattered few were born in the central or eastern districts of Hungary, where most Hungarian Jews resided. In 1900, 36% of all Hungarian Jews lived in the two northeastern regions on both sides of the Tisza River,[51] but only 4% of Hungarian Jews in Vienna were born in this sub-Carpathian area. True, 22% of Hungarian Jewry lived in the two western regions, but that figure is much smaller than the percentage of Hungarian Jews in Vienna from those areas. Within Hungary, 30% of all Jews lived between the Danube and Tisza Rivers, almost all in Budapest, but only 16% of the Hungarian Jews in Vienna were born there.

Like all other immigrants, Jews moved to Vienna for a variety of positive and negative economic, political, and psychological reasons. Jews, however, migrated to the city for reasons which were unique to Austro-Hungarian Jews. Vienna certainly offered them greater economic and cultural opportunities, as well as more prestige and status. It also provided an escape from provincial antisemitism which was often expressed in economic pressure against Jewish merchants and traders, with Jewish poverty the result. Vienna itself was the scene of antisemitic demagoguery, but Czech, Polish, and Hungarian Jews felt such strong linguistic, cultural, and ideological ties to the city that its antisemitism paled beside its great attractiveness to them.

The usual causes of nineteenth-century population movement—agricultural depression, rural overpopulation, increasing fragmentation of landholding, the end of guild restrictions, a declining feudal mentality, and the lure of employment in expanding industry[52]—did not operate in the case of Jews, who were neither peasants nor potential proletariat. General population density, which by exerting pressure on the economic foundations of a region acts as one of the primary motivations for migration,[53] cannot explain why so many Jews moved at the end of the nineteenth century.

Moreover, specifically Jewish population density[54] also does not sufficiently account for Jewish population movement to Vienna. Jews moved to the capital from regions of high Jewish density, such as northeast Galicia where they formed 13% of the population and, concentrated in commerce, provided increasing competition with each other for a livelihood as Jewish population grew. But Jews also moved to Vienna from regions with low Jewish density such as Bohemia (1% of the population) or western Galicia (8%). Moreover, they did not move from all regions of high Jewish density. Both northeast and southeast Galicia had equally high Jewish density, but although many northeastern Galician Jews came to Vienna, few Jews migrated to Vienna from the southeast. Likewise northeast Hungary, just south of the Galician border, had very high Jewish density,[55] but very few Jews in Vienna between 1870 and 1910 were born in this region. The counties with the highest Jewish density in Hungary—the northeastern counties of Máramaros (18%), Ung (11%), and Bereg (14%) [56]—were not sending Jews to Vienna in appreciable numbers. Hungarian Jews in Vienna were almost all from western Slovakia and western Hungary, close to Vienna but considerably lower in Jewish density than sub-Carpathian northeast Hungary. Western Hungarian Jews who migrated to Vienna, however, did come from the three counties with higher than average Jewish density: Pozsony/Pressburg (5%), Nyitra/Neutra (6%), and Sopron/Oedenburg (7%).[57] Jews from the more populous northeast may, of course, have moved to Budapest, while western Hungarian and western Slovakian Jews moved in the 1870s and 1880s to Vienna and only after 1890 to Budapest as well. Nevertheless, other factors besides Jewish population density were at work encouraging Jews to leave certain regions, and discouraging them from leaving others.

Since Jews lived in the cities, urban Jewish overpopulation could have impelled many Jews to move to Vienna. Jewish population density in the towns and cities, however, was in no way the primary impetus to migration. After all, Jews left towns in Bohemia and Moravia with low Jewish population density, towns in Hungary with both high and low Jewish density, and towns in Galicia with extraordinarily high Jewish density (Table 2:8a and 2:8b). In general, Jewish immigrants to Vienna came from towns and cities in which the Jewish density was typical for their native provinces. Thus, for example, 66% of all Galician Jews in Vienna (average 1870–1910) were born in communities which were 20–49% Jewish and an additional 23% in towns which were more than half Jewish. But most Jews in Galicia lived in towns which were in fact preponderantly Jewish.[58] Similarly, Bohemian Jewish men and women came from towns less than 10% Jewish, but almost no towns in Bohemia had higher Jewish density.[59]

No, population pressure, although important, was not the major cause of Jewish migration to Vienna. The first impetus to migration to Vienna was the end of the restrictions on Jewish residence in the cities in general and in Vienna in particular. Bohemian and Moravian Jews had been sharply affected by the eighteenth-century restrictions and eagerly took advantage of the new freedom of movement, residence, and occupation granted to them in 1848 and confirmed in 1859, 1860, and by the Emancipation of 1867. Jews in Moravia, as in many areas of German-speaking Central Europe, had also been

Table 2:8a. Jewish Density of Grooms' Hometown, 1870–1910

	Less than 1%	1–9%	10–19%	20–49%	Over 50%	
			Bohemians			
1870 (13)	23.1%	69.2	7.7	—	—	100.0%
1880 (15)	26.7%	73.3	—	—	—	100.0%
1890 (17)	23.5%	70.6	5.9	—	—	100.0%
1900 (23)	21.7%	78.3	—	—	—	100.0%
1910 (27)	11.1%	85.2	3.7	—	—	100.0%
			Moravians and Silesians			
1870 (16)	—	50.0%	43.8	6.3	—	100.0%
1880 (17)	11.8%	52.9	17.6	17.6	—	100.0%
1890 (26)	3.8%	61.5	23.1	11.5	—	100.0%
1900 (40)	12.5%	60.0	20.0	7.5	—	100.0%
1910 (39)	12.8%	59.0	28.2	—	—	100.0%
			Galicians and Bukovinians			
1870 (5)	—	—	—	80.0	20.0	100.0%
1880 (14)	—	7.1%	—	71.4	21.4	100.0%
1890 (34)	2.9%	—	—	79.4	17.6	100.0%
1900 (61)	1.6%	13.1	—	62.3	23.0	100.0%
1910 (66)	1.5%	9.1	3.0	66.7	19.7	100.0%
			Hungarians			
1870 (37)	—	24.3%	51.4	24.3	—	100.0%
1880 (43)	2.3%	30.2	48.8	18.6	—	100.0%
1890 (42)	4.8%	31.0	38.1	26.2	—	100.0%
1900 (29)	—	27.6%	44.8	27.6	—	100.0%
1910 (34)	5.9%	23.5	50.0	20.6	—	100.0%

Table 2:8b. Jewish Density of Brides' Hometown, 1870–1910

	Less than 1%	1–9%	10–19%	20–49%	Over 50%	
			Bohemians			
1870 (3)	—	100.0%	—	—	—	100.0%
1880 (10)	10.0%	90.0	—	—	—	100.0%
1890 (15)	26.7%	73.3	—	—	—	100.0%
1900 (14)	64.3%	35.7	—	—	—	100.0%
1910 (20)	10.0%	85.0	—	5.0	—	100.0%
			Moravians and Silesians			
1870 (22)	—	31.8%	63.6	4.5	—	100.0%
1880 (16)	12.5%	50.0	31.3	6.3	—	100.0%
1890 (16)	6.3%	50.0	18.8	25.0	—	100.0%
1900 (25)	24.0%	56.0	16.0	4.0	—	100.0%
1910 (32)	9.4%	56.3	25.0	9.4	—	100.0%
			Galicians and Bukovinians			
1870 (4)	—	—	—	50.0%	50.0	100.0%
1880 (14)	7.1%	—	—	78.6	14.3	100.0%
1890 (32)	—	6.3%	—	68.8	25.0	100.0%
1900 (36)	2.8%	8.3	2.8	58.3	27.8	100.0%
1910 (47)	6.4%	6.4	6.4	46.8	34.0	100.0%
			Hungarians			
1870 (32)	—	28.1%	53.1	18.8	—	100.0%
1880 (32)	3.1%	25.0	40.6	31.3	—	100.0%
1890 (20)	5.0%	25.0	25.0	45.0	—	100.0%
1900 (25)	8.0%	40.0	32.0	20.0	—	100.0%
1910 (25)	4.0%	40.0	24.0	32.0	—	100.0%

severely restricted by marriage decrees which only allowed the eldest son to marry and then only after his father's death. In 1798 Emperor Francis II not only confined the Moravian Jews to 52 *Judengemeinden,* and excluded them from the free royal cities, but also prohibited Moravian Jewry from exceeding 5,400 families.[60] When these onorous decrees were annulled, Moravian Jews surged into the previously forbidden free royal cities and the new industrial and commercial ones. Jews left the rural communities and sought their fortunes in the new urban centers. They also left Moravia altogether, primarily for Vienna, and Moravia experienced an absolute and relative Jewish demographic decline in the second half of the nineteenth century.[61] Bohemian Jews also moved to the cities in this period, especially to Prague and Vienna.[62]

More important than population pressures, or the relaxing of traditional restrictions on the Jewish decision to migrate, were economic factors unique to the Jews. Jews, like non-Jews, left certain areas of Austria-Hungary because of economic depressions or long-term regional poverty. In the Jewish case, however, local anti-Jewish boycotts as well as an attempt to create a Polish, Slovak, or Czech business class, squeezed Jewish traders out of the marketplace and forced them to move elsewhere in search of a livelihood.

Poverty combined with anti-Jewish economic pressure certainly prevailed in western Slovakia, for example, the area in which most Hungarian Jews in Vienna were born. In this mountainous region, the soil was not fertile enough to provide farmer or trader with an adequate living.[63] Furthermore, Slovakian nationalists tried to deprive Jewish shopkeepers and petty traders of a means of livelihood. The Catholic clerical party, *Néppárt,* the *L'udová Strana* (People's Party), used antisemitic invective in its attempt to unite the Slovak peasants. In 1906 its spokesman Svetozár Hurban-Vajanský called on the Slovak peasants to boycott Jewish merchants and establish their own shops in the towns and villages.[64] Living close to Vienna and in easy reach of the capital by steamboat or railroad, western Slovakian and western Hungarian Jews, who in any case had linguistic and cultural affinities to Vienna,[65] decided to move to the Habsburg *Residenzstadt.* Only with increased Magyarization at the end of the nineteenth century did they stop migrating to Vienna, choosing instead the Hungarian capital of the Monarchy. On the other hand, Jews in the agriculturally richer land of eastern Hungary were able to live their traditional lives relatively undisturbed and thus rarely moved to Vienna.[66]

In Moravia and Bohemia as well, the growth of Czech nationalism led to the creation of a Czech middle class which sought to replace the Jews in the rural economy. This Czech bourgeoisie provided competition for Jewish traders who had previously held a virtual monopoly on trade. In both provinces this nationalism was coupled with anti-German as well as antisemitic feelings. In their quest for Czech autonomy, Czech nationalists sought to eliminate all Germans from Bohemian and Moravian economic and political life. They regarded the Jews as pro-German and pro-Habsburg because Jews spoke German and voted for the German parties, at least before the German parties became antisemitic; thus anti-German activities generally had anti-Jewish repercussions.[67] Moreover, in Bohemia, Czech nationalists engaged in specifically anti-Jewish economic activities. They formed consumer cooperatives and declared an anti-Jewish boycott, the *Svůj k svému* ("Each His Own"), both developments which were devastating to Jewish shopkeepers in the villages.[68] Recurring anti-German and antisemitic riots in Prague undoubtedly added to the perception that Jews were not particularly welcome in Bohemia.[69]

In Galicia, poverty and antisemitic pressure became especially onorous at the very end of the nineteenth century. Jewish poverty in Galicia was extensive.[70] In large measure, the poverty was induced by the rapid population growth which affected all of East European Jewry in the nineteenth century. Between 1869 and 1900, for example, the Jewish population of Galicia grew from 575,433 to 811,371, or 41%, while Catholic population growth was only about 10%.[71] Since most Jews were traders, a sharp increase in numbers made it difficult for all of them to make a living in Galicia, a relatively impoverished region.[72] This naturally induced poverty was intensified by Polish political pressure and nationalistic attempts to create a Polish bourgeoisie. By trying to ease the credit situation of the peasants through credit unions *(Kołka rolnicze* and *kasy szefczyka)* and cooperatives, the Poles consciously tried to close the Jews out of their traditional role as middlemen in the peasant economy. As early as the 1860s and 1870s, during the struggle for Galician autonomy, Jews had been the target of the movement of the Galician nobles to regain control of the Polish economy. Efforts against the Jews intensified at the end of the century as the National Industry Movement, which sought to form a Polish middle class, endeavored to end Jewish control over certain areas of the economy. In 1893 a Catholic convention in Cracow proclaimed an economic boycott of the Jews in Galicia, and this boycott, which lasted until World War I, had disastrous repercussions on Jewish economic life in the province. Finally, in 1910 Galician authorities prohibited the Jews from selling alcoholic beverages, one of the mainstays of their economic life.[73]

As a result of this economic pressure, combined with fear of pogroms after those of 1898, Galician Jews migrated to the cities of Galicia, to Vienna, to other major cities of Europe, and to the United States.[74] Just as "Austrian," i.e., Galician, immigration to America increased around 1900[75] in response to increased economic and political pressures, so too did Galician immigration to Vienna increase at this time.

Jewish urbanization within Austria-Hungary, then, was induced by general freedom of movement and the desire to make use of new opportunities. It was also caused by population pressures on the economic foundations of Jewish life and by nationalism colored with antisemitism which sought to push Jews out of certain sectors of the economy. Certain factors, however, inhibited Jewish migration from many areas. Besides normal inertia, the primary reason why many Jews remained in their old homes was religious orthodoxy. The mystical and pietistic Hasidic movement, with the intense attachment of its adepts to their charismatic leaders, was an important impediment to the migration of Jews from certain areas of Hungary and Galicia where Hasidism flourished.[76] For example, the Jews of northeastern Hungary were overwhelmingly Hasidic and rarely moved to Vienna.

Similarly, Jews in southeastern Galicia were also mostly Hasidic and seldom moved to the Austrian capital. On the other hand, western Slovakia and western Hungary, the birthplaces of 70% of Hungarian Jews in Vienna, were the homes of non-Hasidic orthodox Jews. The area around Pressburg/Pozsony (today Bratislava) in particular was the base of support for one of the most vigorous anti-Hasidic orthodox leaders of the nineteenth century, Rabbi Moses Sofer.[77] Economic and political incentives, however, frequently overcame religious inhibitions. A very large percentage of Galician Jews in Vienna were born in northeast Galicia, and many Hasidim lived in that part of the province.

The sheer attractiveness of Vienna itself may have been one of the most important reasons why Jews chose to move there. Vienna was the destination of these emigrant Jews because as capital of the Dual Monarchy it offered unparalleled economic and psychological opportunities and advantages. For the Jews who moved to Vienna because of poverty, Vienna offered the hope of economic improvement.[78] To the upwardly mobile Jews of the provinces, Vienna promised both financial gain and increased personal prestige. The music critic Joseph Wechsberg, a Moravian-born Jew, reminisced about Vienna's pre-World War I magnetism:

> When someone thought he was becoming prominent, he might move to Vienna where a man's opportunities were less limited and the rewards were higher. Vienna's attractions remained irresistible to the Germans and German-speaking Jews in Ostrau. . . . My mother's annual visits . . . were considered almost a status symbol at home. It was said, perhaps not jokingly, that some people stayed up late at night trying to discover a relative in Vienna whom they might visit, just as a start.[79]

Moreover, Austro-Hungarian Jews had important cultural and linguistic connections to Vienna and thus it was a logical destination for them. Traditional Jews who spoke Yiddish, a language derived from medieval German, were more likely to feel at home in German-speaking Vienna than in Polish, Czech, or Hungarian cities which sometimes demanded the acquisition of new linguistic skills. By the mid-nineteenth century, many Jews in Bohemia, Moravia, and western Hungary already spoke German and possessed a German cultural orientation. Those who sought some measure of assimilation considered German the language of culture and enlightenment in contrast to Yiddish or "Jargon" on the one hand, and Polish, Czech, or even Magyar on the other. For several generations of Central European Jews, to westernize and modernize were synonymous with acquiring German culture. George Clare recalled that Austrian Jews possessed "that unquenchable thirst to drink deeply of German culture and language." [80] The Viennese Zionist Isidor Schalit noted:

> The Jews, throughout the entire nineteenth century, were entirely German. They were German through their education, because German culture dominated in the multi-lingual Empire. . . . The Jews were German because to them the German people in Austria were the symbol of freedom and progress.[81]

Finally, Jews chose to move to Vienna because they identified it with the liberal, progressive forces which had granted them emancipation in 1867, and with the German Liberal Party to which they were staunchly loyal, even after the Liberals abandoned the Jews and many Austro-Germans embraced antisemitism.[82] Galician Jews in particular revered Vienna as the home of the Liberalism which had freed the Jews from age-old disabilities.[83] Despite the growth of antisemitism in Vienna itself, Austrian Jews continued to regard Franz Joseph's *Residenzstadt* as a kind of political oasis.

Concerned with the preservation of their rights, Austrian Jews staunchly supported the Habsburg multinational Empire. It was only natural for a group described as "the only Austrians in Austria" [84] to choose to live in the city which was the home of the other pan-Austrian institutions: the emperor, the civil service, and the army. Excluded by antisemitism and their pro-Habsburg orientation from the Czech or Polish national camps, Jews would logically move to the Austrian capital.

Characteristics of Jewish Immigrants

The Jews who responded to these challenges and attractions and who arrived in Vienna in the Czech, Hungarian, or Galician waves of migration came from a wide range of economic, cultural, and religious backgrounds. Consequently, they brought with them different expectations of urban life and different attitudes toward the impact of Vienna on their assimilation and their continued Jewish identity. It is, unfortunately, impossible to determine how religious these immigrants were, either when they first arrived, or after years of living in Vienna. It is also impossible to ascertain from computer-readable data the extent to which they had already acculturated and assimilated before they migrated to the *Grossstadt*. It is possible, however, to determine their relative economic prosperity as well as the extent to which Jewish immigrants were urban dwellers before they moved to Vienna. The different levels of wealth and prior urban experience of the Jews in the three waves of migration were important factors in shaping the different attitudes of Bohemian, Moravian, Hungarian, and Galician Jews toward assimilation.

Those Jews who migrated in the early waves of immigration from Bohemia, Moravia, and Hungary were relatively prosperous. Moving to take advantage of new opportunities, these Jews easily achieved a certain measure of wealth and respectability after settling in the city. Bohemian, Moravian, and Hungarian[85] Jews appeared in the same proportions among the prosperous, taxpaying echelons of the Jewish community (Table 2:9) as in the community at large. Just as among the Jewish grooms, one quarter of the IKG taxpayers were from Hungary, and 21% were from Bohemia and Moravia. Jews from these areas were either already members of the middle classes when they arrived, or quickly achieved middle-class status once in Vienna.

The Bohemians were the richest Jewish immigrants to Vienna. In the middle of the nineteenth century, they were represented in the IKG tax rolls above their share in the general Jewish population. In 1869 only 8.6% of the Jewish fathers were Bohemian, but almost 14% of all the new entrants to the IKG tax rolls between 1868 and 1879 had legal residence rights in Bohemia (Table 2:10). Moreover, except for those with Viennese *Heimatrecht*, Bohemians were more likely than any other Viennese Jews to be assessed more than the 20 Kronen minimum tax for the IKG.

The Hungarians, on the other hand, were the least prosperous of the early immigrants. In all likelihood, the Hungarian migration contained a fair number of poor along with the more respectable middle classes. Although, on the average, Hungarians were represented in the tax rolls in proportion to their numbers in the community

Table 2:9. Heimatland of IKG Taxpayers, Composite, 1855–1914*

Land	Number	Percent of Total
Vienna	809	39.1
Other Lower Austria	7	0.3
Bohemia	222	10.7
Moravia	211	10.2
Silesia	32	1.5
Galicia	158	7.6
Bukovina	18	0.9
Other Austria	15	0.7
Hungary	501	24.2
Other Foreign**	95	4.6
	2,068	100.0%

* The IKG only recorded *Heimat* community, not place of birth.

** "Other Foreign" includes 41 Germans, 13 Russians, 13 Rumanians, 10 from other Balkan countries, and 18 others.

Table 2:10. Heimatland of New IKG Members, New Entrants in Each Decade

	1855–67 N = 225	1868–79 N = 394	1880–89 N = 356	1890–99 N = 491	1900–1914 N = 582
Vienna & N.O.	53.3%	21.6%	18.0%	26.1%	69.1%
Bohemia	7.6	13.7	11.8	14.7	6.4
Moravia & Silesia	10.7	12.4	16.3	16.3	5.2
Galicia & Bukovina	2.2	13.2	9.8	11.8	4.5
Other Austria	0.4	1.0	0.3	1.2	0.5
Hungary	22.2	31.7	37.4	25.7	11.2
Other Foreign	3.6	6.3	6.5	4.3	2.9
	100.0%	100.0%	100.0%	100.0%	100.0%

at large, in every decade the number of Hungarians admitted to the tax rolls of the IKG was somewhat lower than the number of Hungarians in the general Jewish community. In 1880, for example, 44.5% of the Jewish fathers were born in Hungary, but in the decade 1880–89 only 37.4% of the new IKG taxpayers possessed Hungarian *Heimat* (Table 2:10 compared to 2:5).

In the decades before World War I, the percentage of Bohemian, Moravian, and especially Hungarian Jews among the new entrants to the IKG tax rolls (Table 2:10) declined considerably. Although, for example, 31.7% of all new entrants were Hungarian between 1868 and 1879, only 11.2% of the new applicants in the final years before World War I were from Hungary. This decline merely reflected the ebb in migration from those areas of the Monarchy during the late nineteenth century, as well as the liberalization of *Heimatrecht* laws in 1910 which permitted many to change their legal residence to Vienna.

Galicians, who comprised the third wave of Jewish immigration to Vienna at the very end of the century, were by far the poorest Jews in Vienna. On the average between 1870 and 1910, 20% of the Jewish community was Galician, but only 8% of all IKG taxpayers during this period came from Galicia. There were two distinct groups of Galician Jews in Vienna. A small group of Galician Jews moved to Vienna in the 1860s and 1870s, probably to take advantage of Viennese opportunities, and they tended to be prosperous, represented in the IKG tax rolls at the same rate as they were in the community at large. In 1869, only 10.5% of all Jewish fathers were born in Galicia, but as many as 13.2% of all new IKG taxpayers between 1868 and 1879 had legal residence in Galicia (Table 2:10). Moreover, before 1880, Galician members of the IKG easily changed their *Heimat* to Vienna, a procedure which required a good bit of money, at a rate higher than any other Viennese Jews. The Galician Jewish masses who arrived in the city at the end of the century, on the other hand, were overwhelmingly poor, and they probably migrated because economic necessity and antisemitism forced the issue. Thus, virtually none of them were sufficiently prosperous to pay IKG taxes. In 1910, at a time of massive Galician influx, 35% of all Jewish fathers were born in Galicia, but only 4% of new *Gemeinde* taxpayers between 1900 and 1914 were Galician. Their status as recent immigrants only partially explains the absence of Galicians in the tax rolls. In general, they simply lacked the economic wherewithal to pay *Gemeinde* taxes in proportion to their share in the Jewish population. As will be later demonstrated, these Galicians of the second and larger wave of Galician immigration to Vienna were less urban and probably had greater attachments to traditional Jewish life than did earlier migrants from that province, or anywhere else.

The richest Jews in Vienna were those who were native to the city. Jews with Viennese *Heimat* were twice as likely to be represented in the taxpaying echelons of the Jewish community as in the community at large. On the average between 1870 and 1910 only 18% of the fathers and 20% of the grooms were Viennese-born, but almost 40% of all IKG taxpayers between 1855 and 1914 (Table 2:9) possessed legal residence rights in Vienna. Moreover, the IKG levied the highest tax assessments on Jews who had Viennese *Heimatrecht.* Before the Jews were emancipated, over half of the new taxpaying members of the IKG had legal domiciliary rights in Vienna, but once Jews began to immigrate in large numbers, the percentage of native Viennese Jews in the IKG tax rolls plummeted (Table 2:10). At the end of the century, the number of Jews with legal residence rights in Vienna grew rapidly so that almost 70% of the new taxpayers after 1900 possessed Viennese *Heimat.* Part of this increase was caused by the 1910 liberalization of the rules for changing *Heimat.* This increase also attests to the growth of a well-to-do second generation of Jews in the capital.

Rich or poor, Jews who migrated to Vienna were familiar with urban life when they arrived in the city. Unlike gentile immigrants, most of whom were born in peasant villages and small towns,[86] Jews who moved to Vienna, like Austrian and Hungarian Jews in general, had lived in large towns and cities, and a considerable number of them had even resided in the other *Grossstädte* of the Dual Monarchy. Only about 5% of the male Jewish immigrants and 3% of the female ones were born in villages of less than 500 people, and 16% of the immigrants of both sexes were born in small towns with 500–1,999 residents. Over a third came from larger towns of 2,000–9,999 people. Most important, almost one-half of the Jewish men and women who moved to Vienna came from cities with over 10,000 inhabitants, including 11–12% who were from large cities with over 100,000 population (Table 2:11).[87] Prior to their migration, most Jews who chose to move to Vienna were more likely than most Austro-Hungarian Jews to live in large cities. This urban experience facilitated their move to the metropolis and hastened their adjustment to an urban life-style. Thus, more easily than most immigrants, Jews made use of the opportunities that Vienna offered.

Not all Jews were equally urban (Table 2:11). Hungarian Jews, typical Jewish immigrants to Vienna, almost never came from villages; one-third of them were from large towns (2,000–9,999), one-third from small cities (10,000–99,999), and 10% from other metropolitan centers. Moravians, on the other hand, were rarely born in *Grossstädte*, but were much more likely than any other Jews in Vienna to come from small or large towns. Although on the average, between 1870 and 1910 a little over half of all Jewish brides and grooms in Vienna were born in towns from 500–9,999 inhabitants, almost three-quarters of Moravian brides and grooms were born in towns of this size. Moravians were also less likely than most Viennese Jews to come from small cities. Bohemian Jewish immigrants differed from Moravian and Hungarian ones in that they were much more likely to come either from villages or large cities with over 100,000 population. Fewer Bohemian brides and grooms were born in large towns and small cities than was true in the general Jewish population, but many Prague Jews did choose to move to Vienna.

The size of the hometowns of Bohemian and Moravian Jewish immigrants to Vienna accurately reflected the settlement patterns of Jews in Bohemia or Moravia.[88] That is, Moravian Jews tended to live in small or large towns and Bohemian Jews in villages, small towns, or in the capital, Prague. As the Jews of Bohemia and Moravia increasingly urbanized in the second half of the nineteenth century, the proportion of Bohemian and Moravian Jewish migrants to Vienna born in villages and small towns declined, and the number born in large towns and cities increased between 1870 and 1910. The percentage of Bohemian Jews in Vienna born in Prague remained the same.

Urbanization within Hungary, however, did not lead to a greater proportion of city dwellers within the Hungarian Jewish community in Vienna. On the contrary, in the late nineteenth century a different sort of Hungarian Jew chose to move to Vienna than had been true earlier. With the passage of time, the small-town Hungarian Jews near the Austrian border provided an ever larger share of Hungarian Jewish migration to Vienna. By 1910, two-and-a-half times as many Hungarian Jewish fathers had been born in small towns of 500–1,999

Table 2:11. Population of Hometown, Jewish Grooms and Brides, Composite, 1870–1910*

Hometown	Overall		Bohemia		Moravia/Silesia		Galicia/Bukovina		Hungary	
Population	Grooms N = 618	Brides N = 473	Grooms N = 95	Brides N = 62	Grooms N = 138	Brides N = 111	Grooms N = 180	Brides N = 133	Grooms N = 185	Brides N = 134
Under 500	4.5%	2.7%	15.8%	14.5%	2.9%	—	1.1%	—	2.7%	0.7%
500–1,999	15.9	16.1	20.0	27.4	21.7	17.1%	6.1	6.0%	20.0	19.4
2,000–9,999	36.9	35.1	29.5	22.6	50.0	53.2	32.8	30.8	34.6	30.6
10,000–99,999	31.4	33.8	14.7	21.0	20.3	22.5	47.2	48.1	32.4	36.6
Over 100,000	11.3	12.3	20.0	14.5	5.1	7.2	12.8	15.0	10.3	12.7
	100.0%	100.0%	100.0%	100.0%	100.0%	100.0%	100.0%	100.0%	100.0%	100.0%

* Viennese-born are not included in this table since the concern was with the immigrants to the city.

inhabitants than was true in 1869 (Table 2:12). Conversely, 31% of the Hungarian Jewish fathers in 1869 had been born in small cities of 10,000–99,999 residents, but only 18% of the Hungarian Jewish fathers in 1910 originated in such cities. The number migrating from the largest cities declined after 1870 and remained constant from 1880 to 1910. Jews in Hungarian cities may have increasingly chosen Budapest over Vienna when they wanted to improve their situations. Small-town Jews in western Slovakia or western Hungary probably continued to move to Vienna because it was so close.

Jews who migrated to Vienna from Galicia were also not typical Galician Jews. In fact, they were much more urban than Galician Jews generally. Whether because of greater poverty, greater mobility, or easier accessibility to the means of transportation, Jews living in the cities of Galicia were much more likely to move to Vienna than any other Jews in the province. Within Galicia, 28% of all Jews lived in cities with over 10,000 residents, and 5.4% lived in the capital, Lemberg.[89] Among Galician Jewish brides and grooms in Vienna, however, over 60% came from cities with more than 10,000 residents and 14% from Lemberg alone. Moreover, despite rapid urbanization in Galicia in the late nineteenth century, between 1870 and 1910 the percentage of Galician Jewish immigrants to Vienna born in large cities declined markedly (Table 2:13).

This decline again reveals the fact that indeed two waves of Jewish migrants left Galicia for Vienna. The first, very small wave in the 1860s and 1870s consisted preponderantly of men and women from the cities of Galicia. In 1869, fully 82% of all Galician Jewish fathers in Vienna (Table 2:13) had been born in cities with more than 10,000 inhabitants, including 24% born in the largest cities of the province. As we have already seen, these Jews were also prosperous, upwardly mobile men and women who sought to take advantage of Viennese opportunities. On the other hand, those Jews who participated in the second, mass wave of immigration at the end of the nineteenth

Table 2:12. Size of Hometown of Hungarian Fathers, 1869–1910

	1869 N = 121	1880 N = 60	1890* N = 63	1900 N = 75	1910 N = 28
Under 500	0.8%	3.3%	—	5.3%	3.6%
500–1,999	11.6	6.7	7.9%	21.3	25.0
2,000–9,999	42.1	48.3	52.4	40.0	46.4
10,000–99,999	31.4	36.7	33.3	24.0	17.9
Over 100,000	14.0	5.0	6.3	9.3	7.1
	100.0%	100.0%	100.0%	100.0%	100.0%

* 1890 figures based on *Heimatland,* not place of birth.

Table 2:13. Size of Hometown of Galician Jewish Fathers, 1869–1910

	1869 N = 33	1880 N = 18	1890* N = 28	1900 N = 49	1910 N = 57
Under 500	—	—	—	2.0%	3.5%
500–1,999	—	5.6%	—	6.1	14.0
2,000–9,999	18.2%	11.1	28.6%	30.6	36.8
10,000–99,999	57.6	44.4	39.3	34.7	29.8
Over 100,000	24.2	38.9	32.1	26.5	15.8
	100.0%	100.0%	100.0%	100.0%	100.0%

* 1890 figures based on *Heimatland,* not place of birth.

century were less likely to have been born in the cities, more likely to come from the smaller towns of Galicia. Thus, in contrast to 1869, only 46% of the Galician Jewish fathers in 1910 came from cities of more than 10,000 residents. In this forty-one-year period, the number of Galician Jewish fathers born in towns with 2,000–9,999 inhabitants doubled from 18% to 37%, and the number born in even smaller towns rose as well. The most striking decline was in the number of Galician Jews in Vienna born in Lemberg. Almost 30% of the Galician Jewish grooms in 1880 were Lemberger, but only 6% were born in the Galician capital in 1910. Moreover, although small-town life does not necessitate poverty, as we have seen, the Jews in the second wave of migration were overwhelmingly poor.

Whatever the size of their hometowns, Jewish immigrants to Vienna, especially those from Galicia and Hungary, came from communities which contained substantial Jewish populations (Table 2:14). About two-fifths of Jewish immigrants to Vienna were born in small Jewish communities, but a large percentage were born in large communities as well. With the exception of Jews from Prague, Jews who immigrated to Vienna from Bohemia and Moravia, like Bohemian and Moravian Jews generally,[90] hailed from small Jewish communities. Fully 80% of Bohemian Jewish grooms and 90% of Moravian grooms came from communities of less than 2,000 Jews. Hungarian Jews in Vienna, on the other hand, were considerably more likely than Bohemian or Moravian Jewish immigrants to have been born in medium or large Jewish communities, including Budapest itself.

Galician Jews in Vienna, like Galician Jews generally, came from very large Jewish communities.[91] In contrast to the overwhelming majority of Bohemian, Moravian, and even Hungarian Jews born in communities of less than 2,000 Jews, only 24% of the Galician grooms were born in such small Jewish communities. Conversely, almost half of the Galician-born Jewish brides and grooms in Vienna came from very large Jewish communities in which between 10,000 and

Table 2:14. Jewish Population of Grooms' and Brides' Hometown, Composite, 1870–1910*

# Jews	Overall		Bohemia		Moravia/Silesia		Galicia/Bukovina		Hungary	
	Grooms N = 617	Brides N = 472	Grooms N = 95	Brides N = 62	Grooms N = 138	Brides N = 111	Grooms N = 180	Brides N = 133	Grooms N = 185	Brides N = 134
Under 500	39.7%	36.7%	69.6%	71.0%	53.6%	40.4%	11.1%	10.5%	38.9%	32.8%
500–1,999	21.9	22.7	9.5	11.3	38.4	51.9	12.8	9.0	23.8	20.1
2,000–4,999	10.5	12.1	1.1	3.2	2.9	—	20.6	21.1	12.4	18.7
5,000–9,999	8.1	8.9	—	—	5.1	7.7	9.4	10.5	14.1	14.9
10,000–99,999	16.9	16.1	20.0	14.5	—	—	46.1	48.9	1.2	0.7
Over 100,000	2.9	3.6	—	—	—	—	—	—	9.7	12.7
	100.0%	100.0%	100.0%	100.0%	100.0%	100.0%	100.0%	100.0%	100.0%	100.0%

* Excluding Viennese-born.

100,000 Jews resided. As indicated above, Jews in these towns were a substantial minority, and sometimes even a majority of the total population.

All of the differences between Czech, Hungarian, and Galician Jews in Vienna may partially explain why there were, in effect, two Jewish communities in the city, one composed of the native-born, Bohemians, Moravians, and Hungarians, and the other composed of Galicians. It was not just their recent status as immigrants that differentiated the Galicians from the other Jews in Vienna. Galician Jews also had a sense of themselves as a distinct group, an Eastern European outpost in a sea of Central European Jews, and they strove to maintain that distinctiveness in Vienna.

To be sure, like Jews in Germany, the already Germanized Jews from Bohemia, Moravia, and Hungary did regard Galician Jews with a measure of contempt and separated themselves from these Polish Jews.[92] George Clare remembered the distaste he felt for his maternal grandmother from Lemberg:

> I was already second-generation Viennese, and Viennese-born Jews felt resentment towards the less assimilated Jews from the East. We were, or rather thought we were, quite different from that bearded, caftaned lot. We were not just Austrian, but German-Austrian. Little wonder that I resented the Yiddish sing-song intonation with which Adele spoke German, a "yoich" sigh at the start and end of almost every sentence.[93]

In fact, all of Clare's grandparents were from Galicia or Bukovina, but they had succeeded in Germanizing and thus shared the general contempt for Eastern Jews. Clare admitted that he long resented the fact that his own mother was born in Galicia.[94]

For their part, Galician Jews had a strong sense of their own identity and the worth of Polish Jewish culture. Resenting the "German" Jewish antipathy to them, Polish Jews consciously created their own culture in Vienna.[95] In a call for the creation of an organization of Polish Jews in Vienna, "L" declared:

> Indeed, the "great" Viennese Jews whose fathers migrated from Bohemia, Moravia, or Hungary consider themselves better than the "Eastern Jews," the Poles or Russians . . .

He urged that Galician Jews band together, "to fulfill important social duties to their Eastern brothers." [96] Galician Jews also sought to preserve Galician Jewish religious culture in "German" Vienna through the establishment of synagogues in which services would be conducted according to Polish customs.[97]

This sense of separateness was translated into marriage preferences. Native-born, Bohemian, Moravian, and Hungarian Jews married each other in proportion to their share in the population and avoided the Galicians. Conversely, Galician Jews almost exclusively chose each other as marriage partners. Most Viennese Jewish marriages (60.6%) involved men and women born in different provinces of the monarchy,[98] but only 5.8% of the Bohemian grooms, 2.1% of the Moravian grooms, and 5.5% of the Hungarian grooms chose Galician brides. Bohemians shied away from Hungarians to some extent as well. Although 12.5% of the native-born brides married Galician men, almost all Jewish brides from Moravia, Bohemia, and Hungary shunned men from Galicia.

Galician Jews, however, overwhelmingly married other Galician Jews. The native-born also had a high endogamy rate, but the Galicians' endogamy rate was twice as high as that of any other Viennese Jews (Table 2:15). (Male/female differences relate to the different proportion of each national group within the male and female populations.) One-quarter of each national group, on the average, married spouses from their province of origin, but half of the Galician grooms and three-quarters of the Galician brides married other Galicians. Due to increased migration, Galician endogamy increased between 1870 and 1910; 51.7% of Galician brides married Galician men in 1880, and 79.6% did so in 1910.

As will be shown later, Galician Jews in Vienna also concentrated more densely in the Jewish neighborhoods of the city. Moreover, Viennese Jews from Galicia participated more actively than other Viennese Jews in movements like Zionism and diaspora Jewish nationalism which sought to revive Jewish national feelings in late Habsburg Vienna. They provided the majority of the rank and file as well as the leadership cadres of these two movements. Galician Jews, coming from regions of greater Jewish density and intensity of Jewish life than other Viennese Jews, may have been more devoted than Bohemian, Moravian, Hungarian, or native Viennese Jews to asserting their Jewish identity and living a more consciously Jewish life. They were probably also more religious.

Table 2:15. Percentage of Grooms and Brides From Each Land Marrying Partners From That Land

	% Grooms	% Brides
Vienna	62.4	33.6
Bohemia	15.4	25.8
Moravia/Silesia	27.7	34.2
Galicia/Bukovina	49.7	72.1
Hungary	34.2	47.9

Urbanization and assimilation were interrelated phenomena, but the fact that Jewish immigrants came to Vienna from large towns and cities did not mean that they were all assimilated or seeking integration into gentile culture. The Jews of Bohemia and Moravia were less urban than other Austrian Jews but assimilated into European culture earlier than Eastern European Jews,[99] and were the majority of the most assimilated Jews in Vienna. Galician Jews, more heavily concentrated in cities than Jews of any other province, were the most religious and the least assimilated, and would provide the demographic foundation for a good deal of assertive Jewish separatism in Vienna.

The fact that Jewish immigrants to Vienna were so urban did, however, prepare them for the necessary adjustments they had to make to life in the capital. Arriving in Vienna with urban experience and urban occupations, the Jews were in a better position than most immigrants to make use of the expanded opportunities they encountered. Many Jewish immigrants were extremely poor, but their previous urban experience meant that they engaged in commercial or artisanal occupations. Not having to work for very low wages at heavy labor, as did immigrants of peasant stock, they were in a better position to improve their economic status. Largely literate, they were able to move into new urban occupations.

3. *From Trader to Clerk: The Occupational Transformation of Viennese Jewry*

IN 1850, the young Sigmund Mayer, later a wealthy businessman and leading member of the Viennese Jewish community, passed his *Matura*, qualifying himself for admission to the university. The young man's mother advised him not to pursue his studies but to enter the family textile business. She argued knowingly that any other kind of career was impossible for a Jew.[1] Mayer did obtain a law degree, but he soon realized that his Jewish origins hindered a career in the bureaucracy, professoriat, or law. Using bad eyesight as an excuse, he took his mother's advice and became a textile merchant.[2]

Although there was a handful of Jewish professionals and industrialists in the 1840s and 1850s, in that period commerce provided virtually the only career open to Viennese Jews unwilling to convert to Christianity. By World War I, however, the dilemma of Mayer and his generation no longer existed to the same extent. The Jews who moved to Vienna and their children took advantage of the economic opportunities available to them in the city after the government lifted the laws which had restricted Jews to petty trade for centuries. Although many Jews continued to trade, in fin-de-siècle Vienna, Jews also flourished as industrialists, professionals, and, to an even greater extent, as clerks, salesmen, and managers. The urban environment served as a major catalyst in the restructuring of Jewish economic preferences in the second half of the nineteenth century.

The pattern of this economic restructuring is somewhat controversial. Mayer, a prolific writer as well as a wealthy merchant, would have his readers believe that the Jews abandoned trade for careers as large-scale industrialists. Generalizing from his own experience as a merchant who turned to manufacturing, Mayer confidently announced in a 1903 article:

> One can safely say that an era of Jewish industry, a time of Jewish industrialists, is becoming more and more apparent, and signifies the establishment of a new epoch in the economic history of Austrian Jewry.[3]

On the other hand, other observers of Viennese Jewry take the model of Jewish intellectuals as paradigmatic, and argue that the main thrust of economic change among Viennese Jews was from trade into the professions and the arts. The Viennese Jewish journalist Arnold Höllriegel reminisced in his memoirs about the expectations of his *Gymnasium* classmates:

> My fellow students were all sons of merchants, doctors and lawyers, but it was our dream to become something else, preferably poets or sculptors. At least five members of my class, which was composed of thirty students, later actually did produce literature and were published.[4]

In his analysis of the Zionist leader Theodor Herzl, the historian Carl Schorske argues similarly that as an intellectual whose father was a merchant, Herzl typified the social mobility of Viennese Jews.[5]

The evidence to be presented here proves that neither approach provides an adequate explanation for the economic and professional change experienced by the Jews of Vienna in the second half of the nineteenth century. The Jews who moved to Vienna from elsewhere in the Dual Monarchy and their Viennese-born children indeed abandoned the traditional trading occupations to which European Jewry had long been relegated. Many Jews did enter the professions, primarily medicine and law, and many others became industrialists, but these two paths of mobility were not representative of the occupational change taking place among Viennese Jewry. Far more typically, Jews joined the ranks of salaried white-collar employees, as clerks, salesmen, and managers in commercial and industrial enterprises. The salient change precipitated by urbanization and consequent opportunities for economic and general assimilation was the transformation of a people famous for its trading ability into a clerical and managerial group.

By choosing new occupations as clerks, salesmen, and managers, Viennese Jews improved their social status and announced their successful acculturation. Certainly men whose fathers had been petty traders, often glorified peddlers with virtually no income, enjoyed a much higher and more secure economic position when they became clerks or managers in the insurance companies, banks, or other large business enterprises in Vienna. Moreover, in order to obtain and hold such jobs, Jews had to speak German well, read and write it fluently, and they had to dress and behave like other Viennese burghers. Since all of these companies did business on Saturday, Jews surely had to reject the strictures of traditional Judaism and work on the Sabbath, which is absolutely forbidden by Jewish religious law. Some clerks may have worked for Jewish firms closed on Saturday, but the majority probably did not.

Nevertheless, despite acculturation and the growing disregard for traditional Judaism, Jewish professional transformation did not herald the disappearance of the Jews through economic assimilation into Viennese society. The restructuring of the professional profile of Viennese Jews did not lead to growing similarity between Jewish and non-Jewish occupational distribution. On the contrary, the statistics show that Jews continued to practice occupations which made them distinct from the society in which they lived. They exchanged the old Jewish occupations in trade for new occupations which were equally identifiable as Jewish. Despite capitalist development in Vienna, there was no parallel increase in the percentage of clerks, managers, and salesmen in the Viennese work force as a whole. Under the influence of the urban environment, Jews created a new typically Jewish pattern of occupational preference.

Because they created a new Jewish occupation, Jewish clerks, salesmen, and managers did not encounter many opportunities for structural assimilation. On the contrary, Jews entered new fields collectively and worked largely in the company of other Jews. The new positions afforded them new opportunities to strengthen their contacts with other Jews. Perceiving their collective needs, and wishing to associate with other Jews in similar circumstances, they organized professional associations at the end of the nineteenth century. Jewish transformations thus continued to mark the Jews as a distinct group and provided Jews with new opportunities for associating largely with other Jews.

In order to determine the occupational distribution of all Jews, and not just youthful grooms and fathers, it was necessary here, as in the preceding discussion of migration, to combine data from all five sample years and create composite statistics (Table 3:1). On the average between 1870 and 1910, two-fifths of all Viennese Jews were merchants, one-quarter were "Business Employees," that is, clerks, salesmen, or managers in industrial or commercial enterprises, 12% practiced artisanal crafts, 11% engaged in the professions, i.e., medicine, law, education, engineering, journalism, and the arts, and 3% worked for the civil service. Only 4% called themselves industrialists or factory owners, and 4% labored in factories as "workers." [6] Despite the prevailing notion that the most prestigious careers in the Monarchy in the imperial or municipal civil service were closed to Jews by antisemitism and the perception of antisemitic exclusiveness,[7] some Viennese Jews did indeed work for the government. True, they rarely worked for the prestigious ministries or services. Some worked for the Finance Ministry, but most pursued careers in the less prestigious Railroad and Post Office Ministries. Their rank within these ministries is unknown. Nevertheless, Jews participated in state service more commonly than one might expect.

This Jewish occupational distribution resulted from the fact that Jews took advantage of the economic opportunities available to them in Vienna. In the city, Jews experienced a profound transformation in their patterns of occupational preference, but the new element introduced by urban opportunities was simply the location of Jewish concentration. Young Jews, and second-generation Viennese Jews, no longer bound by the restrictions which hindered their fathers, came to shun careers as merchants, instead choosing positions as clerks, salesmen, and managers. Despite change, Jews continued to choose different occupations than everyone else.

In their rush into clerical and managerial positions, Viennese Jews did not at all fulfill the expectations of the liberals who had granted them emancipation. During the first half of the nineteenth century, liberals had argued that given the opportunity the Jews would leave the "nonproductive" commercial occupations to which they had long been restricted and would enter more "productive" fields in industry and crafts.[8] Instead, when Jews left trade they found new sources of employment not in the developing industry of a modernizing economy but in the banks, insurance companies, and large business enterprises of Austria's late nineteenth-century capitalist expansion.[9] In this period Vienna developed as a banking center and as the center for the corporate headquarters of many industrial cartels whose plants were located elsewhere. It was also, with its growing population, an important market and distribution center, and it had become the main railroad junction for the entire Monarchy. Jews took ad-

Table 3:1. Occupations of Jewish Grooms, Composite, 1870–1910

	#	%
Civil Servants	21	2.6
Professionals	92	11.3
Industrialists	28	3.5
Merchants	331	40.8
Business Employees	207	25.5
Artisans	97	12.0
Workers	35	4.3
	811	100.0%

vantage of the new opportunities that this business expansion offered. Jews easily moved into these clerical and managerial positions in business. Because they had been merchants and traders in the provinces, Jews arrived in the city with commercial skills and a world view compatible with clerical work. It was an easy step from small-scale trade into the clerical or managerial positions in the insurance companies, banks, and large corporations which opened in Vienna at the time.

The changing occupational preference of Viennese Jews was most typical, of course, among the young. The youthful bias of the sample of Viennese Jewish grooms enables the historian to see precisely the choices made by young Jews in the late nineteenth century (Table 3:2). Between 1870 and 1910, the number of Jewish grooms pursuing careers as merchants declined from 55.6% in 1870 to 33.3% in 1910. At the same time, the popularity of careers as "Business Employees" rose from only 2.8% of those who married soon after the Emancipation to 35.2% of those who married just before World War I. This transformation is even more significant than these figures would indicate. During this period, Jewish immigration increased from decade to decade, especially from those areas of Galicia where traditional Jewish economic patterns still held sway. The new migrants certainly deflated the percentage of business employees and inflated the number of merchants. That even with this influx the change is still so noticeable is a testimony to its depth and strength.

Young Jewish men pursued careers simply not available to the preceding generations. About one-quarter of all the Jewish grooms were business employees, but only 3% of their fathers and fathers-in-law engaged in similar occupations (Table 3:3). Information on the fathers and fathers-in-law is mostly from 1870, 1880, and 1890. These men, therefore, made their career choices when they had relatively limited possibilities. Their sons and sons-in-law took advantage of urban opportunities and entered new careers.

Table 3:2. Occupations of Jewish Grooms, 1870–1910

	1870 N = 72	1880 N = 107	1890 N = 155	1900 N = 206	1910 N = 261
Civil Servants	2.8%	—	1.9%	2.9%	3.8%
Professionals	11.1	7.5%	11.6	13.1	11.1
Industrialists	5.6	1.9	3.9	3.4	3.4
Merchants	55.6	57.0	45.8	33.0	33.3
Business Employees	2.8	15.0	22.6	29.6	35.2
Artisans	19.4	15.9	10.3	13.1	8.0
Workers	2.8	2.8	3.9	4.9	5.0
	100.0%	100.0%	100.0%	100.0%	100.0%

Jews in Vienna rejected, however, many other career paths made possible by urban opportunities. Jews did not abandon their roles as merchants to become artisans as their liberal friends had hoped. In the immediate aftermath of Emancipation some Jews did try to become craftsmen, and the percentage of Jewish artisans in 1870 and 1880 was much higher among the Jewish grooms than among their fathers and fathers-in-law (Tables 3:2 and 3:3). After 1880, however, the movement into artisanry declined considerably, so that by 1910 half as many grooms were artisans as had been the case in 1880. Decline was most noticeable in the clothing industry. Only the number of Jewish carpenters, house painters, and paperhangers increased between 1870 and 1910. This increase, as well as the slight increase in the number of Jewish factory workers at the end of the nineteenth century, resulted from the Galician migration which included some artisans in the construction industry as well as some laborers.

Despite the perceptions of participants like Höllriegel or historians like Schorske, Viennese Jews did not move into the professions in large numbers between 1870 and 1910 (Table 3:2). True, more Jewish grooms practiced such professions as medicine, law, journalism, and engineering than their fathers or fathers-in-law (Table 3:3), but professional occupations accounted for the same percentage (11%) of Jewish grooms in 1910 as they did in 1870. Many Viennese doctors or lawyers were Jewish,[10] but Viennese Jews did not rush into careers in medicine or law in this period. Antisemitic discrimination against Jewish doctors may have contributed somewhat to this phenomenon. The public careers of some Jewish doctors were stymied by antisemites, and Jewish newspapers complained of an unofficial boycott of Jewish doctors.[11] In his play, *Professor Bernhardi* (1912), Arthur Schnitzler, himself a physician, gave articulate and artistic expression to the problem of antisemitism faced by Jewish doctors.[12] Antise-

Table 3:3. Occupations of Grooms' and Brides' Fathers, Composite, 1870–1910

	Grooms' Fathers		Brides' Fathers	
	#	%	#	%
Civil Servants	3	1.3	7	2.9
Professionals	15	6.5	18	7.3
Industrialists	7	3.0	10	4.1
Merchants	144	62.3	142	57.3
Business Employees	5	2.2	9	3.6
Artisans	20	8.7	32	12.9
Workers	—	—	1	0.4
Unclassifiable*	37	16.0	29	11.7
	231	100.0%	248	100.0%

* Mostly people living on pension or other income.

mitism, however, did not prevent the modest, but significant rise in the number of Jewish civil servants between 1870 and 1910. None of the grooms in the sample for 1880 were civil servants, but in 1910, 4% of all Jewish men who married worked for the state or municipal government. The prestigious ministries may have been closed to Jews, but the new services like the railroad and post office, with their need for technically skilled personnel, opened their doors to Jews with the necessary training.

The trend into clerical, sales, or managerial positions was by no means typical only of young Jews, such as grooms, or of poorer Jews. Wealthy Jews were also entering these fields. Even among the older and more prosperous taxpaying members of the IKG, there was a noticeable shift from trade into salaried employment between 1855 and 1914. True, this shift was less conspicuous among these older and wealthier notables than it was in the Jewish community at large. The strongest demographic base for the movement into employment in business concerns was not the wealthy merchant class, of which the IKG was largely composed, but rather the sons of poor traders able to make use of big city opportunities to rise in economic station.

Within the richer echelons of Viennese Jewish society, the youngest were the most likely to chose careers as "Business Employees." Among new entrants to the IKG tax rolls (Table 3:4), the percentage of business employees increased from 2.8% in the years before Emancipation to 28.3% in the fourteen years before the First World War. During that same period, the number of merchants declined from 65% to 38.5%, and the number of professionals, and especially civil servants, increased modestly.

Work as clerks or managers may have been only temporary for many Jews, providing them training for careers as merchants. More prosperous merchants, in particular, often groomed salesmen or commercial employees for careers as entrepreneurs. An investigation of

Table 3:4. Occupations of New IKG Taxpayers, Entering Tax Rolls 1855–1914

	1855–67 N = 177	1868–79 N = 350	1880s N = 319	1890s N = 433	1900–1914 N = 501
Civil Servants	0.6%	2.9%	1.6%	2.5%	5.6%
Professionals	11.3	10.6	9.1	12.5	13.8
Industrialists	8.5	4.6	10.3	6.5	2.8
Merchants	65.0	61.7	47.6	42.5	38.5
Business Employees	2.8	7.1	15.4	21.9	28.3
Artisans	11.9	13.1	16.0	14.1	11.0
Workers	—	—	—	—	—
	100.0%	100.0%	100.0%	100.0%	100.0%

the sources, however, reveals that employment in banks, insurance companies, or large business concerns by no means provided only training for careers as merchants. For most business employees, even the older and richer ones, their choice of career was permanent.

Because the IKG tax rolls recorded all occupational changes, it has been possible to map the career paths of the richer members of the Jewish community.[13] Only 24.6% of all *Gemeinde* taxpayers ever changed occupation at all, and many of these merely retired to live on their pensions. Merchants frequently changed occupation, but the "change" amounted to exchanging one kind of goods traded for another. For example, Julius Nemet from Szerdahely, Hungary, was a grocer when he arrived in Vienna in 1899 but later became a silk merchant; Moritz Neufeld of Temesvar, Hungary, a *Gemeinde* taxpayer from 1891 to 1925, also began as a grocer, but later sold women's clothing; and Filipp Neumann of Nagysurany, Hungary, first kept an inn and then dealt in chickens between 1892 and 1900.[14] This particular kind of occupational change does not reflect any restructuring at all, but was normal for certain kinds of traders who would deal in whatever happened to be available at a given time.

Other *Gemeinde* taxpayers who changed occupation easily crossed the line separating industry and commerce. Josef Paschka, for example, a native-born Viennese hat dealer, became a hat manufacturer. Between 1873 and 1910, David Neumann, also born in Vienna, was a clothing dealer and then a large factory owner. On the other hand, Jakob Mandler from Mährisch Weisskirchen, Moravia, was a merchant when he came to Vienna in 1882; during the five years he lived in the city, however, he tried his hand at plumbing.[15] Almost two-fifths of those *Gemeinde* taxpayers who were artisans or industrialists and changed occupations became merchants, and one-fifth of the merchants who changed careers opened factories, primarily in the clothing, and food and drink industries.

Well-to-do merchants, of course, almost never abandoned trade in order to work as clerks or managers in a corporation. The trend to salaried employment in business was not typical of mid-career changes, especially among the prosperous. Of those who chose careers as business employees, however, relatively few ever changed occupations at all. In fact, only 11% of all clerks, salesmen, or managers who paid taxes to the IKG ever did so. When IKG business employees changed careers, they did become merchants, the role for which they had prepared, but most business employees regarded their new positions as permanent.

Of all Jews in Vienna, it was second-generation Jews, the sons of poor, immigrant traders, who were most likely to pursue clerical managerial, and sales careers. Linguistic, financial, and cultural problems often made it difficult for recent immigrants from Bohemia, Moravia, Hungary, and especially Galicia to abandon trade and work as business employees, but their Viennese-born children, educated in the city, had no such problems seeking employment in the business concerns of the city. Thus, it was among the growing body of native-born Jews that the profound restructuring of Jewish economic preference was the most apparent. The percentage of Viennese-born Jews who abandoned trade for jobs as clerks, salesmen, and managers was extremely high, higher than in any other group of Viennese Jews (Table 3:5). In the period between 1880 and 1910—the 1870 figures were too low to be statistically significant—the percentage of merchants among native-born Viennese Jewish grooms declined from 62.5% to 28.4%. At the same time, the percentage of grooms who were clerks, salesmen, or managers rose from 12.5% to 43.2%. Native-born Viennese Jews followed professional careers less often than most other Jews in the city, but they worked for the civil service more frequently. Surprisingly, fewer Viennese-born Jews were civil servants in 1910 than in 1890.

The movement of Bohemian, Moravian, and Hungarian Jews into positions as business employees was less profound than among the native-born, but more substantial than among Galicians (Table 3:5). The causes for this difference are easy to determine. Many Jews from Bohemia, Moravia, and Hungary arrived in the capital already Germanized or as children in the early waves of migration. Thus they received their education in Vienna and had successfully acculturated. Consequently the proportion of Moravian Jewish grooms employed as clerks, salesmen, and managers rose from 5.9% in 1880 to 34.3% in 1910, and the number of Hungarian grooms who practiced these occupations increased less dramatically from 10.4% to 25% in the same period. The percentage of merchants among both groups of Jews declined considerably during that time. Moravian-born Jews, incidentally, concentrated in the professions more than any other Jews in the city.

Bohemians also entered new careers as business employees, and the percentage of Bohemian grooms who were clerks, salesmen, and managers doubled between 1880 and 1910. But the pattern of Bohemian occupational change was atypical for Viennese Jewry. Unlike other Jews, the Bohemians did not abandon trade to enter the new urban occupations. In fact the proportion of merchants among Jews of Bohemian origin remained constant at one-third. Instead it was the artisanal crafts, and to a lesser extent the ranks of the industrialists, which Bohemian Jews in Vienna abandoned in order to do office work. From the outset, Bohemian Jewish grooms, much more than other Viennese Jews, chose industrial occupations, whether as in-

Table 3:5. Occupations of Jewish Grooms from Vienna, Bohemia, Moravia, Galicia, and Hungary, 1870–1910

	Composite	1870	1880	1890	1900	1910
Viennese*	N = 184	N = 3	N = 8	N = 20	N = 58	N = 95
Civil Servants	4.3%	—	—	10.0%	5.2%	3.2%
Professionals	9.4	66.7%	25.0%	5.0	5.2	9.5
Industrialists	3.8	—	—	—	5.2	4.2
Merchants	31.5	—	62.5	50.0	27.6	28.4
Business Employees	38.0	—	12.5	30.0	37.9	43.2
Artisans	8.7	33.3	—	5.0	12.1	7.4
Workers	4.3	—	—	—	6.9	4.2
	100.0%	100.0%	100.0%	100.0%	100.0%	100.0%
Bohemians	N = 98	N = 13	N = 16	N = 19	N = 25	N = 25
Civil Servants	2.0%	7.7%	—	5.3%	—	—
Professionals	11.2	23.1	12.5%	5.3	8.0%	12.0%
Industrialists	7.1	7.7	6.3	10.5	8.0	4.0
Merchants	31.6	30.8	31.3	26.3	32.0	36.0
Business Employees	28.6	—	18.8	31.6	36.0	40.0
Artisans	13.3	23.1	25.0	15.8	8.0	4.0
Workers	6.1	7.7	6.3	5.3	8.0	4.0
	100.0%	100.0%	100.0%	100.0%	100.0%	100.0%
Moravians and Silesians	N = 130	N = 14	N = 17	N = 27	N = 37	N = 35
Civil Servants	3.1%	7.7%	—	—	—	8.6%
Professionals	14.6	21.4	5.9%	14.8%	16.2%	14.3
Industrialists	3.8	—	—	7.4	2.7	5.7
Merchants	42.3	42.9	70.6	51.9	37.8	25.7
Business Employees	23.8	14.3	5.9	11.1	35.1	34.3
Artisans	10.0	14.3	11.8	14.8	8.1	5.7
Workers	2.3	—	5.9	—	—	5.7
	100.0%	100.0%	100.0%	100.0%	100.0%	100.0%
Galicians and Bukovinians	N = 160	N = 3	N = 14	N = 32	N = 51	N = 60
Civil Servants	1.9%	—	—	—	2.0%	3.3%
Professionals	11.3	—	7.1%	12.5%	15.7	8.3
Industrialists	—	—	—	—	—	—
Merchants	41.3	66.7%	21.4	50.0	35.3	45.0
Business Employees	26.3	—	42.9	21.9	19.6	31.7
Artisans	15.0	33.3	28.6	9.4	21.6	8.3
Workers	4.4	—	—	6.3	5.9	3.3
	100.0%	100.0%	100.0%	100.0%	100.0%	100.0%

* Includes a few Lower Austrians

Table 3:5. Occupations of Jewish Grooms from Vienna, Bohemia, Moravia, Galicia, and Hungary, 1870–1910—Continued

		Hungarians				
	Composite N = 186	1870 N = 33	1880 N = 48	1890 N = 46	1900 N = 27	1910 N = 32
Civil Servants	1.1%	—	—	—	3.7%	3.1%
Professionals	7.0	—	2.1%	8.7%	18.5	9.4
Industrialists	4.3	9.1%	2.1	4.3	3.7	3.1
Merchants	55.4	69.7	68.8	50.0	40.7	40.6
Business Employees	16.1	—	10.4	23.9	22.2	25.0
Artisans	12.9	21.2	14.6	8.7	11.1	9.4
Workers	3.2	—	2.1	4.3	—	9.4
	100.0%	100.0%	100.0%	100.0%	100.0%	100.0%

dustrialists or artisans. To be sure, their participation in industry paled by comparison with that of all Czechs (Jews and non-Jews) in Vienna, 74% of whom pursued industrial occupations in 1910, mostly as workers in the clothing industry.[16] Following emancipation, Bohemian Jews had striven to become craftsmen, and in 1870 and 1880 about one-quarter of the Bohemian Jewish grooms had achieved that goal. By 1910, however, the proportion of craftsmen among Bohemian Jews had declined to 4%. Many Bohemian Jews had put on shirts and ties to join the office staffs of the city. Bohemian Jewish "industrialists," many of whom may have been simply the more prosperous artisans, did likewise.

Changes in occupational structure among Galician Jews in Vienna between 1880—the 1870 sample was too small for statistical analysis—and 1910 reflect, on the other hand, two concomitant factors: the greater occupational traditionalism of the second wave of Galician Jewish migrants, and the same modernizing trends common among all Jewish groups at this time. The Galician grooms sampled from 1880 came with the first, less traditional, wave of Galician migration to Vienna. Only one-fifth of the 1880 grooms were merchants, while two-fifths registered as business employees and a substantial number as artisans. By 1890, however, the second wave of migration had set in, creating a reversal of the 1880 distribution. In the next two decades, most Galician Jewish grooms were recorded as merchants, while few held clerical, sales, or managerial positions. Only in 1910 did the number of Galician Jewish business employees increase while the number of Galician Jews participating in trade decreased to some extent. Like Bohemians, many Galicians abandoned artisanal occupations in order to work in offices.

Richer Jews who had *Heimatrecht* in Vienna, Bohemia, Moravia, Hungary, or Galicia also increasingly found employment as clerks, salesmen, and managers, although presumably they did so at a higher and more remunerative level than those who could not afford to pay IKG taxes. For example, in 1868–79, only 6.9% of new entrants into the *Gemeinde* tax rolls who had legal residence rights in Vienna were business employees, but 27.5% of such new entrants in the 1900s were thus employed (Table 3:6). Similarly, more new IKG taxpayers from Moravia, Bohemia, Hungary, and to a lesser extent Galicia, pursued clerical or managerial careers in the 1900s than in the preceding decades. Unlike Jewish grooms from Bohemia who abandoned artisanship in order to become business employees, Bohemian IKG taxpayers behaved like all other Viennese Jews and left careers in trade in order to become clerks, salesmen, or managers. Native-born Viennese IKG taxpayers were the most likely Jews in Vienna to become civil servants in the late nineteenth century; by the 1900s, 6.4% of all new entrants to the IKG tax rolls with Viennese *Heimat* worked for the imperial or municipal government. Finally, many IKG tax payers with Galician *Heimatrecht* moved into such professions as medicine, law, engineering, and writing. In the first decade after emancipation only 8.3% of all new IKG taxpayers from Galicia practiced a profession, but in the 1900s, 24% did so.

The pattern of occupational transformation among Viennese Jews differed radically from the legendary social mobility of the Jews in New York. The Eastern European Jews who emigrated to New York were skilled laborers when they arrived in the United States. Beginning as poor tailors in the burgeoning garment industry, many became wealthy clothing manufacturers with lightning-like rapidity, and their children entered the professions.[17] The sons of the merchants who immigrated to Vienna, on the other hand, turned to clerical and managerial careers, but both groups of Jews experienced profound upward social mobility, that is, a rise in social status, wealth, and prestige. Working as clerks or salesmen meant guaranteed income and a secure position for the sons of poor traders living at the brink of poverty. Vienna made it possible for Jews to enjoy careers which gave them more security, wealth, prestige, and status than they had enjoyed before.

Because of the concentration of Jews in trade and clerical careers, it is virtually impossible to measure Jewish social mobility by the scales employed by most historians. Such scales place merchants in the very highest rank, along with professionals, civil servants, and upper-level managers. These scales measure the movement of men and women from the blue-collar laboring classes into two white-collar ranks, the highest rank of merchants and professionals, and

Table 3:6. Occupations of IKG Taxpayers from Vienna, Bohemia, Moravia, Galicia, and Hungary, 1855–1914

Vienna and Lower Austria	Overall N = 683	Entered IKG In: 1855–67 N = 91	1868–79 N = 72	1880s N = 55	1890s N = 105	1900s N = 345
Civil Servants	4.7%	1.1%	2.8%	1.8%	5.7%	6.4%
Professionals	16.0	11.0	12.5	20.0	21.0	16.2
Industrialists	5.7	11.0	6.9	12.7	6.7	2.3
Merchants	42.8	63.7	59.7	34.5	30.5	37.4
Business Employees	18.6	1.1	6.9	14.5	17.1	27.5
Artisans	12.3	12.1	11.1	16.4	19.0	10.1
Workers	—	—	—	—	—	—
	100.0%	100.0%	100.0%	100.0%	100.0%	100.0%

Bohemians	Overall N = 186	Entered IKG In: 1855–67 N = 14	1868–79 N = 41	1880s N = 39	1890s N = 62	1900s N = 30
Civil Servants	2.7%	—	2.4%	—	1.6%	10.0%
Professionals	15.1	42.9%	24.4	10.3%	9.7	6.7
Industrialists	8.6	7.1	7.3	12.8	9.7	3.3
Merchants	41.9	42.9	51.2	41.0	45.2	23.3
Business Employees	19.9	—	7.3	15.4	25.8	40.0
Artisans	11.8	7.1	7.3	20.5	8.1	16.7
Workers	—	—	—	—	—	—
	100.0%	100.0%	100.0%	100.0%	100.0%	100.0%

Moravians and Silesians	Overall N = 220	Entered IKG In: 1855–67 N = 20	1868–79 N = 43	1880s N = 53	1890s N = 75	1900s N = 29
Civil Servants	1.8%	—	2.3%	3.8%	—	3.4%
Professionals	6.8	—	16.3	3.8	6.7%	3.4
Industrialists	6.4	5.0%	—	9.4	8.0	6.9
Merchants	53.6	70.0	58.1	52.8	50.7	44.8
Business Employees	18.6	5.0	9.3	17.0	25.3	27.6
Artisans	12.7	20.0	14.0	13.2	9.3	13.8
Workers	—	—	—	—	—	—
	100.0%	100.0%	100.0%	100.0%	100.0%	100.0%

Galicians and Bukovinians	Overall N = 161	Entered IKG In: 1855–67 N = 4	1868–79 N = 48	1880s N = 31	1890s N = 53	1900s N = 25
Civil Servants	2.5%	—	4.2%	3.2%	1.9%	—
Professionals	13.7	—	8.3	9.7	17.0	24.0%
Industrialists	3.1	25.0%	2.1	6.5	1.9	—
Merchants	50.9	75.0	64.6	48.4	39.6	48.0
Business Employees	14.3	—	4.2	9.7	26.4	16.0
Artisans	15.5	—	16.7	22.6	13.2	12.0
Workers	—	—	—	—	—	—
	100.0%	100.0%	100.0%	100.0%	100.0%	100.0%

Table 3:6. Occupations of IKG Taxpayers from Vienna, Bohemia, Moravia, Galicia, and Hungary, 1855–1914—Continued

Hungarians	Overall N = 441	Entered IKG In: 1855–67 N = 37	1868–79 N = 104	1880s N = 121	1890s N = 118	1900s N = 60
Civil Servants	0.9%	—	—	0.8%	1.7%	1.7%
Professionals	6.3	8.1%	4.8%	7.4	7.6	3.3
Industrialists	6.6	5.4	6.7	8.3	6.8	3.3
Merchants	54.6	64.9	66.3	53.7	46.6	45.0
Business Employees	16.8	8.1	6.7	14.9	22.0	33.3
Artisans	14.7	13.5	15.4	14.9	15.3	13.3
Workers	—	—	—	—	—	—
	100.0%	100.0%	100.0%	100.0%	100.0%	100.0%

the second rank composed of clerks, salesmen, small proprietors, and such lesser professionals as teachers or entertainers.[18] These scales pose nearly insurmountable problems for measuring Viennese Jewish social mobility. In the first place, all Viennese Jews would find themselves in the highest two status ranks, even though, in fact, most Viennese Jews enjoyed little social status. Many Viennese Jewish merchants did enjoy a large measure of prestige and wealth, but others lived on the brink of poverty. Jews who called themselves merchants could have been peddlers at one extreme, or wealthy businessmen with world-wide connections at the other. Sigmund Mayer, the prominent textile wholesaler, listed himself as a *Kaufmann* (merchant) in the IKG tax records; Alfred Lederer, whose poverty forced him off the tax rolls of the *Gemeinde,* was also a *Kaufmann.*[19] Scales which place over half of the population in the highest rank are an invalid measure of changing social stratification.

Secondly, the usual scales do not account for many nineteenth-century status differentials because they incorrectly place peddlers, who are, after all, entrepreneurs, in a high-status rank and ignore the true status of certain craftsmen in the nineteenth century.[20] Even the scale devised by Michael Katz, which ranks all nineteenth-century occupations in an order which reflects their true status and wealth,[21] is insufficient for measuring Jewish transformations. Wealth is certainly the best measure of social status,[22] but no adequate measures of Jewish wealth exist for Vienna. Although the *Gemeinde* records contain tax assessments, these tax assessments have proven inadequate as specific wealth indicators because 75% of the members paid the minimum tax and those in the highest brackets engaged in all kinds of occupations. Most Viennese Jews did not pay taxes to the IKG in any case.

If Jewish social mobility is measured according to a modified version of the scale devised by Michael Katz,[23] it appears that Jews experienced no upward or downward social mobility at all between 1870 and 1910 despite radical occupational restructuring (Table 3:7). According to this scale, "high-status" rank includes merchants, professionals, factory owners, upper-level civil servants, and upper-level managers; "medium-status" rank includes clerks, salesmen, business agents, and lower-level civil servants; and "low-status" rank consists of peddlers, artisanal assistants *(Gehilfen),* unskilled workers, and servants. Artisans have been placed in a separate status category because the records did not indicate if craftsmen were masters, journeymen, or shopworkers. Throughout the period, Jews clustered in the high-status careers, rich Jews especially, and few had low social status. Of course, the fact that most Jews were merchants, professionals, or managers, all of which came under the high-status category, caused this clustering in the highest status rank.

Given the nature of Jewish occupational change in Vienna, one might have expected the scale to register downward social mobility, from high- to medium-status ranks between 1870 and 1910. On the contrary, except for a diminishing proportion of artisans, Jewish social status remained virtually unchanged in the decades before the First World War. The continued immigration of merchants who augmented the "high-status" rank and the increasing number of Jewish civil servants, partially explain this lack of change. The growing number of business employees should have augmented the "medium-status" rank, but the diminishing number of Viennese Jewish business agents included in this category and the fact that some "Business Employees" were included in the "high-status" rank, cancelled out any growth of the "medium-status" category.

By conventional standards, a decline in Jewish social status did take place between the generation of the fathers and that of the sons, for the sons of supposedly "high-status" merchants became clerks, salesmen, and managers and thus entered "medium-status" careers (Table 3:8). While 68.9% of the grooms' fathers enjoyed "high" social status, only 51.9% of the grooms enjoyed similar status; conversely, 27.8% of the grooms practiced medium-status careers as compared to 18.5% of their fathers. Moreover, 57% of the grooms practicing "medium-status" occupations had fathers with "high-status" positions. This apparent downward mobility, of course, did not result from any real loss of social status. Rather, this descent into the "medium-status" category as clerks and salesmen was upward social mobility for the sons of men who were in fact peddlers or petty traders.

The sons of many working-class Jews were also able to advance in social status by entering clerical careers, or by becoming merchants and professionals. Of the bridegrooms whose fathers were artisans,

Table 3:7. Occupational Status of Jewish Grooms, 1870–1910, and IKG Taxpayers, Composite, 1855–1914

	Grooms						IKG Taxpayers
	Composite N = 834	1870 N = 73	1880 N = 108	1890 N = 159	1900 N = 217	1910 N = 277	1855–1914 N = 2504
High Status	51.9%	57.5%	47.2%	51.4%	51.2%	51.6%	70.8%
Medium Status	27.8	17.8	31.5	28.3	24.9	31.0	18.1
Artisans	11.6	19.2	15.7	10.1	12.9	7.9	10.9
Low Status	8.6	5.5	5.6	7.5	11.1	9.4	0.1
	100.0%	100.0%	100.0%	100.0%	100.0%	100.0%	100.0%

Table 3:8. Occupational Status of Grooms, Grooms' Fathers, and Brides' Fathers, Composite, 1870–1910

	Grooms N = 834	Grooms' Fathers N = 238	Brides' Fathers N = 256
High Status	51.9%	68.9%	64.1%
Medium Status	27.8	18.5	17.6
Artisans	11.6	9.2	12.9
Low Status	8.6	3.4	5.5
	100.0%	100.0%	100.0%

30% practiced "medium-status" occupations, and 35% pursued "high-status" careers. One-quarter of the sons of artisans practiced "low-status" careers at the time of their marriage (largely as artisanal assistants), but this apparent downard shift was a factor of the life cycle. The sons of men who practiced "low-status" occupations, most of them peddlers, were extremely likely to enter medium- or high-status careers. Only eight of the bridegrooms in the sample had fathers who were peddlers, and most of them entered "medium-status" positions as clerks and salesmen.

There was no true downward social mobility among Viennese Jews. Rich Viennese Jews were extremely successful at maintaining their status.[24] Among taxpaying members of the IKG who changed occupations, fully 85% of those with "high-status" positions maintained that status when they changed jobs, even if they changed jobs repeatedly. Indeed, most IKG taxpayers who changed occupations (641 or 24.6% of all taxpayers) only moved up in social standing. Of the artisans who changed occupations, 68.9% entered "high-status" careers as merchants or industrialists, and 24.4% entered "medium-status" careers. Similarly, four-fifths of those IKG taxpayers who began their careers in "medium-status" positions and who changed jobs entered "high-status" careers.

All of the economic restructuring described thus far by no means led, however, to the economic assimilation of the Jews. Jews changed occupations and rose in social status, but they remained a group apart in Vienna. The rush of Jews into clerical, managerial, and sales positions did not parallel any similar growth in the percentage of business employees in the Viennese work force as a whole in the decades before World War I. Jews transformed themselves in the urban environment but that transformation did not lead to the growing similarity of Jewish and gentile occupational distribution. Jewish change only led to continued Jewish distinctiveness.

Comparing Jewish occupational distribution to the distribution of the Viennese work force as a whole best reveals the unique position of Vienna's Jews at the end of the nineteenth century. In order to compare both groups, it was necessary to employ the categories of the Austrian census which divided the economy into four sectors: "Agriculture," "Industry," "Trade and Transport," and "Public Service and Free Professions." [25] Unfortunately, the Austrian Statistical Central Commission used the fourth sector as a catch-all category, including in it not only military men, civil servants, educators, religious leaders, doctors, lawyers, scientists, writers, artists, and entertainers, but also business employees (secretaries, bookkeepers, clerks, managers, administrators), people living on private income, and men and women in such public institutions as prisons and insane asylums. This category minimizes some of the differences between Jews and all Viennese, but its use is necessary for comparative purposes. This study has not employed the Austrian economic categories for the general discussion of Jewish occupational change because these categories obscure the most important changes in Viennese Jewish economic behavior.

Comparing the Jews in the composite samples to Viennese generally reveals that they clustered in different sectors of the economy in the late nineteenth century (Tables 3:9 and 3:10). As expected, Jews (Table 3:9) concentrated in "Trade and Transport" and in "Public Service and Free Professions." Approximately two-fifths of all grooms, fathers, and IKG members (on the average) engaged in occupations included under Trade and Transport, and a little under two-fifths in occupations included under Public Service and Free Professions. Only one-fifth of the Jews practiced industrial occupations. On the average between 1890 and 1910, over half of the total Viennese work force (Table 3:10) engaged in industrial pursuits, while only one-quarter concentrated in Trade and Transport, and one-quarter in Public Service and Free Professions. Even though Vienna was the commercial and administrative center of the Monarchy, it was not populated in major part by traders and administrators,[26] but rather by those who labored in industry. Jews were an atypical group in the city.

Within each of these economic sectors, Jews and Viennese generally clustered in different branches. In the industrial sector, for example (Table 3:11), Jews shied away from those branches of heavy industry which attracted most Viennese. Only 18.8% of Jewish grooms in industry on the average between 1870 and 1910 were involved in such industries as mining, metals, machinery, stone, chemicals, and gold and silver ("Industry I"), but 27.6% of all Viennese concentrated in industry worked for these industries. In fact, within the category "Industry I" most Jews worked with gold and silver as jewelers, but most Viennese were machinists or metal workers.[27] Similarly, Jews in industry were much less likely than Viennese generally to work

Table 3:9. Occupational Sector of Jewish Grooms and Fathers, Composite, 1870–1910, and IKG Taxpayers, Composite, 1855–1914

Sector	Grooms N = 835	Fathers N = 1075	IKG Taxpayers N = 2507
Agriculture	0.2%	0.3%	0.1%
Industry	19.6	24.7	18.4
Trade & Transport	44.3	50.4	42.2
Public Service & Free Profs.	35.7	24.7	39.2
	100.0%	100.0%	100.0%

Table 3:10. Occupational Sector of Total Viennese Work Force, 1890–1910

Sector	1890 N = 695,393	1900 N = 848,973	1910 N = 1,094,185	Average 1890–1910
Agriculture	1.2%	0.7%	0.9%	0.9%
Industry	55.4	51.5	46.6	51.2
Trade & Transport	21.5	23.5	27.1	24.0
Public Service & Free Profs.	21.9	24.3	25.4	24.9
	100.0%	100.0%	100.0%	100.0%

Sources: Öst. Stat., 33:1, p. viii; 66:1, p. xvi; N.F. 3:1, p. 13*.

either with paper, leather, fur, wood, cork, and straw ("Industry II"), or in the food, drink, and restaurant industries. On the other hand, within this sector of the economy, Jews were just as likely as all Viennese to concentrate in the clothing industry. Unlike their coreligionists in New York, Paris, or London, however, Jews in Vienna did not dominate the clothing industry. Only 3.6% of the total Jewish work force clustered in the garment industry, but 17.8% of all Viennese *Berufstätige* (all those actually working) in 1890 produced clothing.[28] Jews with industrial occupations were twice as likely as Viennese in industry to be in construction, mostly as carpenters, painters, paper hangers, and decorators.

Jews in the Trade and Transport sector of the economy were overwhelmingly traders in goods or money and avoided careers in transport. Only 3% of the Jewish grooms counted in this sector were in transport, but 9.8% were in banking and credit, and 87.2% traded in goods of one sort or another. The Viennese who came under this category, however, often engaged in transport. In 1900, about 38% of those in the commercial sector—including the Jews—traded in goods, 7% in money and credit; 30% were in transport, and about 15% in personal service.[29]

It is within the sector "Public Service and Free Professions" that the staggering differences between Jewish and Viennese occupational

Table 3:11. Comparison of Jews and Total Viennese Work Force Engaged in the Industrial Sector of the Economy, 1900

Branch	Grooms Composite N = 154	Grooms 1900 N = 38	Males Vienna, 1900 N = 313,227
Industry I*	18.8%	10.5%	27.6%
Industry II**	6.5	5.3	16.6
Textiles	4.5	—	4.0
Clothing	19.5	23.7	19.8
Food, Drink, Restaurants	8.4	7.9	15.0
Print, Art	9.7	5.3	4.3
Construction	19.5	28.9	10.3
Unspecified	13.0	18.4	2.5
	100.0%	100.0%	100.0%

* Industry I: Mining, metals, gold and silver, stones and earth, machines and instruments, chemicals.
** Industry II: Paper, leather, fur, wood, cork, straw.
Sources (Vienna): *Öst. Stat.*, 66:2, pp. 7–29; *SJSW* (1901), pp. 73–94.

structure come to light. For the first time in 1900 the Austrian census presented enough detail on this sector to make analysis and comparison possible[30] (Table 3:12). In that year, 7% of all Viennese counted in this sector worked as secretaries, stenographers, and managers *(Privatbeamte).* In sharp contrast, 53.8% of all Jewish grooms, and 51.8% of the grooms who married in 1900, counted in this sector pursued clerical, sales, and managerial occupations. Viennese men who concentrated in "Public Service and Free Professions" worked much more frequently than Jews for the military and police, or the imperial and municipal civil service. Fully one-quarter of all Viennese in this sector worked for the civil service, but only 8.1% of Jewish grooms in this sector did likewise. Jews almost never were employed by the military or police. Jews, however, more commonly than Viennese generally, practiced medicine and law.

Jews also differed markedly from the entire Viennese work force when measured by the social-status ranking devised by the Austrian Statistical Central Commission for the decennial census. This scale, not concerned with class in the modern sense, divided the work force into five "classes": the self-employed *(Selbstständige),* those employed for a regular salary *(Angestellte),* wage earners or workers *(Arbeiter),* day laborers *(Taglöhner),* and family helpers *(Mithelfende Familienangehörige).* The class of *Angestellte* included civil servants as well as business employees, while the worker category included most industrial laborers.[31] As would be expected, comparing Jews to all Viennese on this scale reveals that Jews concentrated in both self-employed and salaried-employed groups, while Viennese overwhelm-

Table 3:12. Comparison of Jewish Grooms and Total Viennese Work Force in "Public Service and Free Professions," 1900*

	Grooms		Males
	Composite N = 284	1900 N = 85	Vienna, 1900* N = 77,359
Military and Police	2.1%	3.5%	40.0%
Civil Service	8.1	8.2	24.3
Education	4.6	5.9	7.7
Medicine	9.5	9.4	4.3
Religion	2.1	1.2	1.8
Law	9.2	9.4	3.8
Art, Theater, Writing, Science	10.9	10.6	11.0
Office Work	53.8	51.8	7.0
	100.0%	100.0%	100.0%

* Omitting people in institutions, "On Income," or "Without Professions."
Source (Vienna): *Öst. Stat.*, 66:2, pp. 62–64.

ingly concentrated in the "worker" classification (Table 3:13). Over half of all Jewish grooms, and almost two-thirds of all male IKG taxpayers were self-employed, but only about a quarter of all male Viennese in the 1900 work force worked for themselves. Moreover, Jews were twice as likely as Viennese generally to hold salaried positions. On the other hand, almost 60% of the male Viennese work force worked for wages in 1900, but under 20% of the Jewish grooms, and 10% of the IKG taxpayers were either artisans or workers.

These differences become even starker when changing occupational preferences are taken into account. Between 1870 and 1910, Jews flocked into the ranks of the *Angestellte* (Table 3:14) and the per-

Table 3:13. Austrian Social Status Ranking of all Jewish Grooms, Male IKG Taxpayers, and 1900 Viennese Work Force

	Grooms N = 827	IKG Taxpayers N = 2238		Male 1900 Viennese Work Force N = 582,486
Self-Employed	53.3%	65.4%		23.2%
Salaried-Employed	29.1	24.5		14.1
Artisans*	10.6	10.0		
Workers**	6.9	0.1		59.8
			Day Laborers	2.4
			Family Helpers	0.5
	100.0%	100.0%		100.0%

* Separate category of artisans created for Jews because sources did not indicate if these artisans were self-employed or worked for others.
** No Day Laborers or Family Helpers indicated in sources on Jews.
Source (Vienna): *Öst. Stat.*, 66:2, p. 49; *SJSW* (1901), pp. 67–68.

centage of Jewish grooms employed on a salaried basis rose from 6.8% to 41.7% in that period. During the same period, however, despite Vienna's capitalist expansion, there was no increase at all in salaried employment among all Viennese (Table 3:15). Between 1890 and 1910, the percentage of *Angestellte* in the Viennese work force remained constant at 12–14% of the entire work force, including the Jews. Most Viennese *Angestellte* worked for the imperial and municipal civil service, while most Jewish employees worked as clerks, salesmen, or managers in the business world. Since the category of salaried employees, especially for private companies, accounts for so many Jews and so few Viennese generally, and since 8–9% of the total Viennese population was Jewish, most Viennese clerks, salesmen, and managers may have been Jewish. Salaried white-collar employment for private companies had become a Jewish profession.

Jews displayed their distinctiveness not only in terms of the new occupations they chose, but also in their ability to rise in true social status. Jewish transformations stand in sharp contrast to the absence of any change at all in the social status of Viennese generally in the late nineteenth century. Vienna, like most European cities, and unlike many American ones, offered its inhabitants few opportunities for

Table 3:14. Austrian Social Status Ranking of Jewish Grooms, 1870–1910

	1870 N = 73	1880 N = 109	1890 N = 155	1900 N = 213	1910 N = 266
Self-Employed	71.2%	66.1%	60.0%	47.4%	44.0%
Salaried-Employed	6.8	13.8	25.8	32.4	41.7
Artisans*	19.2	15.6	8.4	11.3	6.8
Workers	2.7	4.6	5.8	8.9	7.5
	100.0%	100.0%	100.0%	100.0%	100.0%

* Separate category of artisans created for Jews because sources did not indicate if these artisans were self-employed or worked for others.

Table 3:15. Austrian Social Status Ranking of Viennese Work Force, 1890–1910

	1890 N = 695,393	1900 N = 848,973	1910 N = 1,094,185
Self-Employed	31.4%	31.8%	32.1%
Salaried-Employed	13.7	11.6	12.9
Workers	52.1	53.6	48.4
Apprentices*			4.7
Day Laborers	2.9	2.1	0.8
Family Helpers	—	1.0	1.0
	100.0%	100.0%	100.0%

* Apprentices only listed separately in 1910.

Sources: Öst. Stat., 33:1, pp. 1xvi–vii; 66:1, p. 49; N.F. 3:1, p. 145; *SJSW* (1901), pp. 67–68.

social advancement; in most European cities people rarely rose from the laboring classes into the entrepreneurial ones.[32] Yet, in the Austrian capital the Jews did manage, as they did in the cities of the United States,[33] to rise rapidly in social status and prestige. The pattern of Jewish mobility in New York was from blue-collar to white-collar jobs, and in Vienna from one kind of white-collar work to another. In both cases, however, the higher-entry level of Jews into the labor market, along with cultural values which encouraged achievement, ethnic cohesiveness and support systems, and familiarity with urban life-styles and urban occupations, enabled Jews to achieve status and wealth at a much more rapid rate than other immigrants.[34] Other immigrants came largely from peasant backgrounds. Entering the labor force at a lower level and accustomed to servility, they were unable to achieve social mobility with anywhere near the success of the Jews.

Jewish immigrants to Vienna were very successful. They did not become rich, but they were able to change their occupations and rise in social respectability. The change from trade to salaried employment had profound implications for Jewish life in the city. This economic transformation announced that the Jews had acculturated and had disregarded much of the traditional Jewish life-style. But, this transformation did not herald their assimilation into Viennese society. Economically, as in other areas, Jews continued to be a recognized group in Vienna. The change had been a collective one, and Jews remained identifiable to themselves, and to others, as Jews.

Jewish economic change even provided new outlets for Jews to associate primarily with other Jews. Jewish clerks and managers in large companies probably worked with other Jewish clerks and managers. Moreover, perceiving their own special needs and expressing a desire to associate specifically with other Jews in similar positions, Jewish business employees established professional organizations in the last decades before World War I, many under Zionist or Jewish nationalist auspices. Endeavoring to improve Jewish working conditions, these organizations set up free employment agencies and organized employees to bargain for better wages and conditions. At the same time they hoped to instill Jewish national consciousness and Jewish pride among Jewish business employees.[35] Many of these Jewish business employees' associations tried to fight the ravages of the antisemitic boycott and to convince large Jewish firms to hire more Jews. In fact, they and the Jewish press in general complained that large Jewish establishments did not hire enough Jews.[36] The Zionist paper, *Jüdische Zeitschrift,* for example, announced that the firm of Rothschild & Gutmann filled its offices with antisemites and not Jews, thus profoundly disappointing "all of the fathers, who, through bitter sacrifice made it possible for their sons to study . . . and who perhaps therefore hoped that they would be able to have them enter these Jewish international firms *(Weltfirmen)*. . . ."[37]

The existence of these professional organizations was one of the many brakes which Viennese Jews devised to halt their total assimilation into Viennese society, but it was by no means the only device through which Jews declared their continued distinctiveness. Jews in the city also lived largely in the company of other Jews. The creation of Jewish neighborhoods was their most effective means for associating largely with each other and maintaining their group identity.

4. *The Jewish Neighborhoods of Vienna*

THE VIENNA JEWS lived with other Jews. The creation of Jewish neighborhoods in the city served to separate Jews from gentiles and instill more deeply the perception—among Jews and non-Jews alike—that Jews formed a distinct group. Within these neighborhoods, Jews came into contact chiefly with other Jews. Their residential concentration thus hindered them from forming friendships and other intimate relationships with non-Jews. The very existence of Jewish neighborhoods, therefore, acted as a strong brake on structural assimilation into Viennese society. Students of ethnicity have long recognized the importance of such residential concentration for ethnic group survival. Residential clusterings make it easier for members of an ethnic group to befriend and marry each other, call attention to their ethnic distinctiveness, and preserve their ethnic group.[1] Within the Jewish neighborhoods of Vienna, Jews succeeded in maintaining and preserving their Jewish identity.

Whether in the United States or in Europe, Jews have always created Jewish neighborhoods to cater to their religious needs, protect them from antisemitism, or to help preserve Jewish identity. In her recent study of New York Jews between the two World Wars, Deborah Moore argues that the highly concentrated Jewish neighborhoods of New York were the very foundations for heightened Jewish ethnicity there. The wide range of social contacts, as well as the more formal institutions generated in these neighborhoods "created the framework for their [the Jews'] persistence as an ethnic group." In the neighborhood the Jews were able to set the limits of their assimilation and redefine the meaning of Jewishness to fit their new status as middle-class Americans.[2] Similarly in Vienna, the formation of Jewish neighborhoods provided the foundation for continued Jewish identity even when many traditional features of that identity had been removed by upward social mobility and a modicum of integration into gentile society.

Viennese Neighborhoods: An Overview

The creation of Jewish neighborhoods in Vienna took place at a time when the city was expanding aggressively, building monumental public buildings, and creating many new residential areas in which the working, middle, and upper classes were increasingly segregated from each other. Before 1850, the city of Vienna consisted only of the Inner City, still surrounded by walls, a glacis, and moat. In that year, the city incorporated many of the artisanal suburbs *(Vorstädte)* near the walls, ultimately to become districts II–X of the city. In 1890, Vienna annexed other, more distant suburbs (the *Vororte*), creating districts XI–XIX (See Map 4:1). These newly incorporated areas included more artisanal centers, but also villages formerly devoted to viticulture or dairy farming and some resort areas. During this period of expansion, in 1857, the Emperor ordered the destruction of the city walls, and subsequently the city built the famous Ringstrasse around the Inner City. Located on this wide semicircular boulevard were the public buildings of the Empire: the Parliament, City Hall, University, National Theater, Opera, museums, Stock Exchange, and luxurious apartment houses for Austria's new aristocracy of wealth.[3]

Economic changes in the *Gründerzeit*, or period of economic expansion and modernization (1870–1914), were accompanied by a radical shift in residential patterns in the city as one's place of work and residence became increasingly separated. Industrialization led to the general (but not complete) replacement of artisanal workshops with factories. Because land was expensive in the center of the city, factories went up in the northwestern or southeastern outer districts where land was cheap. An industrial zone was created in Ottakring (XVI) and Hernals (XVII), and in Favoriten (X) and Meidling (XII).[4] The existence of this industrial zone on the outskirts of the city led to the formation of working-class neighborhoods there. The industrial proletariat rented damp, dark, and cramped apartments in apartment "barracks" *(Mietkaserne)* newly built for workers in these districts. Living conditions in the new working-class districts were terrible. Unlike the situation in preindustrial Vienna, workers now found themselves segregated residentially from the rest of the population.[5]

The segregation of the working class was part of a larger trend which resulted in separate neighborhoods for people of different classes.[6] The Ringstrasse, for example, became the special address of the upper and upper-middle classes. Along this grand boulevard, huge apartments on the aristocratic model were constructed for the truly wealthy and the socially striving.[7] Aristocrats and newly ennobled bourgeois resided in the Schwarzenbergplatz area of the Ring,

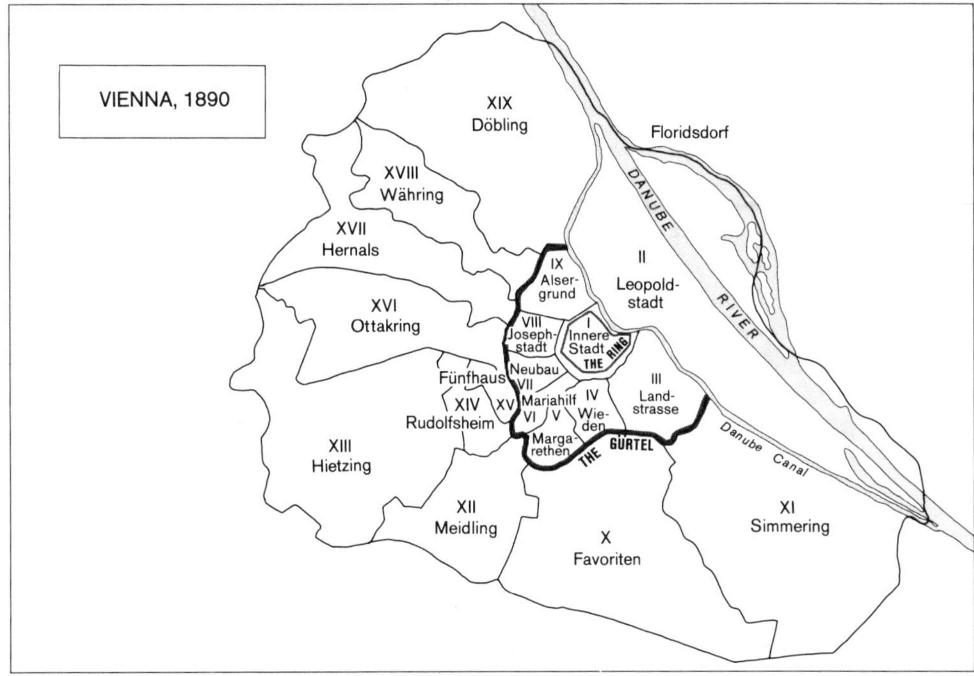

Map 4:1

while the *Grossbürgertum*—businessmen, professionals, and high officials, "the social pillars of ascendant liberalism"—lived in the area between the museums and the university.[8] The entire Inner City, along with Wieden (IV), housed many aristocrats, and became the home of the richest Viennese.[9]

Throughout the period 1870 to 1914, rapid construction in the inner districts (II–IX) destroyed their former artisanal character, establishing them as middle-class residential areas, areas in which residence and work were increasingly separated. Although the wealthy continued to live in the Inner City, it became progressively less residential as banks, corporations, and government agencies opened offices there.[10] The building of the tramway system in the 1870s and 1880s[11] accelerated housing development in districts II–IX. As shops and stores multiplied on such main arteries as Mariahilferstrasse or Währingerstrasse, the inner districts became prime areas for the construction of middle-class apartment houses. Old houses in which artisans had both shops and living quarters were demolished to make way for apartment row houses for the middle classes. In the old artisanal districts of Mariahilf (VI) and Neubau (VII), 80% of the reconstruction resulted in middle-class apartment houses, while in the Alsergrund (IX), the proportion was 70%. The improvements in these old *Vorstädte* led to the displacement of many lower-middle-class Viennese and their transplantation to working-class areas.[12] Districts like Leopoldstadt (II), Landstrasse (III), Mariahilf (VI), Neubau (VII), Josefstadt (VIII), and Alsergrund (IX) became respectably middle class.[13]

Middle- and upper-class neighborhoods also emerged in certain outer districts. Single-family villas became common in the northwest in Währing (XVIII) and Döbling (XIX), and in the southwest in Hietzing (XIII). The *Cottageviertel* in Döbling contained villas for officials, professionals, and businessmen.[14]

Although the trend led toward class differentiation, people of different social ranks did continue to be neighbors in many areas. Between 1870 and 1890, many of the apartment row houses which were built contained "front houses," with modest apartments and indoor plumbing for the middle classes, and "rear houses" in the courtyard which had small apartments and communal toilets for the less prosperous. After 1890, most new construction resulted in middle-class housing alone, but many of these new apartments were dark and small.[15]

The Creation of Jewish Neighborhoods

In the decades before World War I, Viennese Jews chose to live with each other and not with gentiles of similar social class or national origins. Jews of all social classes and from all over the Monarchy clustered in a Jewish section of the city composed of the Leopoldstadt (District II), the Alsergrund (District IX), and the Inner City (District I). Within this section, they were concentrated in certain streets and, as in Prague, probably in certain apartment houses as well.[16] This clustering was by no means restricted to the immigrant generation alone, nor was it typical only of the poor. Within areas of Jewish concentration, poor, middle-class, and wealthy Jews lived on different streets or in different houses, with the wealthy on the avenues and the poor on the side streets and back alleys. But Jews lived with other Jews and not with gentiles with whom they shared economic interests. Some of this Jewish self-segregation may have derived from real and perceived antisemitic hostility. Whether they felt excluded by gentiles or simply desired to live with their own kind, the Jews of Vienna chose housing mainly with their Jewishness in mind.

In selecting fellow Jews as neighbors, Viennese Jews behaved like Jews and other ethnic groups in cities all over the world. In the

1930s, sociologists, especially those of the Chicago School, observed that urban immigrant groups frequently were concentrated in ethnic neighborhoods. But, these sociologists argued, once those immigrants acculturated and became more prosperous, they would surely disperse throughout the city. New immigrants might need to live near each other in order to ease their adjustment to urban life. With the passage of time, however, they would no longer require the comfort of an ethnic enclave and would seek out those with whom they shared economic interests.[17]

Recent historical and sociological studies contradict the findings of the Chicago School. These studies reveal that ethnic concentration persists well beyond the initial immigrant generation, not only among the poor but also among the middle class and rich members of all ethnic groups. In New York, for example, in the 1920s and 1930s, Jews moved out of their immigrant ghettos into new areas of Jewish concentration, different areas for the poor, the middle class, and the rich, but Jewish areas for all.[18] Some scholars continue to argue that social class is the primary factor in neighborhood selection,[19] but most modern urban sociologists, faced with the persistence of ethnic concentrations,[20] have been forced to conclude that ethnicity rather than social class is the primary factor in the determination of who lives with whom. What these sociologists have discovered is that ethnicity and race interact with social class to determine neighborhood selection. Class does not act independently to determine residence; instead it is within ethnic concentrations that differentiation occurs along social class lines. Economic equality does not lead to ethnic or racial integration. In fact, the extent to which social class undercuts racial or ethnic segregation is minimal, and only within each ethnic group do rich and poor keep their distances.[21]

The statistics reveal that separation of Jews from non-Jews was pronounced in Vienna before World War I. According to the frequently used Index of Dissimilarity, which measures the relative integration of groups,[22] about 45% of all Viennese Jews would have had to move in order for them to be disbursed throughout the city in the same way as gentiles. This figure is a bit lower than that for New York Jews,[23] and considerably below the percentage for American Blacks,[24] but it nevertheless reveals a high degree of Jewish residential concentration in Vienna.[25] Between 1880 and 1910, despite acculturation, social mobility, and the constant infusion of new immigrants, the residential concentration of Viennese Jewry remained constant.[26]

As pointed out above, Viennese Jews of all social classes lived primarily in three districts of the city: the Inner City (I), the Leopoldstadt (II), and the Alsergrund (IX) (Table 4:1 and Map 4:2). In 1900, only 12.9% of all non-Jews and 17.8% of all Viennese lived in Districts I, II, and IX,[27] but 55.2% of all Viennese Jews lived there. In 1880, 75% of all Jews in Vienna resided in these three districts. The districts in which Jews were concentrated also had a high Jewish density (Table 4:2 and Map 4:3). In a city in which Jews comprised only 9% of the total city population, they accounted for one-third of the population of the Leopoldstadt, and a fifth of the population in both Alsergrund and the Inner City. At the same time, Jews were underrepresented in Districts XI–XIX, and in III–V and X. Only in Mariahilf and Neubau (VI–VII), and later in Währing (XVIII), did they achieve, and even surpass, their general proportion in the city population.

The single largest Jewish concentration, containing one-half of all Viennese Jews in 1880—no district level statistics were available for 1870—and a third of them in 1910, was in the Leopoldstadt, the location of the seventeenth-century Jewish ghetto.[28] Arthur Schnitzler

Table 4:1. Percentage of all Viennese Jews Living in Each District, 1880–1910

		1880 N = 73,222	1890 N = 118,495	1900 N = 146,926	1910 N = 175,318
I	Inner City	17.1	10.9	7.7	6.2
II	Leopoldstadt	48.3	41.7	35.8	32.4
III	Landstrasse	7.5	6.2	5.6	5.7
IV	Wieden	2.7	2.0	1.7	2.2
V	Margarethen	2.6	2.3	2.0	2.1
VI	Mariahilf	4.3	3.9	4.0	4.7
VII	Neubau	4.2	3.9	4.3	4.6
VIII	Josefstadt	2.3	1.7	2.0	2.7
IX	Alsergrund	9.5	10.1	11.7	12.3
X	Favoriten*	1.5	1.8	2.1	1.9
XI	Simmering		0.4	0.4	0.3
XII	Meidling		1.2	1.1	1.1
XIII	Hietzing		0.6	0.7	1.9
XIV	Rudolfsheim (Sechshaus)		1.9	2.1	2.1
XV	Fünfhaus		1.9	1.6	1.4
XVI	Ottakring		2.9	2.8	2.6
XVII	Hernals		2.8	2.5	2.0
XVIII	Währing		2.9	2.3	2.3
XIX	Döbling		1.1	1.3	2.2
XX	Brigittenau**			7.6	8.1
XXI	Floridsdorf***				1.0
Military				0.5	0.5
		100.0%	100.0%	100.0%	100.0%

* Vienna only included Districts I-X until December 1890 when many suburbs were incorporated into the city as XI-XIX.
** Brigittenau (XX) was part of II until 1900.
*** Floridsdorf was incorporated into the city in 1904.
Sources: Sedlaczek, 1880, Part II, pp. 24, 126–27; 1890, Part II, pp. 50–53, 63–65; *SJSW* (1901), pp. 50–51; (1911), endpaper.

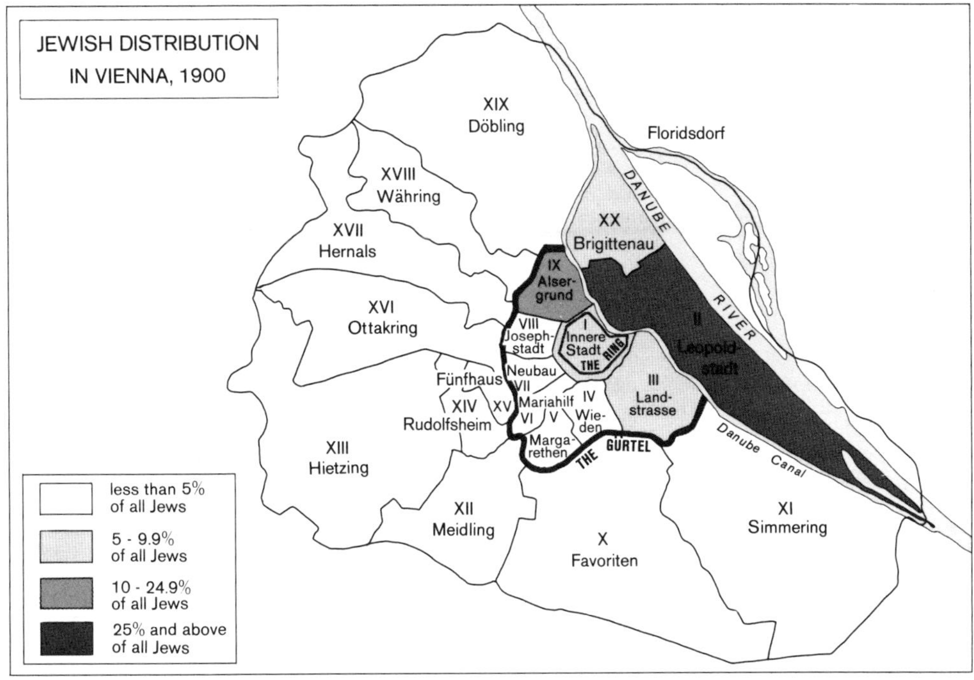

Map 4:2

described the Leopoldstadt of his youth in the 1860s as "fashionable and distinguished." [29] At the end of the nineteenth century, however, the Leopoldstadt, home of many Jewish immigrants, became a "Jewish ghetto" once again in the popular imagination.[30] Sigmund Mayer remarked in his memoirs that the influx of Jews from the provinces changed the Leopoldstadt, making it very noticeably Jewish, with stores closed on Saturday, women wearing wigs to cover their hair in accordance with Jewish laws on modesty, and servants carrying *cholent* through the streets, a traditional dish of beans, potatoes, and meat cooked overnight on Friday and eaten on the Sabbath.[31]

Jews in Vienna avoided all of the working-class areas of the city as well as some of the new middle-class neighborhoods. Very few Jews lived in the proletarian districts inside or outside the *Gürtel*, the semicircular boulevard around Districts III-IX. Jews shunned residence in working-class Ottakring (XVI), Hernals (XVII), Margarethen (V), and Favoriten (X). They also avoided the villa districts of Hietzing (XIII), Währing (XVIII), and Döbling (XIX). Jews rarely chose residence in wealthy Wieden (IV) or in *bürgerlich* Josefstadt (VIII). Some Jews did rent apartments in middle-class Landstrasse (III), Mariahilf (VI),

Table 4:2. Percentage of the Population of Each District Which Was Jewish, 1880–1910

		1880	1890	1900	1910
I	Inner City	17.9	19.1	19.4	20.4
II	Leopoldstadt	29.6	31.0	36.4	33.9
III	Landstrasse	6.0	6.6	6.0	6.3
IV	Wieden	3.4	3.9	4.2	6.0
V	Margarethen	2.8	3.2	2.7	3.5
VI	Mariahilf	4.9	7.2	9.5	12.9
VII	Neubau	4.1	6.4	9.1	11.1
VIII	Josefstadt	3.3	4.2	5.8	8.8
IX	Alsergrund	10.1	14.7	18.2	20.5
X	Favoriten*	2.4	2.5	2.5	2.2
XI	Simmering		1.6	1.5	0.9
XII	Meidling		2.3	2.2	1.8
XIII	Hietzing		1.5	1.7	2.7
XIV	Rudolfsheim (Sechshaus)		4.2	3.9	3.9
XV	Fünfhaus		5.1	5.1	5.4
XVI	Ottakring		3.2	2.8	2.5
XVII	Hernals		4.3	4.1	3.3
XVIII	Währing		4.9	4.0	4.5
XIX	Döbling		4.2	4.9	7.4
XX	Brigittenau**			15.7	14.0
XXI	Floridsdorf***				2.3
Military				3.0	3.1

* Vienna only included Districts I-X until December 1890 when many suburbs were incorporated into the city as XI-XIX.
** Brigittenau (XX) was part of II until 1900.
*** Floridsdorf was incorporated into the city in 1904.
Sources: Sedlaczek, 1880, Part II, pp. 110–15, 126–27; 1890, Part II, pp. 25, 50–53, 63–65; *SJSW* (1901), pp. 50–51; (1911), endpaper.

and Neubau (VII), but they did so much less frequently than in the more Jewish districts.

This residential distribution surely did not depend upon class. Jews lived not in areas which accorded with their economic status but in Jewish areas. Despite some variation, a study of three Jewish sample populations—a cross section of all Viennese Jews (grooms and brides), the more prosperous IKG taxpayers, and destitute Jews receiving charity[32]—shows that all three groups lived in almost the same areas of the city (Tables 4:3 and 4:4). Wealthy Jews resided in the Inner City (I) or Alsergrund (IX), chose apartments in Wieden (IV) only rarely, and continued to live in the Leopoldstadt (II) despite its reputation as home of the Jewish poor. Middle-class Jews lived in the middle-class Alsergrund (IX) and Leopoldstadt, or even in Mariahilf (VI) or Neubau (VII), but almost never in equally middle-class Josefstadt (VIII). Poor Jews shunned residence in the lower-class outer districts in order to live side by side, if not with wealthy Jews, certainly with middle-class Jews in the Leopoldstadt (II) and the

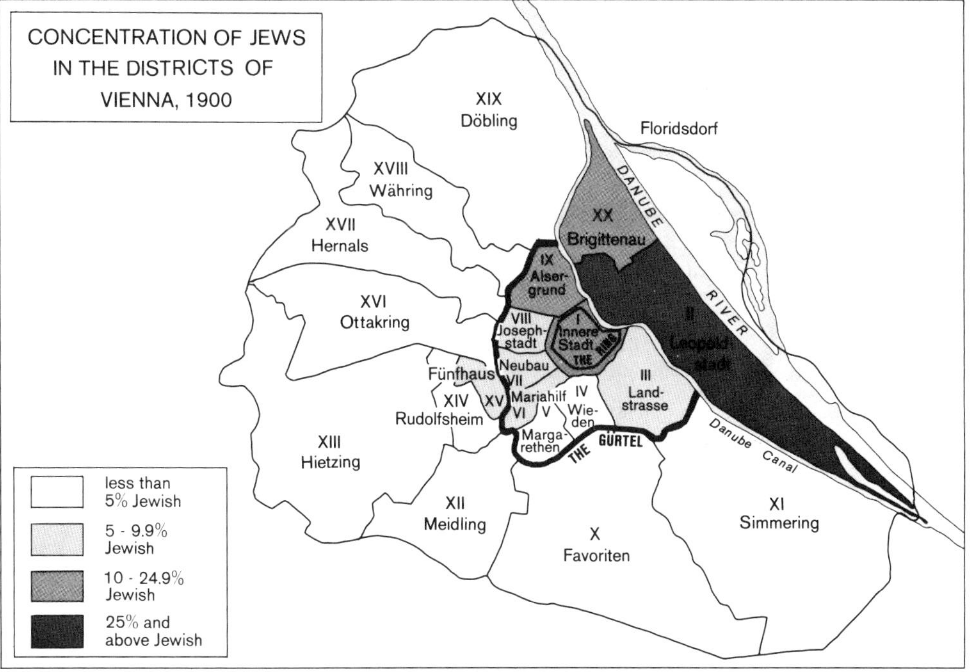

Map 4:3

Alsergrund (IX). Rich, poor, and middle-class Jews lived in middle-class areas, but not because they were all middle class. On the contrary, only about one-third of all Viennese Jews could even afford the minimum tax to the IKG.[33] Jews lived in these areas in order to live with other Jews. Within areas of Jewish concentration, of course, rich and poor did not necessarily dwell side by side.

To be sure, very poor Jews did not reside in the fashionable Inner City next to the truly wealthy. Some poverty-stricken Jews on relief were forced to live far from Jewish neighbors in outer areas like Ottakring (XVI) and Hernals (XVII) where rent was cheap,[34] but most destitute Jews lived alongside most Viennese Jews in the Leopoldstadt (II) and in the Alsergrund (IX) (Table 4:4). Poor Jews were concentrated more than average Viennese Jews in the Leopoldstadt. Over half of those on the charity rolls lived in the second district compared to a third of all Jewish brides and grooms. Jews on charity also lived in the Brigittenau (XX), a very poor section of the Leopoldstadt which was made into a separate district in 1900. Conditions in this area were terrible for the poor Jews who found residence there. In many cases one-room apartments made do for six to ten people.[35] Jews on charity, however, were just as likely as all other Jews to live in the

Table 4:3. Residential Distribution of Jewish Grooms and Brides, Composite, 1870–1910, and IKG Taxpayers, Composite, 1855–1914, and 1896 Sample*

	Grooms N = 881	Brides N = 884		IKG Members N = 1883		1896 IKG*** N = 2269
I	8.6%	9.3%		23.0%		23.6%
II	33.6	36.3		25.1		27.3
III–V, X	9.5	10.4		12.4	III, XI	6.7
VI–VIII	10.2	11.1	VI–VII	11.0	IV, V, X	5.6
IX	9.8	9.8	VIII–IX	14.3	VI–VII	11.0
XI–XIX	11.7	10.5		11.6	VIII–IX	14.9
XX[t]	3.3	4.0		1.6	XII–XV	4.2
Other	13.3**	8.6**		0.8	XVI–XVII	3.7
					XVIII–XIX	3.0
	100.0%	100.0%		100.0%		100.0%

* Districts are grouped here and in the following tables to make analysis easier. Because few Jews lived in III–V, X, and XI–XIX, they were grouped together.

** Those living in the provinces and "imported" to Vienna by their prospective spouses.

*** Sample of every five eligible voters in the 1896 Board elections (CAHJP, AW 48/1). The district groupings here are those used by the IKG as voting districts.

[t] XX appears lower than the census statistics for 1900 and 1910 because the sample is a composite of 1870–1910, and Brigittenau was only separated from the Leopoldstadt in 1900.

Table 4:4. Residential Distribution of those Receiving Charity from the IKG

	1894–1903 Centralstellung für das Armenwesen N = 518	1893–1899 Armenwesen N = 337	1896–1914 Armenamt N = 325
I	1.4%	2.4%	0.6%
II	57.7	57.0	41.8
III–V, X	6.9	9.8	10.8
VI–VII	3.3	2.7	4.3
VIII–IX	10.2	8.0	12.3
XI–XV	3.9	8.0	8.0
XVI–XVII	8.5	8.0	5.5
XVIII–XIX	4.4	4.2	4.6
XX	3.7*	**	11.4
XXI	—	—	0.6
	100.0%	100.0%	100.0%

* Brigittenau was only a separate district after 1900, so the figure is low.
** Brigittenau was not yet a separate district, so its residents are included in II.

Alsergrund, the area of the city characterized by the rising new Jewish middle class. As in New York, comfortable and poor Jews often shared the same neighborhoods.[36]

It was natural, of course, for poor Jews to avoid the poor sections of Vienna. The outer districts were the reserve of the industrial proletariat, and Viennese Jews, no matter how poor, were rarely factory workers. Moreover, even though destitute, these Jews were largely *bürgerlich* in their orientation. Although they could not even eke out a living, poor Jewish traders would naturally seek to live with other *Bürger,* especially if those *Bürger* were fellow Jews. Even working-class Jews, however, did not live in proletarian Favoriten (X) or Ottakring (XVI). More Jewish workers lived in the outer districts than members of the community at large, but most working-class Jews resided in the Leopoldstadt and Brigittenau.

On the other hand, middle-class and wealthy Jews who paid taxes to the IKG were even more concentrated in the Jewish disricts than most Viennese Jews (Table 4:3). Only 52% of the grooms lived in I, II, and IX, but 62.4% of the IKG members did so. Of course, these richer Jews were four times as likely as most Viennese Jews to reside in the Inner City, and they certainly avoided poverty-stricken Brigittenau (XX) and the working-class districts of the city beyond the *Gürtel.* Yet they lived in great numbers in the Alsergrund (IX) and also in Mariahilf-Neubau (VI–VII).

Most strikingly, these prosperous Jews continued to find the "Jewish ghetto" in the Leopoldstadt an attractive place to live, presumably because it was the focus of Jewish life in Vienna. Well-to-do Jews were somewhat less concentrated in the second district than most Viennese Jews, but nevertheless, fully one-quarter of the *Gemeinde* taxpayers did live in the Leopoldstadt along with Vienna's Jewish lower-middle class and poor. Those taxpayers who paid more than the minimum tax—only 21.6% paid more than the minimum—were more likely than the rest to live in the Inner City or Wieden, but a substantial number still maintained their residence in the Leopoldstadt (Table 4:5). A significant percentage of those Jews in the very highest tax brackets also lived in the "Jewish ghetto." After 1900, the IKG instituted a two-class voting system for biennial elections to the Board because it was fearful of Zionist inroads into *Gemeinde* politics. All IKG members voted for twenty-four members, and those who paid over 200 Kronen each year were to elect an additional twelve members.[37] In 1900, a very large percentage of these highly taxed Jews were concentrated in the Inner City, but many of them also lived in the Leopoldstadt. Of the 865 men who paid over K200 in 1900, 412 or 47.6% lived in the Inner City, a rate twice as high as most taxpayers and five times as high as most Viennese Jews. But 124 or

14.3% still lived in the Leopoldstadt. Although this rate was much lower than average for Viennese Jews, it still indicates the persistence of neighborhood attachments even among Jews in the highest tax brackets.

Moreover, when the prosperous Jews who lived in the Leopoldstadt decided to change residence, a very large proportion of them moved to new apartments elsewhere in the second district. IKG taxpayers who lived in the "Jewish ghetto" were more likely than all other prosperous Viennese Jews to remain in their original neighborhood (see Table 4:10). When they moved a second or a third time, prosperous Jews who lived in the Leopoldstadt also had the highest persistence rate. Of those IKG members who moved from original homes in the second district, 67.3% remained in the second district the first time they moved, 62.1% the second time, 51.6% the third, 38.5% the fourth, and 33.6% the fifth. The percentage declined, but apparently the Leopoldstadt continued to attract even the more affluent Jews.

Rich and poor Jews lived together in both Leopoldstadt (II) and Alsergrund (IX), but in all likelihood they lived in different houses, on different streets, and even in different sections of the two districts. The richer Jews probably rented lovely apartments on the main thoroughfares or tree-lined side streets, while the poor resided on the back streets and alleys or in the older, more run-down houses. It was especially easy in the Leopoldstadt, an area in which places of work and residence were not completely separated, for rich and poor to live in close proximity to one another. This hypothesis receives support from the statistical evidence. Although it is not possible to determine the street addresses for all Viennese Jews, those middle-

Table 4:5. Residential Distribution of IKG Members in Each Tax Bracket, First Tax to the IKG, Composite, 1855–1914

Address	K20 N = 1480	K30–99 N = 312	K100–499 N = 60	K500+ N = 9	Second tax K100–499 N = 99
I	19.7%	34.6%	36.7%	77.9%	33.3%
II	27.8	15.1	13.3	—	11.1
III–V, X*	12.6	10.5	18.3	11.1	8.1
VI–VII	11.1	13.1	5.0	—	13.1
VIII–IX	14.6	12.2	15.0	—	18.2
XI–XIX**	11.6	12.5	10.0	11.1	15.2
XX	2.0	0.3	—	—	1.0
Other	0.6	1.6	1.7	—	—
	100.0%	100.0%	100.0%	100.0%	100.0%

* Mostly III and IV, not V and X.

** Mostly XVIII and XIX, and not in working-class areas.

and upper-class Jews who paid IKG taxes[38] can be located on the map. Because the amount of tax assessed varied with income, it is possible to discover how the residential patterns of the middle class within Viennese Jewry differed from those of the upper class.

Jews who paid taxes to the IKG were heavily concentrated in the northeast quadrant of the Inner City, in the adjacent western part of the Leopoldstadt, and in the southeastern section of the Alsergrund. Fully 65.8% of all IKG members lived in those adjacent sections of Districts I, II, and IX. Within these districts, middle-class Jews congregated on certain streets (see Map 4:4). About 35% of IKG taxpayers who lived in the Inner City resided on thirteen streets, in an area bounded by Schottenring to the northwest, Franz Josephs Kai (on the Danube Canal) to the northeast, Rotenturmstrasse to the southeast, and Wipplingerstrasse to the southwest. In the Leopoldstadt, IKG members congregated on the large thoroughfares: Taborstrasse, Rembrandtstrasse, Untere Augartenstrasse, Stefaniestrasse, Praterstrasse, and, on the Danube Canal, along Obere Donaustrasse. They lived between Rembrandtstrasse in the northwest and Franzensbrückenstrasse in the east, between Obere Augartenstrasse and Darwinstrasse in the northeast and the Danube Canal in the southwest. They did not live at all east of the Augarten, north of the Prater (an amusement park), or near the Danube River. In the Alsergrund, almost all the middle-class Jews lived in the southeast part of the district, in the streets bounded by Währingerstrasse and Porzellangasse, south of Grüne Thorgasse. In fact, Jews clustered more compactly in Alsergrund than in either Districts I or II. Over half of Alsergrund's IKG taxpayers lived on eleven streets: Porzellangasse, Liechtensteinstrasse, Währingerstrasse, and the side streets Wasagasse, Kolingasse, Hörlgasse, Berggasse (where Freud lived), and Türkenstrasse (where Theodor Herzl lived).

The richest *Gemeinde* members, those who paid over 200 Kronen a year in taxes to the IKG, clustered in somewhat different areas from the middle-class Jews within the larger Jewish neighborhoods of the city. Within the Inner City, the wealthiest IKG members seem to have congregated on exactly the same streets (Gonzagagasse, Esslinggasse, Franz Josephs Kai, Schottenring) as *Gemeinde* taxpayers in general. In the Leopoldstadt, however, wealthy and not so wealthy *Gemeinde* taxpayers inhabited different sections of the district. Almost all of the very wealthy Jews who lived in the second district lived to the east of the Taborstrasse and not in the densely populated areas of the district to the west of Taborstrasse. Most poorer Jews in the Leopoldstadt undoubtedly lived in the numerous side streets and back alleys between Rembrandtstrasse and Taborstrasse (or north of Rembrandtstrasse in the Brigittenau) which even today are run-

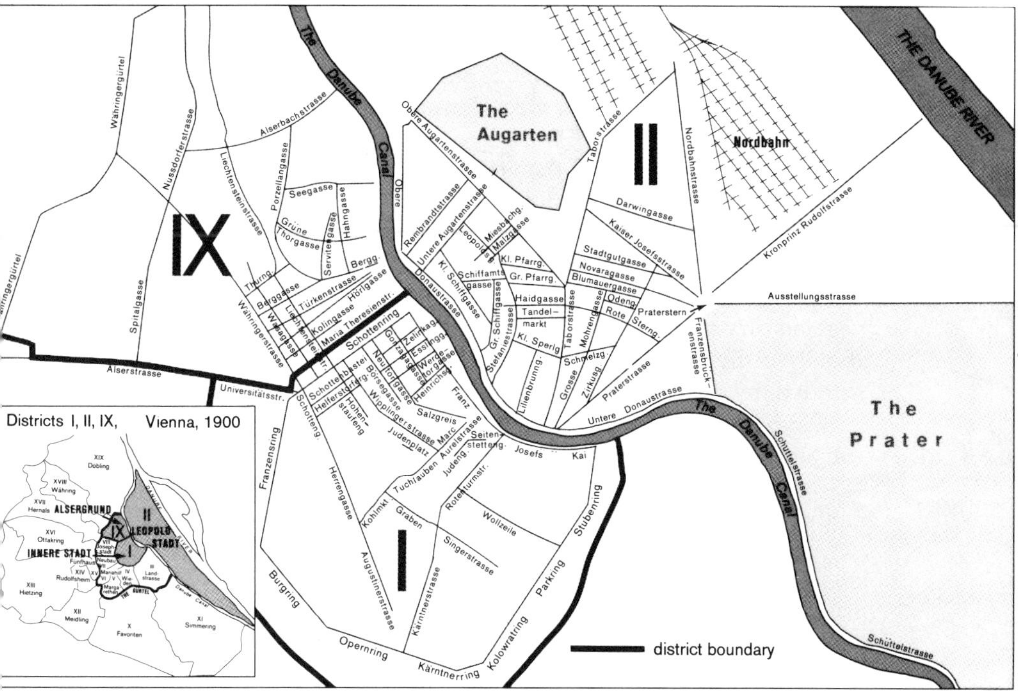

Map 4:4

down, while their economic betters lived on the major thoroughfares and the wealthiest lived beyond the Taborstrasse altogether.

Wealth was not the only reason for internal divisions within areas of Jewish concentration. The occupations which Jews practiced also played an important role in their choice of neighborhood. Merchants lived all over the Jewish districts of Vienna, but Jews practicing other professions did congregate in certain areas (Tables 4:6 and 4:7). In particular, business employees and professionals overwhelmingly chose Alsergrund as their home, and thus the ninth district, with its Jewish population consisting largely of business employees and professionals, became the proper address for a new breed of urban Jew. About 16% of Jewish grooms who were business employees lived in the Alsergrund (Table 4:6), and while only one-quarter of all grooms were clerks, salesmen, or managers, 38.6% of all the grooms residing in the ninth district pursued such occupations (Table 4:7). Alsergrund also contained a higher than average percentage of professionals. Doctors, lawyers, and other Jewish professionals shied away from the Leopoldstadt but did live in the Inner City in large numbers.

Jewish grooms who practiced other occupations also had their favorite neighborhoods (Tables 4:6 and 4:7). Jewish civil servants did

Table 4:6. Residential Distribution of Grooms by Occupation, Composite, 1870–1910

	Unclass.* N = 9	Civil Servants N = 21	Profes-sionals N = 91	Factory Owners N = 28	Merchants N = 326	Bus. Employ. N = 207	Artisans N = 92	Workers N = 35	Overall N = 881
I	—	4.8%	14.3%	3.6%	12.0%	6.3%	8.7%	2.9%	8.6%
II	22.2%	33.3	23.1	10.7	35.0	33.8	39.1	37.1	33.6
III–V, X	—	4.8	13.2	10.7	8.3	11.6	10.9	8.6	9.5
VI–VIIII	—	14.3	6.6	28.6	9.5	10.1	10.9	11.4	10.2
IX	11.1	9.5	14.3	3.6	8.3	15.5	5.4	5.7	9.8
XI–XIX	11.1	14.3	6.6	14.3	8.0	12.1	16.3	20.0	11.7
XX	—	4.8	1.1	—	4.3	1.0	2.2	11.4	3.3
Other	55.6	14.3	20.9	28.6	14.7	9.7	6.5	2.9	13.3
	100.0%	100.0%	100.0%	100.0%	100.0%	100.0%	100.0%	100.0%	100.0%

* Unclassifiable, primarily those living on private incomes.

Table 4:7. Occupations of Jewish Grooms Residing in Each District, Composite, 1870–1910

	I N=76	II N = 266	III–V, X N = 80	VI–VIII N = 83	IX N = 83	XI–XIX N = 87	XX N = 24	Other N = 110
Unclass.	—	0.8%	—	—	1.2%	1.1%	—	4.5%
Civil Servants	1.3%	2.6	1.3%	3.6%	2.4	3.4	4.2%	2.7
Professionals	17.1	7.9	15.0	7.2	15.7	6.9	4.2	17.3
Factory Owners	1.3	1.1	3.8	9.6	1.2	4.6	—	7.3
Merchants	51.3	42.9	33.8	37.3	32.5	29.9	58.3	43.6
Business Employees	17.1	26.3	30.0	25.3	38.6	28.7	8.3	18.2
Artisans	10.5	13.5	12.5	12.0	6.0	17.2	8.3	5.5
Workers	1.3	4.9	3.8	4.8	2.4	8.0	16.7	0.9
	100.0%	100.0%	100.0%	100.0%	100.0%	100.0%	100.0%	100.0%

not share the Alsergrund with business employees or professionals. Avoiding the wealthy Inner City, they tended to live in the Leopoldstadt, close to their jobs with the Nordbahn and Nordwestbahn railroads. Factory owners were unlikely to live in Districts I, II, or IX, the primary areas of Jewish residence in the city, but almost 30% of them lived in Mariahilf or Neubau (VI and VII). Many wealthy factory owners also lived in Wieden (IV) along with the Rothschilds, the Gutmanns, and other ennobled Viennese Jews. Artisans, on the other hand, did not live in these two districts, nor in the Alsergrund. They chose to live in the Leopoldstadt, or to a lesser extent in certain working-class areas. Unskilled workers, however, lived in certain outer districts, as well as in VI and VII, alongside the factory owners, undoubtedly because of the presence of factories in or near these districts.

In the years between 1870 and 1910, Jews in Vienna adjusted their choice of neighborhood to conform to their changing occupations and social status. Contrary to the expectations of the Chicago School of urban sociologists, they did not simply leave their homey immigrant enclave in the Leopoldstadt to move randomly to middle-class areas of the city. Like their counterparts in other cities, as Jews in Vienna acquired more social status they created new Jewish concentrations, middle-class Jewish clusterings in middle-class Jewish neighborhoods. In the late nineteenth century, the rising Jewish bourgeoisie more and more chose residence in the Alsergrund, conveniently located across the Augartenbrücke from the Leopoldstadt, and across the Ring from the Inner City. The Alsergrund, located near the university, was a middle-class, intellectual area. Like many other areas of second settlement, however, it was not the home of middle-class Jews exclusively but contained poor Jews as well. Upwardly mobile Jews also increasingly chose Mariahilf and Neubau (VI–VII) or Währing and Döbling (XVIII–XIX) as their new homes. Meanwhile, the number of Jews in the Leopoldstadt remained high because of the constant infusion of Jewish immigrants there and because many middle-class and wealthy Jews preferred to remain in this Jewish neighborhood.

It was primarily young Jews rather than Viennese Jews generally who moved into these new neighborhoods. A glance at the residential distribution of *all* Viennese Jews in each decade between 1870 and 1910 (Table 4:1) indicates that fewer and fewer chose to live in the Inner City and the Leopoldstadt, while residence rose only modestly in Alsergrund and not at all in Mariahilf (VI), Neubau (VII), Währing (XVIII), or Döbling (XIX). *Young* Jews, however, the grooms, brides, and new entrants onto the IKG tax rolls, increasingly chose Alsergrund (IX), Mariahilf (VI), Neubau (VII), and to a lesser extent Währing and Döbling (XVIII–XIX) as their residence (see Table 4:8). Only about 4% of the grooms lived in the Alsergrund in 1870, but about 15% resided there in 1910. Similarly, in 1910, 16% of the grooms lived in Districts VI–VIII, compared with only 8% in 1900 and 10–11% in 1870–1890. Moreover, between 1870 and 1910, the percentage of Jewish residents in Alsergrund and Mariahilf-Neubau increased steadily. While the Jewish density of Districts I and II remained more or less the same, the Jewish share of the population of the Alsergrund doubled from 10% to 20%, and Jewish density in Mariahilf and Neubau (VI–VII) tripled from 4% to 12% between 1870 and 1910 (Table 4:2). Young Jews also moved to the outer districts in the final decades before World War I. Among the more prosperous IKG taxpayers, the movement of young Jewish men into Alsergrund, Mariahilf, and Neubau began earlier, in the 1890s. During the whole period, of course, the Leopoldstadt and the Brigittenau continued to attract Jews of all ages.

Those Viennese Jews who chose to move to the Alsergrund were overwhelmingly business employees and professionals, and thus between 1870 and 1910, Alsergrund became *the* neighborhood for Jewish professionals and business employees, the "new" urban Jews. In this period, business employees came to shun residence in the Leopoldstadt, moving in ever larger numbers to the ninth district. Only 6.3% of all Jewish clerks, managers, and salesmen who married in 1880 lived in the ninth district—none had in 1870—but fully one-fifth of them (21.5%) lived there in 1910. Likewise, 7% of new members of the IKG who were business employees lived in the Alsergrund in the 1880s and one-fifth did so in the 1900s. Professionals also displayed a growing preference for housing in the Alsergrund. Less than 13% of all the grooms practicing a profession lived in the ninth district in 1880 (5.6% in 1890), but one-fifth did so in 1900 and 1910. Further, less than 10% of the Jewish professionals who entered the *Gemeinde* tax rolls in the 1880s lived in the

Table 4:8. Residential Distribution of Jewish Grooms, 1870–1910 (Omitting Nonresidents)

	1870 N = 84	1880 N = 91	1890 N = 136	1900 N = 191	1910 N = 258
I	14.3%	23.1%	12.5%	6.8%	5.0%
II	32.1	38.5	53.7	41.9	29.8
III–V, X	10.7	13.2	10.3	15.2	7.4
VI–VIII	11.9	11.0	10.3	7.9	15.9
IX	3.6	10.0	9.6	11.5	14.7
XI–XIX	27.4*	4.4	3.7	14.7	16.3
XX	—	—	—	2.1	9.7
	100.0%	100.0%	100.0%	100.0%	100.0%

* Jews living in *Vororte* included in 1870 sample, but not in 1880 and 1890.

Alsergrund, but 20% of them had addresses in this district after 1900.

The changes in the composition of Alsergrund's Jewish population between 1870 and 1910 (Table 4:9) outpaced the movement of Viennese Jews into salaried employment and the professions. In 1870, 1880, and 1890, the Alsergrund, like most Jewish areas, was inhabited largely by Jewish merchants. By 1900, the percentage of merchants in the ninth district had dropped well below the Viennese average. At a time when about one-third of all Jewish grooms were merchants, only one-fifth of all grooms in the ninth district engaged in commerce. On the other hand, the proportion of professionals and business employees in the Alsergrund far exceeded the Viennese Jewish norm. In 1900, only 13% of Viennese Jewish grooms pursued professional careers, but in Alsergrund the proportion of doctors, lawyers, writers, and other professionals was 28.6%. Similarly, in 1910, when 35% of all grooms worked as clerks, salesmen, and managers, such business employees made up half of the grooms from the ninth district. IKG taxpayers from Alsergrund also tended much more than most *Gemeinde* taxpayers to be professionals or business employees. Of IKG members living in the Alsergrund in the 1880s, only 14.3% were business employees, but in the 1900s twice that figure, or 31%, had become clerks, managers, or salesmen.

Jewish business employees also moved into Mariahilf and Neubau, transforming Districts VI and VII from areas with a high percentage of industrialists to areas with a large contingent of *Angestellte*. The period between 1870 and 1910 witnessed a significant decline in the percentage of industrialists in Districts VI–VII. Almost half (45.5%) of all factory owners who entered the IKG tax rolls in the 1880s lived in these two districts, but only 18.8% of those who entered in the 1900s lived there. Similarly, while 14.3% of the grooms from

Table 4:9. Occupational Distribution of Jewish Grooms in the Alsergrund, 1870–1910

	1870 N = 2	1880 N = 9	1890 N = 13	1900 N = 21	1910 N = 38
Unclass.	—	11.1%	—	—	—
Civil Servants	50.0%	—	—	—	2.6%
Professionals	—	11.1	7.7%	28.6%	13.2
Factory Owners	—	—	—	4.8	—
Merchants	50.0	66.7	61.5	19.0	21.1
Business Employees	—	11.1	23.1	38.1	52.6
Artisans	—	—	—	9.5	7.9
Workers	—	—	7.7	—	2.6
	100.0%	100.0%	100.0%	100.0%	100.0%

these districts owned factories in 1890, twenty years later the proportion had declined to 8.1%. At the same time, Mariahilf and Neubau became the home for an ever-increasing number of Jewish business employees. In the 1880s and 1890s, only one-fifth of the grooms from these districts were business employees, but in 1910, clerks, salesmen, and managers made up 37.8% of the group. Among IKG taxpayers, the proportion of employees increased from 14% in the 1880s to 31% in the 1900s.

The outer districts seemed to have attracted a growing number of young Jews in the decades before World War I (Table 4:8). In part, Jewish population growth in Districts XI–XIX merely reflected the 1890 annexation of these districts into the city limits. Additionally, well-to-do young Jews, whether merchants, business employees, or professionals increasingly chose residences in the outer districts, although not in the working-class areas like Ottakring (XVI) and Hernals (XVII). Rather, well-heeled young Jews bought houses in the newly developed villa areas in Währing (XVIII) and Döbling (XIX), i.e., the *Cottageviertel*. At the same time a growing number of poor Jewish artisans chose to live in the districts beyond the *Gürtel*, primarily in working-class Ottakring and Hernals (XVI–XVII). In 1880, 11.8% of all grooms practicing a craft lived in the outer districts, but in 1910, that percentage had risen to 23.8%. In particular, many Galician Jewish craftsmen who arrived in Vienna after the turn of the century resided in Districts XVI–XVII. In 1910, sixteen grooms lived in these two districts, and nine of them had been born in Galicia. Artisans who paid taxes to the IKG did not relocate to the outer districts.

Focusing on the changes in Viennese Jewish residential patterns from decade to decade obscures the choices made by individual Jews who decided to move. Unfortunately, it has been possible to map the changing residential patterns only of those Viennese Jews rich enough to pay IKG taxes.[39] Richer Jews probably moved less often than their poorer brethren,[40] and about a third (35.4%) of *Gemeinde* taxpayers never changed residence at all. Among IKG taxpayers, 24% moved one time, 33% moved two to four times, and 7.4% moved five times or more. Studying the individual residential patterns of well-to-do Jews reveals that while Alsergrund (IX) was a popular new address for Viennese Jews, it did not blossom as a Jewish neighborhood because Jews rejected the Leopoldstadt. On the contrary, the Leopoldstadt (II) and the most prestigious addresses in the elegant Inner City continued to attract Jews from all over Vienna.

The overwhelming majority of *Gemeinde* taxpayers who moved chose to remain in their original district. A comparison of 2,269 IKG voters on the 1896 voting lists with the same voters on the 1906 lists[41] indicates that 24.2% still resided at the same address while another 18.5% lived elsewhere in the same district. Thus 42.7% of all IKG taxpayers in 1906 still lived in close proximity to their 1896 homes. Most intradistrict movement, furthermore, took an individual only around the corner; 40% of those who lived in the first district and moved elsewhere in the Inner City chose new apartments a block or two away, and the rate was even higher in Districts II and IX. Similarly, between 1855 and 1914, about three-fifths of all *Gemeinde* taxpayers who changed residence remained in the same district (Table 4:10). The diagonal of Table 4:10 represents the persistence rate of *Gemeinde* taxpayers in each district, that is, the percent that remained in their original district when they changed residence. As indicated earlier, IKG taxpayers in the Leopoldstadt had a higher persistence rate than any other Viennese Jews paying taxes to the *Gemeinde.*

Many IKG taxpayers who lived in the Inner City chose to leave the first district in this period, and thus the Jewish persistence rate in this district was the lowest in the city. Jews who left the Inner City chose either the new Jewish neighborhood in the Alsergrund or the more traditional Jewish concentration in the Leopoldstadt. Whether because they lost their money or because the Jewish atmosphere of the Leopoldstadt attracted them, 18% of the IKG taxpayers who moved out of the first district crossed the Danube Canal to live in the Leopoldstadt. Indeed most residential transfer between the Inner City and the Leopoldstadt was in the direction of the latter. At the same time, many prosperous Jewish residents of Mariahilf (VI), Neubau (VII), and to a much lesser extent, Alsergrund (IX) and Leopoldstadt moved to the Inner City. Those *Gemeinde* taxpayers whose initial tax was 30–99 Kronen were more likely than those paying the minimum tax to move to the Inner City.

Alsergrund (IX) attracted *Gemeinde* taxpayers from the Inner City and from Mariahilf-Neubau (VI–VII) to a lesser extent, but not particularly from the Leopoldstadt. Undoubtedly, many Jews left their parental homes in the second district to take up residence in the ninth, but already established *Gemeinde* members made this move less frequently. Almost 30% of those who moved to Alsergrund had originally lived in the Inner City. Alsergrund held many intellectual attractions for well-to-do Viennese Jews, and thus a relatively high percentage of *Gemeinde* members who crossed the Ring into the ninth district followed professional careers (28.9% compared with 19.6% overall). Professionals were also more likely to remain in Alsergrund than any other group.

Finally, many residents of Mariahilf, Neubau, and Alsergrund chose to move to Währing and Döbling during this period. The playwright

Table 4:10. Patterns of Residential Movement, IKG Members, Composite, 1855–1914 (Percent) (N = 1055)

First Address		Second Address							
		I	II	III–V, X	VI–VII	VIII–IX	XI–XIX	XX	Other
I	(270)	**42.2**	18.1	9.3	5.9	19.6	4.4	0.4	—
II	(245)	9.0	**67.3**	6.5	4.1	6.1	4.1	2.9	—
III–V, X	(125)	7.2	12.0	**62.4**	6.4	4.8	5.6	0.8	0.8
VI–VII	(115)	12.2	3.5	6.1	**64.2**	11.3	1.7	—	—
VIII–IX	(160)	9.4	9.4	9.4	8.1	**50.0**	11.3	1.3	1.3
XI–XIX	(124)	7.3	4.0	3.2	12.1	10.5	**62.1**	0.3	—
XX	(16)	—	31.3	—	—	18.8	6.3	**43.8**	—

Arthur Schnitzler, for example, was born in the Leopoldstadt, lived at Frankgasse 1 in the Alsergrund in 1896, but at Spöttelgasse 7 in Währing (XVIII) in 1906.[42] This trend became more noticeable in the subsequent residential relocations of IKG taxpayers. About 11% of the taxpayers who left Alsergrund in their first move went to these new fashionable areas; when men and women who had remained in Alsergrund in their first move changed residence again, 18% of them chose new apartments in Währing and Döbling. In particular, those IKG members who paid the highest taxes relocated to these fancy sections.

To recapitulate, Jews in Vienna created Jewish neighborhoods in which Jews of all social classes lived near each other rather than with gentiles with whom they shared economic interests. Although within the Jewish areas Jews divided along class lines, Jewishness and not class was the major criterion by which Jews selected a neighborhood. The transformation of the occupational profile of Viennese Jews between 1870 and 1910 only led to the establishment of new Jewish neighborhoods within which Jews could associate with other Jews of similar background. Jewish neighborhoods served an additional purpose as well. They effectively separated Jews from the gentile immigrants who had come to Vienna from the same areas of the Dual Monarchy as they.

Ethnic/National Ties

In Vienna Jews preferred to live with other Jews, no matter what their national origins, rather than with gentile immigrants with whom they had little in common but similar birthplace. For Viennese Jews, Jewishness superseded all other criteria for neighborhood selection. Thus, for example, Bohemian Jews consciously avoided all areas of the city in which gentile Bohemian immigrants congregated. For the Jews, whose identity derived from their Jewishness and not their geographical provenance, Jewish neighborhoods preserved and ensured that separate Jewish identity. To the rest of the city as well, the Jewish neighborhoods announced that Jews were Jews, and not Bohemians, Galicians, Hungarians, or anything else.

Comparison is really only possible between Jews and gentiles from Bohemia and Moravia, the two Czech provinces which provided Vienna with its largest number of immigrants. Measuring the Jewish/Czech Index of Dissimilarity, that is, the percentage of one group that would have to move in order to be distributed in the same pattern as the other group, reveals that the residential separation of Jews and Czechs was even greater than that of Jews and gentiles generally. In 1900, the Jewish/Czech Index of Dissimilarity was 51.6%,[43] eight points higher than the Index of Dissimilarity for Jews and all Viennese gentiles. Moreover, no matter what their social class, Bohemian and Moravian Jews and gentiles lived in completely different sections of the city, and almost never lived next door to each other.

The Czech community of Vienna, composed of approximately 100,000 men and women from Bohemia and Moravia whose everyday language was Czech, not German,[44] did not concentrate quite as heavily as Jews in certain districts. Nevertheless, wanting to establish some social distance from Germans, they did create Czech neighborhoods in the city. Mostly working class, Bohemians and Moravians in Vienna clustered in Favoriten (District X), which was 17.6% Czech in 1880 and 15.1% Czech in 1910. Working-class Czechs also lived in Ottakring (XVI), which was 11% Czech, and other working-class areas. Czech servant women resided in the homes of their employers in Districts I and IV.[45] Middle-class Czechs, on the other hand, lived in Landstrasse (III), which was 12% Czech, or to a much lesser extent in Districts II, V, and IX.[46]

Table 4:11. Residential Distribution of Bohemian and Moravian Jewish Grooms, Composite, 1870–1910*

District	Jewish Bohemians N = 78	Jewish Moravians/Silesians N = 94
I	11.5%	9.6%
II	26.9	42.6
III	5.1	7.4
IV	2.6	1.1
V	2.6	2.1
VI	7.7	8.5
VII	6.4	—
VIII	1.3	2.1
IX	21.8	10.6
X	3.8	2.1
XI	1.3	1.1
XII	—	1.1
XIII	—	—
XIV	—	4.3
XV	3.8	—
XVI	—	1.1
XVII	1.3	2.1
XVIII	1.3	1.1
XIX	—	—
XX	1.3	3.2
	100.0%	100.0%

* Those actually resident in Vienna.

Most Viennese Czechs lived in Favoriten (X), but almost no Jews from Bohemia or Moravia (or anywhere else) lived in that district or the other working-class districts in which Czechs concentrated (Table 4:11). Much of this difference was caused by the divergent economic status of the two groups. The majority of the Czechs in Vienna worked in factories, while most Bohemian and Moravian Jews practiced middle-class occupations. Consequently, the two groups would be unlikely to live together. Even the middle classes of both groups avoided each other. Middle-class Czechs lived in Districts III, V, and to a lesser extent in IX, but Bohemian and Moravian Jews concentrated, as did most Jews, in Districts I, II, VI, and IX. Czech gentiles and Bohemian and Moravian Jews avoided each other, not only for class reasons, but for cultural ones as well. Bohemian and Moravian Jews who spoke German and identified with German culture[47] would not seek out common residence with gentiles whose everyday language was Bohemian or Moravian. The most important cause of the residential separation, however, was the desire of each group to establish its own identity in the city.

Taking Jewishness as the primary criterion in neighborhood selection, most Viennese Jews did not make distinctions based on geographical origins as long as their neighbors were other Jews. Only for Galician Jews was provincial origin an important issue when they chose housing. The division of the Jewish community into two groups, one composed of natives, Bohemians, Moravians, and Hungarians, and the other composed of Galicians did make itself felt to some limited extent in Viennese Jewish residential patterns. These differences, however, were not as great as those between neighborhoods of German Jews and Eastern European Jews in New York, Paris, or London in the nineteenth century.[48]

As a consequence of the differences between the two groups of Jews, the average Index of Dissimilarity for Jews born in Vienna, Bohemia, Moravia, and Hungary was low, only 25%, indicating the high level of internal integration among these Jews. The Index of Dissimilarity for Bohemian and Galician Jews, on the other hand, was 39%, reflecting the different residential patterns of these two Jewish groups. Moreover, while all Jews in Vienna lived in large numbers in the Leopoldstadt, the Inner City, and the Alsergrund, the Galicians concentrated much more heavily in the Leopoldstadt and the Brigittenau than any other Jews in the city (Table 4:12). An average of 57% of all Galician grooms between 1870 and 1910 lived in these two districts, compared with two-fifths of Hungarian and Moravian Jews and only 30% of Bohemian Jews. Over half of the Jewish grooms from the Brigittenau (XX) were born in Galicia. On the other hand, Galician Jews were less likely than other Jews to live in the Inner City, or Mariahilf-Neubau (VI–VII), but just as likely as the native-born, Moravians, and Hungarians to live in the Alsergrund, which, it will be recalled, contained pockets of poor Jews. Because a large number of Galicians were poor, more of them also lived beyond the *Gürtel* in Districts XI–XIX, mostly in Ottakring and Hernals (XVI–XVII).

Galician Jews concentrated in the Leopoldstadt not simply because of their recent immigrant status or their poverty. Rather they perceived hostility among the more Germanized Jews toward "Polish" Jews and thus probably wanted to live together as a source of comfort and to assert their own self-worth. Even richer Galician Jews in Vienna, those who paid taxes to the IKG, were more likely than any other group of middle-class Jews to live in the densely Jewish Leopoldstadt. In fact, 39.5% of all *Gemeinde* members *zuständig* in Galicia lived in the second district, compared with 25% of *Gemeinde* taxpayers in general. Even when Galicians were more affluent, they still tended to remain in the old Jewish neighborhood, where ethnic attachments were strong. Although they were less concentrated in the second district in 1910 than they had been in the 1870s (34.6% compared with 55.6%), Galicians remained much more likely than any other middle-class Jews in Vienna to live in the Jewish ghetto.

Moravians, Hungarians, and the native-born, on the other hand, were "typical" Viennese Jews. The Bohemians were much less likely than most Viennese Jews to live in the Leopoldstadt (about one-fourth compared with one-third) and the outer districts, but more likely to live in the Inner City, Districts III–V, X, VI–VIII, and especially in the Alsergrund. Richer Jews from these areas were equally integrated.

Table 4:12. Residential Distribution of Jewish Grooms from Each Area of Origin, Composite, 1870–1910

	Vienna* N = 186	Bohemia N = 83	Moravia** N = 100	Galicia[t] N = 169	Hungary N = 155	Other Foreign N = 28
I	10.2%	10.8%	12.0%	5.9%	16.1%	14.3%
II	31.7	28.9	41.0	47.3	42.6	39.3
III–V, X	8.6	13.3	12.0	8.9	12.9	10.7
VI–VIII	15.1	16.7	12.0	5.3	13.5	14.3
IX	10.8	20.5	10.0	10.1	9.7	14.3
XI–XIX	19.4	7.2	10.0	13.0	3.9	3.6
XX	3.2	1.2	3.0	9.5	1.3	3.6
XXI	1.1	1.2	—	—	—	—
	100.0%	100.0%	100.0%	100.0%	100.0%	100.0%

* Includes a few born in Lower Austria.

** Includes Silesians.

[t] Includes those born in Bukovina.

Jews of Vienna, whether new immigrants just off the trains from Galicia or those more established in the city, tended to live together in areas of Jewish concentration. The very fact of this concentration served to strengthen Jewish identity, both in terms of Jewish self-awareness, and in terms of gentile perceptions of Jewish separateness. Jewish self-separation served to weaken the forces for assimilation which the urban environment generated. In the Jewish neighborhoods Jews socialized with other Jews, they married each other, engaged in political debate with those of similar, or opposite mind, and formed organizations to proclaim traditional Jewish ideas or sport new Jewish identities. By living with other Jews, the Jews of Vienna cut off many opportunities for structural assimilation.

Mostly, the Jewish neighborhoods of Vienna made it possible for Jewish acculturation to take place within a Jewish setting. The process of assimilation into Austro-German culture became a Jewish endeavor, a kind of Jewish group effort. Fellow Jews experienced the same problems and shared the same goals. In the neighborhood, Jews went to school together and were introduced into the exciting world of Western culture in each others' company. School provided a major avenue to acculturation, but because Jews went to school with other Jews, their attendance at school did not lead to their total assimilation.

5. *Education, Mobility, and Assimilation: The Role of the* Gymnasium

IN HIS EVOCATIVE recollection of prewar Vienna, *The World of Yesterday,* Stefan Zweig, the son of a Jewish bourgeois, related the experience of his class:

> Every well-to-do family took care to have its sons "educated" if only for purely social reasons. They were taught French and English, they were made familiar with music, and were given governesses at first and then tutors to teach them good manners. But only the so-called "academic" education, which led to the University, carried full value in those days of enlightened liberalism; and that is why it was the ambition of every "good" family to have some sort of doctor's title prefixed to the name of at least one of its sons.[1]

Thus Zweig notes, "As a matter of course I was sent to the *Gymnasium* when I had finished attending elementary school."[2]

For the members of Zweig's "good Jewish bourgeoisie" *Gymnasium* education may have been a given, but this was so only for the upper echelons of Viennese Jewish society. Viennese Jews attended the *Gymnasium* in record numbers. They contributed 30% of the *Gymnasium* students in a city whose Jews made up only 8% of the population.[3] It was not education, however, which provided the Jews in Vienna with the initial thrust to enter the middle classes. Rather, secondary education ensured and enhanced social advancement already achieved through other means. Most Jewish *Gymnasium* students were the sons of respectable bourgeois who wanted their sons to pursue professional careers and thus improve upon a social status gained through commercial success.[4]

Jews were much more successful than most Viennese, however, in using a relatively closed educational system as an avenue of upward social mobility. *Gymnasium* education for Jews was the reserve of an elite, but this elite was much more broadly based than among the non-Jews who provided their sons with such an education. The late nineteenth-century Austrian educational system granted access to more members of the lower classes than ever before, but most *Gymnasium* students were still the scions of the upper ranks of society, noble or bourgeois. This system of education, which provided the only access to university education and hence to most high-status careers, groomed ten-to-eighteen-year-old boys largely derived from the upper classes of society for continued membership in the elite. The army or the priesthood provided children of peasants or workers with alternate paths to the upper echelons of society, but *Gymnasium* education remained an important delineator of class and status barriers in nineteenth-century Central Europe.[5] For a variety of reasons, however, Jews were more able than non-Jews to breech the status barrier.

Gymnasium education not only provided Jews with continued access to high-status careers but also served as a great force for their acculturation and assimilation into the world of European *Kultur* and *Bildung*.[6] Well-versed in Greek and Latin authors, graduates of the *Gymnasium* became heirs to the humanistic tradition in European culture, and could take their place in that most respected rung of society, the intelligentsia. The high percentage of Jewish students in the Viennese *Gymnasien* in the decades before the First World War attests to the high level of acculturation in Viennese Jewish bourgeois circles and to the desire of those middle-class Jews to encourage even further assimilation among the young.[7]

Despite the integration into European culture guaranteed by *Gymnasium* education, however, attendance at secondary school by no means guaranteed the structural or total assimilation of middle-class Viennese Jews. *Gymnasium* students knew more about Tacitus or Cicero than about the Torah, or the Talmud, but their school experience did not lead to their full integration into Viennese society. Middle-class Jews attended secondary schools in which the majority of students were fellow middle-class Jews. School thus did not require them to befriend non-Jews, and their acculturation occurred within the context of a largely Jewish social life. Jews who attended the *Gymnasium* both improved their career opportunities and achieved some ill-defined and never-expressed level of assimilation, but they did not necessarily sever their ties to the Jewish community.

Gymnasium Education and Viennese Jews

Like its counterparts elsewhere in Central Europe, the Viennese *Gymnasium* provided vigorous training in the Greek and Latin classics to those students being groomed for the university and high-status careers in the professions or civil service. The humanistic *Gymnasium* for ten-to-eighteen-year-old boys developed at the end of the eighteenth century out of the church-run Latin schools of the sixteenth century. The educators who constructed the curriculum firmly believed that the study of Latin and Greek grammar was instrumental in developing logical thought patterns; that the study of classical literature was essential for the development of a taste for beauty and simplicity; and that concentration on ancient history and philosophy would inculcate noble and heroic sentiments in young scholars, who afterward could pursue independent academic study and prepare for a profession at the university.[8]

Firmly in state control by 1869,[9] and therefore uniform, the *Gymnasium* curriculum was also rigorous. Students studied Latin, Greek, German language and literature, history and geography, mathematics, physics, and religion, and took electives in French and English. *Gymnasium* boys had only three hours of mathematics or science each week. The core of the *Gymnasium* program was the intensive study of the classics. Depending on grade level, students took between five and eight hours per week of Latin in all eight years of the *Gymnasium*, and between four and five hours per week of Greek from the third to the eighth years. Gymnastics, singing, drawing, and penmanship completed the curriculum.[10]

School authorities expected the students to perform at a very high level. In German class, for example, sixth-year pupils learned Middle High German, studied German literature from its inception to Luther, and poured over the verses of the *Nibelungenlied.* In the seventh year, they studied New High German, literature from Luther to Goethe, and the works of Goethe and Schiller in depth. In the final year, they analyzed German literature from the romantic period to the present.[11] In Greek class the students read the *Iliad* and the *Odyssey,* as well as Plato and Sophocles in the original. Latin grammar and literature formed the very heart of the curriculum, and students studied such authors as Livy, Virgil, Tacitus, Horace, Cicero, Ovid, and Julius Caesar.[12]

Jews began to attend *Gymnasium* at the end of the eighteenth century when the Austrian Emperor Joseph II removed the restrictions against Jewish school attendance and became the first European monarch to encourage the Jews to pursue secular education. In line with his general quest for centralization and Germanization, Joseph wanted the Jews to shed their supposedly negative Jewish ways and begin the process of integration into European society. His *Toleranzpatente* of 1782 abolished the special body tax on Jews and the juridical powers of the autonomous Jewish community. It also called on the Jews to establish schools for their children or send them to Christian schools, learn handicrafts, and attend the secondary schools and universities of the Empire.[13]

Throughout the debate on Jewish emancipation in the eighteenth and nineteenth centuries, Jews and non-Jews alike viewed secular education as the necessary precondition for Jewish participation in European society. Those that desired such participation also hoped that this education would undermine the segregationist influences of the traditional Jewish community and free the Jews for assimilation.[14] The Jews themselves were also eager to acquire secular education in order to practice professions impossible in the traditional Jewish community and to win acceptance by European society. The *Haskalah* movement, or Jewish enlightenment, of the late eighteenth and early nineteenth centuries, encouraged Jews to obtain Western education and become modern Europeans.[15] As a result, many Jews attended the secondary schools and universities newly open to them in the nineteenth century. For most Jewish students, this education provided an exciting opportunity for professional advancement and gentile social acceptance. Some Jewish students also viewed *Gymnasium* and university education as an express ticket to total assimilation and a severing of all bonds with the Jewish community. Most Jews who attended school, however, wanted some level of integration, although they rarely clarified the extent of assimilation they desired.

By the end of the nineteenth century, Jews made up an exceptionally high proportion of the student body in most Viennese *Gymnasien* (Table 5:1). In the decades before World War I, 30% of all *Gymnasium* students were Jews in a city in which less than 10% of the population was Jewish. This extraordinarily high percentage of Jewish students reflects Jewish success in acculturating, and in overcoming the status barriers of the educational system. Jews who chose to educate their sons shunned Vienna's less prestigious schools in favor of the gems of the educational establishment, the humanistic *Gymnasien.*

Jews attended almost all Viennese *Gymnasien* in numbers far exceeding their percentage in the population. In certain schools, those in the areas of Jewish concentration in the Inner City (I), the Leopoldstadt (II), and the Alsergrund (IX), between two-fifths and four-fifths of all the *Gymnasium* students were Jewish from 1875–1910. The Jewish proportion in the schools in Districts I, II, and IX far and away surpassed the Jewish proportion of the population in these districts. Only 34% of the population of the second district was Jewish in 1910, but three-quarters of the students in the two Leopoldstadt *Gymnasien* were Jewish. Similarly, Jews formed only 20% of the residents of the Inner City in 1910, but 40% of the *Gymnasium* students in the first district were Jewish. In the ninth district, Jews made up 20% of the population but two-thirds of the *Gymnasium* students. The proportion of Jewish students was high even in districts which had small Jewish populations.[16]

Jews rarely attended the two most prestigious schools in Vienna: the *Gymnasium zu den Schotten* and the *Theresianische Akademie.* These schools offered the most elite education in Vienna. The *Schottengymnasium,* established by the Benedictine order in the eighteenth century, then reorganized and reopened in 1804, offered the advantages of superior intellectual training with a genuine concern for the community. Many of Vienna's intellectual and political leaders attended this school, which sought to instill a measure of German national consciousness.[17] The *Theresianische Akademie,* originally created in 1746 for the sons of the nobility,[18] attracted the sons of Austria's aristocracy and inculcated aristocratic attitudes and noble sentiments.

In 1875 the *Schottengymnasium* did have a core of Jewish students. At that time, a number of Jews later prominent on the Viennese literary or political scene, men like Victor Adler or Heinrich Friedjung, were students at this elite school.[19] In the ensuing decades, however, fewer and fewer Jewish students attended the *Schottengymnasium,* probably because of its increasingly German nationalist orientation, an orientation which had antisemitic overtones. The *Theresianum,* on the other hand, with the anomalous exception of 1890/91, almost never had any Jewish students at all. The few Jews who did attend this school, like the sons of the Baron de Rothschild, came from families which had been ennobled.[20] It is not clear whether these private schools had restrictive policies against Jews, or whether Jews consciously avoided them because of the church connections and strong German nationalism of the one and the aristocratic tone of the other, a tone which might cause discomfort among the Jewish bourgeoisie.

Jewish presence in the other Viennese *Gymnasien* had already reached its highest level as early as 1875. Despite the growth of the Jewish community between 1875 and 1910, there was no growth in the Jewish percentage of the total *Gymnasium* student body. Jews comprised about 30% of *Gymnasium* students in 1875, and they comprised the same 30% in 1910. Although the number of Jewish students in Viennese *Gymnasien* increased, Jewish *Gymnasium* attendance did not keep pace with Jewish population growth. The Jewish student population increased 123% between 1875 and 1910, but the Viennese Jewish community grew 209% in these years.[21] The significant growth in the Jewish student population in certain schools between 1875 and 1910 resulted from the formation of new or larger Jewish neighborhoods in this period. For example, the increase in the number of Jewish students in the *Maximilian-Gym-*

Table 5:1. Jews in Viennese Gymnasien and Realgymnasien, 1875–1910*

		1875/76			1881/82		
Gymnasium	District	# Students	# Jews	% Jews	# Students	# Jews	% Jews
Akademisches	I	604	227	45.9	472	205	43.4
Franz-Joseph	I	279	123	44.1	304	125	41.1
Sophien	II	512	395	77.1	556	397	71.4
Erz. Rainer	II				472	350	74.2
Staatsgym.	III	311	47	15.1	488	101	20.7
Realgym.	III						
Staatsgym.	IV				231	28	12.1
Elisabeth	V						
Staatsgym.	VI	370	65	17.6	424	112	26.4
Staatsgym.	VII						
Staatsgym.	VIII	382	21	5.5	431	54	12.5
Maximilian	IX	291	95	32.6	419	167	39.9
Karl Ludwig	XII**						
Staatsgym.	XIII						
Staatsgym.	XIV						
Staatsgym.	XVI						
Staatsgym.	XVII				(270	46	17.0)**
Staatsgym.	XVIII						
Staatsgym.	XIX						
Staatsgym.	XXI						
Gym. zu den Schotten	I	434	56	12.9	419	32	7.6
Theresianische Akademie	IV	341	16	4.7	337	4	1.2
Privatgym.	VIII				63	9	14.3
Total		3,524	1,045	29.7%	4,616***	1,584***	34.3%***

Gymnasium	District	1890/91 # Students	# Jews	% Jews	1900/01 # Students	# Jews	% Jews	1910/11 # Students	# Jews	% Jews
Akademisches	I	459	204	44.4	399	139	34.8	531	212	39.9
Franz-Joseph	I	319	138	43.3	290	126	43.4	327	135	41.3
Sophien	II	455	298	65.5	431	305	70.8	509	304	59.7
Erz. Rainer	II	455	313	68.8	431	325	75.4	518	422	81.5
Staatsgym.	III	446	79	17.7	519	89	17.1	627	89	14.2
Realgym.	III							81	38	46.9
Staatsgym.	IV	263	16	6.1						
Elisabeth	V				368	55	14.9	451	61	13.5
Staatsgym.	VI	432	122	28.2	430	122	28.4	399	154	38.6
Staatsgym.	VII							123	17	13.8
Staatsgym.	VIII	453	75	16.6	505	92	18.2	517	108	20.9
Maximilian	IX	383	229	59.8	445	288	64.7	429	285	66.4
Karl Ludwig	XII	328	49	14.9	384	40	10.4	488	43	8.8
Staatsgym.	XIII				227	14	6.2	509	64	12.6
Staatsgym.	XIV							18	1	5.6
Staatsgym.	XVI							174	36	20.7
Staatsgym.	XVII	317	50	15.8	315	59	18.7	450	87	19.3
Staatsgym.	XVIII							447	36	8.1
Staatsgym.	XIX	351[t]	19[t]	5.4	346	79	22.8	343	116	33.8
Staatsgym.	XXI							297	58	19.5
Gym. zu den Schotten	I	443	3	0.7	381	18	4.7	414	34	8.2
Theresianische Akademie	IV	379	76	20.1	382	8	2.1	365	2	0.5
Privatgym.	VIII	76	14	18.4	131	40	30.5	113	28	24.8
Total		5,559	1,685	30.3%	5,984	1,799	30.1%	8,130	2,330	28.7%

* *Realgymnasien* were similar to *Gymnasien,* and frequently joined to them.
** Schools in Outer Districts not part of Vienna until 1890 incorporation.
*** Not including school in Hernals.
[t] Communal in 1890/91; state-run thereafter.

Sources: 1875: *Oesterreichisches statistisches Jahrbuch,* 1875, V, pp. 32–43;
1881: *Öst. Stat.,* 3:2, pp. 32–33; 40–41;
1890: *Öst. Stat.,* 35:4, pp. 30–31, 38–39;
1900: *Öst. Stat.,* 70:3, pp. 32–33;
1910: *Öst. Stat.,* N.F. 8:2, pp. 40–43.

nasium in the Alsergrund (IX) from 33% in 1875 to 66% in 1910 was a consequence of rising Jewish population in the Alsergrund in the decades before World War I. Similarly, the enlargement of the Jewish student body in the schools in Mariahilf (VI) and Döbling (XIX) reflected the creation of similar, albeit smaller, new Jewish residential clusterings in the city.

The early preponderance of Jews in Vienna's prestigious schools, and the fact that their high proportion did not increase was caused by the differences between the waves of migration to the Austrian capital. The earliest Jews to migrate to Vienna were more acculturated and more secure financially than members of later waves of migration to the city. Consequently, Bohemian, Moravian, and Hungarian businessmen who arrived in mid-century were in a better position than later immigrants, mostly traditional Jews from Galicia, to send their sons to *Gymnasium*. Some of the sons of newer immigrants did attend *Gymnasium*, but they were proportionately less likely to do so than the sons of the Jews who had settled in Vienna at mid-century. With the passage of time, of course, many more would probably attend secondary schools.

It is very difficult to estimate the number of Jewish families that sent their sons to *Gymnasium*. In any case, more Jewish families gave their sons an elite education than was true in the population at large. In 1881, for example, only 0.6% of all Viennese were *Gymnasium* students, but 2.2% of the Jewish population were attending *Gymnasium*. In 1910 the figures were 0.4% and 1.3% respectively.[22] In order to estimate the number of families which gave their sons elite education in 1910, it is necessary to multiply the *Gymnasium* student population (8,130) and the number of Jewish students (2,330) each by 10 to take family members and those without *Gymnasium* age children into account, and then divide the resulting figure by the total population of gentiles and Jews, respectively. This procedure reveals that only 4% of the entire Viennese population sent their sons to *Gymnasium*, while 13% of the Jewish families gave their sons the benefits of this elite education.

If they were going to send their sons to secondary school, Viennese Jews wanted the very best available. Jews also attended the *Realschulen*, the less prestigious, more technical secondary schools in Vienna, but they did so in proportions somewhat smaller than for the elite *Gymnasien*. A little over one-fifth of all *Realschule* students in the *Residenzstadt* in the decades before World War I were Jewish (Table 5:2). In the *Realschulen* in the first and ninth district, Jews formed two-fifths of the student body, and in the *Realschule* in the Leopoldstadt between two-fifths and two-thirds of the students were Jewish between 1875 and 1910.

The curriculum at the *Realschulen,* modern by contemporary standards, and therefore rich in mathematics, science, and foreign languages, did not offer Latin and Greek, subjects required for university admission and most high-status careers.[23] *Realschule* graduates could attend the *Technische Hochschule,* the technical or engineering university, and could obtain good jobs in business and industry. Technical careers may have been less open to Jews than such professions as medicine or law, and thus Jews preferred to send their sons to the *Gymnasium* in order to prepare them for the university. In any case, Jews aimed to enhance their status through the very best education available.

The Viennese Jewish penchant for elite education was part of an empire-wide pattern. In Prague, for example, Jews accounted for 46%

Table 5:2. Jews in Viennese Realschulen, 1875–1910 (Percent)

School	1875/76	1881/82	1890/91	1900/01	1910/11
k.-k. *Realschule* in:					
I*		23.4	36.1	30.6	38.6
II	65.4	69.7	39.0	40.7	53.0
II	60.9	42.5	70.6		21.7
III	30.9	22.4	21.0	23.2	22.1
IV*	9.0	6.1	6.9	8.5	9.4
V	11.5	11.6	7.8	5.4	6.9
VI*	10.4	13.4	18.7	18.0	23.5
VII	7.3	7.9	11.7	14.1	20.9
VIII					16.7
IX*	18.3				44.0
X					9.7
XI					3.7
XIII					5.1
XV	(10.4)**	(14.9)**	10.1	12.5	9.8
XVI					7.0
XVIII		(6.7)**	13.7	15.5	13.4
XIX					15.7
XX				61.2	40.8
Privat-Realschule in:					
I	14.7	14.1	15.8	23.2	
III		5.1	13.2	18.0	20.0
VII		5.6	8.9		
VIII	5.1	5.7	3.6		
XII					7.7
XV				8.9	
XVI				13.8	
Total:	21.4%***	19.7%***	22.1%	23.0%	20.9%

* Run by municipal government of Vienna through 1890/91; afterward in state control.
** Not in Vienna before 1890 annexation of the suburbs.
*** Only including schools in District I–X.
Sources: Oesterreichisches statistisches Jahrbuch, 1875, V, pp. 46–47, 50–51; *Öst. Stat.,* 3:2, pp. 42–43; 35:4, pp. 40–41; 70:3, pp. 44–45; N.F. 8:2, pp. 76–79.

of the student body in the German-language *Gymnasien* in 1910.[24] Similarly, in Lemberg, about 50% of the students in the German-language *Gymnasien* and 21% of the students in the Polish-language *Gymnasien* were Jewish in 1900.[25] In Budapest, where Jews were a major force in industry, 35.8% of the *Gymnasium* students, and 48.9% of the *Realschule* students were Jewish in 1911/12.[26]

Education and Mobility

Gymnasium education was generally not a primary vehicle for upward social mobility in Austria. A two-track educational system made it particularly difficult for the sons of workers, shopkeepers, or artisans to obtain higher education. The primary schools designed for the masses, called simply *Volksschulen,* provided basic instruction in the four Rs—Reading, Writing, Arithmetic, and Religion—until age fourteen. The secondary school system admitted students at age ten after four years in the *Volksschule.* Upper-middle-class and upper-class boys fully expected to transfer to the *Gymnasium* at age ten, attend university, and hold the wide range of prestigious positions reserved for *Gymnasium* (and university) graduates alone.[27] Only a few particularly bright lower-class boys were selected at age ten to receive *Gymnasium* education. Those who merely completed the *Volksschule* were doomed to remain lower or lower-middle class.[28] A kind of vicious circle existed: one needed either high social status, exceptional brilliance, or a great deal of ambition to attend *Gymnasium* in the first place. Financial considerations did not provide insurmountable barriers since tuition fees, about 100 Kronen or $25 per year, were low, and could be waived if necessary.[29] Most poor people, however, needing the additional income which their children could earn, could not afford to allow their sons to spend time in secondary school. The cost of proper school attire alone would have been prohibitive.

Unlike most Viennese, Jews did succeed in using this educational system to improve their social status. Elite education did not make possible their initial thrust into respectability, but Jews did use it to fortify already achieved social status and wealth. For the Jewish bourgeoisie, *Gymnasium* education guaranteed a higher-status future for their sons within the limits prescribed by society at large. This education allowed the offspring of a fairly broadly based business middle class to enter the more prestigious world of the professional middle class, as lawyers, doctors, writers, and managers.

Concentrated in mercantile professions and expanding into salaried employment, Jews possessed clear advantages over non-Jews in transcending the barriers of a class-bound educational system. As in the quest for occupational advancement, the economic position and cultural characteristics of the Jews greatly aided them in obtaining higher education. Most working-class Viennese probably never considered sending their sons to the prestigious secondary schools. Coming from peasant backgrounds, many Viennese workers were accustomed to servility toward their social superiors, not to sitting next to them in class. Jews, on the other hand, possessed no tradition of servility. Moreover, no matter how poor they were, Jews practiced bourgeois occupations which prepared them psychologically to advance their sons' careers through education. By the late nineteenth century, Jews had transposed their famous respect for learning from rabbinics to secular academics. In addition, their new economic freedom made the Jews particularly sensitive to the need for security, and they assumed that education would offer that measure of security which wealth, with all its inherent risks, never could. One could always lose one's money in an unwise business deal, but professional status generally insulated a person from the vicissitudes of the market and assured a safe and high position in society. Education and the professions also seemed to offer a haven from the tensions of a hostile environment. Through education Jews thought they could perhaps win a more favorable acceptance among gentiles than they could in the business world. Thus wealthy or not-so-wealthy Jewish businessmen sought to guarantee the positions of their sons through the best possible education.

The following discussion of the social and economic background of Jewish students receiving elite education is based on a careful analysis of those who attended three Viennese *Gymnasien* with high Jewish enrollment: the *Franz-Joseph-Gymnasium* in the Inner City, the *Erzherzog-Rainer-Gymnasium* in the Leopoldstadt (II), and the *Maximilian-Gymnasium (Wasagassegymnasium)* in the Alsergrund (IX).[30] These young Jewish men certainly belonged to the bourgeoisie, and their fathers pursued careers more prestigious than those of typical Viennese Jews (Table 5:3). A higher percentage of fathers of Jewish *Gymnasium* students were merchants, presumably prosperous ones, or industrialists than was true in the Viennese Jewish community at large. Professionals and civil servants, those who certainly hoped to preserve their own level of social status, eagerly sent their sons to *Gymnasium* and did so in proportions higher than their share in both the general Jewish population and among the prosperous IKG taxpayers. On the other hand, Jewish clerks, salesmen, and managers proved less capable than others of sending their sons to *Gymnasium*. Although one-quarter of the Jewish grooms in Vienna between 1870 and 1910 worked as business employees, only 18.6% of the fathers of Jewish secondary school students pursued clerical, sales, or managerial careers. As might be expected, few Jewish artisans or workers sent their sons to *Gymnasium.* Even though many prosperous Jewish artisans lived in Vienna, these men had lower status aspirations for their sons than did other Viennese Jews.

Between 1890 and 1910, changes in Viennese Jewish occupational preference made themselves felt in the kinds of families which sent their sons to *Gymnasium* (Table 5:4). As Viennese Jews increasingly abandoned trade for careers as business employees, many Jewish clerks, salesmen, and managers began to send their sons to *Gymnasium* (Table 5:4) in order to guarantee their sons high-status careers. Business employees remained proportionally less likely than professionals to send their sons to *Gymnasium.* Nonetheless, between 1890 and 1910 there was a 128% rise in the Leopoldstadt in the number of fathers of Jewish *Gymnasium* students who were business employees, and in the Alsergrund (IX) the increase was 209%!

Studying the backgrounds of students in each school separately suggests that a number of Jews did use the educational systems to rise in true social status. To a limited extent at least, some Jews in Vienna's Jewish ghetto, the Leopoldstadt, attended *Gymnasium* to achieve intergenerational upward social mobility (Table 5:4). Students in the Inner City *Gymnasium* came largely from the most prestigious families, and students in the ninth district from homes most typifying the economic transformations of Viennese Jews. The Jewish boys in the *Gymnasium* in the Leopoldstadt, on the other hand, had fathers who enjoyed less social status than the fathers of students elsewhere. Fewer of the Leopoldstadt fathers pursued a profession or owned a factory, and more of them were artisans or salaried business employees. In addition, because of the number of tuition waivers in the *Erzherzog-Rainer-Gymnasium* in District II, it is likely that many

Table 5:3. Occupations of Fathers of Jewish Gymnasium Students in 1890 and 1910, Compared to Occupational Distribution of IKG Taxpayers and Jewish Grooms (Composite)

	Gymnasium Students		IKG %	Grooms %
	#	%	N = 2207	N = 811
Civil Servants	86	5.9	3.6	2.6
Professionals	226	15.5	11.5	11.3
Industrialists	93	6.4	5.8	3.5
Merchants	708	48.5	47.4	40.8
Business Employees	271	18.6	18.7	25.5
Artisans	64	4.4	13.1	12.0
Workers	12	0.8	—	4.3
	1460	100.0%	100.0%	100.0%

Table 5:4. Occupations of Fathers of Jewish Gymnasium Students, 1890/91 and 1910/11

	Overall		Gym. in I		Gym. in II		Gym. in IX	
	1890/91 N = 638	1910/11 N = 822	1890/91 N = 120	1910/11 N = 128	1890/91 N = 306	1910/11 N = 417	1890/91 N = 212	1910/11 N = 277
Civil Servants	3.3%	7.9%	0.8%	4.7%	3.9%	6.5%	3.8%	11.6%
Professionals	15.5	15.5	25.0	29.7	12.7	10.3	14.2	16.6
Industrialists	7.0	6.0	9.2	15.6	3.9	4.3	9.9	4.0
Merchants	57.8	41.2	53.3	39.1	57.8	44.8	60.4	36.8
Business Employees	12.9	23.0	10.0	8.6	15.4	25.7	10.8	25.6
Artisans	3.0	5.5	1.7	2.3	5.2	6.5	0.5	5.4
Workers	0.6	1.0	—	—	1.0	1.9	0.5	—
	100.0%	100.0%	100.0%	100.0%	100.0%	100.0%	100.0%	100.0%

of the Leopoldstadt Jewish fathers who were merchants earned less money and enjoyed much less social prestige than the merchants who sent their sons to school in the Inner City or in the Alsergrund.

Financial assistance made it possible for some less prosperous Viennese Jews to attend *Gymnasium* and rise in social status. Although prestigious secondary schools like the *Schottengymnasium* and the *Theresianische Akademie* granted few tuition waivers, other Viennese *Gymnasien* exempted, on the average, 20% to 30% of their students from tuition payments of about 100 Kronen a year.[31] In the *Gymnasien* in Leopoldstadt (II), Landstrasse (III), Meidling (XII), and Hernals (XVII) about half of the students paid no tuition. The number of free *Gymnasium* places increased in this period, even in the schools in the Inner City which granted few tuition waivers.[32] In Vienna, tuition waivers opened the doors of the *Gymnasium* to more students than in Prussia, where only 10% of the places were "free." [33] Since the number of *Gymnasium* students remained low in the nineteenth century, tuition waivers apparently did not open the educational system widely to the lower classes. Although there is no way to know, it is possible that certain professional groups like university professors or civil servants automatically received these waivers.

About a third (34.4%) of the Jewish students in the three *Gymnasien* studied received tuition exemptions.[34] Jewish students who received tuition waivers came from homes which enjoyed less social status than those of average Jewish *Gymnasium* students. The fathers of students receiving financial aid practiced professions and owned factories less often than the fathers of other students. Moreover, they worked as clerks, salesmen, and managers, and as artisans more often than the fathers of other Jewish *Gymnasium* students. More than half of the boys whose fathers were business employees and artisans received tuition exemptions.

In the Leopoldstadt in particular, tuition exemptions made it possible for the less well-to-do to send their sons to *Gymnasium* and thus rise in social rank. The number of Jewish students needing financial assistance in the *Erzherzog-Rainer-Gymnasium* in District II rose between 1890 and 1910. In 1890, only 30.2% of its Jewish students received tuition exemption; twenty years later fully 50.4% received financial aid. Even though the 1890 statistic is artificially low because of missing information for the first-year class for that year, it is nevertheless apparent that the 1910 classes needed and received considerably more financial assistance than did the 1890 classes. Jews attending the *Franz-Joseph-Gymnasium* in the Inner City did not require financial assistance. Coming from prosperous families, only 5% of them received tuition waivers. As a result of financial assistance and their own ambition, Jews in Vienna employed a relatively closed educational system to make modest advances, solidify earlier gains, and enhance their social position in the city. Most Jewish students in *Gymnasium* were of the middle class to be sure, but that middle class was open to the less respectable as well as the well-to-do.

In contrast to the Jews, only the upper crust of non-Jewish society ever sent their sons to *Gymnasium*. Among Vienna's gentiles, unlike among its Jews, secondary school education merely perpetuated class distinctiveness. Fathers of gentile students in the three *Gymnasien* studied here[35] enjoyed much higher social status and derived from a much narrower stratum of Viennese society than did their Jewish counterparts (Table 5:5). Over one-third of the non-Jewish fathers were either military officers or upper-level bureaucrats, a rate ten times higher than Jewish fathers in 1890, only 3% of whom were civil servants, and of this 3%, most were in low-status ministries. Many of the gentile fathers held professorships at the university, positions which bestowed on them extremely high social status. Moreover, about one-quarter of the non-Jewish fathers were professional, again a rate much higher than the 16% of the Jewish fathers pursuing professions in that year. Thus in 1890, 60% of the gentile students had fathers who were officers, high-ranking civil servants, and professionals, compared with 19% for Jews. On the other hand, the fathers of gentile students were significantly less likely than the Jews to be merchants, factory owners, or business employees, and very few were artisans or workers.

Gentile students not only came from more prestigious homes than Jews but had fathers who belonged to the upper rank of Viennese society. Although most Viennese were working class or lower-middle class, almost no gentile workers or shopkeepers sent their sons to secondary schools. Nor in general did Vienna's gentile businessmen provide their sons with an elite education. It was upper-level civil

Table 5:5. Occupations of Fathers of Gentile Gymnasium Students, 1890/91

	Gym. in I N = 44	Gym. in II N = 37	Gym. in IX N = 55
Military Officers	6.8%	2.3%	5.5%
Civil Servants	18.2	29.7	41.8
Professionals	27.3	24.3	23.6
Industrialists	4.5	5.4	1.8
Merchants	25.0	16.2	14.5
Business Employees	13.6	8.1	5.5
Artisans	4.5	2.7	3.6
Workers	—	10.8	3.6
	100.0%	100.0%	100.0%

servants, military officers, and professionals, only 11% of the Viennese work force, who provided 60% of the non-Jewish students at the humanistic *Gymnasien* in Vienna.[36] For these men, *Gymnasium* education guaranteed that their sons would enjoy the same high level of social prestige as they themselves did.

Immigrants and Natives

Analysis of the national origins of Jewish students[37] reveals that immigrant fathers, like other Jewish fathers in Vienna, attempted to use elite education to confirm or improve the social status of their sons. This fact is especially striking because immigrants were not in a good position to send their offspring to *Gymnasien*. They did so nonetheless, and far more often than fathers of non-Jewish immigrants, who generally chose trade schools to secure their sons' futures.

Certainly most Jewish *Gymnasium* students were Viennese-born. A higher percentage of Jewish students than either grooms, fathers, or IKG taxpayers had been born in the Austrian capital. In 1890, for example 17% of the fathers were Viennese, and 26% of the new entrants to the IKG tax rolls had Viennese *Heimat*,[38] but over two-thirds of the Jewish *Gymnasium* students (on the average) were natives of the city (Table 5:6). Between 1890 and 1910, as the native-born proportion of the Viennese Jewish community grew, so too did the number of students born in the capital. The percentage of Viennese-born students in the schools in Districts I and II rose from two-thirds to more than three-quarters during this period. The differences between the eighth-year classes of 1890, which started school in 1883, and the first-year classes of 1910 are even more substantial. In the *Erzherzog-Rainer-Gymnasium* in the Leopoldstadt (II), only 48% of the eighth-year class in 1890 was native-born, but 75% of the students in the youngest classes in 1910 had been born in Vienna. Similarly, only 45.5% of the class which entered the *Franz-Joseph-Gymnasium* in the Inner City in 1883 were native-born, and 83.5% (or twice as many) of the youngest classes in 1910 were born in Vienna. In the *Maximilian-Gymnasium* in the Alsergrund (IX), Jewish students were always overwhelmingly Viennese-born.

Despite the large proportion of natives, a sizeable number of Jewish students in these three *Gymnasien* came from immigrant families. In 1890, a little under a third (31.6%), and in 1910, about a quarter (24.5%) of the Jewish students had been born outside of Vienna, and probably an even higher percentage were Viennese-born sons of recent Jewish immigrants. This percentage, while considerably smaller than the percentage of immigrants in the Jewish community

Table 5:6. Place of Birth of Viennese Jewish Gymnasium Students, 1890/91 and 1910/11

	Gym. in I		Gym. in II		Gym. in IX	
	1890/91 N = 141	1910/11 N = 140	1890/91 N = 344	1910/11 N = 452	1890/91 N = 244	1910/11 N = 307
Vienna	67.4%	80.7%	63.7%	73.5%	74.2%	73.0%
Other Lower Austria	3.5	2.1	3.5	2.7	5.7	4.9
Bohemia	2.8	4.3	2.3	2.9	3.7	3.9
Moravia & Silesia	4.3	5.7	6.4	3.3	4.5	3.9
Galicia & Bukovina	3.5	2.1	8.7	12.2	2.5	5.2
Hungary	11.3	1.4	9.9	4.2	7.0	3.6
Western Europe	4.3	2.1	1.5	0.7	0.8	2.9
Eastern Europe	2.1	0.7	2.9	0.4	1.6	2.3
Elsewhere	0.7	0.7	1.2	0.2	—	0.3
	100.0%	100.0%	100.0%	100.0%	100.0%	100.0%

generally, was relatively large in view of the difficulties that prevented immigrants from attending elite schools. In the first place, the majority of immigrants arrived in the city as adults who could not attend *Gymnasium*. Moreover, most immigrants would be too busy trying to earn a living to send their children, especially those born in the provinces, to elite schools. In any case, a number of Jewish boys born in Bohemia, Moravia, and Hungary did attend *Gymnasium*, but their numbers decreased as immigration from the Czech lands and Hungary tapered off between 1890 and 1910. Thus, for example, 14.6% of the Jewish boys who started *Gymnasium* in the Leopoldstadt in 1884 and 1885 were Hungarian, but only 4.3% of those who started between 1906 and 1910 had been born in Hungary. Most of the Jews who migrated to Vienna from Bohemia, Moravia, and Hungary did so in the early waves of migration, and so by 1910 few of them had *Gymnasium*-age children any longer.

School-wide statistics for 1890 and 1910 indicate that there was a modest rise in the percentage of Galician-born Jewish students between 1890 and 1910, especially in the *Gymnasium* in the Leopoldstadt, where the proportion of Galicians rose from 8.7% to 12.2%. While this rise in no way corresponds to the large increase in Galician-born Jews in Vienna in this period, it suggests that even among these more traditional Jews many wanted to give their sons an elite education. A closer look at the geographical origins of students in all classes in the *Erzherzog-Rainer-Gymnasium* in District II in 1890 and 1910 reveals that there were nearly as many Galicians in the entering classes in the early 1880s, a time of low Jewish migration from Galicia, as in the classes which began school after 1906, a time of mass migration from that province. In 1890, 9.9% of students in the oldest three grades had been born in Galicia, while in 1910, the proportion in the youngest five grades was 11.6%. The earliest Galician Jews in Vienna, it will be remembered, were acculturated, well-to-do, and consequently sent their sons to *Gymnasium.* The newer immigrants at the end of the century were too poor and less concerned with assimilation or acculturation and hence with *Gymnasium* education than earlier *Galizianer* in Vienna. Thus, despite the very large growth of the Galician Jewish community in Vienna, the number of Galician Jewish students in Vienna did not rise appreciably. It appears, however, that some poor Galicians did send their sons to *Gymnasium,* and that more of them would do so with the passage of time and the decline of tradition. Although only 5.2% of all Jewish students in the sample were Galician, 15.5% of those with tuition waivers had been born in Galicia.

Few recent Jewish immigrants could send their sons to *Gymnasium,* but Vienna's gentile immigrants were even less able to send their sons to prestigious secondary schools. In the three schools under analysis here, as indeed in virtually all of the *Gymnasien* in Vienna, almost all of the gentile students were Viennese or had been born elsewhere in the province of Lower Austria, near Vienna, where few *Gymnasien* existed (Table 5:7).[39] The only *Gymnasium* in Vienna with any substantial number of students who were not born in Vienna was the *Theresianische Akademie,* which catered to the sons of the nobility from all over the Dual Monarchy. In 1895 only 46% of its students were native-born, 12% Lower Austrian or Styrian, 10% Bohemian and Moravian, 5% Galician, 10% Hungarian, and 18% born elsewhere.[40] Most of the students at the more typical *Schottengymnasium* in 1911/12 were either Viennese (79%) or Lower Austrian (11%).[41]

None of the ethnic minorities in Vienna received *Gymnasium* education, least of all the Czechs. With the exception of the *Franz-Joseph-Gymnasium* in the Inner City, which attracted the sons of a

Table 5:7. Place of Birth of Gentile Gymnasium Students, 1890/91

	Gym. in I N = 48	Gym. in II N = 37	Gym. in IX N = 57
Vienna	75.0%	78.4%	80.7%
Other Lower Austria	10.4	8.1	7.0
Bohemia	8.3	—	—
Moravia & Silesia	2.1	8.1	3.5
Galicia & Bukovina	—	2.7	1.8
Hungary	2.1	2.7	3.5
Western Europe	—	—	3.5
Eastern Europe	—	—	—
Elsewhere	2.1	—	—
	100.0%	100.0%	100.0%

few Bohemian noblemen, very few gentiles in the three schools studied were Czech. These schools, located far from Czech concentrations in the city, would be unlikely to contain many Bohemian or Moravian students. But there were virtually no Czech students anywhere else either. Certainly almost no students whose mother tongue was Czech attended Viennese *Gymnasien* or *Realschulen.* In 1910, only 108, or 1.6%, of 7,414 *Gymnasium* students in Vienna cited Czech as their mother tongue.[42] German-language assimilation could easily have obscured the presence of Czechs in the schools, but there were likewise almost no students born in Bohemia or Moravia in the *Gymnasien* in districts close to Czech concentrations in the city. In the *Staatsgymnasium* in Hietzing (XIII), none of the students in 1903/4 had been born in Bohemia.[43] In working-class Hernals (XVII), 9% of the student body was Bohemian in 1885, but in 1895 the proportion had fallen to 3%.[44] Similarly, only 3% of the *Gymnasium* students in the twelfth district in 1890/91 and 1910/11 were Bohemian.[45] The working-class character of the Czech community of Vienna effectively prevented it from obtaining higher education.

In contrast to the Jews, who concentrated their efforts on sending their sons to the most prestigious schools of Austria, gentile immigrants to Vienna sent their sons to trade schools after they had completed the *Volksschule.* A very large proportion of the students in the Viennese trade schools were Czech. Czech-speaking students constituted 23.9% of the student body at the trade schools in Vienna in 1889/90.[46] In 1910, when a great deal of German-language assimilation had taken place among the Czechs in Vienna, they still formed 18.2% of the total trade school student body. In certain schools Czechs constituted a considerably higher proportion. For example, in 1910, in the trade school for tailors, Czechs comprised 67% of the student body, for shoemakers 51%, for carpenters 49%. On the other hand, Czechs provided only 2% of the students in those business schools which trained lower-level clerks.[47]

Jews, on the other hand, rarely attended these lower-class educational institutions. The trade schools could have offered them a certain type of social mobility and assimilation. Working-class Jews, or even Jews who barely made a living as peddlers or commission agents, might have improved their sons' financial and social positions by providing them with manual training and jobs as skilled laborers. In a working-class city greater integration of the Jews into gentile society might have been achieved if more Jews had chosen occupations as craftsmen rather than as intellectuals or professionals or clerks. But in contrast to other immigrant groups in the city, Viennese Jews rarely chose this kind of social mobility and integration. With the exception of certain schools which offered higher status or income to their graduates, or were for trades with which they had been associated traditionally, Jews shunned Vienna's trade schools. Working-class Jews in Vienna, a small group to begin with, either personally provided their sons with the necessary vocational training, or sought social mobility through business or clerical positions. Poor Jews, those who peddled and traded, clearly did not want to improve their sons' chances by encouraging them to pursue careers in manual labor. Rather, they probably viewed trade and commerce and positions as clerks and salesmen as much more promising avenues to a better future than a life devoted to artisanal skills. Antisemitism among Viennese artisans probably also contributed to their avoidance of trade schools.

In most Viennese trade schools, Jews formed an infinitesimal proportion of the student population in both 1890 and 1910 (Table 5:8), much smaller than their proportion in the population at large.[48] Even in schools for the needle trades, Jews constituted only 2% of the student body in the boys' schools and 5% in the girls' schools. Jews only appeared in appreciable numbers in those schools which taught trades that offered more security or prestige than the others. Thus, in 1910, 18% of the students in the school for jewelers and 18% of the students in the school for dental technicians were Jewish, as were 24% in the school for decorators and upholsterers, and 31% in the furrier school. Jews did seek careers as low-level business clerks, and thus 19% of the students in the two "business schools" were Jewish.

Girls' Education

Jews also wanted to educate their daughters. Although the number of girls who received secondary education in Vienna was low, Jews were an extremely prominent group in the higher schools for girls, even more so than at the *Gymnasien.* This education had no career implications. Women were not admitted to the university until the twentieth century (and to the law faculty only after World War I), and they almost never pursued independent careers. Even so Jews did want to "improve" their daughters.

In contrast to boys' education, which guaranteed both social prestige and acculturation and in which a rather broadly based middle class could participate, education for Jewish girls in the period before the First World War was limited to the daughters of the wealthiest and most established Jews in the city. Wealthy Jews probably viewed the education of their daughters as an ornament on their already achieved

Table 5:8. Jews in Viennese Trade Schools, 1910

Type of School	Number of Schools	Number of Students	# Jews	% Jews
General Trade Schools	5	906	14	1.5
Specialty Trade Schools:*				
For Bakers	4	703	8	1.1
Building Trades	5	1,117	3	0.3
Sculptors	1	122	2	1.6
Bookbinders	3	708	36	5.1
Turners	1	171	6	3.5
Electricians	1	287	12	4.2
Coopers	1	123	—	—
Dyers	1	213	2	0.9
Brassworkers	2	356	1	0.3
Farriers	1	263	1	0.4
Hatmakers	1	181	10	5.5
Industrial Painters	1	52	1	1.9
Plumbers	1	358	32	8.9
Jewelers & Goldsmiths	2	636	113	17.8
Tailors	11	3,402	67	2.0
Furriers	1	283	87	30.7
Machinists	1	138	2	1.4
Machine Fitters	4	1,296	12	0.9
Mechanics	4	1,356	13	1.0
Metal Workers	6	1,498	7	0.5
Chimney Flue Sweepers	1	117	15	12.8
Saddlers	1	326	1	0.3
Signpainters	1	78	—	—
Locksmiths	6	2,013	18	0.9
Shoemakers	11	2,228	58	2.6
Upholsterers	1	202	49	24.3
Pocketbookmakers	1	191	14	7.3
Carpenters	10	2,693	25	0.9
Cartwrights	1	133	—	—
Weavers	1	301	25	8.3
Dental Technicians	1	220	39	17.7
		21,765	659	3.0
Speciality Schools for Girls:				
For Seamstresses	19	4,017	197	4.9
Artificial Flower Makers	1	359	14	3.9
Milliners	1	415	50	12.0
Underwear Makers	2	471	8	1.7
		5,262	269	5.1
Guild Schools for Apprentices	32	7,444	147	2.0
Guild Schools for Female Apprentices	3	922	159	17.2
Business Schools	2	5,086	972	19.1
Overall		40,479	2,206	5.4%

* Printers missing in source.
Source: SJSW (1910), pp. 412–25.

high social status. Educated daughters could symbolize the aristocratic pretensions of their parents and could serve to forge alliances with other wealthy families. Moreover, to train one's daughters in English and French indicated both a high level of acculturation and the desire of rich Jewish families to ensure their further assimilation into Viennese bourgeois society.

The state did not establish schools for girls beyond the *Volksschulen* before World War I. Women were not admitted to the prestigious humanistic *Gymnasien* or the *Realschulen* because it was assumed that such an education would be wasted on "mere girls" and would prove distracting to the male students for whom education was a necessity.[49] Various private foundations and organizations devoted to female education did, however, establish "higher" girls' schools, called *Mädchen-Lyzeen,* offering six-year programs for girls from ten to sixteen years old. The graduates of these schools could not attend university, but by 1905 they could become special students *(ausserordentliche Hörerinnen)* in the philosophy faculty of the university and, after three years of study, return to teach in the *Lyzeum.* Graduates of *Mädchen-Lyzeen* were likewise entitled to begin the third or fourth year of a teachers' training school, study pharmacology, take the state stenography examination, or attend the *Wiener Handelsakademie für Mädchen.*[50]

The curriculum in a six-year *Mädchen-Lyzeum* resembled, to some extent, that of the *Realschule* for boys. It did not usually offer Latin or Greek, but did instruct in an array of modern languages. Unlike the *Realschule,* however, the curriculum was not strong in math and science. Electives could be taken in sewing, stenography, typing, and in a few schools, Latin.[51] The *Mädchen-Lyzeum* curriculum was considerably less rigorous than that of the *Gymnasium.* While the boys were studying Latin and Greek, physics and algebra, the girls read *William Tell,* wrote compositions on "The Advantages of Country Life," "An Unlikely Summer Journey," or "The Crucifixion," and gave poetry recitals. *Gymnasium* students read at least three times as many masterpieces of German literature as the girls did.[52]

Two foundations did attempt to equalize education for girls in pre-World War I Vienna. After 1888, the *Verein für erweiterte Frauenbildung* (Society for Expanding Women's Education) attempted to make it possible for Austrian women to go to university and pursue careers reserved for university graduates. In the *gymnasiale Mädchenschule* established by this *Verein* in 1892, girls pursued a regular *Gymnasium* curriculum of Latin and Greek, German, history and geography, religion, mathematics, natural history, and philosophy in a six-year program, increased to seven years in 1901 and eight in 1910. In 1912, the *Verein für realgymnasialen Mädchenunterricht* (Society for the Instruction of Girls in the *Realgymnasium* System) also established a school for girls.[53]

Vienna's richest and most assimilated Jews sent their daughters to *Mädchen-Lyzeen* in numbers far greater than the gentiles of the city. In fact, relatively little space remained for the daughters of the gentile majority. In 1895/96, 57% of all *Lyzeum* students were Jewish,[54] and in 1910 the figure was still 46% (Table 5:9), a figure much higher than the Jewish proportion either in the *Gymnasien* (30%) or in the *Realschulen* (21%). Certain *Mädchen-Lyzeen,* such as the schools named for Dr. Amalia Sobel and Dr. Olga Ehrenhaft-Steindler, were almost totally Jewish; others, such as Eugenie Schwarzwald, were two-thirds Jewish. On the other hand, those *Lyzeen* run by Christian foundations contained no Jewish students at all.

Jewish girls who attended the Inner City's Eugenie Schwarzwald *Mädchen-Lyzeum,* the school studied in depth here,[55] certainly came from the upper classes. They were the daughters of Vienna's most successful and established Jews, those who had already achieved high social status and now wanted to have their daughters become

Table 5:9. Jews in Viennese Girls' Secondary Schools, 1910/11

		# Students	# Jews	% Jews
Gymnasien				
• des Vereines für erweiterte Frauenbildung (8 classes)	I	388	168	43.3
• des Dr. J. Schwarz (1 class)	VIII	7	2	28.6
Mädchen-Lyzeen				
• Hilda von Gunesch	I	24	6	25.0
• Martha Luithlen	I	123	32	26.0
• Eugenie Schwarzwald	I	164	113	68.9
• Dr. Amalia Sobel	I	43	38	88.4
• Chr. Verein zur Förderung der Frauenbildung	I	9	—	—
• Dr. Olga Ehrenhaft-Steindler	I	178	157	88.2
• Berta Freyler	I	131	36	27.5
• Wr. Frauenerwerbverein	IV	236	112	47.5
• Klothilde Liste	V	48	7	14.6
• Sophie Halberstamm	VI	135	52	38.5
• Klosterfrauen-Notre Dame de Sion	VII	124	—	—
• Schulverein für Beamten-töchter	VIII	558	215	38.5
• Rosa Feri-Fliegelmann	IX	167	129	77.2
• Hietzinger Lyzeum-Gesellschaft	XIII	184	51	27.7
• Cottage-Lyzeum der Salka Goldmann	XIX	197	115	58.4
Total: *Lyzeen*		2,321	1,063	45.8%
Lyzeen & Gym.		2,716	1,233	45.4%

Source: Öst. Stat., N.F. 8:2, pp. 68–71, 102–3.

the proper ornament of their upward mobility. These girls came from homes which were even more well-to-do and established than those of the Jewish *Gymnasium* students in general, and even of students in the *Franz-Joseph-Gymnasium* in the Inner City. Most of the girls' fathers were Vienna's Jewish industrialists, large-scale merchants, and high-status professionals, and very few worked as either civil servants or business employees (Table 5:10). In 1910, the number of girls from professional families was greater than in 1890. Moreover, almost all Jewish girls at Schwarzwald were native-born Viennese. In 1890, two-thirds had been born in the capital, and in 1910, three-quarters.

However narrow the group of Viennese Jews who sent their daughters to the *Lyzeum*, the group of gentiles who educated their girls was narrower still. Of the sixty-five non-Jews at Schwarzwald in 1910/11, almost half were the daughters of military officers (12.9%) or high-ranking civil servants (35.5%). Among the gentile fathers, 11% were professionals, 8% were factory owners, only 11% were merchants, 15% business employees, and 2% artisans. Most of the gentile girls were either Viennese or had been born in Lower Austria or Styria.

Education and Assimilation

Secondary school education served the dual purpose of enhancing Jewish social prestige and ensuring that middle-class Jews were properly initiated into European high culture. With its emphasis on the humanistic tradition, *Gymnasium* education offered the Jews an enticing invitation—one they accepted fully—to adopt gentile cultural values as their own and consequently to reject Jewish ideas and concerns.[56] *Gymnasium* education in Central Europe, as steeped in pagan classicism as it was, could easily lure students away from Jewish concerns into the dazzling world of ancient and modern

Table 5:10. Occupations of Fathers of Jewish Students at Schwarzwald Mädchen-Lyzeum, 1890 and 1910

	1890/91 N = 86	1910/11 N = 131
Civil Servants	—	3.8%
Professionals	14.0%	31.3
Factory Owners	18.6	13.0
Merchants	53.5	26.0
Business Employees	10.5	23.7
Artisans	3.5	2.3
Workers	—	—
	100.0%	100.0%

European culture. Certainly religious Jews could label the *Gymnasium* as a Hellenistic and pagan influence and, in the tradition of the Maccabees, oppose the education of their sons in such an avowedly gentile atmosphere. Young men trained there surely knew more about Horace, Cicero, and the *Nibelungenlied* than they did about the Talmud and the Torah. All Jewish students at the *Gymnasium* received two hours of Jewish religious instruction each week, but these two hours could not suffice to inculcate Jewish religious values and knowledge. Arthur Schnitzler, the playwright, gaily described his classmates' lack of respect for their Jewish religious instructors at the *Akademisches Gymnasium* in the Inner City. They talked—or talked back—while the rabbis lectured on the Bible.[57] For many, Judaism paled by comparison to Plato, Sophocles, or Julius Caesar, the real heroes of the *Gymnasium* world.

This humanistic learning exerted a powerful attraction upon the first generation of students exposed to it. Sigmund Mayer, a wealthy Viennese businessman who attended *Gymnasium* in Pressburg/Pozsony in the 1840s observed: "This school was for us Jewish lads practically a charmed *(anmutende)* oasis in the social wilderness that surrounded us." [58] Later students, much more exposed to Western culture than Mayer had been in 1847, were sometimes repelled by what Stefan Zweig called the "dull, pointless learning" and "constant and wearisome boredom," [59] of *Gymnasium* education, but they rejected the hard benches of the *Gymnasium* mainly because they yearned to participate in the exciting life of the city around them. They were reaching beyond the *Gymnasium* to all the delights modern culture had to offer. Arnold Höllriegel, later a journalist, was more interested in Karl Kraus's satirical periodical *Die Fackel,* than his school work at the *Erzherzog-Rainer-Gymnasium* in the Leopoldstadt.[60] All of Stefan Zweig's friends devoured the journals and newspapers, avidly followed literary developments, and insatiably attended theater performances.[61] Zweig wrote: ". . . during our school hours, on our way to and from school, in the coffeehouse, in the theater, on our walks, we half-grown young colts did nothing but discuss books, pictures, music, and philosophy." [62] Schnitzler also grew up in a circle of budding literary types. In his eighth year at the *Gymnasium,* he had "no lack of time" for his literary endeavors: "The theater, concerts, reading, long walks and lengthy talks with friends, my poetizing—all of it could be easily fitted into the day . . .," he recalled.[63]

Beyond the sheer allure of secular learning, the fact that all students had to attend *Gymnasium* classes on Saturday, the Jewish sabbath and day of rest, certainly added to their estrangement from traditional Jewish life and to their assimilation into secular/Christian society.

The need to go to school on Saturday may have prevented the more religious from attending the *Gymnasium.* Many probably attended class, but did no writing on that day because, according to Jewish law, writing is prohibited on the Sabbath. Peer pressure and pressure from school officials must have been great and presumably led to a situation in which students naturally accepted school mores and hence the mores of a non-Jewish world. Many students may have also resented their Jewish origins for having placed them in this situation. Finally, the connection between secular and Christian culture in the *Gymnasium* must not be overlooked. In Austria classrooms had a large crucifix prominently displayed on the walls. Jewish students were reminded daily that the state in which they lived was not really secular but avowedly Christian.[64]

Even though it thrust young Jews into European culture, however, *Gymnasium* education in Vienna apparently did not often lead to the establishment of intimate relationships between Jews and gentiles. Structural assimilation was *not* the end product of elite education for Jews. Jews attended schools which were overwhelmingly Jewish. Two-thirds of all Viennese Jewish *Gymnasium* students attended school in Districts I, II, and IX, schools in which 40% to 80% of the students were Jewish. The school environment neither forced nor encouraged Jewish boys to become friends with non-Jews, and the situation was the same for Jewish girls who attended largely Jewish schools. Non-Jews were the outsiders in these schools. A classmate of Arthur Schnitzler's who later became a German nationalist showed his new friends his class picture and lamented, "Just take a look, what a lot of Jews I had to go to school with." [65] Even the most assimilated Jews in Vienna went to school with other Jews. Arnold Höllriegel, who wrote that his Judaism meant little to him, remembered that "in our class, there were very few Christians, and these were often Protestants, which, in Catholic Vienna of that time, almost always meant baptized Jews." [66] All of Höllriegel's later associates were also Jewish.[67]

Höllriegel's case was by no means unique. Arthur Schnitzler also recalled that almost all of his *Gymnasium* friends and intimates had been fellow Jews. He noted that: "A certain separation of Gentiles and Jews into groups which were not kept strictly apart (nor was there any idea of such a division into 'parties') could be felt always and everywhere, also therefore in school." [68] If Schnitzler detected a Jewish/gentile separation in the late 1870s, surely in the following decades, when antisemitism was more overt, this separation became even more institutionalized. The *Gymnasium* simply did not provide Jews, even Jews who might have wanted to shed all Jewish association, with much impetus to meet and become close to non-Jews.

The large percentage of Jews in each class must have also limited peer pressure to write on the Sabbath for those who still clung to religious tradition enough to care. If, in the Leopoldstadt, the area which was most likely to have Sabbath-observing Jewish *Gymnasium* students, 80% of every class was Jewish, then those who would not write on Saturday were rather likely to find support from other similarly observant students, and the difficulties in solitary observance were minimized. Of course, assimilated Jews might exert even cruder pressure than gentiles on the still-observant. Nevertheless, the traditional were more likely to find support in such a Jewish environment than in a more gentile one.

In short, at the *Gymnasium*, middle-class Jews absorbed the European cultural legacy in the company of other Jews. They were initiated into secular learning as a group. Despite complete acculturation, Jewish *Gymnasium* students experienced no compulsion to meet and befriend gentiles. Acquiring secular knowledge was a Jewish group activity, and the group nature of this experience modified and attenuated assimilation. An educated Jew was not an anomaly in a (hostile) gentile environment, but rather enjoyed the company of other similarly educated and acculturated Jews.

Moreover, it was the graduates of *Gymnasium* and university who created the political and intellectual movements which rejected the dominant assimilationist mentality of the Viennese Jewish community in the early twentieth century. Students, mostly at the university, first formulated Zionism and diaspora Jewish nationalism which challenged the nineteenth-century Jewish quest for assimilation. They called upon the Jews to assert their nationhood, and they yearned for the creation of a political framework to bring that nationhood to fruition. Their *Gymnasium* training by no means urged these young men to sever their ties to the Jewish community. Some well-educated Jews did intermarry or convert from Judaism, but their education was not the primary factor in that disaffection.

6. *Intermarriage and Conversion*

TO SOME EXTENT most Viennese Jews tried to acculturate and integrate into the larger society. Some Jews in Vienna went further than most and assimilated totally, a number of them—some famous, most not—taking the ultimate steps to renounce their affiliation with the Jewish people. Through intermarriage and through the formal act of converting from Judaism, some Viennese Jews declared that they were no longer tied to the history and destiny of the Jewish people, that they desired total incorporation into the society in which they lived. They wanted to cease being Jews and disappear into the gentile world.

Intermarriage—marriage to non-Jews—resulted from indifference to Jewishness, from the conscious renunciation of Jewish identity, or from the fact that Jews met and wanted to marry gentiles. No matter what the motivation, however, intermarriage ultimately led to total assimilation. Although some Jews who intermarried did continue to regard themselves as Jews, and raise their children accordingly, intermarriage usually meant the creation of non-Jewish families and the end of Jewish identity.[1] According to the sociologist Milton Gordon, intermarriage is the final stage in the process of ethnic assimilation.[2]

Since Jews are separated from gentile society by religion as well as ethnicity, conversion was another option for the Jew who wished to assimilate totally. By consciously and actively rejecting Judaism, the convert definitively (or so he hoped) broke with the Jewish people and with all its memories and expectations. The Jewish apostate expected that by renouncing Judaism and embracing Christianity he would become a fully accepted member of the majority. Generally this expectation was realistic. Until racial antisemitism provided a nearly insurmountable obstacle to Jewish assimilation, the gentile world willingly accepted the baptized Jew as an equal.[3]

The names of famous Viennese Jews who took the final steps to conversion and total assimilation readily come to mind: Gustav Mahler, Arnold Schoenberg, Karl Kraus, Otto Weininger, and Victor

Adler. These were joined by hundreds of others. In fact, Viennese Jews converted to Christianity at a rate higher than Jews anywhere else in the Dual Monarchy, Prague and Budapest included. To some extent the freer urban environment did accelerate disaffection from Judaism and the Jewish people. Opportunities for career and marriage available to the already baptized certainly sweetened the renunciation of Jewishness.

The number of men and women who married non-Jews or who renounced their Jewish affiliation was, however, never high enough to threaten the perpetuation of Jewish group identity in the Habsburg capital. The extent of conversion and intermarriage did not herald any soon-to-be-realized amalgamation of Viennese Jews into Viennese gentile society. Certainly antisemitism retarded Jewish assimilation by serving notice that even baptized Jews would not find acceptance. Yet in Vienna relatively few Jews sought total alienation from their origins. Moreover, many of those who did convert realized the futility of their actions and returned to the Jewish people.

Intermarriage

In Vienna, a Jew could not marry a non-Jew without prior conversion of the Jewish or the non-Jewish partner. Thus intermarriage was a much more radical step than elsewhere in Central or Western Europe or in America. With the introduction of civil marriage at the end of the eighteenth century or early nineteenth century in France or Germany, Jews and Christians in those countries could easily marry each other. In Hungary, civil marriage became an option for such partners after 1894. In Austria, however, despite the existence of civil marriage, marriage between Jews and Christians was forbidden by law. For a mixed couple to marry, one of the partners had to convert either to the religion of the other or to the neutral category, *konfessionslos,* "without religious affiliation."[4] This legal impediment minimized the numbers of Jews and gentiles who married each other and inflated the numbers who chose to convert.

Despite a steady rise in the number of Viennese Jews marrying non-Jews before World War I, the intermarriage rate remained low (Table 6:1), well below 10% of all Jews who married. In this calculation, intermarriage means the marriage of Jewish with *konfessionslos* individuals. In 1910, for example, 946 Jewish women married, 64 of them to non-Jews, and 972 Jewish men married, 91 of them to non-Jewish, that is *konfessionslos* women.[5] The cumulative intermarriage rate, that is, the percentage of all Jews in Vienna married to non-Jews, was, of course, considerably lower than the yearly rates presented in Table 6:1.

On the other hand, the true intermarriage rate was probably somewhat higher than indicated in these statistics. They are based on an unavoidably faulty source: the marriages of Jews and people who declared themselves *konfessionslos.* All those Jews who converted to Christianity, or became *konfessionslos* prior to their marriage with gentiles, elude statistical discovery. The records permit conclusions only regarding those Jews who made some minimal commitment to Jewish life by not converting themselves, but by requiring instead that their prospective spouses renounce any formal religious affiliation. Those Jews who converted in order to intermarry—and these may have been the most likely to have married in order to assimilate fully—do not appear in the records.

Even so, it is clear that the number of mixed marriages was lower in Vienna and in other Austrian cities like Prague,[6] than it was in most cities in Europe in which assimilating Jewish communities resided, and much lower than in America today. In Berlin, for example, between 1901 and 1904, 17.9% of the Jewish men who married, and 12% of the Jewish women, chose non-Jewish spouses.[7] Either a great many intermarrying Jews in Vienna disappeared into the Christian or *konfessionslos* categories, or the Austrian requirement of prior conversion successfully dissuaded many Jews from marrying gentiles.

In addition, intermarriage may have been less common in Vienna than elsewhere because of the twin influences of antisemitism and the rich, creative Jewish culture of the city. Antisemitism could easily reduce contact—and hence marriages—between Jews and gentiles. Moreover, the large array of Jewish organizations and the rich variety of Jewish ideologies which they affirmed—whether Zionist, conventionally religious, or integrationist—acted as a brake on intermarriage and structural assimilation.[8] Furthermore, the Jewish community of Vienna was continually augmented by the immigration of more traditional Jews from Galicia who rarely married non-Jews.

Those Jews who did intermarry did so for a wide range of reasons. Although social mobility provided no automatic inducement to in-

Table 6:1. Intermarriage Rates, Viennese Jews, 1895 and 1910

	1895	1910
Jewish Men	5.0%	9.4%
Jewish Women	2.6%	6.8%
Average	3.8%	8.1%

Sources: SJSW (1896), pp. 34–35; *SJSW* (1910), pp. 49–50.

termarry,[9] presumably some Jews married non-Jews because they wanted to facilitate advancement to the upper strata of society, or to consolidate gains already achieved, or because newfound status provided greater opportunities for intermarriage. Others intermarried because they were indifferent to Judaism or consciously desired assimilation. Most, however, probably married non-Jews because they happened to meet and wanted to marry a particular gentile man or woman. As one sociologist has noted about American Jewry, "The Jew who intermarries, then, generally does so because he wishes to *marry* rather than because he wishes to intermarry." [10]

Analysis of records kept by the IKG of marriages between Jews and people who declared themselves *konfessionslos*[11] reveals that in Vienna two types of Jews intermarried: one group belonged to the rising middle class, and the other belonged to the lowest classes. As in the case of conversion (to be discussed below), these groups split along gender lines. Men who chose to intermarry generally belonged to the middle class, while intermarrying women tended to come either from the lower-middle class or from the working classes. The middle-class men and women may well have expected intermarriage to improve their social standing, but when lower-class Jewish women intermarried, they did so not because they wanted to rise in social status but because they met and desired to marry fellow workers.

Jewish men who intermarried pursued careers as business employees or merchants (Table 6:2). Almost half of the Jewish men who married *konfessionslos* women identified themselves as business employees. The other upwardly mobile group, however, is most conspicuous in its absence; *none* of the Jewish grooms who married *konfessionslos* brides in this admittedly small sample (N = 30) were professionals. Undoubtedly, professionals did intermarry, but doctors, lawyers, and writers who could most expect career advantages from family alliances with gentiles, would want to maximize those advantages by converting from Judaism before they married non-Jewish women. On the other hand, some business employees who intermarried remained nominally Jewish. Jewish artisans and workers rarely married gentile women. Jewish men in mixed marriages do not seem to have married for money. Few of the *konfessionslos* brides lived in the wealthy neighborhoods in the Inner City or Wieden. Unfortunately, information on the occupation of the brides' fathers was not available.

Jewish women who married *konfessionslos* men belonged to both the middle and lower classes. Almost half (45.9%) of the Jewish brides of *konfessionslos* husbands (N = 24) married business employees, while 25% married professionals or civil servants, and 25% married artisans or workers. Only one married a merchant. Of the

Table 6:2. Occupations of Jewish Grooms Who Married konfessionslos Brides (Number)

Civil Servants	1
Professionals	—
Industrialists	1
Merchants	8
Business Employees	16
Artisans	2
Workers	1
	N = 29*

* One groom did not list profession.

ten brides for whom occupation was listed, six worked in the needle trades, an occupation which gave them considerable contact with gentile workers. On the other hand, wealthy Viennese Jewish women rarely married gentiles, at least not without prior conversion to Christianity. None of the brides who married *konfessionslos* men lived in the Inner City or Wieden.

Most Jews who intermarried did not live in areas of Jewish concentration, in neighborhoods where the presence of a large number of Jews would deter such matches. One-quarter of both men and women who intermarried had homes in the second district, but Jewish men who married *konfessionslos* women were most likely to live in Mariahilf-Neubau (VI–VII), and the outer districts, while the Jewish women who married non-Jews mostly resided in the Josefstadt (VIII), the Alsergrund (IX), and the outer districts.

A look at the place of origin of intermarrying Jews also produces an interesting pattern. Those who chose *konfessionslos* partners had been born in Vienna, Bohemia, or Moravia generally speaking. In the decades before World War I, only one-fifth of Viennese Jewry were natives of Vienna, but 63.3% of the Jewish men who married *konfessionslos* women and 56.5% of the Jewish women who married non-Jews had been born in the Austrian capital. Jews from the more traditional areas of Jewish settlement in Hungary and Galicia only rarely intermarried. Among the Jewish men who intermarried, 10% came from Galicia and 3% from Hungary, while among the women the figures were 4% and 9%, respectively. When Jews intermarried, they chose partners who were either native-born or Czech, as would be expected given the ethnic composition of the Viennese population.

To sum up, intermarriage in Vienna was a reality, and the numbers involved grew from decade to decade. But its extent did not imply the imminent demographic decline of the Jewish community of the *Reichshauptstadt*. Despite the fears it evoked in the Jewish community, neither did conversion to Christianity.

Conversion

Conversion to Christianity was also on the rise in Vienna in the final decades before the First World War. Between 1868, when the interconfessional law first required converts to inform the authorities of the step they had taken,[12] and 1903, the year of a study by the Jewish demographer Jakob Thon, 9,085 Viennese Jews left Judaism.[13] Only 7 Jews converted in 1868, but 512 converted in 1910 (Table 6:3).

The number of Jews converting in Vienna in the years before World War I did not cause a serious decline in Jewish numbers in the city. These numbers certainly alarmed the entire Jewish community, Zionists and non-Zionists alike, but the proportion of the Jews of Vienna actually converting, or even entertaining notions of doing do, was very small. For example, in 1900, 0.04% of all Jews in the city converted, a total of 559 converts. The cumulative percentage was, of course, higher than this figure, but it too represented only a tiny fraction of the Jews of Vienna.

Vienna's Jewish conversion rate far outranked that of any other city in the Dual Monarchy or elsewhere in Europe. Outside of Vienna, Austrian Jews almost never converted either to Christianity or to *Konfessionslosigkeit*. Even in the provincial cities Jews rarely converted. In Lemberg, Galicia in 1900 only about 30 Jews converted, and in Brünn, Moravia 19 Jews left Judaism in 1890. Virtually no Jews in Prague ever accepted baptism.[14] In Berlin, the home of an assimilating Jewish community with a high intermarriage rate, far fewer Jews converted than in Vienna. Between 1872 and 1902, only 2,812 Berlin Jews (about 94 per year) converted to Christianity.[15]

The causes for the relatively high rate of Jewish conversion in late Habsburg Vienna are complex. Contemporary observers and objective scholars have always linked conversion with the twin desire of upwardly mobile Jews to ensure the success of their careers and to assimilate fully. The fact that most converts were young and single and thus in a position to make major career and life decisions, has led observers to conclude that Jews went to the baptismal font to

Table 6:3. Converts from Judaism, 1868–1919 (Number)

	Male	Female	Total
1868	2	5	7
1870	22	17	39
1880	61	49	110
1890	169	133	302
1900	315	244	559
1910	255	257	512

Sources: Thon, p. 70; *SJSW* (1900), p. 374; *SJSW* (1910), pp. 366–72.

advance their careers, marry non-Jews, and disappear. By removing the stigma of their Jewish origins, these Jews hoped they could break down the barriers to full integration in society.[16]

The idea that Jews converted to Christianity in order to follow certain careers and participate in European culture dates from the end of the eighteenth century. During the debates on Jewish emancipation, many liberals who argued in favor of civic, social, and legal equality for Jews expected Jews to embrace Christianity either as a precondition or as a result of their new rights.[17] In the years between 1780 and the end of the Napoleonic wars, many wealthy European Jews converted because they were attracted by European culture and society, and understood that at that time Judaism precluded gentile acceptance.[18] David Friedlaender, for example, the disciple of the Jewish philosopher Moses Mendelssohn, attempted to convert in 1799. By no means a believing Christian, Friedlaender regarded baptism as the necessary entrée into fashionable Berlin society.[19] The Protestant authorities in Berlin rejected such a cynical conversion, but other Jews, such as Heinrich Heine, or the father of Karl Marx, converted with similar goals in mind.[20] The number of such converts was small, but they did come from the upper echelons of Jewish society. Although the conversion movement never presented a demographic threat, it did cause considerable psychological agitation in the Jewish community.[21]

During the nineteenth century, conservatives and liberals alike continued to insist that conversion was virtually a prerequisite for integration into European society.[22] Moreover, many Jews converted to Christianity because in the Christian state certain careers remained closed to the unbaptized. Sigmund Mayer, for example, could not pursue a legal career in the 1850s because, in his own words, "I could not bring myself to make the break *(zu dem Schritt entschliessen).*"[23] Mayer remained a prominent businessman like his father, but those who did make the break entered fields which excluded professing Jews. Even with the introduction of legal rights at the end of the century, many Jews still found that conversion opened a multitude of doors that paper rights never could. A substantial number of famous European men of politics and letters were ex-Jews whose careers had been stymied by their religious origins. By converting, these men severed all ties to their past in order to achieve present desires.

In Vienna at the end of the nineteenth century, many famous and not-so-famous Jews converted in order to enhance their careers. The experience of prominent Jews reinforced the notion that conversion and career advancement were intimately connected. Gustav Mahler, the composer and conductor, certainly converted for the sake of his conducting career. The son of a Bohemian Jewish liquor dealer, Mahler held a variety of conducting positions in Germany, Austria, and Hungary, and then accepted baptism in 1897 because, in the words of his wife Alma Mahler Werfel, "He was afraid lest otherwise he might find it difficult as a Jew to get his engagement in Vienna." [24] According to her account, Cosima Wagner, the wife of composer Richard Wagner, had tried to block Mahler's appointment as conductor of the Vienna Opera because he was a Jew. Thus Alma Mahler argued, "he had had to be baptized before he could aspire to such a high position under the Royal and Imperial exchequer." [25] Others were also tempted to convert in order to gain promotions. George Clare, a Viennese Jewish memorist, recalled that his grandfather, an excellent medical diagnostician, was advised that if he converted he would be appointed court physician. Unlike Mahler, Dr. Klaar turned down the offer.[26]

Other prominent Jews converted for less pointedly careerist motives. For some, conversion was the natural consequence of secular education. Sigmund Mayer reported that in the 1840s his university friends considered it a given *(selbstverständlich)* that he would convert. He remained Jewish not so much out of belief or even as a point of honor (as many were to do at century's end in the face of virulent antisemitism), but because he did not wish to hurt his family.[27] For others, conversion was the result of estrangement from Judaism and a desire to assimilate fully, coupled with a knowing resentment of the barriers to full integration posed by Jewish origins. Victor Adler, leader of the Austrian Social Democrats, was the son of a wealthy Bohemian Jewish businessman in Vienna. As a youth, he saw Judaism as a kind of ghetto wall separating him from the world of European culture. In particular, he felt insulted that the antisemites attempted to deny him, a Jew, membership in the German nation. He converted to Protestantism, not because of religious conviction, but to end his status as a pariah, to obtain, in Heine's words, "the entry ticket to European culture." [28] In 1913 he wrote in his testament:

> I only became a Protestant in order to make the separation *(Lostrennung)* from Judaism more fundamental and easier for my children, and to spare them the idiotic annoyances *(blödsinnige Scherereien)* which are caused by *Konfessionslosigkeit* in Austria.[29]

The satirist Karl Kraus also converted in order to ease his total assimilation into Western culture. A vituperative critic of all things Jewish, Kraus urged total assimilation through acceptance of the religion of the majority despite his later aversion to Catholicism.[30]

Jewish observers of the time associated increasing conversion with conscious assimilationism. In April 1902, an author identified as "M.S." wrote a series of articles in the large-circulation, non-Zionist Jewish weekly newspaper *Oesterreichische Wochenschrift* attributing the rise in the number of apostates to the coming of age of the generation that had grown up between 1859 and 1888, the heyday of assimilationism in Vienna. In this "liberal" period, Jews ignored Jewish education and all traditional and ritual aspects of Jewish life. Jewish women in particular received no Jewish training. The author called for a return to a more profound Jewish sensibility and better Jewish education. In a telling aside, "M.S." observed that at least antisemitism helped fill the synagogues.[31]

The Zionists and Jewish nationalists went further than most observers in linking conversion to career advancement and the desire for assimilation. Regarding baptism as an absolute betrayal of the Jewish people, Zionists in Vienna regularly published "lists of shame" of all those who had converted.[32] All converts, the Zionists believed, came from the world of high finance or the *Berufsintelligenz.*[33] They vehemently charged that the children of the wealthiest Viennese Jews were running over each other in their haste to embrace Christianity. In a 1902 article, one Zionist writer remarked sarcastically that when a Viennese Jew reached his first 100,000 Kronen, conversion was *de rigueur.* If they themselves did not convert, then surely their children and grandchildren accepted baptism.[34] The Jewish nationalist newspaper *Jüdisches Volksblatt* editorialized that "there is hardly one [wealthy] family that has not given thought to conversion." [35]

Thus both prominent participants and contemporary critics believed that Jews converted because they consciously sought career advancement and total integration. This attitude, however, derived from a narrow focus on male apostates, many of whom were, in fact, professionals or civil servants trying to enhance their careers by renouncing Jewish affiliation. Not all Viennese Jewish converts had such goals in mind. Lower-class Jews—largely women—also were baptized at the end of the nineteenth century (see below), and not because they sought civil service sinecures or consciously desired assimilation. On the contrary, they probably converted in order to marry non-Jews whom they met in the workshops and factories of the city. These lower-class conversions may even have led to a higher level of Jewish-gentile integration than middle-class conversions ever could. In any case, male conversion was a middle-class and female conversion both a middle- and lower-class phenomenon. Both the rising classes and those on the lowest rungs of the socioeconomic ladder converted to Christianity.[36] A wider range of factors must be adduced to explain Jewish apostasy in Vienna than has commonly been employed.

Conversion for the sake of marriage may have been as important as conversion for the sake of career advancement in Vienna, or even more important. Jewish critics chided Vienna for the fact that its conversion rate was higher than in notoriously assimilated Berlin,[37] but the fact remains that in order for a Jew and a non-Jew to marry, one of them had to convert. This legal stipulation increased the rate of conversion from Judaism. Most lower-class converts, and indeed probably even a good many middle-class ones, changed religion simply to marry someone outside of the faith. Gentiles also converted to Judaism for the same purpose.[38] Moreover, some Jews converted for genuine religious reasons, because they consciously preferred Christianity.

Whether for reasons of career enhancement or marriage, most converts changed religion for pragmatic reasons. Conversion for reasons of personal belief may have been the exception. Although Vienna was a predominantly Catholic city, only half of all Jewish converts accepted baptism in the Roman faith. On the average, about one-quarter of all Jews who left Judaism chose the Evangelical Church (Lutheran or Reformed), and another quarter decided to declare themselves "without religious affiliation." [39] For some Jewish converts, Protestantism may have appeared more palatable than ornate, ritualistic Catholicism. Certainly for those who wanted to convert for pragmatic reasons and believed neither in Judaism nor in Christianity, *Konfessionslosigkeit* provided an easy solution to a legal or personal problem. Declaring themselves without religion allowed Jews guiltless separation from the Jewish people. Conversion due to religious conviction may have been more pronounced among female converts, a higher percentage of whom chose to affiliate with the Catholic Church than was true among the male apostates.[40]

Only a systematic study of the backgrounds of those men and women who severed their ties to the Jewish people can reveal the true relationship between social status and conversion. The analysis here is based on a study of a sample of men and women (N = 1037) who formally renounced Judaism in 1870, 1880, 1890, 1900, and 1910.[41] In this group of converts, 53.3% (552) were male and 46.7% (483) were female,[42] although in contrast to the later years sampled, over half of the converts were female in 1870 and 1880.

As would be expected, the statistics reveal that most converts were young and single. More than three-quarters of both sexes (76.1%) had not yet married, 19.1% were married, 1.9% divorced, and 2.9% widowed.[43] As for the age of converts, most were in their twenties and thirties, although women, due to their earlier age at marriage, were younger on the average than the male converts. Two-fifths (39.9%) of the male converts were in their twenties, and 28.5% in their thirties; among the women the figures were 47.9% and 26.7%, respectively.[44] The mean age of converts was 30–34, although about 16% of all converts were over 40. Conversions late in life resulted from second marriages or parental deaths which released the more timid from the guilt of hurting their families' sensibilities. Most Jews apostatized as individuals; only 12.5% converted with their parents, children, spouses, or siblings, many of them children under seven who automatically converted with their parents. Two-thirds of all married converts renounced Judaism alone, either to pave the way for spouses and children to follow or to follow already converted husbands and wives.

Career advancement certainly tempted many young Jewish men to convert from Judaism. An extremely high percentage of male converts were either civil servants or professionals[45] (Table 6:4), those whose careers would profit most from a convenient change of religion. Fully two-fifths of all male converts were professionals or civil servants, and another 12% were students, that is, young men being groomed for these sorts of careers. Apostates were twice as likely as Jews generally to be professionals, civil servants, or students. Many of the professionals worked as actors, musicians, or singers, in occupations with a great deal of public exposure, but many were ordinary doctors, lawyers, and the like, who simply felt that cutting their ties to Judaism would help them in their careers.[46]

Conversion for these men not only assured their own career advancement, but also enhanced the social prestige and economic comfort already won by their parents. Most male apostates came from upper-middle-class homes; of their fathers, 16.7% were civil servants, 18.3% were professionals, and 47.6% were merchants. Those Jewish civil servants, professionals, and students who converted were

Table 6:4. Occupations of Jewish Converts, Composite, 1870–1910

	Male N = 370	Female N = 105
Civil Servants	10.8%	1.9%
Professionals	28.6	18.1
Students	12.4	2.9
Industrialists	0.5	—
Merchants	15.9	6.7
Business Employees	21.6	6.7
Artisans	3.5	35.2
Workers	6.5	28.6
	100.0%	100.0%

not the sons of small businessmen or artisans and did not represent the first generation of their families to achieve success. Rather, they were the sons of other civil servants and professionals. Over half (52.4%) of the converts who were professionals or *Beamte* and 63.6% of the students had fathers who pursued careers as civil servants or professionals.

The percentage of professionals and civil servants among converts only increased in the years between 1870 and 1910 (Table 6:5). This increase cannot be explained by a huge expansion in the number of Jewish professionals or *Beamte* in this period. Rather, the stepped-up rate of conversions in these two groups was probably a reaction to growing antisemitism. Feeling more vulnerable than they had in the halcyon days after the Emancipation, many Jewish doctors, lawyers, actors, and civil servants, especially older ones in their forties and fifties, sought to escape their origins through conversion.

Antisemitism had a reverse effect on students, however. The percentage of converts who were students *decreased* from 19% in 1890 to 8% in 1910. Antisemitic agitation seems to have made younger Jews, especially those at the university, more conscious of their Jewishness and more intent on asserting their Jewish identity.[47] In general, antisemitism seems to have induced older Jews to convert in order to escape and younger Jews to defy the antisemites through a more vigorous defense of Judaism. Between 1890 and 1910 the number of converts under nineteen years of age also decreased sharply. In 1880, 23.5% of the 34 converts recorded for that year were under nineteen; in 1910, only 7.3% of 343 converts were children or adolescents. Teenagers were less likely to convert on their own, and parents must have recognized the futility of escaping antisemitism through baptizing their small children.

Jewish industrialists, merchants, and artisans, on the other hand, did not find that conversion enhanced their careers and, despite their

Table 6:5. Occupations of Male Converts from Judaism, 1870–1910

	1870 N = 1	1880 N = 5	1890 N = 96	1900 N = 149	1910 N = 119
Civil Servants	—	—	7.3%	10.7%	14.3%
Professionals	100.0%	20.0%	18.8	32.9	31.1
Students	—	—	18.8	12.1	8.4
Industrialists	—	—	1.0	0.7	—
Merchants	—	40.0	19.8	16.1	11.8
Business Employees	—	—	19.8	20.8	25.2
Artisans	—	20.0	6.3	2.0	2.5
Workers	—	20.0	8.3	4.7	6.7
	100.0%	100.0%	100.0%	100.0%	100.0%

proportion in the Viennese Jewish work force, seldom appear among converts (Table 6:4). Zionist charges notwithstanding, neither did the very wealthiest Viennese Jews convert in this period. Only business employees converted at a rate which paralleled their share of the Viennese Jewish work force; about one-fifth of the converts were clerks, salesmen, and managers, while about one-quarter of Jewish men in Vienna were so employed. Between 1890 and 1910, however, the percentage of Jewish clerks and managers who converted remained the same despite a rapid rise in the percentage of Jewish business employees in Vienna (Table 6:5). These men either experienced less antisemitic pressure at work than professionals, or, working largely in the company of other Jews, were in a better position to withstand such pressure where it existed. They may also have simply been more strongly attached to their Jewishness than were professionals or civil servants.

Most Jewish women who converted came from the lower classes, and probably accepted baptism in order to marry fellow gentile workers. Fully 63.8% of the female converts who registered occupations worked as artisans, especially as seamstresses, dressmakers, or milliners, as unskilled workers *(Handarbeiterinnen)*, or as servants. Most female apostates came from homes which enjoyed much lower social status than the homes of male converts. Only 5.6% of the fathers of Jewish men who converted were artisans or workers, but 17.5% of the female converts had fathers who practiced such occupations. The fathers of most of these female converts were merchants (46.8%) although 9% were industrialists and 19.3% were professionals or civil servants.

The percentage of working-class Jewish women who converted from Judaism did decline between 1870 and 1910. The proportion of artisans and workers among female apostates dropped from 79.3% (of those who listed occupation) in 1890 to 50% in 1910. Probably because of increased antisemitism among Viennese artisans,[48] fewer working-class Jewish women wanted to marry non-Jews. But antisemitism had the reverse effect on female Jewish clerks and professionals, most of whom worked as governesses and actresses. In 1890, only 3.4% of the female converts who listed occupation were clerks, while in 1910, the proportion was 10.9%. More significantly, 3.4% of the women who left the Jewish fold in 1890 practiced a profession, but about one-quarter (23.9%) were professionals in 1900 and 1910.

Middle-class Jewish women, those who did not list occupation in the conversion records, also embraced Christianity or *Konfessionslosigkeit* at the end of the nineteenth century. Women who had no careers obviously did not convert to smooth their career paths. Rather they converted either for genuine religous reasons or to marry gentiles.

They may have hoped thereby to enhance the social status of their families, escape the stigma of Jewishness, or simply to marry men whom they loved. For women then, no matter what their class, conversion generally resulted from the desire to marry.

Conversion out of religious conviction or for the sake of marriage was by no means the preserve of Jewish women alone. Gentiles—mostly lower-class Catholic women—converted to Judaism in the late nineteenth century, presumably in most cases to marry Jews. In a sample of 476 men and women who converted to Judaism in 1870, 1880, 1890, 1900, and 1910,[49] 142 were baptized Jews who returned to Judaism (see below), while 334 were individuals of gentile origin who embraced Judaism. Most of these proselytes (314) were female, and 89% of these women were single. The majority of female Jewish proselytes came from working-class homes. Among the 79 female proselytes who listed their occupation, 30.4% were artisans and 22.8% were workers. Although 19% were professionals, most of these worked as actresses and singers. The few men who converted to Judaism in order to marry Jewish women also worked as artisans (31.3%) or workers (22.9%). About 15% of the male proselytes pursued professional careers, again, mostly in the theater.

Converting to Christianity may not have been the sole preserve of an aspiring middle class, but clearly it did result from life in the metropolis. About 47% of both male and female Jewish converts had been born in Vienna (Table 6:6). Converts to Christianity were twice as likely as Viennese Jews in general to be native-born Viennese. Between 1870 and 1910, the percentage of Vienna-born apostates grew. Professionals, students, and female business employees born in Vienna were especially likely to convert.

On the other hand, birth in areas of greater Jewish traditionalism acted as a kind of brake on Jewish apostasy. Jews born in Galicia, the province where the most traditional Jewish life-style prevailed,

Table 6:6. Place of Birth of Converts from Judaism, Composite, 1870–1910

	Male N = 530	Female N = 472
Vienna & Lower Austria	45.7%	48.7%
Bohemia	12.1	12.5
Moravia & Silesia	12.1	11.0
Galicia & Bukovina	8.1	5.9
Other Cis-Leithanian Austria	0.4	1.5
Hungary	14.0	15.9
Western Europe	4.3	2.5
Eastern Europe	3.4	1.9
	100.0%	100.0%

almost never chose to sever their ties to the Jewish people (Table 6:6). About one-fifth of all Viennese Jews were Galician, but they produced only 8% of the male and 6% of the female converts. Very few Galician females of the working class converted, and only among civil servants of Galician origin was there any appreciable number who left Judaism. Moreover, despite increased immigration from Galicia, the percentage of Galician-born converts remained small, and it even declined somewhat among male apostates between 1870 and 1910. In 1910, when 35% of new Jewish fathers were Galician-born, only 5% of the men who converted from Judaism came from Galicia. Galicians of all social strata, especially the lower classes, were too traditional to countenance apostasy.

Jews from less traditional Bohemia and Moravia converted in proportion to their share of the Jewish population of the city, but Hungarian Jews, coming from areas of somewhat greater Jewish traditionalism, were represented less frequently among the converts than their numbers in Vienna would warrant. This greater traditionalism in general did not suffice to deter lower-class Jewish men and women from Hungary from conversion. In fact, a large proportion of all artisans and workers who left Judaism were of Hungarian origin. Hungarians produced only about 15% of all converts, but 42% of the male artisans, 19% of the male workers, 19% of the female artisans, and 38% of the female workers who converted from Judaism had been born in Hungary.

For all groups—rich and poor, male and female, Czech, Hungarian, and native Viennese—conversion from Judaism was connected to large-scale urbanization. The demographer Arthur Ruppin correctly assessed one potential impact of the urban environment on Jewish loyalties.[50] Most converts from Judaism had been born either in Vienna or in Prague, Budapest, or the other metropolitan centers of the Dual Monarchy, not in the small towns in which a more traditional way of life prevailed. Almost two-thirds of all converts, male and female alike, came from cities with over 100,000 population (Table 6:7). Very few apostates hailed from villages or small towns, although a fair number came from large towns and small cities. Among those converts not born in Vienna, 25.9% of the men and 23.2% of the women came from Budapest, Prague, Brünn, Lemberg, or Trieste, a much higher proportion than the 12% of the grooms and 13% of the brides born in those cities.

Bohemian, Moravian, and Hungarian converts were more likely than all Jews in Vienna from those provinces to hail from the provincial *Grossstädte*. For example, while only 20% of Bohemian grooms came from Prague, 40.7% of the Bohemian male converts had been born in the Bohemian capital. Similarly, while only 11%

Table 6:7. Population of Hometown, Male and Female Converts, Composite, 1870–1910*

	Male N = 450	Female N = 406
Under 500	1.1%	1.7%
500–1,999	5.1	4.9
2,000–9,999	14.9	13.8
10,000–99,999	14.4	15.5
Over 100,000	64.4	64.0
	100.0%	100.0%

* Including Viennese-born.

of the Hungarian Jews in Vienna came from cities with over 100,000 inhabitants, 35% of the Hungarian Jewish converts had been born in such cities.

Jewish converts in Vienna rarely came from medium-sized cities with high Jewish density. Most of such cities were in Galicia, and few converts came from that province. High Jewish density, especially in the restrained atmosphere of a large town or small city, easily counteracted the forces which led to conversion in the larger communities with low Jewish population density.

High Jewish density acted as a deterrent to Jewish conversion within Vienna itself as well. Before their conversion, Jews who renounced Judaism were less likely than most Viennese Jews to live in the Jewish neighborhoods of Vienna (Table 6:8). In 1900, for example, only 17% of the male converts and 22% of the female converts lived in the heavily Jewish Leopoldstadt. Most of the Jewish converts in 1900 and 1910 lived scattered all over the city. The fact that they were not concentrated in Jewish areas may have provided them with the opportunities for conversion in the first place. Jewish neighborhoods created environments in which Jews met and married each other. Viennese Jews who either consciously or unconsciously chose gentile neighbors were more likely than other Jews to marry gentiles, and to convert in order to do so.

Once they had converted, Jewish apostates generally continued to live in their old neighborhoods. Of the small proportion for whom evidence exists (96 out of 1,037 in the sample),[51] most tended to live in the same district, often in the same houses, as they had prior to their conversion. Three-quarters of those who lived in Districts I and II and two-thirds of those in Districts IX and XI–XIX remained in the same neighborhood ten and twenty years after their conversion.

Table 6:8. Residential Distribution of Male and Female Jewish Converts, 1870–1910

	1880*		1890		1900		1910	
	Male N = 12	Female N = 13	Male N = 42	Female N = 39	Male N = 238	Female N = 180	Male N = 251	Female N = 178
I	25.0%	46.2%	26.2%	25.6%	16.4%	13.9%	16.3%	13.5%
II	16.7	38.5	23.8	38.5	16.8	22.2	13.9	14.0
III–V, X	—	—	7.1	5.1	18.5	20.0	18.7	25.8
VI–VIII	—	7.7	14.3	7.7	12.2	12.2	15.5	14.6
IX	50.0	7.7	19.0	15.4	17.2	16.7	14.7	14.0
XI–XIX	8.3	—	9.5	7.7	17.6	13.9	19.9	13.5
XX	—	—	—	—	1.3	1.1	0.8	4.5
	100.0%	100.0%	100.0%	100.0%	100.0%	100.0%	100.0%	100.0%

* Too few converts in 1870 to allow for significant statistical analysis.

Was Conversion Successful?

Converts tried to renounce their ties to Judaism and the Jewish people, but many of these conversions had limited success. Many gentiles, antisemites, other Jews, even the converts themselves continued to regard converts as Jews. Despite baptism, such prominent converts as Heinrich Heine, Karl Marx, Benjamin Disraeli, and Gustav Mahler remained Jews in the popular mind. Gentile society remembered the origins of Jewish converts for a very long time, and only with the passage of generations could a convert really blend into the society at large.[52]

The rise of racial antisemitism at the end of the nineteenth century guaranteed that conversion would no longer provide an automatic entry ticket into European society.[53] Even baptized Jews were still biologically members of the "inferior" Semitic race because baptismal waters could never remove the taint of Jewish origins. For many potential converts, remaining Jewish became a point of honor in the face of this new kind of anti-Jewish animosity. Heinrich Bermann, a character in Arthur Schnitzler's novel *Road to the Open* (1907), emphasized the ineffectiveness of conversion in the face of such antisemitism. He states to his friends:

> That's why I'll admit, into the bargain, that in spite of my complete indifference to every single form of religion, I would positively never allow myself to be baptized, even if it were possible—though that is less the case today than ever it was—of escaping once and for all Anti-Semitic bigotry and villainy by a dodge like that.[54]

In an atmosphere filled with antisemitism, conversion frequently did not convince the convert either, and hence some Viennese converts like Mahler or even Karl Kraus, continued to possess something of a Jewish sensibility despite the formal renunciation of their origins. Alma Mahler, a Catholic, recalled that Christmas "meant nothing" to her husband. Although he was attracted by Catholic mysticism and not by Judaism, he nevertheless understood that others—and even he himself—considered him a Jew. She reminisced:

> . . . he was not a man who ever deceived himself, and he knew that people would not forget he was a Jew because he was skeptical of the Jewish religion and baptized a Christian. Nor did he wish it forgotten, even though he frequently asked me to warn him when he gesticulated too much, because he hated to see others do so and thought it ill-bred.[55]

Mahler felt three times homeless: "as a native of Bohemia in Austria, as an Austrian among Germans, and as a Jew throughout the world."[56]

Many converts, recognizing that antisemitism made conversion useless, or realizing that they were proud of their heritage in the face of antisemitic attacks, even converted back to Judaism. The most famous of such "returnees" was Arnold Schoenberg, who slowly reaffirmed his Jewish identity in response to the hostility he perceived around him. In 1923, for example, he wrote to the artist Wassily Kandinsky:

> . . . I have at last learned the lesson that has been forced on me during this year . . . and that I shall never forget. . . . It is that I am not a German, not a European, indeed perhaps scarcely even a human being (at least the Europeans prefer the worst of their race to me), but that I am a Jew. . . . I am content that it should be so! [57]

Schoenberg reembraced Judaism officially when Hitler became Chancellor of Germany in 1933.[58]

Not all returnees announced their reaffiliation with Judaism in as public a manner as Schoenberg, but a considerable number of baptized Jews did reconvert to Judaism at the end of the nineteenth century. In the sample of 476 proselytes to Judaism in 1870, 1880, 1890, 1900, and 1910,[59] 142 (30%) were Jews who had left Judaism and were returning to their people. About 45% had been Catholic, 20% Protestant, and 33% *konfessionslos.* Men formed almost two-thirds of this group, and women only one-third.

Of the sample group, approximately one quarter (26.1%) returned to Judaism in 1870, and more than half (54.9%) did so in 1900 and 1910. Those that returned in 1870, just three years after the Emancipation in 1867, must have reaffirmed their Judaism in a mood of great optimism. They hoped that the granting of civil and political rights to Jews would obviate the need to convert in order to enter European society. They rejoined their people because they felt that Judaism would no longer be an impediment to their participation in society. Those that returned to Judaism in 1900 and 1910 did so, presumably, because antisemitism made them realize the ineffectiveness of conversion or simply as a point of honor in the face of attack.

Those who returned to Judaism in 1870 had converted to Christianity or become *konfessionslos* in the 1830s, 1840s, and 1850s, when it really had been impossible to follow certain careers as a Jew. Of the 1870 returnees, 35% were returning after twenty years, and 78% after ten years. Those who returned to Judaism after 1890, in contrast, did so after a short time as gentiles. In 1910, 29.3% had been non-Jews for one year or less, 32.8% for two to five years, and 20.7% for six to ten years, with very few having been non-Jews for more than ten years. They had converted in order to improve their careers and returned when they realized that antisemitic barriers still prevented their acceptance.

The men in both groups of "returnees" appear to have converted out of Judaism in the first place in order to advance their careers. A very high percentage of the returnees were professionals (Table 6:9). Even as early as 1870, when few Viennese Jews were professionals or civil servants, 17% of the returnees practiced professions, and 9% worked as civil servants. In 1890 and 1900, almost half pursued professional careers. Clearly, obstacles to professionals of Jewish origins in the last decades before World War I induced many to return to Judaism. The number of business employees among returnees to Judaism also rose significantly between 1870 and 1910, but this rise resulted from the occupational transformation in Viennese Jewry in this period. Baptized Jewish women who returned to Judaism came from the middle classes, and they presumably reaffirmed Judaism either because they recognized the ineffectiveness of their conversion for winning gentile acceptance or as a point of honor in the face of rising antisemitism.

Table 6:9. Occupations of Male Converts Returning to Judaism, 1870–1910

	1870 N = 23	1880 N = 11	1890 N = 9	1900 N = 13	1910 N = 30
Civil Servants	8.7%	18.2%	—	7.7%	3.3%
Professionals	17.4	27.3	44.4%	46.2	23.3
Students	—	—	11.1	—	3.3
Merchants	34.8	27.3	22.2	23.1	30.0
Business Employees	4.3	9.1	22.2	23.1	30.0
Artisans	30.4	9.1	—	—	6.7
Workers	4.3	9.1	—	—	3.3
	100.0%	100.0%	100.0%	100.0%	100.0%

Along with the memoir literature, the statistics demonstrate that conversion did not always imply the final severing of all ties to the Jewish people and total integration of the former Jew into the gentile world. The atmosphere of pre-World War I Vienna was simply too antisemitic, too hostile to the Jews to allow for a smooth process of complete assimilation. Some less famous converts might have won gentile acceptance more easily than could Mahler or Schoenberg, but given the antisemitic environment, combined with the low rate of Jewish apostasy, conversion did not spell the end of Jewish life in Vienna. The Jews continued to be a viable ethnic group in the city. They continued to identify themselves as Jews and they built a strong organizational framework to assure their group survival.

7. *Organizational Networks and Jewish Identity*

THE JEWS OF VIENNA practiced similar professions, lived in the same neighborhoods, attended school together, and married each other. They also forged an extensive network of Jewish organizations which allowed them to associate primarily with other Jews. Through this varied network of organizations Viennese Jews provided themselves with an efficient brake against total assimilation. From the legally mandated religious community—the *Israelitische Kultusgemeinde*—and a host of charitable and literary societies, to the political organizations which worked for Jewish rights at home and abroad, these groups institutionalized the fact that Jewish association need not be restricted to the religious sphere alone. The social connections established in these organizations made it possible for most Viennese Jews to enjoy a Jewish social life.

Jewish communities have always spawned a myriad of social, philanthropic, and religious societies,[1] but antisemitic tensions in late Habsburg Vienna accentuated the need for separate Jewish organizations to fight for Jewish rights and vigorously to defend Jewish identity. Antisemitism prompted the Jews to take stock of their Jewishness, ascertain the meaning and the limits of assimilation, and discover new justifications for continued Jewish identity. Bitterly divided on their response to the antisemitic challenge, Viennese Jews forged organizations to articulate and institutionalize divergent reformulations of the meaning of Jewishness in the modern world. All of the factions—those who continued to believe in assimilation, the political Zionists and Jewish nationalists who rejected assimilation and called for Jewish national rebirth, or the members of defense organizations which declared Jewish pride while struggling against antisemites—all created extensive institutional structures to affirm their own version of Jewish identity in an avowedly hostile world.

The Jewish organizations of Vienna thus served a dual function, providing a forum for the assertion of Jewish identity and enabling

Jews of different political persuasions to enjoy a nearly totally Jewish social life. Every subgroup in the Viennese Jewish community—the rich, middle class and poor, recent immigrants and longtime residents, integrationists and Jewish nationalists—created its own institutions which helped it to assert its own brand of Jewish identity and to provide a rich forum for interchange with fellow Jews.

Religious, Charitable, and Social Organizations

The *Israelitische Kultusgemeinde* (IKG) administered the religious affairs of the Jewish community of Vienna. As early as 1852 the Austrian government authorized the *Gemeinde* (as it was commonly called) to be the sole agency to manage the religious, educational, and philanthropic needs of the Jews of the city. According to the 1867 statutes, revised in 1890, functions of the *Gemeinde* included the establishment and maintenance of synagogues, supervision of such religious concerns as kosher meat, ritual baths, Passover matzah, and cemeteries, recording of Jewish vital statistics, and oversight of certain Jewish charitable institutions, including a Jewish hospital.[2] Although the interconfessional law of 1868 permitted only one *Gemeinde* in each city, the *Israelitische Kultusgemeinde* serviced the religious needs only of the Ashkenazic Jews in Vienna (those from Central and Eastern Europe). Jews from the Ottoman Empire or the Balkans who lived in Vienna had their own "Turkish" *Gemeinde* which provided religious services for the few thousand Jews of Sephardic extraction in Vienna.[3] All Jews in the city belonged to the *Gemeinde,* but only about one-third of all householders were able to pay the taxes, ranging from 20 to 1,000 Kronen per year, which supported *Gemeinde* activities.

The leadership of the IKG derived from the richest and most powerful circles of Viennese Jewry. Serving the *Gemeinde* provided a source of honor and prestige for wealthy Jewish businessmen, industrialists, and lawyers, who saw themselves as the natural leaders of Viennese Jewry. The Board was composed of twenty men before 1890, twenty-four until 1902, and thirty-six thereafter; those who sat on it, often for decades, were elderly, wealthy, frequently ennobled.[4]

Restricted as it was to religious and charitable matters, the *Gemeinde* did not satisfy the associational needs even of Vienna's wealthy Jewish elite. From the earliest days of modern Jewish settlement in the Habsburg capital, a whole range of humanitarian and charitable organizations existed which provided opportunities for Jewish notables to receive honor within the Jewish community and associate with each other, while at the same time helping Vienna's Jewish old, poor, sick, and orphaned to whom the *Gemeinde* could not pay adequate attention. As in most other Jewish communities, there was a burial society *(Chevra Kadisha),* institutions for the blind, deaf, dumb, and orphaned, foundations to provide poor brides with dowries and needy school children with shoes, clothing, scholarships, and summer camps, and general purpose charities to provide assistance to the poor. Most of these organizations received subvention aid from the IKG.[5]

Vienna's Jewish notables also sought to alleviate the sufferings of persecuted Jews, whether they lived in the Austrian provinces of Galicia and Bukovina, or outside the Dual Monarchy in Russia, Romania, or the Middle East. The same men who formed the *Gemeinde* Board also served as directors of such organizations as *Verein zur Förderung der Handwerke unter den inländischen Israeliten* ("Society for the Encouragement of Handicrafts among Austrian Jews"), which sought to apprentice Jewish boys in trade, the *Hilfsverein für die notleidende jüdische Bevölkerung in Galizien* ("Society for Aid to the Suffering Jewish Population in Galicia"), and the *Israelitische Allianz zu Wien* ("Vienna Israelite Alliance"), an offshoot of the French Jewish charitable organization, the *Alliance israélite universelle.*[6] The Vienna *Allianz* established modern schools in Galicia and provided assistance to persecuted and impoverished Jews anywhere. It engaged in behind-the-scenes diplomacy on behalf of Jews in Romania, Persia, Morocco, and Bulgaria, and aided pogrom victims in Russia and in Austria itself. In 1899, for example, it helped the victims of the anti-Jewish riots which accompanied the Hilsner ritual murder trial in Polna, Bohemia. The *Allianz* also gave advice and financial assistance to Jewish emigrants enroute to America.[7]

Vienna's Jewish notables organized to improve the conditions of poor Jews who suffered the economic consequences of the antisemitic boycott of Jewish shops in Vienna itself. Such organizations as the *Verein zur Unterstützung jüdischer Handwerker und Kleingewerbetreibender* ("Society for the Support of Jewish Artisans and Independent Craftsmen"), established in 1888 by Wilhelm Stiassny, Sigmund Taussig, Bela Taussig, Arthur Kuranda, and other wealthy Viennese Jews who served on the IKG Board, provided poor Jewish artisans with loans and sickness and death benefits.[8] In addition, the Viennese Jewish elite organized the *Verein zur Hebung der Gewerbe in Wien und dessen Vororte* ("Society for the Improvement of Industry in Vienna and Its Suburbs"), and the *Verein für unentgeltlichen Arbeitsnachweis* ("Society for a Free Labor-Exchange").[9]

Wealthy Jews in the city also united for social and humanitarian purposes in two chapters of B'nai B'rith, the international Jewish fraternal organization. The members of *Wien* (1895) and *Eintracht*

("Harmony") (1903) saw themselves as men from "the best circles of Vienna Jewry" and as "a phalanx of high-principled, intelligent, and educated Jews, an ethical society." Both chapters devoted themselves to the idea that one could be both a Jew and a "modern man." Deriving its leadership from the same circles as the IKG, B'nai B'rith sought to deflate anti-Jewish prejudice not through public action, but through what it considered proper Jewish public and personal conduct.[10] B'nai B'rith supported the work of the humanitarian organizations mentioned above, and worked tirelessly on behalf of Russian Jewish pogrom victims, those Jews who suffered during the Balkan Wars, and poor Jews in the Austrian capital. *Eintracht,* for example, ran the Toynbee Hall Jewish settlement house in Brigittenau (XX) after its original Zionist directors were no longer able to do so in 1904. Both chapters sponsored lectures on Jewish and general topics, including Freud's early lectures on the interpretation of dreams.[11] In 1911 the B'nai B'rith opened a youth organization, the *Jüdischer Jugendbund,* to inculcate its values among the younger generation of Viennese Jewish notables.[12] B'nai B'rith provided both an opportunity for secular Jews to experience their Jewishness profoundly, and an important framework within which members of the Viennese Jewish elite could associate primarily with each other.

Vienna's wealthiest and most prominent Jews did not find themselves alone in their humanitarian and charitable work on behalf of other Jews. Middle-class and poor Jews also organized to help others less fortunate and to socialize with each other. Moreover, many Jews organized self-help organizations which offered sickness and death benefits to members, perhaps because they resented the condescending tone of the charities run by the notables. Among these societies were the *Kranken-, Witwen-, und Waisenunterstützungs-Verein: Chesed Shel Emes* ("Society for Support to the Sick, Widowed, and Orphaned: Act of True Kindness"), and *Wohltätigkeits- und Krankenunterstützungs-Verein: Mazmiah Jeschua* ("Society for Benevolence and Support for the Sick: Growth of Salvation").[13] The decades before World War I witnessed the growth of women's charitable organizations which provided bourgeois Jewish women with the opportunity to fulfill the nineteenth-century ideal of female philanthropy. These women's groups provided food, clothing, even summer camps to poor school children, and worked for the education of Jews in working-class areas of the city.[14] Moreover, Jews organized special interest associations and *Tempelvereine* ("Synagogue Societies") to build new synagogues.

Alongside the general charitable and social organizations of Jews in Vienna, an extensive network of immigrant religious, cultural, and social organizations existed. Immigrants, especially those from Galicia, felt scorned by and excluded from the Germanized Jewish establishment, and they proudly created a Galician-Jewish subculture in Vienna. Even wealthy Galician Jews joined in this separate Galician Jewish community.

The basic unit of immigrant community life was the *Landsmannschaft,* that organization of people from the same town or district found in all areas of Jewish immigrant settlement in Western Europe and America. *Landsmannschaften* provided sickness and death benefits to members, and more importantly functioned as centers of social life where people from the same town could establish warm connections with old friends and neighbors. Shunning the official community, they sought financial assistance and sociability largely from each other. Most of the *Landsmannschaften* in Vienna were composed of Galician Jews, but many Hungarian and Moravian Jews founded such organizations as well.[15]

Yiddish-speaking Jewish immigrants did not have much success in creating a strong Yiddish culture in Vienna. No Yiddish newspapers appeared in cities in Germany with large Eastern European populations, and the same was true in Vienna. The German-language milieu perhaps explains this absence. Since Yiddish was linguistically close to German, Yiddish speakers did not face much difficulty reading the German-language press once they had mastered the Gothic script. Moreover, German-speaking Jews deprecated Yiddish as *Jargon* and may have placed difficulties in the way of those wishing to create a Yiddish press.[16]

Moreover, Jewish immigrants to Vienna did not write great Yiddish literature in this period as did Eastern European immigrants in New York, London, and Paris. Organizations like *Jüdische Kultur* did sponsor "evenings" for Yiddish poetry readings and lectures on Yiddish literature,[17] but apart from these "evenings" the only active public Yiddish culture in Vienna was the Yiddish repertory theater. In the final years before World War I, one, sometimes two, Yiddish repertory theaters performed the classics of the Yiddish stage in Vienna. The *Jüdische Bühne* ("Jewish Stage"), a repertory group under the direction of M. Siegler, performed at the Hotel Stefanie on the Taborstrasse in the heart of the Leopoldstadt, providing regular seasons of plays by Avrom Goldfadn, Jakob Gordin, Lateiner, Perez Hirschbein, and others. The *Jüdisches Theater-Variété* performed similar melodramas in Yiddish.[18]

Immigrant Jews in Vienna focused more attention on their religious needs than on Yiddish culture. Galician (and Hungarian) Jews in Vienna established many *Bethäuser,* prayer rooms, where they conducted services as they had back home. These Jews found the more formal religious services in the *Gemeinde* temples uncomfortable. Wealthier Jewish immigrants from Galicia also established their own synagogues which would be both "Polish" and consonant with their middle-class or upper-class respectability. Annoyed both by the noisy orthodox *Bethäuser,* and by the German tone of the official IKG synagogues, they resolved to create their own decorous and modern temple, in which services would be conducted according to the "Polish rite," that is, using the Polish melodies. The *Israelitischer Bethhaus-Verein, Beth Israel,* organized in 1882, sought to build a synagogue that would be "a spiritual home for the Jewish people [of Polish origin] in the metropolis of the Empire." Ignaz Jolles of the building committee assured Viennese Jewry that this "light and clean" synagogue would not be the scene of zealotry nor "a fortress of opposition to religious enlightenment" but a modern, orthodox synagogue for services conducted according to Polish-Jewish customs and melodies.[19] After raising money in the 1880s and 1890s from such wealthy Galician Jews in Vienna as Arthur Edler von Mises, and conducting a lottery in 1891 and 1892 with the assistance of Galician-born polemicists Saul Raphael Landau and Josef Samuel Bloch, the *Verein* built a synagogue at 29 Leopoldsgasse in the Leopoldstadt in time for the 1893 High Holidays.[20]

Galician Jews in Vienna did not content themselves with religious and social organizations. Their spokesmen called for political agitation within the Jewish community to combat the contempt for "Polish" Jews among the Germanized Jewish elite and to ensure equal representation for *Ostjuden* (Eastern European Jews) in Jewish communal affairs. In an article in the Jewish weekly *Oesterreichische Wochenschrift* in April, 1908, an author named J. Grobtuch noted: "In no other *Weltstadt* is such an animosity against Galician Jews so predominant as in Vienna." He called on all Galician Jews in the city to organize in order to obtain better conditions. Grobtuch himself shied away from direct confrontations; he merely demanded more jobs for Galician-Jewish clerks and salesmen who faced discrimination at the hands of antisemites and "antisemitic" Jews alike.[21]

Responding to Grobtuch's suggestion in the pages of S. R. Landau's Jewish nationalist weekly, *Neue National-Zeitung,* a writer identified as "Dr. K" agreed that the animosity against Polish Jews in Vienna, especially in the halls of the IKG, was staggering and necessitated an organization of Galician Jews. He quarreled, however, with Grobtuch's aversion to political action. On the contrary, he argued, a Galician Jewish organization should engage in political struggle to elect self-conscious Galician Jews to the Board of the *Gemeinde* to ensure representation for Galician interests there. He called on the already existing Galician-Jewish organizations such as the *Kaufmän-*

nischer Unterstützungsverein: Osten ("Society for the Protection of Merchants: The East"), organized in 1876 to provide loans and grants-in-aid to Galician Jews in Vienna, to unite in a strong new organization of all *Ostjuden* in the capital.[22]

Two years later, in 1910, the *Verband der östlichen Juden in Wien* ("Federation of Eastern Jews in Vienna") was founded to "raise the feeling of solidarity among the Jews of eastern origin in Vienna, as well as to protect and further their interests in social, material, and economic areas." The organization appealed to all those dissatisfied with the present condition of Eastern European Jews in Vienna, where Galician Jews were held in contempt by Jews from the Czech lands and Hungary. It urged its members to engage in political action to overcome that contempt. The Federation also sought to provide legal and financial assistance to poor Galician Jews in the city, and to persecuted Jews in Eastern Europe. Primarily, however, it saw itself as the center of Galician-Jewish social life in Vienna.[23]

One group of orthodox Galician Jews organized to protect the special interests of very religious Galician Jews in the city. In October 1903, this group opened a chapter of *Machzike Hadath* ("Strengtheners of the Faith") to unite the orthodox for political action. *Machzike Hadath,* originally founded in 1879 in Galicia, argued that the *Gemeinde* Board and the Jewish establishment ignored the needs of orthodox Galician Jews. In addition to serving the religious needs of Jewish migrants enroute to America, *Machzike Hadath* strove to unify the Polish-Jewish community of the capital.[24]

Political Organizations

Alongside these charitable and social organizations, Viennese Jews established political movements to fight for individual Jewish rights or for Jewish national equality. Political and racial antisemitism in the Habsburg capital forced the Jews not only to worry about their position but also to reexamine their assimilationist goals. As a result, they created three new movements to deal with the problem of antisemitism and to redefine what it meant to be a Jew in Austria. The first response of the Jews in Vienna was to create the *Oesterreich-Israelitische Union* ("The Austrian-Israelite Union"), which sought to defend Jewish rights against the increasingly violent attacks of the Austrian antisemites. Viennese Jews subsequently created Zionism, which sought to establish a Jewish state in the land of Israel, and diaspora Jewish nationalism, which regarded Zionism as utopian fluff and demanded the recognition of the Jewish nation within a nationally federated Austria.

These three political movements assumed radically different postures on the nature of modern Jewish identity. Both the Zionists and the Jewish nationalists, many of whom were from highly assimilated homes,[25] rejected the Jewish commitment to assimilation which was now a century and a half old. Declaring that antisemitism had revealed the emptiness of the assimilationist hope, they argued that a tough, assertive Jewish nationalism would be the best response to the antisemitic challenge. Those Jews who continued to desire integration into Austrian society decried Jewish nationalist and Zionist separatism and loudly affirmed their Austrian identity, but antisemitism in late Habsburg Vienna forced all but the most extreme assimilationists to assert their Jewish identity with equal pride. The members of the *Oesterreich-Israelitische Union,* who certainly defined themselves as patriotic Austrians, asserted a strong Jewish pride and a sense of the common origin and destiny of the Jewish people. Although the Zionists charged the *Union,* and the Viennese Jewish establishment of which it was an integral part, with assimilationism and treason, the *Union,* composed of the leaders of Viennese Jewry, was prepared to encourage a forceful assertion of Jewish identity in the face of the anti-Jewish hostility which it encountered.

The Integrationists

In the years after the Emancipation in 1867, the leaders of Viennese Jewry sought the integration of the Jews into Austrian, that is Austro-German, society. These notables maintained that Judaism was a religious confession which in no way interfered with full participation in Austrian culture and society. Throughout the second half of the nineteenth century, Viennese Jewish leaders, like Jewish spokesmen elsewhere in Western and Central Europe, denied that the Jews were—or wanted to be—a group apart.[26] Adolf Jellinek, chief rabbi of Vienna until his death in 1893, most clearly articulated this view in the pages of the Jewish weekly newspaper *Die Neuzeit,* which voiced the opinion of the IKG leadership. In 1884 Jellinek wrote, "For all intents and purposes, the Jews are subject to the same ethnic influences as all other citizens." [27] In an article written shortly before his death, he argued that the Jews "belong to one and the same stock *[Stamm],* profess the same articles of faith, but are no longer a separate nation. A king without land is no sovereign, a people *[Stamm]* without independent political and cultural life can never more appear as a nation." [28]

Jellinek and other Viennese Jewish integrationists also asserted the intimate connection between Jews and liberalism, the force which had emancipated the Jews in 1867. One writer for *Die Neuzeit,* for example, affirmed in 1870 the "intimate union" of the Jews "with the constitutional state and with the idea of liberalism which dominates it." "We stand and fall with the modern state," he declared.[29] Such Jews optimistically hoped that all barriers to the integration and assimilation of the Jews would fall as a reward for their loyalty. Jews would participate as individual human beings in a rosy Austrian future. Many Jews continued to affirm their integrationist aspirations well after the antisemites decided that they were unfit for membership in European society.

Antisemitism did galvanize into action a younger generation of Viennese Jewish integrationists. As they organized to combat the new threat, this younger group also asserted a new pride in shared Jewish origins. In 1886, in response to the virulent antisemitism of the 1880s, they established the *Oesterreich-Israelitische Union* (OIU). Predating the similar *Central-Verein deutscher Staatsbürger jüdischen Glaubens* ("Central Organization of German Citizens of the Jewish Faith") in Germany by seven years, the OIU was an organization which, like its German sister, would later distance itself from Zionism and Jewish nationalism, but would always declare its devotion to the principled and assertive struggle against antisemitism and to the strengthening of Jewish identity.[30] Composed primarily of businessmen and industrialists from the same circles which provided leadership for the IKG (minus the noblemen), the *Oesterreich-Israelitische Union* identified strongly with Habsburg Austria while at the same time asserting a large measure of Jewish pride.

The original impulse for such a defense organization came from Josef Samuel Bloch, a Galician-born rabbi in the Viennese suburb of Floridsdorf (later District XXI). Bloch, a feisty Jewish parliamentary deputy from Galicia, worked tirelessly against antisemitism. In 1883 he publicly humiliated the antisemite August Rohling, professor in Prague and author of *Der Talmudjude,* a vicious rewriting of Eisenmenger's seventeenth-century antisemitic classic, *Entdecktes Judentum.* Bloch forced Rohling to sue him for libel and then withdraw his suit.[31]

In the next year, Bloch founded the weekly newspaper *Oesterreichische Wochenschrift,* which he owned and edited until after World War I. Bloch used this widely read newspaper as his major weapon against what he deemed the twin enemies of antisemitism and assimilationism.[32] Although he later opposed the Zionist movement, Bloch did want his newspaper to "thrill national feelings" and

> rouse a feeling of kinship among all who belonged to the Jewish race and to make them conscious of their inescapable fate, as well as at the

> same time arousing a noble pride in their common past of four thousand years unparalleled alike in suffering and glory.[33]

Bloch used his newspaper to strengthen Jewish self-respect, inculcate Jewish knowledge, and counteract "treason and apostasy." The weekly sought to spread knowledge of Jews and Judaism, both within the community, and (hopefully) in the outside world.[34]

In the very first number of the *Oesterreichische Wochenschrift*, Bloch called on the Jews to establish a political organization which would serve the dual function of fighting antisemitism and intensifying Jewish pride.[35] On March 4, 1885, together with several other young men, he decided to establish an organization whose task would be

> to precipitate a joint, resolute political action on all questions concerning Judaism, to influence the improvement of religious instruction, to spread knowledge about Jewish history in Jewish circles, to elevate and foster Jewish consciousness *[Stammesbewusstsein]*, to create a front against the rapidly spreading "semitic antisemitism," and as much as possible, to suppress all tendencies which seek to sharpen religious and racial antagonisms.[36]

On April 24, 1886, they formally constituted the *Oesterreich-Israelitische Union*. Bloch never dominated the new organization. Probably because of his belligerent personality, he was never president and never held office. In his tradition, however, the *Union* perceived its mission as winning young alienated Jews back to the Jewish fold and waging a spirited campaign against antisemitism.

In the early years of the *Union's* existence, its leaders placed greatest emphasis not on defense activities but on the need to reinstill Jewish pride among very assimilated Jews. At the constituting meeting, Dr. Sigmund Zins asserted that the OIU's first task would be to fight self-hatred within the Jewish camp. He pledged the OIU to

> the internal struggle against the shameful self-surrender *[Selbstpreisgebung]* and degradation [of alienated Jews] and to the retrieval of the younger generation, which is practically totally estranged from us [and] from our glorious . . . tradition.[37]

Although the OIU statutes did mandate that the organization act as a lobbying group for Jewish interests in the Austrian parliament, the statutes placed greater emphasis on the desire of the fledgling organization to improve the quality of Jewish education as the first line of defense against disaffection among the young and against antisemitism in Vienna. In addition, the OIU wanted to encourage Jewish scholarship and train modern religious leaders. Its initial defense agenda consisted of deflating misconceptions about the Jews by precipitating public discussions on Jewish issues.[38]

Although the OIU wanted to defend Jewish interests, its leaders quickly pointed out that the new *Union* had no hidden separatist agenda. On the contrary, these young Viennese businessmen asserted their loyalty to Austria and the Habsburgs. Dr. Zins stated at the opening meeting of the *Union* in 1886:

> We emphasize the duties of the Austrian Jews to a straightforward *Austrian patriotism* and to political brotherhood with the peoples and nations among whom they are born and raised, in whose literature they are educated by preference and in whose economic and cultural life they participate . . .[39]

Yet he and the other leaders of the OIU firmly believed that alongside their Austrian identity, even their German-, Czech-, or Polish-Austrian identity, there was still room for them to be Jews. Dr. Zins announced:

> We find that patriotism and national feeling of the Austrian Jews in the different kingdoms and lands by no means excludes Jewish consciousness and its preservation . . .

It was still the duty of the Jews to preserve their own heritage, and to protect their rights against attack. They were not fighting for *Judenrecht* (Jewish rights), Zins argued, but for the *Menschenrechte der Juden,* the "human rights of the Jews." [40]

As the antisemites in Austria intensified their anti-Jewish campaigns and as the antisemitic parties expanded their power bases, the *Union*'s role as a defender of Jewish rights and of the Jews became primary and more explicit. In the first issue of its monthly periodical in October 1889, the *Union* issued its battle cry:

> Jews, band together, be united in the defense against the contemptuous attacks! This is the password of the *Oesterreich-Israelitische Union!* The organization shall be a center for you, the headquarters for the successful defense of our position. The organization seeks to awaken interest in public life among our coreligionists, and will work tirelessly so that each Jew will become a fighter for this holy task.[41]

This 1889 call to action only grew louder with the years.

In its activity against antisemitism, the *Union* engaged in activities similar to those of the *Centralverein* in Germany. By 1897 the *Union* opened a *Rechtsschutzbureau,* a "legal rights office", to engage in legal actions on behalf of Jewish rights and to collect evidence on those who attacked Jewish individuals or the Jewish people in newspapers, meetings, or representative bodies in all of Cisleithanian Austria.[42] At the twelfth General Assembly held April 23, 1898, spokesmen argued that they had established the *Rechtsschutzbureau* so that Jews, no longer able to remain silent in the face of antisemitism, could "loudly and decisively speak up and bring to bear all legal means which exist for the defense of our rights." [43] This office, the focus of all OIU activity, worked on such problems as antisemitism in the press, the Hilsner ritual murder affair, antisemitic activities in Galicia, the boycott, various legal battles in which Jews were engaged, as well as in the struggle of Viennese Jews to change *Heimat*.[44]

Many people in the *Union* were saddened by the need to fight for Jewish rights, but Maximilian Paul-Schiff, president in 1901, announced: "Today we have the full right and the sacred duty to think of *ourselves* first." [45] By 1903 the OIU finally added a clause to its statutes which acknowledged the primarily defensive posture of the organization. This clause stated: "The organization sees its task as the safeguarding of the general and political rights of the Jews and as helping [guarantee] those rights to those practicing the Jewish religion." [46]

In 1910, when the OIU celebrated its twenty-fifth anniversary, it prided itself on its political and defense accomplishments. The *Rechtsschutzbureau* had intervened in 5,000 cases and the organization boasted 7,000 members.[47] The *Union* congratulated itself that Jews were no longer relying on the ineffectual German Liberals, but had turned to assertive self-reliance and defense activity. While many members of the *Union* remained somewhat ambivalent about a separate Jewish organization fighting for Jewish rights, and Sigmund Mayer, president after 1905, even labeled the organization a "Schande für das Land" ("a shame for the country"), most felt that the antisemitic attacks of the late nineteenth century had made the strong posture of the OIU necessary.[48]

Viennese Zionists, however, regarded the *Union*'s leaders as a group of traitorous assimilationists. While they congratulated the *Union* for its defense activities, its "patriotic Jewish work," [49] the Zionist and Jewish nationalist press charged that *Union* activities on behalf of Jewishness were shamefully inadequate.[50] The Jewish nationalist newspaper *Neue National-Zeitung* reserved its nastiest comments for OIU president Sigmund Mayer. In May 1907 the newspaper charged that the OIU only pretended to represent Jewish interests; it was, in fact, only a clique of careerists who did not have the real interests of the Jews at heart, but only "personal vanity and organizational stewardship" (*Vereinsmeierei*, a play on Mayer's name).[51] In 1911, the newspaper editorialized that "Herr Sigmund Mayer, despite his large factories and his immense knowledge, is only a Jewish organizational great, but no great Jew." [52] The Jewish nationalists pounced on the fact that Mayer's son had converted to Christianity in order to advance his civil service career as proof of Mayer's lack of Jewish commitment.[53]

Mayer had been, in fact, an arch-exponent of the assimilationist philosophy, but even he felt obligated to return to the Jews once the antisemitic movement erupted. In his memoirs he recalled:

> I had actually forgotten that I was a Jew. Then the antisemites brought me to this unpleasant discovery. I knew I could not change this accident of birth, but it went against my disposition and temperament to hold my tongue when I was attacked for no other reason but that my father, grandfather, etc., back to Abraham were Jews; yes, this must be responded to.[54]

Mayer felt completely alienated by the Jewish atmosphere at the *Union* when he attended his first meeting, but the antisemitic atmosphere in Vienna prompted him to take an active role. In 1894 he became a political strategist and director of the *Rechtsschutzbureau* of the OIU, and in 1905, its president. He saw his role there as "instilling the Jews with a feeling of security and the courage to resist." [55]

Zionist charges notwithstanding, the *Oesterreich-Israelitische Union*, with its Jewish defense activities, rich lecture series, and its nonnationalist Jewish consciousness, did fulfill an important role in the social and political life of Jewish Vienna. Although the organization was unsympathetic to Zionism or Jewish nationalism, and in fact feared the dangerous consequences of both movements for the Jews of Austria, like the *Centralverein* in Germany[56] it nevertheless served to define a certain kind of Jewish identity in fin-de-siècle Vienna. Neither Zionist nor nationalist, nor as aggressively Jewish as Bloch may have wanted, the OIU called for a large measure of Jewish pride and assertiveness among Vienna's assimilated middle- and upper-class Jews who felt bewildered by the antisemitic hostility which surrounded them.

Jewish university students also responded to the antisemitic crisis by parrying anti-Jewish hostility and asserting Jewish pride. Jewish students, finding themselves excluded from German student associations by rowdy antisemitism at the university,[57] created their own cultural and social student organizations. Some of these organizations advocated radical Jewish national solutions to the problem of antisemitism.[58] All of them provided an escape from insults, degradation, and provocation, and an important institutional setting within which

Jewish students associated with one another and developed their own brand of assertive Jewishness. Many nonnationalist students became more conscious of their Jewish identity than they might have been had the antisemites not forced them to associate almost exclusively with each other.

The *Jüdisch-Akademischer Juristenverein* ("Society of Jewish Academic Law Students"), for example, created by Jewish law students excluded from the *Deutsch-Akademischer Juristenverein,* came to see its role as "strengthening the self-consciousness of Jewish law students," who suffered terrible humiliation in the face of German nationalist antisemitism. The *Akademischer Verein jüdischer Mediziner* ("Academic Association of Jewish Medical Students") similarly worked to organize Jewish medical students at the university.[59] The most important of the nonnationalist Jewish student organizations, however, was the *Jüdisch-Akademische Lesehalle* ("Jewish-Academic Reading Hall"). Sponsoring lectures and symposia, all the reading clubs at the University of Vienna served as important nuclei of university cultural life and, until the 1880s, contained a substantial number of Jewish members. In the 1880s, these organizations became more and more nationalist and antisemitic and ultimately barred Jews from membership.[60] In 1893, annoyed that Jews were excluded from the very liberal organizations which they had helped found, *Kadimah,* the first Jewish nationalist dueling fraternity, called for the creation of a reading hall for Jewish students which would serve as "a spiritual center for Jewish students" who "were closed out of almost all student organizations." *Kadimah* hoped that the *Lesehalle,* which would be neutral on the Jewish national issue, would join the struggle against antisemitism.[61]

The following year, the new *Jüdisch-Akademische Lesehalle* opened with a literary and defensive agenda. The *Lesehalle* saw its role as providing Jews with a forum for social and intellectual discourse and fostering "Jewish consciousness" among the students. Avoiding overt political issues, the *Lesehalle* strove to be a neutral center for all Jews at the university, a focus of intellectual stimulation and Jewish sociability.[62] Like its German prototype, the *Lesehalle* offered a wide range of lectures on Jewish and non-Jewish topics. In 1896, for example, Rabbi Moritz Güdemann spoke on the "Jewish Mission," Bernard Münz on the writer Tolstoy, and Sigmund Freud "On the Meaning of Dreams."[63] The *Lesehalle* received more subvention aid from the IKG than any other Jewish student group.[64]

In 1896 the Jewish nationalists and nonnationalists struggled for control of the *Lesehalle.* The nationalists, led by *Kadimah,* unsuccessfully tried to forge the Reading Club into an instrument of Jewish nationalist politics. As a result of the struggle, the *Lesehalle* changed its name to *Lese- und Redehalle jüdischer Hochschüler in Wien* ("Reading and Speaking Hall of Jewish University Students in Vienna"). It continued its neutrality on the nationality question[65] and provided a place for Jewish students at the university to associate largely with other Jews and feel that they were not alone in the face of frequently erupting antisemitic violence.

The Zionists

The *Oesterreich-Israelitische Union* asserted the pride of Vienna's middle-class Jews, but it never questioned the desire of those Jews for assimilation and integration. In the meantime, two other movements arose in fin-de-siècle Vienna which did call into question the whole thrust of Jewish assimilation in nineteenth-century Europe. Both the Zionists, who worked for the establishment of a Jewish state in Palestine, and the Jewish nationalists, who called for Jewish national autonomy in the diaspora, rejected the notion that the Jews as individuals could—or should—be integrated into the European nations. Both asserted that the Jews were a separate nation and were entitled to independent national development whether in their own land or in some kind of Austrian federation. Both movements were forged not by traditional religious Jews but by young Jews, many from assimilated homes, who, struck by the antisemitic backlash, wanted to return to the Jewish people and Jewish national identity.[66] Vienna's middle-class Jewish youth rejected the assimilationist ideology of the notables and struggled to assert a new kind of Jewishness in the Habsburg capital.

Zionism emerged as a strong political movement only after the 1896 publication of *The Jewish State* by Theodor Herzl, a prominent Viennese journalist, *feuilleton* editor of the *Neue Freie Presse,* and an assimilated Jew.[67] But Zionism predates Herzl in Vienna by thirteen years. In 1883, three university students, Nathan Birnbaum, Reuben Bierer, and Maurice Schnirer, strongly influenced by Peretz Smolenskin's ideas of Jewish national rebirth and offended by the exclusion of the Jews from the German nationalist student corporations, organized *Kadimah* as a Jewish nationalist club at the university. The new organization pledged to fight antisemitism, raise Jewish national consciousness, resist assimilation, and work for the Jewish colonization of Palestine.[68] Initially composed mostly of Eastern European Jews (with the exception of Birnbaum), *Kadimah* gradually enlisted more and more Western European Jews and became a Jewish dueling fraternity. It defended Jewish honor by dueling with the antisemites who insulted the Jewish name, at least before the antisemites declared the Jews unworthy of rendering satisfaction.[69]

The Zionism espoused by the students of *Kadimah* strongly resembled the Zionist goals of the Russian organization *Lovers of Zion,* and indeed *Kadimah* members participated in a tiny *Lovers of Zion* chapter, *Admath Jeschurun,* in Vienna.[70] Like *Lovers of Zion, Kadimah* wanted to establish an asylum in Palestine for the Jews who suffered from persecution in Europe, but they did not actively seek a Jewish state. Nathan Birnbaum, the ideologue of *Kadimah* who later in life became a Yiddishist and the leader of the anti-Zionist Orthodox *Agudas Yisroel* in Lemberg,[71] announced these goals in an 1892 speech which he reprinted in his newspaper *Selbstemancipation.* He argued that Zionism was "the belief that for this asylum and gathering place . . . there can be only *one* land in the world: the old national home of the Jews . . . Palestine." [72]

Zionism meant more than Palestine for members of *Kadimah;* for them Zionism was the struggle against assimilationism and for the recognition of Jewish national identity. Assimilation, *Kadimah* declared in its propaganda, was national suicide.[73] Contrary to the vain hopes of its proponents, assimilation had not eradicated anti-Jewish prejudice. In the first number of his newspaper *Selbstemancipation,* Birnbaum bitterly lamented:

> A feeling of painful, bitter disappointment overcomes us when we must see how vain and frivolous our hopes were about an ultimate cessation of the dominant prejudices against us, about ultimate social equality with our Christian fellow-citizens. All the means that we employed, under which we live, in order to adapt, did not suffice to exorcise the spectre of Jew-hatred . . . or to prevent the growth of this demonic impulse in intensity and in extent.[74]

There was only one solution, he declared: "The borrowing of foreign [culture] has not helped us at all; let us now try [to see] if self-conscious confidence in our own ability *[Kraft]* will not yield better fruit! . . . So let us now undertake to provide once more a national future for our people! " Jews must set aside all hope in assimilation: "The weed of the assimilation disease must be uprooted from home and school," and in its place "the fertile seeds of self-worth" must be planted, he declared. Jewish nationalism should replace moribund assimilationism as the new Jewish ideology.[75]

Speaking in 1894 at the celebration of *Kadimah*'s twenty-fourth semester, Isidor Schalit, a Galician-born member of *Kadimah,* later a leader of Austrian Zionism, articulated the limits of assimilation set by this group of educated and acculturated Jews. The desire for assimilation, he argued, had been a positive force for the generation which had struggled for emancipation, but modern "assimilationism" sought to break loose from Jewishness, and was, consequently, unacceptable. The Jews should by all means participate in the cultural and public life of the countries in which they lived, but "this assimilation need not be transformed into a slavish, denigrating imitation" of all that mocked Jewish tradition.[76] These Zionists viewed their commitment to Jewish nationalism in universal terms. In contradistinction to the integrationists, these early Zionists wanted to participate in and contribute to modern secular culture as Jews, not as individual human beings.

Following *Kadimah*'s lead, other dueling and non-dueling Jewish nationalist clubs flourished at the university. Organizations like *Unitas* and *Gamala* also longed to fight antisemitism and assimilationism by fostering a sense of belonging to the Jewish people.[77] Young Viennese Jewish men and women organized Zionist literary circles. *Kadimah* itself promoted two such cultural organizations to encourage Jews to learn Hebrew and Jewish history.[78] Young women also engaged in Zionist activity, and founded the *Verein jüdischer junger Damen: Miriam* ("Society of Young Jewish Ladies: Miriam") for the colonization of Palestine and *Literarischer Geselligkeitsverein jüdischer Mädchen: Moria* ("Literary-Social Society for Young Girls: Moriah"). *Moria* promoted the study of Jewish history, literature, and the role of women in the Jewish past and assisted in the "national work of reviving Jewish national consciousness *[Stammesbewusstsein]*." Leaving the realm of politics to their brothers, husbands, and cousins, these women sought to create a strong foundation for the new Jewish national movement. By 1896 the organization boasted forty members and met for biweekly lectures on matters of concern to national-minded Jewish women.[79]

In 1892 the *Kadimah Alte Herren* ("Alumni Members") attempted to forge a viable political Zionist movement. In his newspaper Birnbaum called for the creation of a Zionist party.[80] *Kadimah* activists and other members of *Admath Yeschurun* like Schnirer, Brainen, Oskar Kokesch, and S. R. Landau constituted themselses as *Zion: Verband der österreichischen Vereine für Colonisation Palästinas und Syriens* ("Zion: Federation of Austrian Organizations for the Colonization of Palestine and Syria"), a coalition of Austrian *Lovers of Zion* groups. In May 1893 they and others set up the *Wien* chapter of *Zion*.[81] The organization sought to raise money and support the new Jewish settlements in Palestine, but Birnbaum and *Kadimah* proved unsuccessful in their attempt to create a mass activist party.

It took Herzl's megalomania and utopian vision to forge the political Zionist movement. Many years later, Isidor Schalit described the excitement that he and his fellow *Kadimahianer* felt upon reading Herzl's call to action. Perhaps not literally, but certainly emotionally, Schalit raced to Herzl's house and cried:

> Herr Doktor, what you have written is our dream, the dream of many young people. What we have sought for so many years but not found is the word that you have now pronounced: the Jewish state. Come with us and lead us and we will create what men are capable of creating.[82]

The members of *Kadimah* provided Herzl with his first followers in Vienna and the early leadership in the fledgling World Zionist Organization. In May 1896 they and the members of the other Zionist groups in Vienna formally offered themselves to Herzl as co-workers in the new enterprise.[83] They had finally found a leader.

Theodor Herzl's vision was simple. In *The Jewish State* (1896) he declared antisemitism to be an insoluble problem for the assimilated Jews of Europe. The only solution to the Jewish problem, he declared, was for the Jews to establish their own state. Once the Jews left Europe, antisemitism would subside and the Jewish state would be integrated into the family of nations.[84] Herzl did not remain satisfied with a passive role as visionary. He convened annual World Zionist Congresses and he spent the last eight years of his life, until his premature death in 1904 at age forty-four, negotiating with kings and sultans for a charter for a Jewish homeland in Palestine. Political Zionism was the quest for a magical charter which would confer international approval on his utopian venture.[85]

The Zionists who followed Herzl's marching orders espoused a full-blown Jewish nationalism and rejected assimilationism as the solution to the Jewish problem. They did, however, unconsciously continue the assimilationist belief that the Jews were working for the salvation of mankind. But unlike the assimilationists, they saw the Jewish role in national, not individual terms. Adolf Böhm, who served for a time as president of the Zionist Central Committee of Western Austria and later wrote the classic history of the Zionist movement, argued that by no means did Zionists reject European culture. Rather, they sought "the recognition that the Jews must once again become a complete nation *[Vollnation]*." Only as a nation in their own land could the Jews reunite the strands of nationalism and universalism inherent in Judaism, enter the family of nations, and then make fruitful contributions to universal culture.[86]

After Herzl galvanized European Zionists into action, political Zionism flourished in Vienna. Zionism and Zionism's solution to the Jewish problem were by no means universally accepted in Herzl's home city, but they did make deep inroads among the younger generation of middle-class Viennese Jews, providing them with a new secular form of Jewish identity. The Central Zionist Office, which directed international Zionist affairs, was located in Vienna from 1897 until 1905, when it moved to Germany a year after Herzl's death. Thus for a time the leaders of world Zionism and of Viennese Zionism were the same men,[87] and they worked tirelessly both to support Herzl's diplomatic activities and to inculcate Zionist ideology among Viennese Jews. They proceeded to open chapters of *Zion,* the official organization of the political Zionists, all over Vienna. Some chapters remained chapters in name only (e.g., the one in Landstrasse), but most chapters sponsored lively programs and participated actively in Zionist agitation. The largest *Zion* chapters were *Wien* (the original chapter), *Leopoldstadt/Praterstrasse, Fünfhaus* (in District XV), and *Mariahilf-Neubau* (VI-VII). With 240 members, the chapter in Districts VI and VII, the home of a rising Jewish middle class, was the largest in the city. The Zionists also organized separate Zionist organizations for women such as the *Erster zionistischer Frauenverein in Wien* and the *Zionistischer Frauenverein in Fünfhaus,* as well as ones for young girls such as the *Verein jüdischer Mädchen, Hadassah,* which sponsored lectures and study sessions.[89]

The Zionists succeeded in creating a kind of alternative community for their adherents. They established Hebrew-speaking clubs, school associations, credit unions, choirs, kindergartens, literary societies, youth groups, and sport clubs,[90] and they pitched these societies not just to the assimilated middle class, but to Vienna's poor and lower-middle-class Jews as well. The most important Zionist youth organizations in Vienna probably were the sport clubs, the *Turnvereine,* which gave Jewish boys a chance to play soccer or practice gymnastics, hear Zionist propaganda, and fulfill the Zionist dream of "normalizing" the Jewish people through physical exercise. By 1913 seven such Jewish sport clubs devoted to the physical and national revival of the Jews existed.[91] Young Zionists also established a chapter of *Blau-Weiss,* the German-Jewish youth movement, in 1913.[92]

The Zionists always found their strongest supporters at the University of Vienna. Increasing antisemitism at the university even forced nonnationalist Jewish students to form separate social clubs. In a hostile atmosphere in which Jews were socially excluded and physically attacked, Zionism and Jewish nationalism flourished. With *Kadimah* and the other pre-Herzlian fraternities as models, a large number of new Zionist clubs opened after the appearance of *The Jewish State.* Jews in the different faculties, Jews from each province of Austria, and Jews from abroad all formed their own Zionist organizations, some considering themselves dueling fraternities and others not. Membership ranged from twenty to fifty in such organizations as *Bar Kochba* (formed by Galicians), *Iwria* (Silesians), *Erez Israel* (Romanians), and the *Vereinigung zionistischer Hochschüler.*[93] Zionist students also created cultural clubs like *Jüdische Kultur* to provide intellectual programs on Yiddish and Hebrew culture, and tried to work together to propagate Zionist ideology, promote Jewish study, and establish a Jewish dormitory, *Mensa,* and placement service.[94] All of the Zionist organizations at the university received financial assistance from the IKG, with *Kadimah* receiving more aid than any other Jewish nationalist group.[95]

Not content to organize only the middle-class Jews who sought a return to Judaism, Viennese Zionist leaders tried to win over the more traditional, poor Jews living in the Leopoldstadt and Brigittenau, whom they considered natural supporters of the Zionist idea. In December 1900 Viennese Zionist leaders took the lead in establishing and staffing a Jewish Toynbee Hall, a settlement house modeled on Arnold Toynbee's settlement houses in London, which provided lectures, courses, concerts, and sociability all with a Zionist flavor, for the poor Jews of the Brigittenau (District XX) and nearby Leopoldstadt. The Zionist organizers, all of them bourgeois, embarked upon this task in a spirit of *noblesse oblige,* yet they honestly wanted to help Vienna's poor Jews, "improve" them by introducing them to European and Jewish culture, and win them to Zionism.[96] Dr. Leon Kellner, the chairman of the Toynbee Hall committee, remarked at its opening: "The purpose of the Jewish Toynbee Hall is [to create a setting in which] the prosperous and intelligent devote a few hours a day to the poor and less educated, in order to strengthen them morally and spiritually for the battle of the coming days." [97] The Zionists hoped to offer the poor a sense of Jewish community as an alternative to working-class cafés.[98]

To achieve its purpose, the Jewish Toynbee Hall in the Brigittenau offered a rich lecture and course schedule to hundreds of Jewish artisans, clerks, peddlers, and housewives. In one week in February 1901, for example, Zionist students and others lectured on the Bible, the economic conditions of the Jews, the situation of the Jews in pre-Christian Italy, school hygiene, Jews and usury, Lessing's play *Nathan the Wise,* and astronomy. The Hall provided concerts, Sunday outings, and courses in Hebrew, French, English, stenography, and bookkeeping. The girls from *Hadassah* and *Moria* served tea and cookies every night. By 1903 the number of lectures had grown and included such diverse subjects as women in art and literature, modern Jewish poetry, the secular Jewish poetry of the Middle Ages, Zionist thinkers Ahad Ha'am and Theodor Herzl, literary greats like Heinrich

Heine, Shakespeare, and Dickens, Austrian law, infant diseases, and dueling.[99]

The original directorate of the Toynbee Hall included Zionists, Jewish nationalists, and a few members of the IKG Board like Gustav Kohn. By 1904–5, financial difficulties forced the Zionists to hand over control of the Toynbee Hall to the B'nai B'rith.[100] The Toynbee Hall, along with a second settlement house opened in late 1905 in Fünfhaus (District XV), continued to offer a rich array of lectures on Jewish and non-Jewish culture, and on practical matters. In 1910 Toynbee Hall sponsored 103 lectures, 23 concerts, 22 Bible "evenings," and courses in English, singing, and stenography, all extremely well attended. It also offered special programs for children, and provided clothing and medical care to the needy.[101]

The Zionist leadership also attempted to organize Jewish workers, shop clerks, and low-level business employees for the Zionist cause. Schalit recalled that in 1897 or 1898, when he was serving as editor of the Zionist weekly, *Die Welt,* Herzl entrusted him with the task of spreading Zionism among Jewish workers. Since few Viennese Jews were proletarian, the Zionists agitated among petty clerks, trying to co-opt already existing organizations of Jewish clerks into the Zionist camp. In 1899 the Zionists established the *Vereinigung jüdischer Handlungsgehilfen und Privatbeamten* ("Organization of Jewish Shop Clerks and Business Employees").[102]

In this effort to organize Jewish petty clerks, mainstream Zionists faced competition from left-wing socialist and labor Zionists also active in Vienna in these years. *Poale Zion* ("Zionist Workers"), a group which agitated for a socialist Jewish homeland among Jewish workers in Eastern Europe, tried to spread its version of Zionism among the Jewish store clerks of Vienna, especially between 1900 and 1903, the years when Ber Borochov, the leading intellectual of *Poale Zion,* lived in Vienna. Attempting to win the Jewish poor away from the Social Democrats, these Zionists argued that the socialists were not committed to improving the situation of the Jews. They offered practical inducements to join the Labor Zionists by establishing free employment agencies and courses in Hebrew, stenography, and bookkeeping. Many organizations of Zionist clerks and salesmen were organized and collapsed; others lasted. In 1903 six such organizations existed, each with forty to one hundred members. In October 1905 the *Allgemeiner jüdischer Arbeiterverein* ("General Jewish Workers Organization") and the *Verein jüdischer Handelsangestellter* ("Organization of Jewish Business Employees") united in a local chapter of international *Poale Zion.*[103]

Vienna was also the home of religious Zionist, non-Zionist, and even anti-Zionist activity on behalf of Jewish colonization in Palestine.

In 1912 the religious Zionists constituted themselves as a chapter of international *Mizrachi,* the religious Zionist organization, and in 1914 Mizrachi Youth opened a chapter in the city.[104] In 1899 Zionists and non-Zionists joined together to form *Karmel,* an agency to market the products of Jewish colonies in Palestine.[105] In 1904 the *Gemeinde* Board itself, anti-Zionists all except for Oskar Marmorek, tried to deflate Zionist efforts by establishing a non-Zionist Colonization Society. Along with several Viennese rabbis and members of the OIU like Bloch and Zins, this organization encouraged the settlement of (Russian) Jews in Palestine, but was opposed to Herzl's political movement to create a Jewish state.[106]

Finally, Jewish territorialism, the movement to find a Jewish homeland anywhere in the world, found adherents in Vienna. In 1906, many former Zionists and Jewish nationalists organized a chapter of the International Territorialist Organization (ITO), a group which had left the World Zionist Organization in 1905 when the WZO failed to support the establishment of a temporary Jewish homeland in Uganda. Aghast at the sheer number of pogroms in Russia, the Jewish territorialists wanted to find a homeland—any homeland—for the Jews. Many important non-Zionists such as Josef Bloch, editor of the *Oesterreichische Wochenschrift,* became members of the Vienna chapter of the ITO.[107]

The large number of Zionist organizations in Vienna cannot suffice to indicate the extent to which Zionism attracted Viennese Jews in this period. Many of these organizations may have existed only on paper or as mouthpieces for a few argumentative men and women. Even so, the number of Viennese Jews who paid the "shekel," the official dues, to the World Zionist Organization,[108] indicates that while the majority of Viennese Jews were not Zionists, Zionism was certainly a force to be reckoned with in the Viennese Jewish community. In 1902 there were 872 shekel-payers in Vienna, an increase of 14% over the 762 who paid their dues to the Zionist movement in 1899. There were more shekel-payers in the city of Vienna than in all of Bohemia, Bukovina, Moravia, Hungary, and France. To be sure, the number of shekel-payers in Vienna paled by comparison to the numbers who officially identified with Zionism in Russia and Galicia, the areas in which Zionism was the most popular, or even in Germany.[109] Nevertheless, more Jews affiliated with Zionism in Vienna than in other Germanized areas of Austria such as Prague, where Jews found greater acceptance by the German elite than they did in Vienna.[110]

Zionism appealed mostly to young Jews in Vienna. Although the shekel-payer lists did not indicate occupation, 11% of the affiliated Zionists in Vienna identified themselves as students, and others may also have been students. Furthermore, only 25% (215) of the male shekel-payers could be located in the IKG voter eligibility lists.[111] Those who could pay the shekel could certainly afford the IKG taxes, but in order to appear on the voter lists IKG members had to be at least thirty years old and taxpayers for at least three years.[112] Many Viennese shekel-payers must have been in their twenties or early thirties.

Unfortunately, it is impossible to determine if Zionism had greater appeal among the rich or poor. Viennese Jewish poor may have found Zionism immensely attractive, but they could not afford to pay the shekel and formally affiliate with the movement. All the shekel-payers belonged to the respectable middle class, and their occupational distribution was typical for such Jews (Table 7:1). Most of the shekel-payers who could be traced in the IKG voter eligibility lists, and these were the older, middle-class Zionists, were professionals, merchants, or artisans. Zionism did not appeal, it appears, to civil servants.

Zionism found its greatest strength primarily in the new middle-class Jewish neighborhoods of the city, in Alsergrund (District IX) and in Mariahilf-Neubau (Districts VI–VII).[113] Just as Zionist organizational strength lay in Districts VI and VII, so too most "card-carrying" Zionists lived there. Only 8% of all Viennese Jews lived in Mariahilf-Neubau, but 17.4% of all affiliated Zionists resided in the two districts. Similarly, only 12% of all Jews rented apartments in the Alsergrund, but 16.2% of the Zionists lived in District IX. Surely many poor Jews in the Leopoldstadt (II) or Brigittenau (XX) sympathized with Zionism but were unable to pay the shekel. Thus although 36% of all Viennese Jews lived in the Leopoldstadt, only 27.4% of all shekel-payers resided in that district. The strength of Zionism in these new Jewish neighborhoods had an important impact on the course of Jewish communal politics in Vienna in the early twentieth century.

Table 7:1. Occupations of Viennese Jews Who Paid the Shekel to the World Zionist Organization in 1902

(N = 214)	
Civil Servants	1.4%
Professionals	15.4
Industrialists	8.4
Merchants	47.7
Business Employees	9.8
Artisans	13.6
Workers	—
"On Private Income"	2.8
	100.0%

Diaspora Jewish Nationalism

More unusual than the rise of Zionism was the emergence of diaspora-centered Jewish nationalism in fin-de-siècle Vienna. This movement asserted that the Jews could be recognized along with Germans, Hungarians, Czechs, Poles, and South Slavs as one of the nations of Austria-Hungary. Like Zionism, the Jewish nationalists rejected assimilation and called for the self-conscious assertion of Jewishness. Unlike the Zionists, who saw the natural development of Jewish nationalism only on the soil of Palestine, the diaspora nationalists desired Jewish national development within a nationally federated Austria. They fervently hoped that their vision of nonterritorial national autonomy for all nations, including the Jews, under the protective wings of a strong supranational Austria would finally end the strident nationality conflict which was the central issue of politics in the Dual Monarchy.

Diaspora Jewish nationalism could only have arisen within a multinational state like Austria, where the conflict among the nationalities for a share in political power was the order of the day.[114] Hungarian nationalism had been assuaged somewhat by the Compromise Agreement of 1867 under which Hungary controlled its own internal affairs, but the Czechs, Poles, Ruthenes, Slovaks, Slovenes, Serbs, Croats, Italians, Romanians, and Germans all battled for greater political independence from the highly centralized Austrian government. The situation was particularly complicated for the Jews. In the 1870s, the Jews of Austria had identified with the Austro-Germans, but the rise of antisemitism and exclusivistic nationalism in the 1880s excluded Jews from all the national groups in Austria.[115] While Jewish leaders continued to insist that the Jews could be good Germans (or Poles), the Germans, Czechs, Poles, and others vociferously denied the Jews membership in their respective national groups. By the late 1890s, the exclusion of the Jews from all national camps was well-nigh complete, and the Jews, as one historian has described them, remained the only *Austrians* in Austria.[116]

Jewish diaspora nationalism thus arose within the context of Jewish exclusion from all the national camps in a multinational political system in which national affiliation was imperative. Many young Jews came to the conclusion that the only solution to the Jewish dilemma was vigorous affirmation of Jewish nationhood and the demand that the Jews be given, not a share in political power, but recognition of their legitimacy as a nation in Austria. This Jewish nationalism was an empire-wide movement. Strongest in the major centers of Jewish life in Galicia and Bukovina, it was also a dominant force in Vienna, especially among university students.[117]

It might be claimed that Zionism and diaspora nationalism were incestuous movements in Vienna. Their adherents certainly often worked together for common goals. The first expression of Jewish nationalism was *Kadimah,* the Zionist organization created at the university in 1883. The rise of political Zionism and the pronounced commitment of Austrian Zionists to *Gegenwartsarbeit,* diaspora work to raise Jewish national consciousness,[118] accelerated the development of diaspora Jewish nationalism. In order to win recruits for Zionism, Austrian Zionists allied themselves with the diaspora nationalists to agitate for the recognition of the Jewish nation in Austria. Many of the diaspora nationalists, on the other hand, had once been Zionists, but for a variety of philosophical and personal reasons had split from Herzl and Herzl's movement.

The central argument in Jewish nationalist polemics was that the Jews were not, could not be, and would not ever wish to be Germans, Czechs, Poles, or hyphenated versions of these groups. To be a Jew meant belonging to the Jewish nation. Thus the Jewish nationalists rejected assimilation as "the outmoded style of the past century," and as "a big mistake." [119] Richard Rappaport, leader of the *Jüdischer Volksverein,* a non-Zionist Jewish nationalist group, repudiated the assimilationist view that the Jews were merely a religious group and argued:

> The Jews are not only a religious community *[Confessionsgemeinschaft],* but rather, through their origins, their thousands of years of history, their culture . . . and above all, through their own feeling, a *Nation.*[120]

He repeatedly affirmed in his newspaper the *Jüdisches Volksblatt:* "The Jews are a people; [they] want to and must remain one." [121]

The classic expression of the Jewish national argument came from the pen of the Zionist Heinrich York-Steiner in Bloch's *Oesterreichische Wochenschrift* in 1907:

> We Jews are by nationality neither German nor Czech, not Frenchmen or Englishmen. Whoever maintains the opposite . . . places us Jews in a false light and besmirches our character.

While a German Jew might speak, think, and even feel German, York-Steiner emphasized, he was a Jew of German culture, not a German, but a Jew.[122]

As a consequence of their belief in Jewish national identity, Jewish nationalists advocated the fight not for the equality of the Jews as individuals, but rather for the equality of the Jewish nation.[123] Urging an end to Jewish reliance on traditional political allies, one spokesman called for a Jewish political party to fight for Jewish national rights. He declared: "Nine-tenths of all Austrian Jews, [despite] disunity and disagreements, today are sure that they must, and can, further their citizen rights as *Jews,* not as Germans, Czechs, or Poles."[124] The *Jüdische Volkspartei* ("Jewish Peoples' Party"), which the Jewish nationalists created in 1902, eschewed chauvinistic nationalism, but vowed to assert Jewish national rights and demand equality of the Jews with the other nations of Austria. In order to achieve this equality, the party advocated the adoption of universal suffrage with proportional minority group representation for elections to the Austrian *Reichsrat.* The party also sought to heighten Jewish national consciousness, improve Jewish education, and wrench control of the *Gemeinde* from the assimilationist leaders who dominated it. Finally, the *Jüdische Volkspartei* pledged itself to alleviate the plight of the Jewish poor through the establishment of credit unions, free employment agencies, and bureaus to deal with the problems of Jewish workers in general and Jewish apprentices in particular.[125]

The long-range goal of the diaspora nationalists was the establishment of national autonomy for the Jewish people in a future Austrian federation of autonomous nationalities. Hermann Kadisch most clearly articulated the demands for Jewish autonomy in his book *Jung-Juden und Jung-Oesterreich* ("Young Jews and Young Austria"), written in 1912. Kadisch recognized that national autonomy based on territory was impractical for the territorially dispersed Jews. National autonomy, he insisted, should be based on personal affiliation. Moreover, at a time when other Austrian nationalities demanded more than mere national autonomy, Kadisch realistically acknowledged the Jewish need for a continued imperial framework. He urged the establishment of a greater Austrian *Völkerstaat,* a union of autonomous national groups, with a strong central government which would guarantee liberal civil rights. In this *Völkerstaat,* no nation would dominate, and Jews could continue to be loyal to the greater whole while at the same time being true to their own national identity.[126]

Realizing the utopian quality of these goals, Kadisch presented short-term demands as well. Like Richard Rappaport, he called for universal (manhood) suffrage with proportional representation for the national minorities, including the Jews. Influenced by the Zionists, he called for the official recognition of Hebrew as the national language of the Jews, and for the equality of Hebrew with other languages in state offices and in court. He also desired the opening of departments of Jewish history, literature, and Hebrew at the Universities of Vienna, Prague, Lemberg, Cracow, and Czernowitz, the creation of a national federation of Jewish communities, and certain measures to help the Jewish poor.[127]

In these demands, the Jewish nationalists were undoubtedly influenced by Karl Renner and Otto Bauer, Austrian Marxists, who in 1899 formulated a theory of national autonomism designed for the peculiar constellation of political forces in Austria. At the Brünn Convention of the Austrian Social Democrats, Renner called for the transformation of the Dual Monarchy into a federation of member nations. These "nations," determined not on the basis of territory, but rather on the basis of personal affiliation, would control primary national interests, while the central authorities would administer foreign affairs, the military, and the economy.[128] Renner and Bauer categorically excluded the Jews from this program, but Jewish nationalists, scattered all over the Monarchy, could easily find nonterritorial national autonomy appealing. Jewish nationalists were also influenced by Simon Dubnow, a Russian Jewish historian who provided the theoretical underpinnings for a movement toward national cultural autonomism for the Jews in Russia.[129]

By asserting a separate Jewish national identity in Austria, Jewish nationalists attempted, like their assimilationist parents, to find a viable road to integration into Austrian society. They naively believed that the other nationalities, including the antisemites among them, would be more receptive to a Jewish national position than they had been to the prior Jewish strategy of individual assimilation. Like assimilationism before it, Jewish nationalism could serve to integrate the Jews into the Austrian polity.[130] Moreover, in their affirmation of the continued existence of Habsburg Austria, diaspora nationalists maintained the Jewish tradition of loyalty to the Habsburg state structure. They saw no conflict between being modern men of culture, Jewish nationalists, and good Austrians, contributors to a rosy Austrian future.[131] While the other nationalities clamored for independence or full territorial autonomy, the Jewish nationalists clung to the hope for a strong unified Austria. Through their new ideology the Jews could continue to be the "only Austrians in Austria."

Jewish nationalist agitation, like all nationalist agitation in Austria, grew more forceful in the years which preceded the 1907 introduction of universal manhood suffrage for parliamentary elections. In the two or three years before the election, Jewish nationalists, allied with the Zionists, mounted a public campaign for national autonomy and the recognition of the Jewish nation. In 1907, when the government ruled out national autonomy, they agitated for minority representation (and Jewish representation) in the new parliament. At the same time they tried to wrest control of the *Israelitische Kultusgemeinde* from its integrationist leaders. In both these campaigns they asserted their new brand of Jewish identity which clashed with that of the older leaders of the Jewish community. In the conflict over parliamentary and Jewish communal elections, both sides sharpened their arguments and their understanding of the meaning of Jewishness in late Habsburg Vienna.

8. *The Struggle: Jewish Nationalists vs. Assimilationists*

ZIONISTS and Jewish nationalists on the one hand, and members of the Viennese Jewish elite on the other, clashed not just in their respective definitions of Jewishness, but on how to implement those definitions in public life. Two major battles ensued: one over the political posture of the Jews during the heated parliamentary elections of 1907, the first to be held on the basis of universal manhood suffrage, and the other a power struggle for control of the *Israelitische Kultusgemeinde* itself. In both cases the antisemitism of Viennese politics and Zionist/Jewish nationalist attacks forced the leaders of Viennese Jewry to rethink their assumptions about Jewish assimilation. The potential anti-Jewish consequences of universal manhood suffrage and the Zionist bid for control of the *Gemeinde* prompted the Viennese Jewish notables to formulate a new version of assertive Jewish behavior in the Habsburg capital.

Parliamentary Elections of 1907

During the agitation which preceded the adoption of universal manhood suffrage, Jewish nationalists and Zionists unsuccessfully pressed for their long-range goals of Jewish autonomy and proportional national minority and Jewish representation in parliament. As early as 1905, Benno Straucher, a Jewish parliamentary deputy from Bukovina, had urged national voting curias, including a Jewish curia, for the 1907 election as the only solution to the nationality conflict.[1] If such curias were adopted, then each of the Austrian nationalities would vote as a body for a predetermined number of candidates who would represent their national interests in the *Reichsrat,* and the nationalities would feel adequately represented in the Austrian parliament. On December 12, 1905, the Jewish nationalists more boldly called for national autonomy and "the national equality of the Jews with the other Austrian nations." [2] At the same time, in an attempt to control the Jewish national movement, Austrian Zionists began to agitate for Jewish national autonomy in Austria. In January 1906, Isidor Schalit, head of the Austrian Zionist organization after Herzl's death, demanded the institutionalization of national autonomy in Austria and the recognition of Jewish nationality. In an official policy statement, Austrian Zionists affirmed the primacy of work for Palestine but argued that "in Austria in particular, citizens of Jewish nationality also have an inviolable right to protect and nurture their national life within [the country's] borders." [3]

In 1906 Zionists and Jewish nationalists began to work together for their common goals. In January an informal coalition of the two movements called for proportional representation and a Jewish curia, especially in Galicia and Bukovina, in the upcoming elections.[4] The following month Schalit visited the Minister of the Interior, Graf Bylandt-Rheidt, to make a formal request for national autonomy, proportional voting, and a Jewish curia. The minister informed Schalit that the government would not introduce national voting curias under any circumstances. Bylandt-Rheidt also tried to discourage Schalit from pursuing proportional minority voting because it would only strengthen the hands of those who sought to harm the Jews.[5] In July of 1906, at a meeting in Cracow, Zionists and Jewish nationalists formalized their alliance in the Jewish National Party, which continued to demand autonomy for Jews and other Austrian nationalities.[6]

With both national autonomy and minority curias ruled out by the government, Jewish nationalists and Zionists concentrated their efforts on electing men personally committed to representing the Jewish nation in the Austrian parliament. In the elections of 1907 the Jewish National Party ran candidates in Galicia, Bukovina, and parts of Vienna where potential Jewish voting blocs existed. Isidor Schalit himself ran for parliament from the fifth Viennese voting district, a section of the Leopoldstadt with a substantial Jewish population. The Party called on the Jews to

> elect only men who through their feelings and thoughts [are] Jewish, who through love for their people and consciousness of their great task are committed [to the Jewish nation], who campaign on the basis of a *Jewish program,* and who consider it their duty to join only a *Jewish Club* [in parliament].[7]

The electoral campaign in 1907 provided Jewish nationalists and Zionists with a perfect opportunity to propagate their ideas of Jewish national rebirth among Austrian Jews. The Zionists in particular viewed this election, in which all men could vote, as a means of asserting their own leadership in the Jewish nationalist camp.[8] Although the World Zionist Organization did not want to waste its money or energy on electoral politics, under Isidor Schalit's leadership Austrian Zionists expected to gain a great deal from the political fray. Schalit tried to convince David Wolffssohn, the skeptical president of the World Zionist Organization, that by working to elect committed Jewish nationalists to the Austrian parliament the Zionists could propagate Zionism, and, more importantly, firmly establish themselves as the rightful leaders of the Jewish national struggle.[9] With their greater organizational resources, the Zionists easily dominated the Jewish National Party.

Zionist electoral propaganda emphasized the Jewishness of the Zionist candidates and denounced all other Jewish candidates for their lack of Jewish consciousness. In Vienna, Zionist newspapers presented Schalit as a man proud to be a Jew, as a man who would work for Jewish honor and represent the Jews *qua* Jews in the *Reichsrat*.[10] The Zionist press, especially the political Zionist *Jüdische Zeitung*, depicted the other candidates from the Leopoldstadt as insufficiently Jewish to represent the Jews. This newspaper labeled Dr. Gustav Kohn, a *Gemeinde* vice-president, as a black-hearted reactionary, an opponent of electoral reform even within the IKG, and most disparagingly, as a doddering old man with a German heart who knew nothing of things Jewish. The Zionists castigated Dr. Julius Ofner, the Social-Political candidate, as a man completely devoid of Jewish consciousness and as emotionally German. The best thing one could say about him, the Zionists charged, was that he had not converted.[11]

Although he did not affiliate with the Jewish National Party, the Viennese Jewish nationalist Saul Raphael Landau also called for the election of Jewish deputies who would scorn the very notion of assimilation and would represent specifically Jewish interests. With no favorite candidate of his own, Landau denounced all of the candidates who ran for parliament from the Leopoldstadt and from the largely Jewish Kai section of the Inner City. In particular, Landau attacked Dr. Julius Ofner because the candidate was a self-proclaimed German nationalist, despite his Jewish origins. "It is certainly thoroughly funny *[urdrollig]*," Landau observed, "how Dr. Ofner, in gatherings of Polish and Hungarian Jews, solemnly asserts his German-ness . . ." Arguing the necessity for Jewish nationalist candidates, and appreciating Schalit's candidacy, Landau realistically feared that the Viennese electorate was not yet ready for Jewish national representatives.[12]

The Zionist candidate was not successful in Vienna. Receiving 529 out of 9,398 votes cast, Schalit lost to Julius Ofner in the Leopoldstadt.[13] His defeat was probably caused by inadequate planning, lack of electoral expertise, and the unpopularity of his cause among those who voted. The Zionists, nevertheless, congratulated themselves on their attempt "to annihilate the assimilationist politics of the Jews of Austria" and were confident in their ultimate victory.[14] They expressed great delight with the election of four Jewish national deputies from Galicia and Bukovina, Adolf Stand, Benno Straucher, Arthur Mahler, and Heinrich Gabel, who constituted themselves as the Jewish Club in parliament on June 18, 1907. The Club voted to work for the "rights, interests, and welfare" of all Austrian Jews, not just for their own constituents, to seek the official recognition of Jewish nationality and the Yiddish language, and to field attacks on Jews and Judaism in parliament and in Austria at large.[15] Saul Raphael Landau was also initially ecstatic about the formation of the Jewish Club by men who were "Jews only, total Jews, representatives of the *Jewish* people, fighters for the Jewish people." In almost messianic tones Landau hailed the creation of this four-member parliamentary club as a new chapter in Austrian and Jewish history.[16]

Four years later, in the 1911 *Reichsrat* elections, the Zionists and Jewish nationalists again unsuccessfully sought to return Jewish nationalist deputies to parliament. In Vienna the Zionist candidate Robert Stricker lost to Julius Ofner in the Leopoldstadt. Of the four members of the Jewish Club, only one, Benno Straucher, was reelected.[17]

After their second failure, Viennese Zionists decided to organize the Leopoldstadt, the "center of Jewish life in Vienna," more effectively. They established the *Jüdischer Volksverein für die Leopoldstadt* ("Jewish People's Organization for the Leopoldstadt") to lobby among Jews of the second district. The program of the new organization reiterated the familiar demands of the Jewish nationalists and Zionists—national autonomy, economic assistance to the Jews through full employment, the lifting of statutes which discriminated against Jewish artisans, and through credit unions, and concern for Jewish national culture and consciousness. Presided over by Robert Stricker, the interwar leader of Viennese Zionists, the *Verein* attempted to convert the Leopoldstadt Jews to Zionism.[18]

While the Zionists strove for Jewish curias and for Jewish national representatives in the Austrian parliament, members of the Viennese Jewish establishment vehemently opposed such activity. Fearing the political and economic antisemitic consequences of Jewish nationalism, they articulated their stern opposition both to the recognition of Jewish nationality and to the election of avowedly Jewish national candidates. Labeling the Jews anything else but Austrian citizens would be the first step, they worried, in curtailing Jewish rights. In an article discussing the possibility of national curias in Moravian provincial elections in 1905, for example, the monthly periodical of the *Oesterreich-Israelitische Union* reminded its readers "that a Jewish curia will be a Pariah-curia in the present mood in Austria." [19] The *Union*'s leaders feared that a Jewish curia in Moravia or anywhere else would only please the antisemites, who firmly believed that the Jews were a group apart. They argued:

> The exceptional position, which the Jews would be assigned through a special voting curia, would provide the first satisfaction for antisemitic longings and desires. With the recognition of the Jews as a nationality, their former position as citizens would receive a fundamental blow.[20]

Above all, Jewish leaders feared the terrible economic consequences of the establishment of national curias. They speculated, and were convinced, that if the Jews were considered a separate nation, then the Germans, Czechs, Poles, and others would hasten to bar Jews from the free professions and certain kinds of commerce.[21] Regarding the establishment of Jewish curias as flying in the face of the past 150 years of Jewish history, the OIU declared "We will have nothing to do with political and economic suicide," and successfully lobbied against such curias.[22]

On the issue of Jewish national representatives in the 1907 election, however, Viennese Jewish notables faced a major dilemma. They calculated that universal manhood suffrage guaranteed the demise of the Liberals, who appealed only to the *haute bourgeoisie,* and the victory of the parties which promised to alleviate the economic plight of the masses, that is, the Social Democrats who appealed to the industrial proletariat, and the antisemitic Christian Socials who appealed to the artisans and shopkeepers threatened by economic liberalism and capitalist expansion. A parliament elected on the basis of universal suffrage would be one in which the large number of political antisemites would feel completely free to condemn the Jews. Jewish leaders certainly desired *Reichsrat* deputies who would repudiate antisemitic attacks, but by 1907 Jews could no longer rely on the Liberals, and no other political party could afford to lose votes by defending the Jews publicly.[23] The antisemitism of the electoral campaign, the realities of Austrian democracy, and the pressure of the Jewish nationalists forced Jewish leaders to support Jewish parliamentary candidates who might represent ill-defined "Jewish interests," and, hopefully, defend the Jews against antisemitism.

It was difficult for the Jewish establishment to reach this decision. Its political posture had been set at the time of the Emancipation in 1867. At that time, despite their nearly universal commitment to political Liberalism, Viennese Jewish notables decided that Jews should participate in Austrian politics as individuals, not as Jews. On the eve of the June 1870 parliamentary elections, *Die Neuzeit,* which more or less expressed the opinion of the IKG Board, exorted its readers to vote and exercise their civil rights, but without showing any solid Jewish front. "The Jew as citizen does not have to have the same political interests and program as the Jew in the synagogue." [24] The editors of *Die Neuzeit* reproached a Jewish parliamentary candidate who did appeal to Jewish voters on Jewish issues; they reminded their readers that "We want no Jewish politics, no parliamentary deputies [elected] out of [a sense of] common religious community *[Glaubensgenossenschaft]*." Proudly proclaiming their Austrian identity, and fearing that this man sadly misunderstood the meaning of religious freedom,[25] they relied on the Liberals to defend their interests.

Despite the growing electoral strength of the antisemites in the 1880s and 1890s, the Jewish establishment refused to acknowledge the need for Jewish politics or a Jewish vote. While they hoped for a spirited defense of Jewish rights against the antisemites, they were unwilling to admit that there were Jewish issues in politics. The editors of *Die Neuzeit* asserted in 1890 that "the Jews are Austrians, are proud of naming Austria their fatherland; they are true to emperor and empire, and will surpass their share in the population in love of Fatherland." [26] Jewish leaders did, however, reveal a measure of ambivalence on the issue of Jewish defense. They expressed their disappointment that most Jewish deputies did not speak up for Jewish interests and applauded Josef Samuel Bloch for his vigorous refutation of antisemitic insinuations in the *Reichsrat. Die Neuzeit* repeatedly urged Bloch's Galician district to reelect him.[27]

Throughout the 1890s, the entire Viennese Jewish establishment from the IKG to the OIU persisted in its devotion to the German Liberal Party and its successors, despite the fact that the Liberals had abandoned the Jews. Jewish leaders, who were themselves convinced Liberals, simply believed that middle-class Jews had no alternatives. They could not vote for the antisemitic Christian Socials or the antibourgeois Social Democrats. Thus the establishment's press urged the Jews of Vienna, and indeed all of Austria, to vote for Liberal candidates in the naive hope that they might defend Jewish rights in parliament. In the 1890s, even Bloch and the *Oesterreich-Israelitische Union,* the most assertive members of the Jewish establishment, believed Liberalism was best for Vienna and supported

Liberal candidates for parliament, most of whom were indifferent to the Jews. Unhappy that Dr. Heinrich Jacques, the Liberal representative of the Inner City in the late 1880s and early 1890s, was not particularly concerned with fighting antisemitism, the *Union* nevertheless supported him in the 1891 elections.[28] In the special election of 1892 to replace Jacques after his death, the *Oesterreichische Wochenschrift* urged its readers to vote for the ex-Liberal Democrat, Ferdinand Kronawetter. Recognizing that Kronawetter was unconcerned with Jewish affairs, the *Oesterreichische Wochenschrift* supported him "not from the standpoint of Judaism . . . [but] rather from the Viennese standpoint . . ." [29] In October 1892, the newspaper labeled him "an ideal politician, a pure optimist, an enthusiast, if you will, a human savior—what could be bad? We need just such a [man] in our pessimistic times." [30] In the 1897 elections, the OIU supported progressive candidates Ferdinand Kronawetter, Constantin Noske, Julius Ofner, and Carl Wrabitz, although the *Oesterreichische Wochenschrift* did lament bitterly that these "Jewish deputies have no backbone to stand up for Jewish interests." [31]

In the 1907 elections, the *Oesterreich-Israelitische Union* was divided on the issue of electing Jewish representatives. In the excitement which preceded the May elections, two separate factions of the *Union* attempted to push the organization in conflicting directions on this issue. One group probably inspired by Bloch but led by Sigmund Fleischer, called for the election of deputies pledged to represent Jewish, although not Jewish nationalist, interests. Sigmund Fleischer realistically recognized the need for a new political strategy for Austrian Jews. Fearing that universal suffrage would only strengthen the antisemites and the left, he also recognized that the Jews could expect no support from the liberal parties. The Jews, he argued, had to change tactics, "not out of a change in our way of thinking, but because of the shifting of political power relationships caused by universal suffrage." [32] Thus, Fleischer stated, almost against their will, the Jews must unite and elect Jewish deputies to parliament:

> Since they no longer consider us Germans, Czechs, or Poles of the Jewish religion, but rather see [us] as a special class of the population, separate from our Christian fellow citizens, we are obligated to be in truth what we were falsely designated: an independent political group. As such, we actually have the possibility of making ourselves noticed and creating a powerful, energetic representation in the new parliament.[33]

Consequently, Fleischer recommended that in certain districts of Vienna, and in Galicia and Bukovina, the Jewish majorities return Jewish deputies, men who would not be ashamed to be Jews, "*com-*

plete Jews who are always ready bravely and automatically to enter the fray for the equal rights of our coreligionists and fellow Jews *[Glaubens- und Volksgenossen]*."[34]

In February 1907, with Fleischer's faction still dominant, the OIU-sponsored "Central Electoral Committee for the Protection of Jewish Interests in the Parliamentary Elections" supported liberal candidates who pledged themselves to represent "specifically Jewish interests," that is, who would counter antisemitic attacks. In the Kai section of the Inner City, the Electoral Committee supported Wilhelm Anninger, a one-time OIU president and founder of its *Rechtsschutzbureau*. Anninger, the Committee felt, would best represent the businessmen and Jews of the district. He was a self-made man as well as a "*Jew* with every fiber of his heart," a Jew "ready to fight." [35] The *Union* had a harder time deciding who to support in the Leopoldstadt. It reluctantly supported Josef Bloch because it feared that the four Jewish candidates in the district—Bloch, Ferdinand Klebinder (Old Liberal), Dr. Julius Ofner (Social Political), and Dr. Isidor Schalit (Zionist)—would split the Jewish vote and give the mandate to a Christian Social.[36]

Bloch eagerly advocated his own candidacy in the pages of his newspaper. A man of great conceit, he presented himself as someone with a great deal of parliamentary savvy and as the best "Jewish" candidate. He declared himself a fierce and proven fighter for Jewish rights, and reminded his readers how he alone had defended Jewish honor in parliament in the 1880s and 1890s. His notion of what it meant to be a "Jewish" candidate differed markedly from that of the Zionists and Jewish nationalists. While they talked in terms of the recognition of the Jewish nation in Austria, he pronounced his opposition to the centrifugal forces of nationalism which were tearing his beloved Austria asunder. Although he stated that the Jews were not Germans or Poles, neither did he see them as members of a separate nation. He saw no conflict between his vision of a supra-national Austria and the self-conscious assertion of Jewishness. He presented himself as the only one who could truly represent the interests of a Leopoldstadt constituency.[37]

In April 1907, it became clear that Bloch had to withdraw his candidacy because the Social Democrats would never support him in the event of a run-off election. As an alternative candidate the OIU's Central Electoral Committee chose Dr. Gustav Kohn, a vice-president of the *Gemeinde*. Bloch, his newspaper, and his supporters praised Kohn as a tireless worker for Jewish causes. Much less feisty than Bloch, Kohn promised to take a strong position against anti-semitism and to invigorate Jewish life.[38] At the same time, Anninger withdrew from the race in the Inner City, and for election from that district the OIU supported Kamillo Kuranda, the son of Ignaz Kuranda, an Austrian Liberal politician and former president of the IKG.

The candidates of Fleischer's faction received the warm support of the editors of *Die Wahrheit* (Truth), which, after the demise of *Die Neuzeit,* more or less expressed the opinion of the *Gemeinde* Board. Believing that "there are no special Jewish interests," and that the best Jewish defense was a sound legal system, *Die Wahrheit* nevertheless wanted to see parliamentary deputies defend the Jews. It urged its readers to vote for candidates who would represent Jewish interests, that is, for Kamillo Kuranda in the Inner City and Gustav Kohn in the Leopoldstadt.[40] It recommended the election of the Jew, Kohn, not the "un-Jew," Ofner, arguing that

> the Jewish voters of the . . . Leopoldstadt, who are not indifferent to the future of their children, their adherence to religion and stock *[Stamm],* who feel called to protect the honor of the Vienna *Kultusgemeinde* from hateful reproaches, and who are concerned with the welfare of all Viennese Jewry, must not be fooled by the un-Jewish phrases of Dr. Ofner and his followers, but must give their votes on May 14 to an independent and Jewish-minded man, Dr. Gustav Kohn, to guard their Jewish point of view, and to look after their general interests as citizens.[41]

Worrying that a split Jewish vote would give the mandate to a Social Democrat or a Christian Social, *Die Wahrheit* hoped that Ofner would withdraw from the race.[42]

In early May 1907, Sigmund Mayer and his circle wrested control of the *Union* from those who wanted to elect "Jewish" representatives to the *Reichsrat.* They convinced—or manipulated—the OIU to support liberal or progressive candidates who were not particularly concerned with Jewish affairs. Although they recognized the dangers to Austrian Jewry of universal manhood suffrage, this old guard remained loyal to the notion that only liberal candidates could or should defend Jewish rights in Austria. A man in his seventies, who had reached maturity in the heyday of the Jewish-Liberal partnership and who could not accept the realities of Austrian political life dominated by antisemitism and exclusivistic nationalism, Mayer argued in a classic statement of Jewish faith in Liberalism and Austria:

> We are not only Jews, we are above all very good citizens. Yes, I would like to believe that especially we Jews in Austria are above all the best Austrians. While the nationalists, Slavs, or Germans only want a national [Austria], the clericalists, only a clerical [Austria], the feudalists, only a feudal [Austria], the Socialists a Socialist Austria, we Jews want an Austria *sans phrase.*[43]

Under Mayer's guidance, the OIU transferred its allegiance to one of the Liberal candidates, Dr. Julius Ofner, a man of Jewish origins running as a Social Political in the Leopoldstadt. In contradistinction to Fleischer's arguments, Mayer boldly asserted that Ofner was the best protector of the Jews precisely because "he was not a specifically Jewish representative." [44]

Furious with the change in *Union* policy, Bloch charged in his newspaper that support for Ofner had been engineered by a group of die-hard assimilationists who railroaded the motion through at a meeting in which few of those present were genuine OIU members. The "coterie" had brought in two hundred false members to tip the vote in its favor. Support for Ofner, Bloch announced, was a denial of all that the OIU stood for.[45] *Die Wahrheit* agreed with Bloch's allegations of shady deals. Asserting that *Union* president Maximilian Paul-Schiff did not want to back Gustav Kohn because they disagreed on some petty IKG issue, *Die Wahrheit* expressed its conviction that a small coterie of non-Jewish Jews had illegally forced their views on the whole organization.[46]

The *Union*, of course, denied any misconduct. In the aftermath of the election, in which both Kuranda and Ofner won mandates, the OIU tried to justify its support for Ofner in the face of the accusations against it. It also asserted defiantly that Ofner was the "spirit of our spirit." [47] Whether the charges were true or not cannot be determined. Perhaps the OIU simply behaved realistically in backing a professional politician and not just a Jew who chose to run for parliament. Even Bloch admitted that Ofner's politics were not radically different from Kohn's.[48] In any case, those who had tried to steer the *Union* to somewhat separatist Jewish politics had not been successful.

For his part, ever the proud Jew, Bloch welcomed the Jewish Club elected in 1907 to parliament. Ignoring its Jewish national program, which he opposed, he was pleased that self-conscious Jews could now defend Jewish honor in the *Reichsrat*. On June 21, 1907 he wrote:

> The Jews have done what has been so often desired in these pages, they now have representatives of Jewry without other considerations, without other thoughts, without other goals. They are justly proud of these representatives.

Bloch praised Straucher, Mahler, Gabel, and Stand for their modern progressive politics, for their Jewish consciousness, and for their courage. He wished them luck and hoped that all Jews would abandon foolish assimilationism.[49]

Gemeinde Elections

More important than the 1907 electoral campaign in the reformulation of Jewish identity in Vienna was the acrimonious battle between the Zionists and Jewish nationalists on the one hand and the Jewish establishment on the other for control of the Jewish community. In this battle the factions crystallized their opposing definitions of the meaning of Jewishness and the limits of assimilation in the Habsburg capital. Although the Zionists were unsuccessful in winning a majority on the *Gemeinde* Board until 1932, their polemics precipitated a rethinking of the meaning of Jewishness and forced the Jewish establishment to a stronger assertion of Jewish identity.

In order to raise Jewish consciousness and become the leaders of world Jewry, the international Zionist movement vowed in 1898 to "conquer" the organized Jewish communities of Europe.[50] In Vienna, the birthplace of modern political Zionism, Zionists immediately began their bid for control of the IKG. In every subsequent *Gemeinde* election, held biennially to replace one-third of the Board, the Viennese Zionists, sometimes allied with the Jewish nationalists and other dissatisfied elements, waged a tireless campaign to elect themselves to the Board.

Zionist polemics from 1898 to 1912[51] reiterated three basic themes. In the first place, the Zionists charged that the leaders of the IKG were "assimilationists," who, through their slavish aping of European culture, were forgetting their own people and were guilty of treason. The leadership of such men could only lead to the destruction of the Jewish people. In 1900, for example, Zionists accused the Board of being a "sad caricature of a Jewish council." As a child of Liberalism and assimilationism, "it wanted to have nothing to do with Judaism." [52] Likewise, after their defeat in 1908, Zionists described the *Gemeinde* leaders as "stockbrokers, bank directors, factory owners, large merchants [who] flock to the 'urn,' a parade-like deployment of elements who have been estranged from Judaism . . . for a long time." [53] After every defeat, the Zionists interpreted the votes they did receive as a protest against "the old system of assimilation." [54]

As part of their charge that Board members were indifferent to Jewish concerns, the Zionists eagerly pointed out that many of the children of *Gemeinde* leaders had converted to Christianity. In 1904 Oskar Marmorek, an architect and Zionist leader until his 1909 suicide, charged that almost "the entire coming generation . . . is before or already on the other side of the baptismal font." [55] Zionists repeatedly emphasized the connection between asimilationism and the abandonment of the Jewish people. In the 1906 campaign, the *National-Zeitung* editorialized that

> the old, old-Liberal, fanatically assimilatory clique [will] no longer order other men. One part has died off, another has been baptized, and the rest [are] too compromised to be taken seriously.[56]

The second theme of Zionist polemics against the *Gemeinde* was that the IKG was a thoroughly undemocratic and plutocratic institution. Zionist spokesmen decried the rules which stipulated that only taxpayers could vote in *Gemeinde* elections, rules which excluded two-thirds of Viennese Jewry from the decision-making process. In particular, they railed against the two-class voting system which gave unfair advantage to the rich. According to this system, introduced by the IKG in 1900 presumably to prevent a Zionist takeover,[57] all 12,000 eligible IKG voters elected twenty-four members to the Board, while those men who paid over 200 Kronen a year elected an additional twelve Board members. In 1908 Egon Zweig denounced the *Gemeinde* oligarchy with particular vehemence. In a speech entitled "Electoral Theft on the Seitenstettengasse" (the street in the Inner City on which *Gemeinde* offices were located), he attacked the stringent residency requirement, the disenfranchisement of women, and the special curia for the wealthy.[58] When the Zionists lost, the *Jüdische Zeitung* charged the IKG leaders with "franchise theft" and blamed the plutocratic voting structure for the assimilationist victory.[59]

Undoubtedly believing that universal suffrage in Jewish communal elections would lead to their own automatic victory, the Zionists promised if elected to introduce democracy to the Seitenstettengasse.[60] In all their electoral propaganda, the Zionists demanded universal, equal, and direct voting rights for Viennese Jewish men in IKG elections. They also called for total revamping of the IKG tax-assessment system, and a lowering of the minimum tax from 20 to either 10 or 5 Kronen. Finally, in an attempt to attract more voters, they called for public Board meetings, pensions and insurance for *Gemeinde* employees, and reorganization of the charity administration.[61] In 1902, for example, the Zionists, along with the Jewish nationalists and United Oppositional Temples, urged

> whoever is for setting aside the class system, for equal rights for all IKG taxpayers, against the impoverishment and downfall of the Jewish middle class, for modern . . . welfare, . . . for a good Jewish education for our youth, for the raising of Jewish consciousness, for a virile goal-oriented Jewish popular representation

to vote for their candidate list on November 23.[62]

Finally, the Zionists argued that if they were elected they would create a Jewish community which was truly Jewish. They pledged to establish a vibrant "Jewish People's Community" *(Jüdische Volksgemeinde)* to replace the emasculated "Israelite" religious community. They wanted a *Gemeinde* which would assert Jewish national identity and thus serve all Jewish needs, not just the religious needs of a narrow, taxpaying elite.[63] Although the Zionists admitted that a Jewish state was their ultimate goal, as self-appointed representatives of the Jewish national spirit and the Jewish future they were determined to promote Jewish national consciousness among Viennese Jewry. They pledged that under their leadership the Jewish community would encourge the "economic, physical, and spiritual" uplifting of the Jewish people through more spirited Jewish religious instruction, the construction of Jewish *Volkshäuser*, libraries, and settlement houses, and economic efforts to alleviate the antisemitic boycott.[64] The Jewish nationalist Saul Raphael Landau, who did not support the Zionist candidates for personal reasons, echoed the need to replace the "German-Liberal-assimilatory" Israelite community with a truly Jewish *Gemeinde*.[65]

At the same time that they attacked *Gemeinde* leaders, the Zionists offered Viennese Jewish voters a chance to elect Zionists to the IKG Board. In 1898 the Zionists had insufficient time to prepare a candidate list, but in every subsequent biennial election the Zionists, sometimes allied (as in 1900–1904) with the Jewish nationalists and the "Oppositional" Temple Societies (Orthodox or perhaps Galician), did urge *Gemeinde* members to vote for their lists of candidates. World Zionist leaders Isidor Schalit, Adolf Böhm, Eisig Torczyner, Oskar Marmorek, and Egon Zweig regularly appeared on the lists of Zionist candidates. In the years 1900, 1902, and 1904, prominent non-Zionist nationalists like Richard Rappaport, and a few less objectionable members of the IKG establishment itself, also appeared on the Zionist lists.[66]

The Zionists never received a mandate from the IKG electorate before World War I. Their candidate lists could not attract sufficient votes to take over the *Gemeinde* Board.[67] Nevertheless, the Zionists were by no means unsuccessful in their attempt to attract middle-class Viennese Jews to their antiassimilationist Jewish national views. In 1900 Isidor Gewitch, president of the Leopoldstadt-Praterstrasse chapter of *Zion*, was elected to the IKG Board as a two-year replacement member.[68] In 1906 two Zionist candidates, Isidor Schalit and Adolf Brecher, received enough votes to force a run-off election, which they subsequently lost.[69] In addition, to the dismay of the Zionist leaders, Oskar Marmorek managed to insinuate himself onto the official list in 1904.[70] In 1912 nervous *Gemeinde* leaders co-opted two Zionists, Robert Stricker and Dr. Jakob Ehrlich, onto the official list, and hence onto the *Gemeinde* Board.[71]

More significant than these relatively insignificant victories was the extent to which Zionism appealed to those Viennese Jews comfortable enough to pay the 20 Kronen minimum annual tax to the *Gemeinde.* Although voter turnout for *Gemeinde* elections was notoriously low (about 4,000 of the 12,000 eligible voters voted), the Zionist lists received between 25% and 45% of the total votes cast in every election. In 1902, for example, 27% of the 4,735 votes cast went to the Zionist-Jewish national candidates. In 1906 they received 42% of the vote, but two years later, in 1908, only 22%. In 1910 they rallied and received 34% of the vote.[72]

The Zionists found their strength not in the older areas of Jewish settlement in the Inner City or the Leopoldstadt, where wealthy Jewish businessmen scorned Zionism and the poor were not qualified to vote, but in the new areas of Jewish concentration, in neighborhoods which served as home for the new breed of Viennese Jew. Most noticeably, they often won decisive majorities and at the very least 40% of the vote in Mariahilf-Neubau (Districts VI–VII), the districts which also had the largest number of shekel-payers and the strongest chapter of *Zion.* Secondarily, the Zionists received many votes in the Alsergrund (District IX). The Zionist candidates won most of their votes in these two areas. While in 1902 only 30% of the voters in these districts voted Jewish national/Zionist,[73] by 1906 between 50 and 60% of the voters in Mariahilf-Neubau as well as Alsergrund (IX) and Währing (XVIII) voted for the Zionists. In that year the Zionists won 42% of the overall vote, but an absolute majority of 65% in Mariahilf-Neubau, 52% in Währing and Döbling (XIX), and about 45% in Alsergrund, Landstrasse (III), and the Leopoldstadt.[74] On the other hand, they received very few votes in the Inner City. In the prewar period, the Zionists never surpassed their 1906 peak. In 1908 they received an absolute majority in no district, winning only 11% of the vote in the Inner City, 42% of the votes in Mariahilf-Neubau, and 25% of the votes in the Alsergrund. In 1910 they managed to win half of the votes in Mariahilf-Neubau, 43% in Alsergrund, and 41% in Währing and Döbling.[75]

Gemeinde leaders and their supporters were startled by the ferocity of the Zionist denunciation and the extent to which the Zionists were able to muster support within the community. Prior to the Zionist attempt to "conquer" the *Gemeinde,* support for the IKG leadership was more or less universal, at least among the qualified voters, few of whom even bothered to vote.[76] While individual men or particular policies aroused opposition, this was loyal opposition, supportive of the IKG system as a whole. Bloch, for example, opposed Emanuel Baumgarten of the IKG Board and lobbied vigorously against him in his paper in 1889. But Bloch filled his newspaper with praise for other members of the IKG Board, men like Dr. Gustav Kohn, Heinrich Klinger, and Alfred Stern. Bloch asserted that there was "total harmony and reciprocal confidence between the voters and the members of the Board." [77]

Faced with heated Zionist agitation after 1898, the supporters of the IKG responded to all the charges leveled against them with denunciation of the Zionists for behaving in as rowdy and despicable a manner as the Viennese antisemites. In 1900 the Central Electoral Committee, composed of the OIU, the *Politischer Volksverein,* and the United Temple Societies, accused the Zionists of manipulating the "little man" in much the same way as the demagogic antisemitic mass parties did: through promising services to the poor, sending electoral propaganda in the mail, in short, for behaving like a modern political party. They speculated that the Zionists even made more promises to ordinary people than did Dr. Lueger, the leader of the Christian Social Party.[78]

In the following years, the established leaders repeatedly equated Zionist tactics with antisemitic tactics. In 1902 the *Oesterreich-Israelitische Union* branded Zionist charges of corruption on the Seitenstettengasse as childish and a shameless washing of dirty laundry in public.[79] The *Oesterreichische Wochenschrift* editorialized:

> It would seem as if the administration of the Viennese Israelite Religious Community were delivered into the unclean hands of mercenary bands of booty hunters and profit mongers. Men who have become grey in honorable, devoted work, sacrificing for the Jewish people, whose character inspires reverence, whose name enjoys honor even among opponents, were suddenly before the whole world, accused of corruption and venality. In unbelievable competition with antisemitic models, they [the Zionists] have made the methods of political battle their own.[80]

In 1908 the supporters of the IKG charged that the Zionist use of insults and other "antisemitic" tactics would only play into the hands of the antisemites themselves. They feared that antisemitic orators would gleefully repeat the insults leveled by the Zionists at the Jewish establishment. In the aftermath of the election, the *Oesterreichische Wochenschrift* repeated its annoyance with the "Christian-Social battle methods" of the Zionist opposition.[81]

Furthermore, fearing loss of power, the supporters of the *Gemeinde* defended oligarchic control of the IKG. They couched their arguments in conservative economic terms. Even before the Zionist challenge, *Die Neuzeit* had defended control over IKG affairs by the wealthiest men in the community. In a classic conservative argument, *Die Neuzeit* noted that only the wealthy had sufficient spare time to run communal institutions and that only they could be trusted to remain above party politics or infighting, set a good tone, and truly represent the Jews.[82] While in 1898 the OIU had argued that Board members should not come solely from Vienna's richest families,[83] during the height of the electoral battle in 1902 *Die Neuzeit* continued to defend plutocratic control. Although critical of the new rules which enabled the wealthiest men in the community to elect twelve extra Board members—rules which were introduced in that year as a hedge against a possible Zionist takeover of the *Gemeinde*—*Die Neuzeit* nevertheless consoled its readers by observing that Vienna's richest Jews were tireless workers who could afford dispassionately to administer Jewish communal affairs.[84]

Arguing against the Zionist call for democracy at the IKG, the defenders of the system argued that universal suffrage in IKG elections would be unnecessary, absurd, untraditional, and wrong. They flatly asserted that there was no place for democracy in Jewish communal politics. In 1906, for example, one writer for the monthly journal of the OIU noted that universal suffrage for parliament made sense because everyone paid at least indirect taxes to the government. Since poor Jews paid no indirect taxes to the *Gemeinde* they had no legitimate right to vote.[85] Tactless as he was, Bloch stated what must have been in the minds of other supporters of the IKG as well: there was no precedent for democracy in the Jewish community.[86]

IKG supporters opposed universal suffrage in part because they assumed it would only lead to the economic decline of the *Gemeinde*.[87] A Board elected by all Viennese Jews, including the poor, would presumably go on a wanton spending spree. Even earlier, in 1893, when Sigmund Fleischer of the OIU urged lower *Gemeinde* taxes and universal suffrage in *Gemeinde* elections, Bloch vehemently opposed such democracy at the *Gemeinde*. He feared that universal suffrage would only result in an unprecedented drain on *Gemeinde* financial resources.[88]

The IKG notables were unwilling to democratize the *Gemeinde*, but in order to ensure their role as the rightful leaders of the Jewish community they were not above borrowing many other specific planks of the Zionist reform program. The Central Electoral Committee regularly advocated improved Jewish social welfare and religious instruction and lower minimum taxes. In 1904 the Committee called for lowering the minimum tax to 10 Kronen, helping those who suffered from the ravages of the antisemitic boycott, and introducing open competition for IKG contracts.[89] In 1908 it urged an overhaul of the IKG Board, new methods of tax assessment, and the improvement of Jewish religious instruction.[90] Some of these reforms had been suggested by the OIU and the *Politischer Volksverein* even before the Zionist challenge. In 1896 Hermann Fialla, the president of the *Politischer Volksverein,* an organization which sought to fight antisemitism and reform the IKG, called for a less oligarchic *Gemeinde,* a more representative Board, lower minimum taxes, and more assertive leadership.[91] In that year the *Oesterreich-Israelitische Union* also called for an enlarged *Gemeinde* Board, lower minimum taxes, and greater concern for Jewish education and Jewish consciousness at the IKG.[92] Neither Fialla's group nor the OIU, however, ever challenged the leadership itself and always backed candidates from the inner circle.[93]

Fearing fantastic Zionist experiments, the members of the Central Electoral Committee depicted themselves as the true reformers. They promoted the adoption of "healthy reform" by "men who are free from any lust to power, who, if they accept a mandate, are motivated by only one wish: to develop further the Viennese *Kultusgemeinde.*"[94] Charging that the Zionists only wanted to destroy, they cast themselves in the role of men interested in slow reform, in the nonrevolutionary improvement of Jewish communal administration. There was, to be sure, a certain disingenuousness about their concern for reform. While elaborating its program, the Central Electoral Committee continued to support candidates who had served on the IKG Board for decades without manifesting any reforming zeal.

The fundamental argument of the supporters of the IKG system was that only they were Jewish enough to serve Viennese Jewish interests. Just as the Zionists attacked the IKG notables for being insufficiently conscious of their Jewish identities, so too did the Viennese Jewish leaders attack the Zionists for their ignorance of Judaism. The two groups differed with respect to their definitions of Jewishness, with the Zionists espousing a national definition and the Viennese Jewish leaders a religious definition, but each group was eager to attack the other for its failure to be sufficiently Jewish. For example, in the 1900 election, the first real squaring-off between the Zionists and the establishment, one writer for the *Oesterreichische Wochenschrift* denounced those who "euphemistically call themselves Zionists" as self-complacent careerists, only concerned with destroying the IKG, not with reconstructing it, and above all, as being unconcerned with religious affairs.[95] In 1910 when the Zionists accused the son of Wilhelm Stiassny, a prominent member of the IKG Board for three decades, with converting in order to further his career in the civil service, a writer for Bloch's newspaper demurely pointed out that Dr. Sigmund Stiassny was a good and loyal Jew who had said *Kaddish* (the memorial prayer for the dead) for his father, while the Zionist candidates knew Hebrew about as well as they did hieroglyphics.[96] The Central Electoral Committee presented its lists of wealthy men, those who had been on the IKG Board for years, as the best Jews and as the best guardians of Jewish interests.

The Zionists did prod the Viennese Jewish establishment into articulating Jewish pride forthrightly in the final years before World War I. In order to deflate the Zionist campaign against them, Jewish notables called for the proud assertion of Jewish identity and even borrowed Zionist Jewish-consciousness terminology to do so. Their attempts to depict themselves as staunch Jews attest to the success of the Zionists in fomenting stronger assertions of Jewish identity in the entire Jewish community. In 1904 the Central Electoral Committee called for a Jewish (not Israelite) *Gemeinde,* concerned with Jewish values, possessing *jüdisches Solidaritätsgefühl* (feeling of Jewish solidarity). Borrowing the very language of Zionists, the Committee advocated the "valuing and strengthening of the worth of Judaism, the revitalization and reinvigoration of our Jewish consciousness *[Stammesbewusstsein].*" [97] In 1908 their electoral platform sounded like an echo of the Zionist spirit:

> It is the holy duty of the Board, through suitable measures in the field of religion and education, to strengthen the Jewish consciousness of our youth, and to check the disastrous movement of apostasy.[98]

Not content to mount a counteroffensive alone, the Central Electoral Committee also tried to co-opt individual Zionists onto the "official" lists in order to still the Zionist campaign. Only in 1912, in the hope of creating internal peace and unity, did the Central Electoral Committee succeed in bringing two Zionists onto the official lists. At that time they gave Robert Stricker a six-year mandate, and Dr. Jakob Ehrlich a two-year replacement mandate.[99]

In the aftermath of the 1912 election, Dr. Oswald Byk, writing in the *Oesterreichische Wochenschrift,* praised the compromise agreement, and suggested that the responsibility of power would tame the Zionists. Hoping "that the Zionist party contains no Lueger," he prayed that the Zionists would not be agitators, but a responsible internal opposition, catalysts for the discussion of new ideas.[100] Not all observers agreed; some even feared a Zionist-inspired free-for-all on the Seitenstettengasse. But most *Gemeinde* supporters breathed a sigh of relief that the worst of the internal fray had passed and Jews could now work together against the common antisemitic enemy.[101]

Zionists and Jewish nationalists were unsuccessful in their attempts to convince the majority of Viennese Jews that the Zionist definition of Jewishness was correct. Nevertheless, the Zionists succeeded in precipitating a public discussion about the nature of Jewish identity in fin-de-siècle Austria. They prodded the established elite into rethinking the meaning of Jewishness in a hostile world. The Zionist challenge and the antisemitic attacks forced most Jews in Vienna to be more assertively Jewish. In the prewar period, the Jewish nationalist and Zionist perspective appealed only to a third of Viennese Jewry. By the 1930s, the majority of Viennese Jews were Zionists and Zionism was replacing the assimilationist ideology of the nineteenth century. The first steps had been made toward replacing that ideology in the last decade before the First World War.

Conclusion

JEWISH ASSIMILATION in late nineteenth-century Vienna—and presumably in other European cities as well—was a group phenomenon. Jews acculturated into the larger culture and society, adopted the cultural tastes and styles of Austro-German society, but did so in the company of other Jews. They thus gave the whole process of assimilation a Jewish cast. As a result, instead of merging into the larger society, Jews developed new social patterns and new modes of behavior which continued to mark them as Jews to themselves and to the outside world. Moreover, since assimilation was a group effort, Jews avoided structural assimilation and consequent ethnic dissolution. By living in the same neighborhoods, going to school together, and befriending and marrying each other, in short, by associating primarily with other Jews, Viennese Jews ensured Jewish group survival in the Habsburg capital. They also created the mechanisms which made it possible for them to defend themselves and justify their continued existence when such justification became necessary.

This process of assimilation was accompanied by high expectations and deep-seated worries. Viennese Jews certainly hoped that they could win gentile social acceptance both as Austrians and as Jews, but they knew that the antisemites, a very important segment of the Viennese and Austrian political spectrum in the decades before World War I, working assiduously to deny them such acceptance. Racial antisemites insisted that Jews were aliens, were incapable of any European identity, were totally unworthy of membership in European society—indeed, were the avowed enemy of that society. Other antisemites would have accepted the Jews on the condition that they cease being Jewish. Viennese Jews did not want to forgo Jewishness just for the sake of total acceptance, but neither did they want to forgo gentile acceptance for the sake of their Jewishness. They dealt with this dilemma by justifying continued Jewish existence through traditional integrationist formulas or new Zionist and Jewish nationalist ideologies. Whether keeping a low profile or loudly asserting their national identity, Viennese Jews probably hoped that antisemitism would fade and they would ultimately find acceptance as Austrian Jews.

Austria never did accept them. After the First World War, the Jewish community of Vienna grew to over 200,000.[1] At the same time antisemitism flourished in the First Austrian Republic. Demands to remove the Jews became especially shrill after the rise of Hitler to power in Germany in 1933 and the installation of a right-wing government in Austria in 1934. Austrian antisemites may have been even more vicious toward the Jews in the 1930s than were their counterparts in Germany. After the *Anschluss* (union) of Austria with Nazi Germany in 1938, Viennese Jews scrambled to leave Austria and S.S. Colonel Adolf Eichmann, in charge of "emigration" matters, eagerly assisted them. Those who failed to get visas were deported to the death camps during World War II.[2] Austria became virtually *Judenrein,* but antisemites continued to denounce and attack the nonexistent Jews in postwar Austria.

The success of the Nazis and the end of Austrian Jewry should not obscure the positive achievements of nineteenth-century Viennese Jews. They tried to forge a Jewish and a European identity, and sincerely believed that they could do so. The conditions in Austria may not have been conducive to such an identity, but they had no way of knowing that. Moreover, whether the antisemites accepted them or not, the Jews of late Habsburg Vienna were in fact Austro-Germans who held fast to their sense of belonging to the Jewish people.

Appendix I
Sources and Sampling Techniques

MOST STUDIES of social structure and social mobility in past societies employ the relevant manuscript censuses which provide much more detail about personal, family, and social life than do published, aggregated census returns. Unfortunately, a 1927 fire at the Viennese Palace of Justice destroyed pre-World War I Viennese manuscript censuses, except for 1857. Birth and marriage records, however, proved to be excellent sources for this book. These records were kept by the organized Jewish community, the *Israelitische Kultusgemeinde* (IKG), which served as the official registrar for all Jewish births, deaths, marriages, and conversions in Vienna from 1794–1938. Although the death records contained no particularly interesting information, the marriage records listed such important information as place of birth, profession, and residence of both bride and groom, and often that of their fathers as well. The birth records contained similar information on the parents of newborn children. I developed two cross-sectional data bases from these two sets of records, one of 947 grooms and brides, and the other of 1,387 fathers and mothers, selected by recording every fourth Jewish birth and marriage in Vienna in 1869 or 1870, 1880, 1890, 1900, and 1910.

In order to obtain information on the more affluent taxpaying members of the community, I collected a data base from the tax records of the IKG. The Jewish communal tax-assessment records were organized alphabetically in card files, one card per taxpayer to the IKG, for the whole period between 1855 and 1931. Due to water damage incurred during several moves of the archive during and after World War II, only files Ko-Q are still extant. The sample from the tax records includes 2,609 heads of household, a sample which represents one-third of those IKG taxpayers recorded in the extant files for some period of time between 1855 and 1914. Biased against the Viennese Jewish lower classes, these records provide information on geographical origin (*Heimat*, or place of original legal residence rights), profession and professional change, residence and residential change, transiency and wealth of an important sector of the Jewish community.

Gymnasium registration records provided the source material for the chapter on education and assimilation. Still located in the offices of each *Gymnasium*, these records noted each student's religion, place of birth, father's profession, address, and whether the student received financial aid. I developed a data base of 1,857 Jewish students, representing all Jewish students in three Viennese *Gymnasien* and one *Mädchen-Lyzeum* (secondary school for girls) in 1890/91 and 1910/11. The three *Gymnasien* chosen for close analysis were those which had substantial Jewish student bodies and whose records were still extant and readily available: the *Franz-Joseph-Gymnasium* in the Inner City, the *Erzherzog-Rainer-Gymnasium* in the Leopoldstadt (II), and the *Maximilian-Gymnasium* in the Alsergrund (IX). In order to obtain similar information on girls in secondary schools, I used the 1890/91 and 1910/11 records of the *Mädchen-Lyzeum Eugenie Schwarzwald* (I), which now that the *Gymnasien* are coeducational, are located at the Viennese Board of Education. In the total sample, 15.1% (281) attended the school in District I, 42.9% (796) the school in District II, 29.7% (551) the school in District IX, and 12.3% (229) the *Mädchen-Lyzeum.* Despite rising enrollment between 1890 and 1910, the distribution in the four schools remained the same.

Analysis of Jewish conversion to Christianity is based on a study of two sample populations of Jewish converts to Christianity, one collected from the conversion records kept by the *Israelitische Kultusgemeinde,* and the other from the baptismal records of nine selected Catholic parishes in Vienna. Since converts had to notify their mother "church," their new church, and the city authorities, the organized Jewish community had excellent records of converts, which included age, place of birth, marital status, profession, and home address of all Jews leaving Judaism. Unfortunately, these records were extant only after 1890. Recording data on every other Jew who left Judaism in 1890, 1900, and 1910, I created a sample of 721 converts. In order to augment these records with material from the decades before 1890, I consulted Catholic parish baptismal records which recorded similar information as well as the profession of the convert's father. I collected data on all Jews (N = 316) who received baptism in parishes in the Inner City, the Leopoldstadt, and the Alsergrund, the areas of greatest Jewish population density in Vienna, in 1870, 1880, 1890, 1900, and 1910. In the Inner City I used the baptismal records of *St. Stephan,* the main Cathedral of Vienna, *St. Michael bei den P.P. Barnabiten, Zu unserer lieben Frau bei den Schotten,* and *St. Peter.* In the Leopoldstadt I consulted the records of *St. Leopold, St. Johann von Nepomuk,* and *St. Josef bei den P.P. Karmelitern.* In the Alsergrund, I used the records of the *Votivkirche* and *Maria-Verkündigung bei den P.P. Serviten in der Rossau (Rossau-Kirche).* The *Schotten-Kirche* was the most popular place for the Jews who sought baptism. Duplicate names for 1890–1910 were removed to form a total sample of 1,037 converts. Unfortunately, I could not augment the sample with information on converts to the Evangelical (Lutheran or Reformed) Church because of a combination of administrative confusions and archivists' vacations. This omission is not serious because most such conversions occurred after 1890 and were therefore reported in the IKG records.

Appendix II
Jewish Organizations in Vienna

Humanitarian Organizations

Achwah: "Jüdische Brüder" zur Ausspeisung unbemittelter Juden
Aktionscomité zur Unterstützung hilfsbedürftiger Hausierer in Wien
Allgemeiner Krankenunterstützungsverein: "Montefiore"
Allgemeiner Studentenunterstützungsverein in Wien
Allgemeiner Unterstützungsverein "Menschenliebe"
Allgemeines oesterreichisch-israelitisches Taubstummen-Institut
Armenanstalt der israelitischen Cultusgemeinde in Wien
Baron Hirsch Stiftung
Bildungs- und Unterstützungsverein: "Ansche Dath wu Zedek"
B'nai B'rith "Wien"
Chewra Kadischa: Verein für fromme und wohltätige Werke
Die Brüder: Verein zur Bekleidung armer Schulkinder (XX)
Einheit
Eintracht (B'nai B'rith)
Erster oesterreichischer Hilfsverein für kranke zugereiste Juden in Wien
Erster oesterreichischer Rechtsschutzverein für Hausierer in Wien
Erster Wiener isr. humanitärer Heirats-Ausstattungs-Verein "Hachnasath Kalah"
Erster Wiener israelitischer Reconvalescentenheim für arme jüdische Frauen und Kinder
Erster Wiener Lehrmädchenhort
Fides (to clothe children)
Geselligkeitsverein Dananna
Geselligkeitsverein "Flott Wien"
Hilfsverein für die notleidende jüdische Bevölkerung in Galizien
Humanitärer Geselligkeitsverein "Benei Zion"
Humanitärer Geselligkeitsverein "Rudolfsbund"
Humanitärer Geselligkeitsverein "Societas"
Humanitärer Geselligkeitsverein "Treubund" (zur Bekleidung armer Kinder)
Humanitärer Verein "Bikur Cholim"
Humanitärer Verein "Greisenschutz"
Humanitärer Verein "Kinderschutz" zur Erhaltung einer Ferienkolonie

Humanitärer Verein "Marpe Lanefesche" (Seelenheil)
Humanitärer Verein Thorath-Chesed zur Unterstützung armer Talmudschüler
Humanitärer Verein "Tiferes Bachurim"
Humanitärer Verein "Tischgesellschaft"
Humanitärer Verein zur Unterstützung jüdischer Kurbedürftigen
Israelitische Allianz zu Wien
Israelitischer Hilfsverein "Maskil el Dal"
Israelitischer Humanitätsverein für die westlichen Bezirke Wien "Nachlos Jeschurun"
Israelitischer Humanitätsverein zur Ausstattung heiratsfähiger Mädchen
Israelitischer Humanitätsverein in dem X. Bezirke
Israelitischer Jünglingsverein "Tiferes Bachurim"
Israelitische Kinderbewahranstalt
Israelitischer Kindergarten in Wien
Israelitischer Wohltätigkeits- und Krankenunterstützungsverein: "Mazmiach Jeschua"
Israelitischer Wohltätigkeitsverein für den III. Bezirk
Jüdischer Bildungs- und Geselligkeitsverein für den XVI. und XVII. Bezirk
Jüdischer Bildungs- und Unterstützungsverein "Schomrei Hadath"
Jüdischer Bildungsverein "Raschi"
Jüdischer Jugendbund (B'nai B'rith)
Jüdischer Mittelschulverein
Jüdischer Schulverein für den IX. Bezirk
Jüdischer Schulverein im X. Wiener Gemeindebezirk
Kaiser Franz Josef Ferienheim
Kaufmännischer Unterstützungsverein "Osten"
Kinderheim
Kreditinstitut für jüdische Gewerbetreibende und Beamte
Krankenunterstützungsverein "Ansche Emmes"
Krankenunterstützungsverein "Chesed Shel Emes"
Krankenunterstützungsverein "Gomle Chesed"
Krankenunterstützungsverein "Lewias Chen"
Krankenunterstützungsverein "Oseh Chesed"
Krankenunterstützungsverein "Tomech Lechaloim"
Krankenunterstützungsverein "Selbsthilf"
Krankenunterstützungs- und Leichenverein "Chewra Bikur Cholim"
Kranken-, Witwen- und Waisenunterstützungsverein "Chesed Shel Emes"
Landstrasse Freunde
Leopoldstädter Kinderschutz
Leopoldstädter Krankenunterstützungsverein "Nächstenliebe"
Liga zur Bekämpfung des Mädchenhandels
Mädchenunterstützungsverein
Mädchen-Waisenhaus
Stefaniebund
Talmud Thorah Verein
Theodor Schwarz Tischgesellschaft
Theresien-Kreuzer Verein zur Unterstützung armer israelitischer Schulkinder
Unterstützungsverein Brigittenau

Unterstützungsverein Collegialität
Unterstützungsverein jüdischer Hochschüler aus Galizien in Wien
Unterstützungsverein "Pikuach Nefesch Maskil el Dal"
Unterstützungsverein "Tomech Ewionim" für arme jüdische Zugereiste
Verein "Achwah" (rituelle Volksspeisehalle)
Verein "Chonen Dalim"
Verein "Esrath Israel"
Verein für das israelitisches Blinden-Institut
Verein für israelitische Feriencolonien "Gomlei Chesed"
Verein für unentgeltlichen Arbeitsnachweis
Verein für unentgeltliche Arbeitsvermittlung an jüdische Hochschüler
Verein jüdische Toynbee-Halle
Verein Kinderfreunde von Ottakring und Hernals
Verein oesterreichisches Seehospiz
Verein zur Ausspeisung armer israelitischer Schulkinder für den XII., XIII., XIV., XV. Bezirk
Verein zur Ausspeisung armer israelitischer Schulkinder für den XVI. und XVII. Bezirk
Verein zur Beförderung der Handwerke unter den inländischen Israeliten
Verein zur Bekleidung armer alter Männer (israelitischer Confession)
Verein zur Erhaltung einer isr. Kinderbewahr-Anstalt
Verein zur Errichtung von Volksküchen nach israelitischem Ritus
Verein zur Errichtung jüdischer Jugend- und Volksbibliotheken
Verein zur Hebung der Gewerbe in Wien und dessen Vororte
Verein zur Gründung und Erhaltung von Heimstätten für verkrüppelte, schwache, und reconvalescente Kinder jüdischer Confession
Verein zur Rettung verlassener jüdischer Kinder
Verein zur unentgeltlichen Verpflegung Brustleidender auf dem Lande
Verein zur Unterstützung armer kranker Israeliten
Verein zur Unterstützung armer Mediziner
Verein zur Unterstützung israelitischer Handwerker und Kleingewerbetreibender
Verein zur Unterstützung mitteloser israelitischer Studierender in Wien
Verein zur Versorgung hilfsbedürftinger Waisen der israelitischen Kultusgemeinde
Volksküchenverein nach jüdischem Ritus in der Brigittenau
Witwen und Waisenfond: Verein Montefiore
Wohltätigkeitsverein: Frauenhort
Zentralstelle für das jüdische Armenwesen
Zentralstelle für jüdische Wanderarmenvorsorge in Oesterreich
Zwanglos (to clothe children)
II. Leopoldstädter Volksküche (nach israelitischem Ritus)

Women's Humanitarian Organizations

Brigittenauer Israelitischer Frauenwohltätigkeitsverein
Floridsdorfer Israelitischer Frauenwohltätigkeitsverein

Frauenhort
Hietzinger Israelitischer Frauenwohltätigkeitsverein
Israelitischer Frauenwohltätigkeitsverein
Israelitischer Frauenwohltätigkeitsverein für Hausarme
Israelitischer Frauenwohltätigkeitsverein in VI und VII
Israelitischer Frauenwohltätigkeitsverein in der Josefstadt (VIII)
Israelitischer Frauenwohltätigkeitsverein für den XVI. und XVII. Bezirk
Israelitischer Frauenwohltätigkeitsverein in Wieden und Margarethen
Israelitischer Frauenwohltätigkeitsverein in XVIII
Israelitischer Frauenwohltätigkeitsverein in Döbling
Israelitischer Frauenwohltätigkeitsverein in Alsergrund
Israelitischer Frauenwohltätigkeitsverein "Providenzia"
Jüdischer Frauenwohltätigkeitsverein "Zuflucht"
Leopoldstädter Israelitischer Frauenwohltätigkeitsverein
Mädchenunterstützungsverein
Mariahilf Israelitischer Frauenwohltätigkeitsverein
(Polnischer) Israelitischer Frauenwohltätigkeitsverein für Hausarme in Wien
Schutzdamencomité für das Israelitische Mädchen-Waisenhaus

Miscellaneous Nonpolitical Organizations

Allgemeines Oesterreich-israelitisches Bund
Bureau für jüdische Statistik in Oesterreich
Cantoren Bildungs-Anstalt
Commandit-Gesellschaft Karmel
Gesellschaft für Sammlung und Conservierung von Kunst und historischen Denkmälern des Judenthums
Israelitischer Literaturverein Mendelssohn
Jüdisches Bildungsheim
Jüdisches Museum
Komité zur Pflege und Förderung der modernen jüdischen Literatur
Verband der östlichen Juden in Wien
Verband der Religionslehrer an den osterr. Mittelschulen
Verein für jüdische Geschichte und Literatur
Verein Hasomir: Verein zur Pflege ostjüdischer Kunst und Literatur
Verein Jehuda Halevy
Verein jüdisches Studentenheim
Verein zur Unterstützung der Colonisation Palästinas
Versammlung jüdischer Architekten

Landsmannschaften

Geselligkeitsverein Ung. Broder
Humanitärer Geselligkeits-Verein der Holleschauer
Humanitärer Geselligkeits-Verein der Pohrlitzer in Wien
Humanitäts- und Geselligkeits-Verein der Triescher
Humanitärer Verein der Eisenstädter

Humanitärer Verein der Frauenkirchener
Humanitärer Verein der Gross-Meseritscher in Wien
Humanitärer Verein der Mattersdorfer
Humanitärer Verein der Tarnower in Wien
Humanitäts-Verein der Trebitscher
Humanitärer Unterstützungsverein der Kolomeaer und Umgebung in Wien
Krankenunterstützungs-Verein der Lemberger in Wien
Krankenunterstützungs-Verein der Brodyer in Wien
Die Tarnopoler
Die Szeniczer
Verein der Rzeszower

Synagogue or Religious Organizations

Achdus Israel, Bethaus-Verein in II
Adass Jisroel, Bethaus-Verein in II
Auhel Jacob, Bethaus-Verein in II
Beth Israel: Syn.-Verein nach polnisch-jüdischem Ritus
Bethaus-Verein Freundschaft und Brüderlichkeit
Beth Hamidrasch Ohel Abraham
Beth Hachneseth, Bethaus-Verein in III
Bethaus-Verein in II
Bene Brith, Bethaus-Verein in XX
Brigittenauer Bibelschule
Chasidim, Bethaus-Verein in II
Chewra Beth Hatfila, Bethaus-Verein in IX
Edelsinn, Bethaus-Verein in XVI
Israelitischer Bethaus-Verein in II
Israelitischer Bethaus-Verein Am Volkert in II
Israelitischer Bethaus-Verein in III
Israelitischer Bethaus-Verein Emunas Awes
Israelitischer Bethaus-Verein in IX (Bet Hatefilah)
Israelitischer Religionslehrerverein, Esra
Israelitischer Tempel-Verein für Wieden und Margarethen
Israelitischer Tempel- und Schulverein in VI
Israelitischer Tempelverein für die beiden Gemeindebezirke Mariahilf und Neubau
Israelitischer Tempelverein für Josefstadt
Israelitischer Tempelverein für den X. Gemeindebezirk
Israelitischer Tempelverein für den XIX. Bezirk
Israelitischer Tempelverein für den XI. Berzirk
Israelitischer Tempelverein für Voslau
Liwias Chen, Bethausverein in II
Machasike Tora in Wien
Machzike Ha-Dath
Mikdosch M'at Bethausverein in II
Leopoldstädter Bethausverein Montefiore in II

Oesterreichisch-ungarischer Cantoren-Verein
Polnisch-jüdischer Bethausverein "Bichur Chomim" in XX
Schomer Israel: Tempelverein nach poln.-jüd. Ritus in III
Schönlatern Bethaus-Verein in I
Tempelverein in I
Torath-Emet in III
Thora Ez Chaim in II
Verein der Sabbatfreunde: Schomrei Shabbat
Verein Tifilas Neurim in II
Verein zur Wahrung der Interessen des orthodoxen Judenthums

Political Organizations (Nonnationalist)

Israelitisch-politischer Verein: Gleichheit
Israelitischer Wählerverein (XVI und XVII)
Jüdischer Wählerverein
Oesterreich-Israelitische Union
Politischer Volksverein

Zionist Organizations

1) *Political Zionists*

"Zion": Verband der oesterreichischen Vereine für Colonisation Palästinas und Syriens
Einzel Verein "Wien" des Verbandes "Zion"
Innere Stadt "Zion" (I)
Leopoldstadt-Praterstrasse "Zion" (II)
Landstrasse "Zion" (III)
Wieden-Margarethen "Zion" (IV–V)
Mariahilf-Neubau "Zion" (VI–VII)
Josefstadt "Zion" (VIII)
Alsergrund "Zion" (IX)
Favoriten "Zion" (X)
Rudolfsheim-Fünfhaus "Zion" (XIV, XV)
Wien-Döbling "Zion" (XIX)
Erster zionistischer Frauenverein
Wiener zionistischer Frauenverein
Frauenortsgruppe "Zion"
Verein zionistischer Frauen und Mädchen in Fünfhaus
Humanitärer Verein "Bikur Cholim," Erster zionistischer Frauenverein
Verein jüdischer Mädchen, Hadassah
Literarischer Geselligkeitsverein jüdischer Mädchen, Moria
Verein jüdischer junger Damen, Mirjam
Wiener zionistische Vereinigung
Verband jüdischer Frauen für Kulturarbeit in Palästina
Zionistische Centralcomité für West-Oesterreich

Zionistische Distriktscomité für Innen-Oesterreich
Jüdischer Volksverein für die Leopoldstadt

2) Religious Zionists

Misrachi
Misrachi Jugendbund
Verein orthodoxen Zionisten

3) Socialist Zionists

Achwah: Bildungs- und Unterstützungsverein der jüdischen Arbeiter und Privatangestellen
Allgemeiner jüdischer Arbeiterverein
Brigittenau Verein jüdisch-jugendlicher Arbeiter
Jüdisch-nationaler Arbeiterverein
Jüdischer Verein jugendlicher Arbeiter
Klub zionistischer Arbeiter
Poalei Zion
Verein jüdischer Handelsangestellter
Verein Poalei Zion

4) Zionist Sport Clubs

Erster Wiener jüdischer Turnverein
Ha-Koach Sportklub
Jüdischer Turnverein in Döbling
Jüdischer Turnverein in der Leopoldstadt
Jüdischer Turnverein in X
Jüdischer Turnverein in XVII: "Massada"
Maccabi
Turnverein Zion (Fünfhaus)

5) Other Zionist Organizations

Admath Jeschurun (forerunner to "Zion")
Benai Zion
Blau-Weiss
Hebräischer Konversations-Klub
Jüdischer Bürgerverein "ITO" in Wien
Jüdischer Gesangsverein
Los- und Spar-Verein Leopoldstadt-Praterstrasse
Macabäa
Safah Berurah: Hebräischer Sprach- und Sprech-Verein
Verein für Hebräische Sprache und Kultur
Vereinigung jüdischer Handlungsgehilfen und Privatbeamten
Zionistischer Volksverein

Jewish Nationalist Organizations

Allgemeiner jüdischer Arbeiterverein
Bildungs- und Unterstützungsverein der jüdischen Arbeiter und Privatangestellten: Achwah
Jordania: Vereinigung jüdischer Handelsangesteller; Verein von Beamten und Handelsangestellten
Jüdische Kultur
Jüdische National-Partei
Jüdischer Volksverein
Jüdischer Volksverein für die Leopoldstadt
Jüdischer Volksverein für den IX. Bezirk
Jüdischer Volksverein für den XVI. und XVII. Bezirk
Verein Beth Ha'am: Jüdisches Volksheim
Verein israelitischer Fleischselcher und Fleischverkäufer
Verein jüdischer Handelsangestellter
Verein jüdischer jugendlicher Arbeiter in Brigittenau

Zionist and Jewish Nationalist Student Organizations

Akademischer Verein "Gamala"
Akademischer Verein "Jüdische Kultur"
Bar Giora: Vereinigung jüdischer Hochschüler aus den südslavischen Ländern
Bar Kochba: Vereinigung jüdischer Hochschüler aus Galizien
Chejruth: Vereinigung poale-zionistischer Hochschüler
Esperanza
Herzl Klub
Iwria
Jüdisch-Akademische Ferialverbindung Emuna
Jüdischer National-Studentenchor
Jordania
Judäa
Kadimah
Leo Pinsker
Libanonia
Ness Zionah
Russisch-jüdischer wissenschaftlicher Verein Zion
Unitas
Verband der jüdisch-akademischen Verbindungen
Verband der jüdisch-nationalen Finken an der Wiener Hochschulen
Verein Erez-Israel der jüdisch-rumanischen Hochschüler zu Wien
Verein ehemaliger zionistischer Hochschüler
Verein jüdischer Toynbeehalle
Verein zionistischer Hochschüler Theodor Herzl
Verein zionistischer Studenten
Vereinigung zionistischer Hochschüler
Vereinigung absolv. Handels- und Exportakademiker: "Neure Yehuda"

Vereinigung jüdischer Hochschüler zur Pflege der jüdischen Sprache und Kultur, "Hat'chijah"
Zephira

Nonnationalist Student Organizations

Akademischer Verein jüdischer Mediziner
Akademischer Verein jüdischer Frauen
Jüdisch-Akademische Lesehalle
Jüdisch-Akademischer Juristenverein
Jüdisch-Akademischer Philosophenverein
Jüdisch-Akademischer Techniker-Verband
Lese- und Redehalle jüdischer Hochschüler
Theologischer Verein
Unterstützungsverein jüdischer Mediziner
Verein jüdischer Hochschüler: Mensa Academica Judaica
Verein jüdischer Hörer der Hochschule für Bodenkultur
Verein jüdischer Veterinär-Mediziner: Libanonia

Notes

1. Introduction

1. For general works on Viennese culture and its modernist development see Carl E. Schorske, *Fin-de-Siècle Vienna: Politics and Culture* (New York, 1980); William M. Johnston, *The Austrian Mind: An Intellectual and Social History 1848–1938* (Berkeley, Calif., 1972); Allan Janik and Stephen Toulmin, *Wittgenstein's Vienna* (New York, 1973); and William J. McGrath, *Dionysian Art and Populist Politics in Austria* (New Haven, 1974).

2. Carl E. Schorske, "Politics and the Psyche in *fin-de-siècle* Vienna: Schnitzler and Hofmannsthal," *American Historical Review* 66, no. 4 (1961), p. 940.

3. William A. Jenks, *Vienna and the Young Hitler* (New York, 1960), p. 222. Jenks quotes Hitler: "Vienna was and remained for me the hardest, but also the most thorough school of my life."

4. In addition to general works on Viennese culture, see Hans Kohn, *Karl Kraus, Arthur Schnitzler, Otto Weininger: Aus dem jüdischen Wien der Jahrhundertwende* (Tübingen, 1962); Solomon Liptzin, *Germany's Stepchildren* (Philadelphia, 1944); idem, *Richard Beer-Hofmann* (New York, 1936); idem, *Arthur Schnitzler* (New York, 1932); Lucy Dawidowicz, "Arnold Schoenberg: A Search for Jewish Identity," in *The Jewish Presence: Essays on Identity and History* (New York, 1977), pp. 32–45; Frederic V. Grunfeld, *Prophets without Honour: A Background to Freud, Kafka, Einstein and Their World* (New York, 1979); and Josef Fraenkel, ed., *The Jews of Austria: Essays on Their Life, History and Destruction* (London, 1967). For an excellent discussion of the meaning of Jewish participation in German culture generally, see Peter Gay, "Encounter with Modernism," and "The Berlin Jewish Spirit," in his *Freud, Jews and Other Germans: Masters and Victims in Modernist Culture* (Oxford and New York, 1978), pp. 93–168 and 168–88.

5. Jakob Wassermann, *My Life as German and Jew*, trans. S. N. Brainin (New York, 1933), p. 186.

6. Friedrich Heer, "Judentum und 'oesterreichischer Genius,'" in *Land im Strom der Zeit* (Vienna, 1958), p. 295.

7. Kohn, p. 12.

8. In his memoirs, one of the members of *Jung Wien*, Stefan Zweig, argued that Jews filled a gap created by the cultural indifference of aristocrats and petite bourgeoisie; see Stefan Zweig, *The World of Yesterday* (New York,

1943), pp. 20–22. Many scholars have suggested that the fact that Jews were both cosmopolitan and marginal to traditional society enabled them to produce modern art; see, for example, Kohn, p. 4. István Deák, *Weimar Germany's Left-Wing Intellectuals: A Political History of the Weltbühne and Its Circle* (Berkeley, Calif., 1968) makes a similar argument about Jews in Weimar Germany.

9. See, for example, Max Grunwald, *Vienna* (Philadelphia, 1936), p. 417, where Grunwald, a Viennese rabbi, asserts "no where did the Jews become so assimilated as they did in Vienna." See also N. H. Tur-Sinai, "Viennese Jewry," in Fraenkel, p. 315; Hugo Gold, *Geschichte der Juden in Wien: Ein Gedenkbuch* (Tel Aviv, 1966), p. 36. The notion that assimilated Jews were *the* Jews is certainly implicit in such works as Dennis B. Klein, *Jewish Origins of the Psychoanalytic Movement* (New York, 1981), pp. 1–8.

10. Milton Gordon, *Assimilation in American Life: The Role of Race, Religion and National Origins* (New York, 1964), pp. 71, 77.

11. Ibid., pp. 69–70, 80–81.

12. Arthur Ruppin, *The Jews of Today*, trans. Margery Bentwich (New York, 1913), p. 98. Ruppin wrote extensively about Jewish urbanization. See his *Soziologie der Juden* (Berlin, 1930); *The Jewish Fate and Future*, trans. E. W. Dickes (London, 1940); "Die Juden als Stadtbewohner," in Alfred Nossig, ed., *Jüdische Statistik* (Berlin, 1903), pp. 424–29; and articles in *ZDSJ*.

13. Ruppin, *Jews of Today*, pp. 98–99, 174, 185–91, 206.

14. Ruppin, *Jewish Fate and Future*, p. 244.

15. Arthur J. May, *Vienna in the Age of Franz Joseph* (Norman, Oklahoma, 1966); Heinrich Rauchberg, *Die Bevölkerung Oesterreichs auf Grund der Ergebnisse der Volkszählung vom 31. December 1890* (Vienna, 1895), p. 136; idem, "Der Zug nach der Stadt," *Statistische Monatsschrift* (Vienna) 19 (1893), p. 149.

16. Grunwald, *Vienna*, pp. 292–95, 406–9; Wolfgang Häusler, "Toleranz, Emanzipation und Antisemitismus: Das österreichische Judentum des bürgerlichen Zeitalters (1782–1918)," in Anna Drabek et al., *Das österreichische Judentum: Voraussetzungen und Geschichte* (Vienna and Munich, 1974), pp. 97–103; Hans Tietze, *Die Juden Wiens: Geschichte-Wirtschaft-Kultur* (Leipzig and Vienna, 1933), pp. 181–228; Sigmund Mayer, *Die Wiener Juden 1700–1900: Kommerz, Kultur, Politik* (Vienna and Berlin, 1917), pp. 309–35; Theodor Haas, *Die Juden in Mähren: Darstellung der Rechtsgeschichte und Statistik unter besonderer Berücksichtigung des 19. Jahrhunderts* (Brünn, 1908), p. 22; idem, "Statistische Betrachtungen über die jüdische Bevölkerung Mährens in Vergangenheit und Gegenwart," in Hugo Gold, ed., *Die Juden und Judengemeinden Mährens in Vergangenheit und Gegenwart* (Brünn, 1929), p. 594.

17. On Viennese antisemitism, see John Boyer, *Political Radicalism in Late Imperial Vienna: Origins of the Christian Social Movement 1848–1897* (Chicago and London, 1981); Peter G. J. Pulzer, *The Rise of Political Anti-Semitism in Germany and Austria* (New York, 1964); Andrew G. Whiteside, *The Socialism of Fools: Georg Ritter von Schönerer and Austrian Pan-Germanism* (Berkeley, Calif., 1975); Kurt Skalnik, *Dr. Karl Lueger: Der Mann zwischen den Zeiten* (Vienna and Munich, 1954); Paul Molisch, *Geschichte der deutschnationalen Bewegung in Oesterreich von ihren Anfängen bis zum Zerfall der Monarchie*

(Jena, 1926); Carl E. Schorske, "Politics in a New Key: An Austrian Triptych," *Journal of Modern History* 39 (1967), pp. 343–86; Dirk van Arkel, "Antisemitism in Austria" (Ph.D. Dissertation, University of Leiden, 1966).

18. Vicki Baum, *Es war alles ganz anders: Erinnerungen* (Berlin, Frankfurt, and Vienna, 1962), pp. 21, 44. Many memorists mention the Jewishness of their grandparents but give no hint of any Jewish content in their own lives.

19. Arnold Höllriegel (Richard Arnold Bermann), "Die Fahrt auf dem Katarakt (Autobiographie ohne einen Helden)" (unpublished memoir, Leo Baeck Institute, n.d.), p. 25. Unless otherwise indicated, all translations from the German are my own.

20. Gertrude Berliner, "From My Family: Fiction and Truth" (unpublished memoir, Leo Baeck Institute, 1958), p. 5. The importance of gentile maids in introducing Jews to Christian religious practice and gentile customs in general needs study.

21. Toni Cassirer, "Aus meinem Leben mit Ernst Cassirer" (unpublished memoir, Leo Baeck Institute, 1949–50), p. 4.

22. Arthur Schnitzler, *My Youth in Vienna,* trans. Catherine Hutter (New York, 1970), p. 13.

23. Ibid., p. 48.

24. Martin Freud, "Who Was Freud?" in Fraenkel, p. 204; Klein, pp. 45, 59–60; Ernest Jones, *The Life and Work of Sigmund Freud* (Harmondsworth, Eng., 1961), pp. 121, 125, 139, 146; Reuben M. Rainey, "Freud As Student of Religion: Perspectives on the Background and Development of His Thought" (Ph.D. Dissertation, Columbia University, 1971), p. 115; and the works on Freud's Jewishness listed in n. 29.

25. Ernst Waldinger, "Darstellung einer jüdischen Jugend in der Wiener Vorstadt," in Fraenkel, pp. 273–75.

26. Elias Canetti, *The Tongue Set Free: Remembrance of a European Childhood,* trans. Joachim Neugroschel (New York, 1979), p. 86.

27. Zweig, p. 116.

28. Schnitzler, p. 146.

29. Martin Freud, pp. 204, 207; Jones, pp. 287, 422; Rainey, pp. 114–117; Klein even argues that Freud felt uncomfortable with non-Jews in the psychoanalytic circle, p. 93. The scholarship on Freud's Jewishness is extensive. See especially Marthe Robert, *From Oedipus to Moses: Freud's Jewish Identity,* trans. Ralph Manheim (Garden City, N. Y., 1976); David Bakan, *Sigmund Freud and the Jewish Mystical Tradition* (Princeton, N.J., 1958); John Murray Cuddihy, *The Ordeal of Civility: Freud, Marx, Levi-Strauss, and the Jewish Struggle with Modernity* (New York, 1974); Ernst Simon, "Sigmund Freud, the Jew," *LBIYB* 2 (1957), pp. 270–305; and Willy Aron, "Notes on Sigmund Freud's Ancestry and Jewish Contacts," *YIVO Annual for Jewish Social Science* 11 (1956/57), pp. 286–95.

30. As quoted in Robert, p. 35; Rainey, p. 98.

31. Theodor Herzl, *The Jewish State,* trans. Harry Zohn (New York, 1970), p. 80.

32. Schnitzler, pp. 6–7.

33. Ibid., p. 131.

34. Ibid., pp. 131, 13.

35. Zweig, p. 66.

36. Jones, p. 462. Klein also argues (pp. 54–55) that antisemitism in Vienna caused Freud proudly to assert his Jewishness, but that Freud's pride was by no means only defensive.

37. As quoted in Jones, p. 573.

38. Klein, pp. 56–58, 62; Robert, ch. 2; Jones, p. 49; Rainey, pp. 98, 117–20. Klein goes so far as to argue that Freud's Jewish pride laid the foundations for psychoanalysis (p. 62).

39. Jones, pp. 285, 650n. The importance of Freud's connection with B'nai B'rith is detailed in Klein, ch. 3.

40. As quoted in Jones, p. 650.

41. See standard works on Viennese Jewry: Grunwald, Mayer, Tietze, and Häusler; see also Gustav Fall, *Die rechtliche Stellung der Juden in Oesterreich* (Vienna, 1892).

42. Aryeh Tartakower, "Jewish Migratory Movements in Austria in Recent Generations," in Fraenkel, p. 289.

43. The birth, marriage, and death records of the Jews of Vienna from 1784–1938 are housed in the present offices of the *Israelitishe Kultusgemeinde* in Vienna, Wien XIX, Bauernfeldgasse 4. The IKG tax records are part of an extensive archive of the Vienna Jewish community, which, thanks to the clearsightedness of the *Gemeinde* Board, survived World War II. The IKG archive is located at the Central Archives for the History of the Jewish People in Jerusalem. The archive is approximately 450 meters of shelf space, and contains enough material for hundreds of monographs on the Jews of Vienna. The tax records are files AW 805/1–25. The *Gymnasium* registration records are in bound volumes *(Hauptkatalogen)* in the *Gymnasien* themselves. Conversion records were kept by the IKG and exist in bound volumes for the period after 1890 at the IKG office in Vienna. For more details on these sources and information on sampling techniques, see Appendix I.

2. The Creation of Viennese Jewry

1. The process of urbanization in Europe has not been studied adequately. The basic study of nineteenth-century urbanization is probably still Adna F. Weber, *The Growth of Cities in the Nineteenth Century: A Study in Statistics* (1899; reprint, Ithaca, New York, 1963). More recent studies of urban growth in Germany and Austria include Wolfgang Köllmann, "The Process of Urbanization in Germany at the Height of the Industrialization Period," *Journal of Contemporary History* 4 (1969), pp. 59–76; idem, "Zur Bevölkerungsentwicklung ausgewählter deutscher Grossstädte in der Hochindustrialisierungsperiode," *Jahrbuch für Sozialwissenshaft* 18 (1967), pp. 129–44; and William Hubbard, "Der Wachstumsprozess in den oesterreichischen Grossstädten, 1869–1910; eine historisch-demographische Untersuchung," *Kölner Zeitschrift für Soziologie und Sozialpsychologie* 16 (1973), pp. 386–418.

2. For a history of *Heimatrecht* in Austria, see L. Spiegel, "Das Heimatrecht und die Gemeinden," *Schriften des Vereines für Sozialpolitik* 112 (1907), pp.

7–49; *Öst. Stat.*, N.F. 2:1, p. 7; Heinrich Rauchberg, *Die Bevölkerung Oesterreichs auf Grund der Ergebnisse der Volkszählung vom 31. December 1890* (Vienna, 1895), pp. 149–52, 164–70; and Stephan Sedlaczek, *Die k.-k. Reichshaupt und Residenzstadt Wien: Ergebnisse der Volkszählung vom 31. December 1880* (Vienna, 1887), p. 17. Despite liberalization of the *Heimatrecht* laws in 1910 it was still difficult to change *Heimat.*

3. *Öst. Stat.*, N.F. 2:1, p. 7*. In 1910, due to liberalization of the laws of *Heimatrecht*, more people (67%) lived in the communities in which they had legal residence rights.

4. Heinrich Rauchberg, "Die Heimatsverhältnisse der Bevölkerung Oesterreichs nach den Ergebnissen der Volkszählung vom 31. December 1890," *Statistische Monatsschrift* (Vienna) 18 (1892), pp. 351–52; idem, *Bevölkerung*, p. 157; *Öst. Stat.*, 32:2, p. vii.

5. A problem for the Habsburg historian is that almost all towns have more than one name. The Austrian administration bequeathed German names to most places, but the original Czech, Polish, or Magyar names were frequently used. In addition, since World War I, the successor states have either reverted to the non-German place names, or, in an attempt at linguistic unification, have foisted a new name on an old place. As far as possible this book will employ the German names of all towns and cities. This usage was chosen because it was historically accurate for the period under discussion, and because the Jews, the focus of this study, almost always used the German names. English names for Austrian or Hungarian cities were used only for those places most commonly known by their English names: Vienna not Wien, Prague, not Prag or Práha. In addition, in fairness to the Dualist compromise, this book will use both the German and Magyar names for Hungarian cities, towns, and counties.

6. Heinrich Rauchberg, "Der Zug nach der Stadt," *Statistische Monatsschrift* (Vienna) 19 (1893), pp. 125–26.

7. Undertaken for military purposes, all censuses through 1857 enumerated only the *einheimisch* population, that is the people who possessed *Heimatrecht* in a given community. Beginning in 1869 all censuses counted the actual population of all localities. See Rauchberg, *Bevölkerung*, p. 149, and "Die Heimatsverhältnisse," p. 345. The first really accurate census was that of 1890. Adna Weber, who greatly admired this census, called it a "combination of American ingenuity in the way of electrical tabulating machines, and of German thoroughness and completeness in working up the results," which "produced a statistical document far and away superior to any other census" (p. 94).

8. Hubbard, p. 386; Rauchberg, "Der Zug nach der Stadt," pp. 137–38.

9. *Bevölkerung und Viehstand von Böhmen, Bukowina, Dalmatien, etc. nach der Zählung vom 31. Dezember 1869* (Vienna, 1871), IV *(Galizien)*, pp. 2–9; *Öst. Stat.*, N.F. 2:1, p. 157.

10. Ibid.

11. *Bevölkerung und Viehstand . . . 1869*, XI *(Nieder-Oesterreich)*, pp. 2–13; *Öst. Stat.*, N.F. 2:1, p. 33*; *SJSW* (1910), p. 25. See Table 2:1 for population of Vienna from 1857–1910.

12. *Publications statistiques hongroises* 27 (1900), pp. 64–86; *Ungarisches statistisches Jahrbuch* (1900), p. 13. In 1880 Budapest was the ninth fastest growing city in Europe. Josef Körösi, *Die Hauptstadt Budapest im Jahre 1881; Resultate der Volksbeschreibung und Volkszählung,* 3 vols. (Berlin, 1881–83), I, pp. 3–4.

13. On the overseas migration of the Jews, see Wladimir Kaplun-Kogan, *Die jüdische Wanderbewegung in der neuesten Zeit (1880–1914)* (Bonn, 1919); Jacob Lestschinsky, "Die jüdische Wanderung, ihre Ursachen und ihre Regelung," *Archiv für Wanderungswesen* 1 (1928/29), pp. 127–31, 168–72 and 2 (1929/30), pp. 20–25; idem, *Jewish Migration for the Past Hundred Years* (New York, 1944); Mark Wischnitzer, *To Dwell in Safety: The Story of Jewish Migration Since 1880* (Philadelphia, 1948); Samuel Joseph, *Jewish Immigration to the United States from 1881 to 1910* (New York, 1914); and Moses Rischin, *The Promised City: New York's Jews 1870–1914* (1962; reprint, New York, 1970).

14. The only work on Jewish urbanization was done by Arthur Ruppin. For his works, see ch. 1, n. 12.

15. The May Laws of 1882 and subsequent czarist legislation sought to drive the Jews out of rural areas by prohibiting new Jewish settlements in villages, and then redefining both "new settlement" and "village." See Simon Dubnow, *History of the Jews of Russia and Poland from the Earliest Times to the Present Day,* 3 vols., trans. I. Friedlaender (Philadelphia, 1916–20).

16. Ruppin, "Die Juden als Stadtbewohner," in Alfred Nossig, ed., *Jüdische Statistik* (Berlin, 1903), pp. 426–27; idem, *The Jews of Today,* trans. Margery Bentwich (New York, 1913), p. 102.

17. Jakob Thon, *Die Juden in Oesterreich* (Berlin, 1908), p. 19. For postwar analogues see Jacob Lestschinsky, "The Jews in the Cities of the Republic of Poland," *YIVO Annual of Jewish Social Science* 1 (1946), pp. 156–77.

18. For example, in 1900 Jews formed 27.7% of the population in Lemberg, 28.1% of the population in Cracow, and 31.9% of the population in Czernowitz. In Brody, 68.6% of the population was Jewish, and in Sadagora in the Bukovina, 76.2% of the inhabitants were Jewish. Jews constituted 45% of the population in such Galician county seats as Tarnopol, Stanislau, and Zloczow. See *Öst. Stat.,* 63:1, pp. 78–79, 98–99, 108–9, 124–25; Austria, k.-k. Statistische Central-Commission, *Gemeinde-Lexikon der im Reichsrathe vertretenen Königreiche und Länder, 1900,* 14 vols. (Vienna, 1903–8), IX, *Böhmen,* X, *Mähren,* XI, *Schlesien,* XII, *Galizien,* and XIII, *Bukowina.*

19. *Publications statistiques hongroises* 27 (1900), pp. 84–85.

20. *Bevölkerung und Viehstand . . . 1857,* "Nieder-Oesterreich," pp. 2–3; *Öst. Stat.,* 63:1, pp. 48–49; Thon, pp. 7–8.

21. For history of the Jews in Vienna in the *Toleranzperiode,* see Ludwig Bato, *Die Juden im alten Wien* (Vienna, 1928); and Nikolaus Vielmetti, "Vom Beginn der Neuzeit bis zur Toleranz," in Anna Drabek et al., *Das österreichische Judentum: Voraussetzungen und Geschichte* (Vienna and Munich, 1974), pp. 59–82. This period is also treated in the standard histories of Viennese Jewry including Max Grunwald, *Vienna* (Philadelphia, 1936); Hugo Gold, *Geschichte der Juden in Wien: Ein Gedenkbuch* (Tel Aviv, 1966); Sigmund Mayer, *Die Wiener Juden 1700–1900: Kommerz, Kultur, Politik* (Vienna and

Berlin, 1917); Hans Tietze, *Die Juden Wiens: Geschichte-Wirtschaft-Kultur* (Leipzig and Vienna, 1933); and Gerson Wolf, *Geschichte der Juden in Wien (1156–1876)* (1876; reprint, Vienna, 1974).

22. Israel Jeiteles, *Die Kultusgemeinde der Israeliten in Wien mit Benützung des statistischen Volkszählungsoperatus vom Jahre 1869* (Vienna, 1873), p. 42.

23. Akos Löw, "Die soziale Zusammensetzung der Wiener Juden nach den Trauungs- und Geburtsmatrikeln, 1784–1848" (Ph.D. Dissertation, University of Vienna, 1952), pp. 161–63.

24. On an empire-wide basis, Jewish population growth was also more rapid than general growth. In fact, between 1857 and 1869 the Jewish population of Austria grew 32.4% while the total population expanded only 10.2% (Gustav Schimmer, *Die Juden in Oesterreich nach der Zählung vom 31. December 1880* [Vienna, 1881], p. 4). In part, this difference was caused by the fact that in the earlier census Jews were seriously undercounted, especially in Galicia, where the overwhelming majority of Austrian Jews lived. Between 1869 and 1880, Jewish growth in Austria was 22.3% while the general growth rate was 9.7%. Between 1880 and 1890, Jewish and general growth rates were equal at about 13%. See *Öst. Stat.*, 32:1, p. xvii.

25. Thon, p. 4; Leo Goldhammer, *Die Juden Wiens: Eine statistische Studie* (Vienna and Leipzig, 1927), p. 10. For an interesting discussion of the relationship of natural increase and migration in the expansion of Austrian cities see Hubbard, "Wachstumsprozess."

26. For Vienna in general, see *Öst. Stat.*, 32:2, pp. lx–lxiii; Rauchberg, "Der Zug nach der Stadt," Table X, p. 143. A rate of 40% native-born was about average for Central European *Grossstädte* in the late nineteenth century. In 1880, 43% of the population of Budapest had been born in the city. See Körösi, *Budapest . . . 1881*, II, p. 16. For Jews, see following discussion.

27. Rauchberg, *Bevölkerung*, pp. 105, 133–36; idem, "Der Zug nach der Stadt," Table X, p. 143. Prague, Brünn, and Lemberg, for example, only attracted immigrants from Bohemia, Moravia, and Galicia, respectively. For every 100 residents in Prague in 1890, 406 were born in the city, 126 in the surrounding district, and 420 elsewhere in Bohemia, so that Bohemians comprised 95% of Prague's residents in 1890. Brünn's residents were 94% Moravians, and Lemberg's, 94% Galicians. Budapest as well consisted mostly of Hungarians (91%) in 1890; see Josef Körösi and Gustav Thirring, *Die Hauptstadt Budapest im Jahre 1891; Resultate der Volksbeschreibung und Volkszählung*, 3 vols. (Berlin, 1894–98), II, pp. 13–14.

28. For a discussion of the origin of Viennese immigrants, see Rauchberg, *Bevölkerung*, p. 134.

29. Most of the following discussion deals with grooms rather than fathers because the marriage records provided more complete data than did the birth records.

30. *Bevölkerung und Viehstand . . . 1857*. This census included Hungarian population figures because it was done before the Compromise Agreement of 1867 in which Austria and Hungary became independent in internal affairs, including the census.

31. Anson G. Rabinbach, "The Migration of Galician Jews to Vienna, 1857–1880," *Austrian History Yearbook* 11 (1975), pp. 44–54 argues that the

largest wave of migration from Galicia arrived between 1857 and 1869, and that the period 1880–1910 witnessed a gradual decline in the migration of Jews from Galicia to the capital. My findings, on the contrary, indicate an increase in Jewish migration to Vienna in the later period. Mr. Rabinbach did not employ primary sources, and it seems that his conclusions are incorrect. See Marsha L. Rozenblit, "A Note on Galician Jewish Migration to Vienna," *Austrian History Yearbook* (forthcoming).

32. In 1766 the Empress Maria Theresa ordered Bohemian and Moravian Jews to record their births and circumcisions. In 1784, her son Joseph II extended the order to Vienna. See Julius Rosenfeld, *Die Matrikelführung der Israeliten in Oesterreich nach den bestehenden staatlichen Vorschriften* (Vienna, 1913).

33. Löw, p. 179. Löw must have miscalculated somewhat because his figures do not add up to 100%.

34. Peter Schmidtbauer, "Zur sozialen Situation der Wiener Juden im Jahre 1857," *Studia Judaica Austriaca* 6 (1978), p. 62. Schmidtbauer studied a sample of the Jewish population in the Inner City and the Leopoldstadt, a sample which accounted for 46.9% of the Jews in Vienna in 1857.

35. In his study of the 1869 census, Jeiteles (pp. 56–57) found 3.4% of the Jews in Vienna to be Viennese, 11.3% Bohemian, 20.9% Moravian, 13% Galician, and 46.3% Hungarian. Jeiteles derived these figures from the number of Jewish families rather than the number of Jewish individuals in Vienna.

36. Much work has been done on population transiency in American cities. See for example, Michael Katz, *The People of Hamilton, Canada West: Family and Class in a Mid-Nineteenth-Century City* (Cambridge, Mass., 1975), pp. 20–21, 122, 127–31; Stephan Thernstrom, *The Other Bostonians: Poverty and Progress in the American Metropolis, 1880–1970* (Cambridge, Mass., 1973), ch. 2; Peter Knights, "Population Turnover, Persistence and Residential Mobility in Boston," in *Nineteenth-Century Cities: Essays in the New Urban History*, ed. Stephan Thernstrom and Richard Sennett (New Haven, 1969), pp. 258–74. In a paper delivered to the American Historical Association in December 1979, William Hubbard reported great population transiency in the Austrian city of Graz in the nineteenth century.

37. Thomas Kessner, *The Golden Door: Italian and Jewish Immigrant Mobility in New York City 1880–1915* (New York, 1977), pp. 142, 147–48.

38. In his study of Hamilton, Ontario, Michael Katz, pp. 127–31 found that the persistence rate of the wealthy was much higher than that of the less prosperous.

39. In Hamilton only about one-third of the population retained its residence in the city from decade to decade (Katz, p. 122).

40. The Jewish preference for family migration has been discussed in the literature on mass migration of Jews to the United States. See for example, Samuel Joseph, pp. 127–32; Lestschinsky, *Jewish Migration*, p. 8. The Galician Jews who fled to Vienna during World War I also came with their families. See Aryeh Tartakower, "Jewish Migratory Movements in Austria in Recent Generations," in Josef Fraenkel, *The Jews of Austria: Essays in Their Life, History and Destruction* (London, 1967), p. 291.

41. Rauchberg, *Bevölkerung,* pp. 101–2, 111; idem, "Der Zug nach der Stadt," pp. 130, 138; idem, "Heimatsverhältnisse," p. 353; Weber, pp. 276–78.

42. *Öst. Stat.,* 63:1, pp. lii, 3; 63:2, p. 55.

43. Regions of the Austrian provinces used in Table 2:7 are those officially designated by the Austrian Statistical Central Commission; see, for example, *Öst. Stat.,* 32:2, p. viin. For a list of *Bezirke* in each region, see ibid. For Hungary, the regions used here are those employed in the *Ungarisches statistisches Jahrbuch,* which divided Hungary proper into seven regions along its principal rivers: the Left Bank of the Danube, Right Bank of the Danube, between the Danube and Tisza, Right Bank of the Tisza, Left Bank of the Tisza, between the Tisza and Maros, and Transylvania, as well as Fiume and Croatia-Slavonia. To place Jewish hometowns into these provinces and regions, I employed the Austrian Statistical Central Commission's *Allgemeines Ortschaften-Verzeichniss der im Reichsrathe vertretenen Königreiche und Länder nach den Ergebnissen der Volkszählung vom 31. December 1900* (Vienna, 1902), and its *Gemeinde-Lexikon der im Reichsrathe vertretenen Königreiche und Länder bearbeitet auf Grund der Ergebnisse der Volkszählung vom 31. December 1900* (Vienna, 1903–8). The *Allgemeines Ortschaften-Verzeichniss* recorded the population of every commune in Austria, and the *Gemeinde-Lexikon* broke down the population of every commune by religion. For Hungarian towns and cities, I used *Publications statistiques hongroises* (1900).

44. Figures on regional origin for general population from Rauchberg, *Bevölkerung,* p. 119; idem, "Heimatsverhältnisse," pp. 385–86.

45. Ibid.

46. Rauchberg, *Bevölkerung,* p. 129.

47. Rauchberg, *Bevölkerung,* p. 119; "Heimatsverhältnisse," pp. 385–86.

48. Rauchberg, *Bevölkerung,* p. 135; "Der Zug nach der Stadt," p. 148.

49. Based on figures provided in *Gemeinde-Lexikon . . . 1900, X, Mähren.*

50. Based on figures provided in *Gemeinde-Lexikon . . . 1900,* XII, *Galizien.*

51. Based on figures provided in *Ungarisches statistisches Jahrbuch* (1900) and *Publications statistiques hongroises,* n.s. 1 (1900).

52. Rauchberg, *Bevölkerung,* pp. 91, 136, 146–47; idem, "Der Zug nach der Stadt," pp. 149, 169; Weber, pp. 158–220; Köllmann, "The Process of Urbanization, " pp. 59–61; E. A. Wrigley, *Population and History* (New York, 1969), pp. 146–202.

53. Wrigley, ch. 5.

54. Austrian Jewish population density calculated from figures provided in the *Gemeinde-Lexikon . . . 1900.*

55. Hungarian Jewish population density calculated from figures provided in *Ungarisches statistisches Jahrbuch* (1900), and *Publications statistiques hongroises,* n.s. 1 (1900).

56. Ibid.

57. Ibid.

58. See *Gemeinde-Lexikon . . . 1900,* XII, *Galizien.*

59. Ibid., IX, *Böhmen.*

60. Theodor Haas, *Die Juden in Mähren: Darstellung der Rechtsgeschichte und Statistik unter besonderer Berücksichtigung des 19. Jahrhunderts* (Brünn, 1908), pp. 7, 14; idem, "Statistische Betrachtungen über die jüdische Be-

völkerung Mährens in Vergangenheit und Gegenwart," in Hugo Gold, ed., *Die Juden und Judengemeinden Mährens in Vergangenheit und Gegenwart* (Brünn, 1929), p. 593.

61. Haas, *Die Juden in Mähren,* pp. 22–23, 29, 56; idem, "Statistische Betrachtungen," p. 594; Leo Goldhammer, "Die Juden Mährens," in Hugo Gold, *Die Juden und Judengemeinden Mährens,* pp. 598–99.

62. Ruth Kestenberg-Gladstein, "The Jews between Czechs and Germans in the Historic Lands, 1848–1918," in *The Jews of Czechoslovakia,* 2 vols. (Philadelphia, 1968), I, pp. 27–37.

63. Körösi, *Budapest . . . 1881,* II, pp. 31–32; Körösi and Thirring, *Budapest . . . 1891,* II, pp. 14–16; Josef J. Barton, *Peasants and Strangers: Italians, Rumanians, and Slovaks in an American City, 1890–1950* (Cambridge, Mass., 1975), pp. 27–34.

64. Livia Rothkirchen, "Slovakia: I. 1848–1918," in *The Jews of Czechoslovakia,* I, pp. 77–78.

65. Ibid., p. 80. Rothkirchen notes that German was the everyday language of most western Slovakian Jews, even though the antisemites accused the Jews of working for increased Magyarization.

66. Aryeh Sole, "Subcarpathian Ruthenia: 1918–1938," in *The Jews of Czechoslovakia,* I, pp. 126–27.

67. Haas, *Mähren,* pp. 54–55; Kestenberg-Gladstein, pp. 32–34, 43–47.

68. Kestenberg-Gladstein, p. 40.

69. Ibid., p. 44; Gary B. Cohen, *The Politics of Ethnic Survival: Germans in Prague, 1861-1914* (Princeton, 1981), pp. 82, 235, 237–42.

70. Raphael Mahler, "The Economic Background of Jewish Emigration from Galicia to the United States," *YIVO Annual of Jewish Social Science* 7 (1952), p. 255; Kaplun-Kogan, p. 5; Siegfried Fleischer, "Enquête über die Lage der jüdischen Bevölkerung Galiziens," in Nossig, ed., *Jüdische Statistik,* pp. 209–31. This last work was commissioned by the *Oesterreich-Israelitische Union,* a Viennese Jewish defense organization, after the 1898 pogroms in Galicia.

71. Fleischer, pp. 217–18; A. Korkis, "Zur Bewegung der jüdischen Bevölkerung in Galizien," in Nossig, ed., *Jüdische Statistik,* p. 311; *Bevölkerung und Viehstand . . . 1869,* IV *(Galizien); Öst. Stat.,* 63:1, p. xxxiii. Part of this rapid Jewish growth was simply increasingly accurate census enumeration of Jews in Galicia.

72. Piotr S. Wandycz, *The Lands of Partitioned Poland, 1795–1918* (Seattle and London, 1974), p. 223; Fleischer, pp. 214–18.

73. Fleischer, pp. 219–20; Korkis, p. 313; Kaplun-Kogan, pp. 8–10; Wandycz, pp. 220–26; Mahler, pp. 259–60; Rabinbach, pp. 50–52; Max Rosenfeld, "Die jüdische Bevölkerung in den Städten Galiziens 1881–1910," *ZDSJ* 9, no. 2 (February 1913), pp. 19–20; "Galicia," in *Encyclopedia Judaica* (1970), XVI, 1329.

74. Fleischer, p. 209; Max Rosenfeld, "Bewegung der jüdischen Bevölkerung in Galizien von 1895–1910," *ZDSJ* 9, no. 12 (December 1913), p. 173, estimates that between 1902 and 1911, 152,590 Jews left Galicia for the United States.

75. Austrian (i.e., Galician) immigration to America leaped from approximately 7,000 in 1898 to 11,000 in 1899 and 17,000 in 1900 and remained at about that yearly rate until World War I (Rischin, p. 270). See also Joseph, pp. 109–12.

76. Students of the mass migration of Jews to America have also recognized that both the religiously learned and the Hasidim who feared the deleterious effects of American freedom on religious observance tended to remain in Eastern Europe. See, for example, Irving Howe, *World of Our Fathers* (New York and London, 1976), p. 27. The most poignant description of the effect of America on religious observance was made by Abraham Cahan in his novel *The Rise of David Levinsky* (New York and London, 1917).

77. Rothkirchen, pp. 74–75; "Hungary," *Encyclopedia Judaica* (1970), VIII, 1095.

78. Although urban reformers have often considered cities unpleasant for the working classes, in fact, the city offered the poor all kinds of advantages. See Hsi-Huey Liang, "Lower-Class Immigrants in Wilhelmine Berlin," *Central European History* 3 (1970), pp. 94–111.

79. Joseph Wechsberg, *The Vienna I Knew: Memories of a European Childhood* (Garden City, New York, 1979), p. 137.

80. George Clare, *Last Waltz in Vienna: The Rise and Destruction of a Family, 1842–1942* (New York, 1982), p. 86; P.G.J. Pulzer, "The Austrian Liberals and the Jewish Question, 1867–1914," *Journal of Central European Affairs* 23 (1963), pp. 132–33; Lucy Dawidowicz, *The Golden Tradition: Jewish Life and Thought in Eastern Europe* (New York, 1967), p. 70; Kestenberg-Gladstein, pp. 32–34, 43–45; Hans Kohn, "Before 1918 in the Historic Lands," in *The Jews of Czechoslovakia,* I, pp. 17–18.

81. Isidor Schalit, typescript *Erinnerungen* of Kadimah, CZA, A 196/19, p. 31. For a good discussion of the German orientation of Prague Jews, see Gary B. Cohen, *Politics of Ethnic Survival,* and idem, "Jews in German Society: Prague, 1860–1914," *Central European History* 10 (1977), pp. 28–54.

82. Pulzer, "The Austrian Liberals," pp. 131–42; Walter B. Simon, "The Jewish Vote in Austria," *LBIYB* 16 (1971), pp. 97–121; William A. Jenks, "The Jews in the Hapsburg Empire, 1879–1918," *LBIYB* 16 (1971), pp. 155–62; Robert Kann, "German-Speaking Jewry during Austria-Hungary's Constitutional Era (1867–1918)," *Jewish Social Studies* 10 (1948), pp. 239–56; and standard works on Viennese Jews listed in ch. 2, note 21.

83. Dawidowicz, p. 34.

84. Werner Cahnmann, "Adolf Fischhof and His Jewish Followers," *LBIYB* 4 (1959), p. 116; A. J. P. Taylor, *The Habsburg Monarchy, 1809–1918: A History of the Austrian Empire and Austria-Hungary* (1948; reprint, Chicago and London, 1976), p. 17. For a contemporary statement, see Sigmund Mayer, *MONOIU* 19, no. 5 (May 1907), p. 15.

85. The IKG tax rolls recorded the place where each member had *Heimatrecht,* not where he or she was born.

86. Rauchberg, *Bevölkerung,* p. 126; idem, "Der Zug nach der Stadt," pp. 146, 149; Weber, ch. 4.

87. Size of hometowns of Jews in Vienna calculated from *Gemeinde-Lexikon . . . 1900, Allgemeines Ortschaften-Verzeichniss . . . 1900,* and *Publications*

statistiques hongroises, n.s. 1 (1900). The following discussion is based on analysis of the two cross-sectional samples but applies equally to the richer IKG members.

88. Calculated from *Gemeinde-Lexikon . . . 1900,* IX, *Böhmen,* and X, *Mähren.*

89. Thon, p. 19.

90. Jewish population of hometown from *Gemeinde-Lexikon . . . 1900,* IX, *Böhmen,* and X, *Mähren.*

91. Ibid., XII, *Galizien.*

92. The antipathy of German or other Western Jews to Eastern European Jews typified Jewish communities in Western Europe and America. See, for example, Rischin, pp. 95–111; Howe, pp. 229–33; Paula Hyman, *From Dreyfus to Vichy: The Remaking of French Jewry, 1906–1939* (New York, 1979), pp. 115–52; and Jack L. Wertheimer, "German Policy and Jewish Politics: The Absorption of East European Jews in Germany (1868–1914)" (Ph.D. Dissertation, Columbia University, 1978).

93. Clare, p. 31.

94. Ibid., p. 67.

95. See for example, J. Grobtuch's call for an organization of Galician Jews in Vienna, *OW* (17 April 1908), pp. 292–93, and the response to his call in *NNZ* (29 May 1908), pp. 3–4.

96. *NNZ* (10 June 1910), pp. 1–2.

97. *OW* (18 November 1892), p. 859. See also *Jahresberichte* of the *Israel. Bethaus-Verein Beth Israel,* CAHJP, AW 1423/1.

98. Among mothers and fathers in the Jewish birth records, an even higher percentage were born in the same province. Jews in the birth sample were often married in the provinces before they migrated to Vienna.

99. Thon, p. 4, notes that the Jews of Western Austria, i.e., Bohemia and Moravia, "durch ihren ganzen sozialen Charakter wesentlich mit den deutschen Juden übereinstimmten."

3. From Trader to Clerk

1. Sigmund Mayer, *Ein jüdischer Kaufmann 1831 bis 1911: Lebenserinnerungen* (Leipzig, 1911), p. 148.

2. Ibid., pp. 158–59, 162.

3. Sigmund Mayer, "Das ökonomische Entstehen und Entwicklung der Wiener Judenschaft," *MONOIU* 15, no. 2/3 (February/March 1903), pp. 28, 24–30 (=CAHJP, AW 2863/2); idem, *Ein jüdischer Kaufmann,* pp. 199–200.

4. Arnold Höllriegel, "Die Fahrt auf dem Katarakt (Autobiographie ohne einen Helden)" (unpublished memoir, Leo Baeck Institute, n.d.), p. 14.

5. Carl E. Schorske, "Politics in a New Key: An Austrian Triptych," *Journal of Modern History* 39 (1967), p. 367.

6. In order to analyze Jewish occupational preference in Vienna, and best account for the unique distribution of the Jewish work force, I have grouped occupations according to type, and not according to sector of the economy or social status. This schema resembles, to some extent, one used by Peter M. Blau and Otis D. Duncan, *The American Occupational Structure* (New

York, 1967). I did not use the Austrian Statistical Central Commission's division of the work force into the various sectors of the economy (Industry, Trade, etc.) because this division obscured the profound changes in Jewish occupational preference. The Austrian categories will be used later, however, in order to compare Jews with Viennese generally. I have not used the social mobility scales used by American social historians because they proved incapable of measuring professional change among Viennese Jews. For a discussion and critique of these scales see below, pp. 58–61. The discussion of Jewish occupational change is based on the sample of Jewish grooms and not Jewish fathers because the marriage records contained more complete data than the birth records.

7. For example, see Mayer, *Ein jüdischer Kaufmann*, p. 476.

8. For example, see Christian Wilhelm von Dohm, *Über die bürgerliche Verbesserung der Juden* (Berlin and Stettin, 1781–83).

9. Gunther Chaloupek, "Der unvollendete Boom: Die Entwicklung der Wiener Wirtschaft in der Ära des Liberalismus," in Verein für Geschichte der Stadt Wien, *Wien in der liberalen Ära* (Vienna, 1978), pp. 31–43; Iván T. Berend and György Ránki, *Economic Development in East-Central Europe in the Nineteenth and Twentieth Centuries* (New York, 1974); Herbert Matis, *Oesterreichs Wirtschaft 1848–1913: Konjunkturelle Dynamik und gesellschaftlicher Wandel im Zeitalter Franz Joseph I* (Berlin, 1972); Heinrich Benedikt, *Die wirtschaftliche Entwicklung in der Franz-Joseph-Zeit* (Vienna, 1958); Hans Mayer, ed., *Hundert Jahre oesterreichischer Wirtschaftsentwicklung, 1848–1948* (Vienna, 1949); Eduard März, *Oesterreichische Industrie- und Bankpolitik in der Zeit Franz Josephs I* (Vienna, 1968); Geoffrey Drage, *Austria-Hungary* (London, 1909); and Richard Rudolph, *Banking and Industrialization in Austria-Hungary: The Role of Banks in the Industrialization of the Czech Crownlands, 1873–1914* (Cambridge and New York, 1976).

10. In fact, at the end of the nineteenth century, Jews formed a very substantial proportion of all medical and law students at the university. In the winter semester 1900, Jews comprised 22.8% of the law students, 39.6% of the medical students, and 18.2% of the philosophy students (*Öst. Stat.*, 70:3, pp. 2–5). In 1890, Jews had formed 48.7% of the students in medicine (*Öst. Stat.*, 35:4, pp. 2–5).

11. "Die jüdischen Ärtze in Wien und Oesterreich," by Medians, *OW* (9 September 1898), pp. 654–55; George Clare, *Last Waltz in Vienna: The Rise and Destruction of a Family, 1842–1942* (New York, 1982), pp. 21–23.

12. Arthur Schnitzler, *Professor Bernhardi*, trans. Hetty Landstone (New York, 1928).

13. Because of population transiency, community-wide occupational change from decade to decade does not reflect the sum of the occupational changes made by all individuals. Many students of social mobility, therefore, trace individuals from one census to another. See for example, Michael Katz, *The People of Hamilton, Canada West: Family and Class in a Mid-Nineteenth-Century City* (Cambridge, Mass., 1975) and Stephan Thernstrom, *The Other Bostonians: Poverty and Progress in the American Metropolis, 1880–1970* (Cambridge, Mass., 1973). Among Viennese Jews, it is only possible to trace the individual career paths of taxpaying members of the IKG.

14. Examples taken from IKG tax records, CAHJP, AW 805/1–25.

15. Ibid.

16. Monika Glettler, *Die Wiener Tschechen um 1900: Strukturanalyse einer nationalen Minderheit in der Grossstadt* (Munich and Vienna, 1972), pp. 61–62, 64.

17. Moses Rischin, *The Promised City: New York's Jews 1870–1914* (1962; reprint, New York, 1970), pp. 51–75, 272; Thomas Kessner, *The Golden Door: Italian and Jewish Immigrant Mobility in New York City 1880–1915* (New York, 1977), pp. 33–34, 37–38, 59–70, 109–11, 117–18, 125–26. For a classic statement of this social mobility see Abraham Cahan's novel, *The Rise of David Levinsky* (New York and London, 1917).

18. See Thernstrom, Appendix B, pp. 289–302; Kessner, pp. 50–51, both of which are based on Alba Edwards, "A Social-Economic Grouping of the Gainful Workers of the United States," *Journal of the American Statistical Association* 28 (1933), pp. 377–87.

19. CAHJP, AW 805/10, 805/4.

20. For a good critique of the standard social mobility scale see Katz, pp. 9, 71–74.

21. Katz, pp. 53, 142, Appendix II; idem, "Occupational Classification in History," *Journal of Interdisciplinary History* 3 (1972), pp. 63–88. Katz has developed a six-scale ranking of nineteenth-century occupations in which Level I consists of merchants and professionals, Level II consists of clerks, minor officials, and small proprietors; Level III of skilled artisans; Level IV of low-status occupations including peddling and semi-skilled work; Level V consisting of low-status workers such as unskilled laborers; and Level VI consisting of unclassifiables like students, women, pensioners.

22. Katz, *The People of Hamilton*, pp. 81, 139–40, 156.

23. Lacking much of the necessary detail to place different proprietors or artisans in different ranks, I collapsed Katz's scale into four ranks: "High Status" composed of merchants, professionals, factory owners, upper-level civil servants, and upper-level managers; "Medium Status" composed of clerks, salesmen, business agents, and lower-level civil servants; "Artisans"; and "Low Status," composed of artisanal assistants, peddlers, unskilled workers, and servants.

24. In North American cities, the rich were also more able than others to maintain their social status. See Katz, *The People of Hamilton*, pp. 149, 155–59.

25. Described in detail in *Öst. Stat.*, 66:1, pp. ii–x, and used in all census reports and in *SJSW*. Katz also urges study of the work force on a horizontal level. See Katz, *The People of Hamilton*, p. 51; and idem, "Occupational Classification," pp. 81–82.

26. Katz, *The People of Hamilton*, p. 52, also found that Hamilton, Ontario, a commercial city, had a large proportion of skilled and unskilled laborers.

27. *Öst. Stat.*, 66:2, pp. 7–29 displayed the numbers of Viennese in each branch of what I call "Industry I" and "Industry II."

28. *Öst. Stat.*, 33:1, pp. xxiv–xxv.

29. *Öst. Stat.*, 66:2, pp. 29–37, 60–62.

30. *Öst. Stat.*, 66:2, pp. 62–64.

31. For a full description of this schema see *Öst. Stat.*, 66:1, pp. x–xi. The nature of the marriage and birth records made necessary certain revisions in this schema for purposes of discussion of the Jews. I have created a separate category of "artisans" for the Jews because the sources did not specify if a craftsman was a master, and therefore independent, or a journeyman, and therefore a worker. Moreover, I have eliminated the last two Austrian categories, "Day Laborers," and "Family Helpers," because birth and marriage records did not indicate if grooms or fathers worked in those capacities.

32. For social mobility in a nineteenth-century German city, see David F. Crew, *Town in the Ruhr: A Social History of Bochum, 1860–1914* (New York, 1979), pp. 78–86. Crew argues that there was much less social mobility in Germany than in contemporary American cities. See William Hubbard's forthcoming study of social mobility in Graz, Austria. On American social mobility, see Thernstrom; Katz, *The People of Hamilton;* Kessner; Sidney Goldstein, *Patterns of Mobility, 1910–1950: The Norristown Study* (Philadelphia, 1958); Humbert S. Nelli, *Italians in Chicago, 1880–1930* (New York, 1970); and S. M. Lipset and Reinhard Bendix, *Social Mobility in Industrial Society* (Berkeley, Calif., 1959).

33. In Boston, for example, Thernstrom (p. 152) found Jewish social mobility to be twice as high as that of any other religious or ethnic group in the city. For an especially interesting comparison of Jewish and Italian social mobility in New York City, see Kessner.

34. Kessner, pp. 167–74; Thernstrom, pp. 149, 168–73.

35. See appeal of the *Jüdischer Handlungsgehilfen-Verband* in *JZ* (26 September 1913), p. 6; *JZ* (8 October 1913). There were many organizations of Jewish *Angestellte* in Vienna. For a list, see Appendix II.

36. Appeal to hat manufacturers by *Verein jüdischer Handelsangestellter: Achwah* to cease discriminating against Jewish office workers, *Die Welt* 6, no. 35 (1902).

37. *JZ* (13 August 1910), p. 2.

4. Jewish Neighborhoods of Vienna

1. Stanley Lieberson, *Ethnic Patterns in American Cities* (New York, 1963), pp. 6, 10, 189.

2. Deborah Dash Moore, *At Home in America: Second Generation New York Jews* (New York, 1981), pp. 4, 5, 61–62.

3. Hans Bobek and Elisabeth Lichtenberger, *Wien: Bauliche Gestalt und Entwicklung seit der Mitte des 19. Jahrhunderts* (Graz, 1966); Franz Baltzarek, Alfred Hoffmann, and Hannes Stekl, *Wirtschaft und Gesellschaft der Wiener Stadterweiterung*, vol. V in Renate Wagner-Rieger, ed., *Die Wiener Ringstrasse: Bild einer Epoche* (Wiesbaden, 1975); Arthur J. May, *Vienna in the Age of Franz Joseph* (Norman, Okla., 1966); Carl E. Schorske, "The Ringstrasse, Its Critics, and the Birth of Urban Modernism," in *Fin-de-siècle Vienna: Politics and Culture* (New York, 1980), pp. 24–115.

4. Bobek and Lichtenberger, pp. 86, 94, 103, 113, 118; Gunther Chaloupek, "Der unvollendete Boom: Die Entwicklung der Wiener Wirtschaft in der Ära des Liberalismus," in Verein für Geschichte der Stadt Wien, *Wien in der liberalen Ära* (Vienna, 1978), pp. 34–35.

5. Bobek and Lichtenberger, pp. 91–92, 117; Eugen von Philippovich von Philippsberg, *Wiener Wohnungsverhältnisse* (Berlin, 1894), pp. 16–26; Peter Feldbauer and Gottfried Pirhofer, "Wohnungsform und Wohnungspolitik im liberalen Wien," in *Wien in der liberalen Ära,* p. 156; Charles O. Hardy, *The Housing Problem of the City of Vienna* (Washington, D.C., 1934), pp. 10–18; and Felix Czeike and Walter Lugsch, *Studien zur Sozialgeschichte von Ottakring und Hernals* (Vienna, 1955), pp. 44–67.

6. Bobek and Lichtenberger, pp. 86, 116.

7. Schorske, pp. 53–54.

8. Ibid., p. 60; Baltzarek, Hoffmann, and Stekl, pp. 293–99, 305–6, 332–36.

9. The relative wealth of districts can be determined by calculating the percentage of the population of each district who were live-in servants. Calculations are based on *SJSW* (1901), pp. 67–68. Servants composed between 3% and 9% of the population in most Viennese districts, but in District I, servants formed 22.6% of the population and in District IV, they formed 12.4% of the population. For a discussion of the connection of the number of servants to a family's wealth, see Michael Katz, *The People of Hamilton, Canada West: Family and Class in a Mid-Nineteenth-Century City* (Cambridge, Mass., 1975), p. 28.

10. Bobek and Lichtenberger, pp. 90, 95–96, 105–6.

11. Chaloupek, p. 37; May, pp. 37–38.

12. Bobek and Lichtenberger, pp. 86–90, 97, 104, 109, 112–16.

13. Based on percentage of population who were live-in servants. In 1900, servants formed 8% to 9% of the population of these districts, while they formed only 2% to 3% in most other districts (*SJSW* [1901], pp. 67–68).

14. Bobek and Lichtenberger, pp. 92–93; 102, 117.

15. Ibid., pp. 88–89, 91–92, 105–6, 109.

16. Gary B. Cohen, *The Politics of Ethnic Survival: Germans in Prague, 1861–1914* (Princeton, N. J., 1981), p. 136, found that despite the absence of Jewish neighborhoods, Jews in Prague lived in apartment houses which were almost totally Jewish. Jews were accepted participants in German public life in the Bohemian capital, but they lived with fellow Jews. See also idem, "Jews in German Society: Prague, 1860–1914," *Central European History* 10 (1977), p. 49. Unfortunately, the absence of the manuscript census makes it impossible to determine if Jews lived in "Jewish" apartment houses. In 1857, the only year for which the manuscript census is available, Peter Schmidtbauer, "Zur sozialen Situation der Wiener Juden im Jahre 1857," *Studia Judaica Austriaca* 6 (1978), p. 59, found that many Jews did live in houses with a Jewish majority, especially in the Leopoldstadt.

17. Ernest W. Burgess, "Residential Segregation in American Cities," *Annals of the American Academy of Political and Social Science* 140 (1928), pp. 105–15; idem, "The Growth of the City: An Introduction to a Research Project," in Robert E. Park, Ernest W. Burgess, and Roderick D. McKenzie, *The City* (Chicago, 1925), pp. 47–62; Louis Wirth, *The Ghetto* (Chicago and London,

1928, 1956); Paul Frederick Cressey, "Population Succession in Chicago, 1898–1930," *American Journal of Sociology* 44 (1938), pp. 59–69.

18. Moore, pp. 30–32.

19. Wade Clark Roof, Thomas L. Van Valey, and Daphne Spain, "Residential Segregation in Southern Cities: 1970," *Social Forces* 55, no. 1 (September 1976), pp. 59–71; Sam B. Warner, Jr., *Streetcar Suburbs: The Process of Growth in Boston, 1870–1900* (1962; reprint, New York, 1973), p. 46.

20. Lieberson, p. 45 and *passim.*

21. Nathan Kantrowitz, *Ethnic and Racial Segregation in the New York Metropolis: Residential Patterns among White Ethnic Groups, Blacks, and Puerto Ricans* (New York, 1973), esp. pp. 3–9, 34–52; A. Gordon Darroch and Wilfred G. Marston, "The Social Bases of Ethnic Residential Segregation: The Canadian Case," *American Journal of Sociology* 77 (1971), pp. 491–510; Karl E. Taeuber and Alma F. Taeuber, *Negroes in Cities: Residential Segregation and Neighborhood Change* (Chicago, 1965); idem, "The Negro as an Immigrant Group: Recent Trends in Racial and Ethnic Segregation in Chicago," *American Journal of Sociology* 69 (1964), pp. 347–82; Avery M. Guest and James A. Weed, "Ethnic Residential Segregation: Patterns of Change," *American Journal of Sociology* 81 (1976), pp. 1088–1111.

22. The Index of Dissimilarity measures the proportion of one population which would have to move to achieve similarity of residential distribution with another population. The scale runs from zero to 100, with zero indicating complete integration, and 100, complete segregation. A score of 70 is very high. The formula for the Index is

$$D = \sum_{i=1}^{n} \left| \frac{x_i - y_i}{2} \right|$$

where x is the proportion of one population in a census tract, and y is the proportion of another population in the same tract, and the Index (D) is the sum of the absolute values of the differences in the percentage of the two populations in each census tract, divided by two. The Index is discussed in Lieberson, p. 30; Otis D. Duncan and Beverly Duncan, "A Methodological Analysis of Segregation Indexes," *American Sociological Review* 20 (1955), pp. 210–17; and Taeuber and Taeuber, *Negroes in Cities*, pp. 195–245.

23. Moore, p. 31, found that the Index of Dissimilarity for New York Jews rose from 40 in 1920 to 60 in 1930 and 1940. Kantrowitz, p. 29, found that in 1960 the Index of Dissimilarity for New York Jews and other groups in the city ranged between 50 and 60.

24. Kantrowitz, p. 25, found that the Black/White Index of Dissimilarity in New York in 1960 was 80.

25. The Index probably would be higher if population figures were available for smaller areas than the districts. Sociologists recognize the need to determine the Index of Dissimilarity on small population units. See, for example, Roof, Van Valey, and Spain, p. 64.

26. In 1880, the Jewish/gentile Index of Dissimilarity in Vienna was 43.2; in 1890 it was 48.5; in 1900, 45.3; and in 1910, 44.2. The Index was calculated on the basis of population figures provided in *SJSW* (1901), pp.

50–51; *SJSW* (1911), endpaper; Stephan Sedlaczek, *Die k.-k. Reichshaupt- und Residenzstadt Wien: Ergebnisse der Volkszählung vom 31. December 1880* (Vienna, 1887), part II, pp. 110–15, 126–27; idem, *Die definitiven Ergebnisse der Volkszählung vom 31. December 1890 in der k.-k. Reichshaupt- und Residenzstadt Wien* (Vienna, 1891), part II, pp. 50–53, 63–65.

27. *SJSW* (1901), p. 50.

28. See standard works on Viennese Jewry cited in ch. 2, note 21, and Adalbert Klaar, *Die Siedlungsformen Wiens* (Vienna, 1971), p. 51.

29. Arthur Schnitzler, *My Youth in Vienna,* trans. Catherine Hutter (New York, 1970), p. 14.

30. See, for example, May, p. 39, who likened the Leopoldstadt to the "ghetto quarter of an East European town."

31. Sigmund Mayer, *Ein jüdischer Kaufmann 1831 bis 1911: Lebenserinnerungen* (Leipzig, 1911), p. 463.

32. Before World War I, Jewish charity in Vienna was not centrally administered, and thus the records of charity disbursements were not generally housed in the IKG archives. I found three charity files in the Vienna collection of the CAHJP: *Centralstellung für das Armenwesen, 1894–1903* (AW 1890), *Armenwesen, 1893–99* (AW 1899), and *Armenamt, 1896–1914* (AW 1897). Discussion of the residential patterns of destitute Jews is based on the addresses of the men and women found in these files. These charity records are spotty and not as good a source as the other records consulted.

33. In 1896 approximately 10,000 Jewish men paid taxes to the *Israelitische Kultusgemeinde* (Israelitische Cultusgemeinde Wien, *Verzeichnis der im Gemeindegebiete wohnhaften Wähler für die Neuwahl des Cultus-Vorstandes im Jahre 1896,* CAHJP, AW 48/1). Multiplying this number by 5 to account for family dependents, only 50,000 of the 145,000 Jews in Vienna at the end of the nineteenth century could afford to pay the IKG tax.

34. Czeike and Lugsch, pp. 15, 33.

35. N. Chameides, "Das Reservoir der armen jüd. Bevölkerung Wiens," *Die Wahrheit* (6 February 1903), p. 5.

36. Thomas Kessner, *The Golden Door: Italian and Jewish Immigrant Mobility in New York City 1880–1915* (New York, 1977), pp. 158–59; Jeffrey S. Gurock, *When Harlem Was Jewish 1870–1930* (New York, 1979), pp. 27–28, 36–39.

37. The IKG established a new curia of *höherbesteuerte Wähler* on December 4, 1900 (CAHJP, AW 50/3, 51/5). The 1900 list of highly taxed IKG members is contained in Israelitische Cultusgemeinde Wien, *Verzeichnis der im Wiener Gemeindegebiete wohnhaften höherbesteuerten Wähler für die Neuwahl des Cultusvorstandes und der Vertrauensmänner im Jahre 1900,* CAHJP, AW 50/10.

38. Addresses mapped from a sample of every fifth eligible IKG voter in the 1896 IKG election, and every fifth IKG member who paid over 200 Kronen in 1900. Addresses from *Verzeichnis der im Wiener Gemeindegebiete wohnhaften Wähler . . . 1896,* CAHJP, AW 48/1, and the *Verzeichnis der im Wiener Gemeindegebiete wohnhaften höherbesteuerten Wähler . . . 1900,* CAHJP, AW 50/10.

39. Fortunately, the IKG rolls recorded each taxpayer's address as well as the new address of the taxpayers who changed residence.

40. The rich had a much lower transiency rate as well. See ch. 2, notes 36–39.

41. *Verzeichnis der im Wiener Gemeindegebiete wohnhaften Wähler . . . 1896* and *Verzeichnis der im Wiener Gemeindegebiete wohnhaften Wähler für die Wahlen in den Kultusvorstand und der Vertrauensmänner im Jahre 1906,* CAHJP, AW 48/1 and 53/1.

42. *Verzeichnis der im Wiener Gemeindegebiete wohnhaften Wähler . . . 1896,* p. 86 (CAHJP, AW 48/1); *Verzeichnis der im Wiener Gemeindegebiete wohnhaften Wähler . . . 1906,* p. 156 (CAHJP, AW 53/1).

43. Jewish/Czech Index of Dissimilarity based on those whose everyday language *(Umgangssprache)* was Bohemian or Moravian, and those whose religion was Jewish; figures cited in *SJSW* (1901), pp. 50–51, 54.

44. *SJSW* (1901), p. 60. There is a problem determining the exact number of Czechs in Vienna. Surely the actual number is higher than the number who gave Czech as their everyday language. Birth in Vienna and German language assimilation obscured the number of Czechs residing in the Austrian capital. For a discussion of this problem, see Monika Glettler, *Die Wiener Tschechen um 1900: Strukturanalyse einer nationalen Minderheit in der Grossstadt* (Munich and Vienna, 1972), pp. 29–31.

45. Glettler, pp. 44, 54, 56–57; *SJSW* (1901), p. 54. Gettler's figures are somewhat higher than those in *SJSW.*

46. Glettler, pp. 54, 56–57.

47. Hans Kohn, "Before 1918 in the Historic Lands," in *The Jews of Czechoslovakia,* 2 vols. (Philadelphia, 1968), I, pp. 17–18; Ruth Kestenberg-Gladstein, "The Jews between Czechs and Germans in the Historic Lands, 1848–1918," in *The Jews of Czechoslovakia,* I, pp. 32–34, 43–45; Joseph Wechsberg, *The Vienna I Knew: Memories of A European Childhood* (Garden City, N.Y., 1979), p. 148; Cohen, "Jews in German Society," p. 37.

48. In New York City, for example, German Jews lived "Uptown," and Eastern European Jews lived "Downtown," on the Lower East Side. See Moses Rischin, *The Promised City: New York's Jews 1870–1914* (1962; reprint, New York, 1970), pp. 76–111; Moore, p. 21.

5. Education, Mobility, and Assimilation

1. Stefan Zweig, *The World of Yesterday* (New York, 1943), p. 28.

2. Ibid.

3. See below, Table 5:1. For proportion of Viennese population which was Jewish, see Table 2:1.

4. Zweig himself argued that for many Jewish bourgeois, money was only a stepping stone to real status and intellectual careers (Zweig, p. 11). Zweig overstated the case, but understood the reality of the Jewish quest for education in the nineteenth century.

5. There is no good scholarship on Central European education. In English, see James E. Russell, *German Higher Schools: Their History, Organization and Methods of Secondary Education in Germany* (New York, 1899); Frederich E. Bolton, *The Secondary School System of Germany,* International Education

Series, 47 (n.p., n.d.). Both of these books are based on Friedrich Paulsen, *Geschichte des gelehrten Unterrichts auf den deutschen Schulen und Universitäten vom Ausgang des Mittelalters bis zur Gegenwart,* 2nd rev. ed. (Leipzig, 1896–97). Wilhelm Löwy, *Das Unterrichtswesen in Wien,* vol. II, *Mittel- und Hochschulen* (Vienna, 1891) is only good for the history of certain special *Gymnasien.* For information on the class-bound nature of education, see Russell, p. 171.

6. While most sociologists assume that education leads to greater assimilation, there is little empirical research on this subject. See Steven Martin Cohen, "Socioeconomic Determinants of Interethnic Marriage and Friendship," *Social Forces* 55 (1977), pp. 997–1010; and Selma Berrol, "Education and Economic Mobility: The Jewish Experience in New York City, 1880–1920," *American Jewish Historical Quarterly* 65 (1975/76), pp. 257–71.

7. For the role of *Gymnasium* and university education in the assimilation of German Jews, see Monika Richarz, *Der Eintritt der Juden in die akademischen Berufe: Jüdische Studenten und Akademiker in Deutschland* (Tübingen, 1974).

8. Russell, pp. 74, 122; Ernst Springer, "Das Mittelschulwesen," in *100 Jahre Unterrichts-Ministerium 1848–1948; Festschrift des Bundesministeriums für Unterricht in Wien* (Vienna, 1948), p. 115.

9. Robert Kann, *A History of the Habsburg Empire, 1526–1918* (Berkeley, Calif., 1974), p. 351.

10. Curricula drawn from *Gymnasium* yearbooks, for example, *VII. Jahresbericht über das k.-k. Franz-Joseph-Gymnasium in Wien (I), 1880/81* (Vienna, 1881), pp. 58–63; *Jahresbericht des k.-k. Sophien-Gymnasiums in Wien, II, für das Schuljahr 1909/10* (Vienna, 1910), p. 46; *Jahresbericht des kais.-kön. Obergymnasiums zu den Schotten in Wien am Schlusse des Schuljahres 1896* (Vienna, 1896), pp. 91–97. For a comparison with Prussian schools, see Russell, p. 123.

11. For example, see *VII. Jahresbericht über das k.-k. Franz-Joseph-Gymnasium in Wien (I), 1880/81,* pp. 58–63.

12. For example, see *Jahresbericht des kais.-kön. Obergymnasiums zu den Schotten in Wien . . . 1896,* pp. 91–97; Bolton, p. 189.

13. Jacob Katz, *Out of the Ghetto: The Social Background of Jewish Emancipation, 1770–1870* (Cambridge, Mass., 1973), pp. 162–64; Raphael Mahler, *A History of Modern Jewry 1780–1815* (New York, 1971), pp. 229–33.

14. Katz, pp. 64–71.

15. Mahler, pp. 152–72; Katz, pp. 66–68, 124–31; Michael A. Meyer, *The Origins of the Modern Jew: Jewish Identity and European Culture in Germany, 1749–1824* (Detroit, 1967), pp. 11–56.

16. For the Jewish proportion of the population of each district in Vienna, see Table 4:2.

17. William J. McGrath, *Dionysian Art and Populist Politics in Austria* (New Haven, 1974), pp. 27–33.

18. Löwy, p. 7.

19. McGrath, pp. 27–32.

20. Alphonse de Rothschild was one of the students to pass the *Abitur,* the exam which qualified young men for university study, at the *Theresianum* in 1896. See *Jahresbericht des Gymnasiums der k.-k. Theresianischen Akademie in Wien, 1895/96* (Vienna, 1896), p. 93.

21. See Table 2:1.

22. Based on population figures in Table 2:1.

23. Curricula drawn from yearbooks of several Viennese *Realschulen*, including *Zweiter Jahresbericht über die k.-k. Staatsrealschule im IX. Wiener Gemeindebezirk, 1905/06* (Vienna, 1906), pp. 20–22; *XI. Jahresbericht der II. k.-k. Staatsrealschule im II. Wiener Gemeindebezirke veröffentlicht am Schlusse des Schuljahres 1913/14* (Vienna, 1914), pp. 48–51. On Prussian *Realschulen*, see Russell, pp. 127–28.

24. *Öst. Stat.*, N.F. 8:2, pp. 48–55. As early as 1875, Jews formed 45% of the student body in the German-language *Gymnasien* in Prague, *Oesterreichisches statistisches Jahrbuch* (1875), V, pp. 32–37. In Prague, Jews rarely attended the Czech-language schools. In 1910, only 3.8% of the students in those *Gymnasien* were Jewish (*Öst. Stat.*, N.F. 8:2, pp. 52–55).

25. *Öst. Stat.*, 70:3, pp. 38–41. For 1910 figures see *Öst. Stat.*, N.F. 8:2, pp. 56–59. In Lemberg no Jews attended the Ruthene-language *Gymnasium*.

26. Péter Hanák, ed., *Magyarország törtenete, 1890–1918* (History of Hungary), 2 vols. (Budapest, 1978), II, pp. 881–83. I would like to thank István Deák for providing me with this information.

27. Russell, pp. 190, 192, 427; Bolton, p. 33.

28. Bolton, p. 29; Springer, p. 120.

29. *SJSW* (1900), p. 397n. Tuition in Prussian *Gymnasien* was roughly similar; see Russell, p. 152. For a discussion of tuition waivers, see below.

30. These schools were chosen because they possessed excellent records of registration from the nineteenth century. The *Franz-Joseph-Gymnasium* is now the *Bundesgymnasium, I,* Stubenbastei 6–8; the *Erzherzog-Rainer Gymnasium* is now *II. Bundesgymnasium, II,* Wohlmutgasse 3; and the *Maximilian-Gymnasium* is now the *Bundesgymnasium, IX,* Wasagasse 10. For a discussion of sampling techniques, see Appendix I.

31. *Öst. Stat.*, 3:2, pp. 32–33; 35:4, pp. 30–31; 70:3, pp. 32–33.

32. Ibid.

33. Russell, p. 152.

34. Unfortunately, many of the records consulted did not mention if students received tuition exemptions or not. In particular, the *Wasagassegymnasium* in the Alsergrund did not indicate financial aid in the students' registration records. Nevertheless, this statistic conforms to the Viennese average.

35. In order to determine the occupation of fathers of non-Jewish students, I took a control sample of every fourth non-Jewish student at the *Gymnasien* in the Inner City and the Leopoldstadt, and of every third gentile student in the *Gymnasium* in the Alsergrund in 1890/91.

36. In Germany as well, David Crew found that the *Gymnasium* functioned "not to aid social mobility but rather to ensure status continuity." See David Crew, *Town in the Ruhr: A Social History of Bochum, 1860–1914* (New York, 1979), p. 94. Working-class children rarely attended *Gymnasium* (pp. 93–94).

37. Because the *Gymnasium* records indicated place of birth, and not place of *Heimat,* it is impossible to know if the Viennese-born children of Jewish immigrants to Vienna attended *Gymnasium,* and which groups of Viennese Jews were the most likely to give their sons elite education.

38. See Tables 2:5 and 2:10.

39. For other Viennese *Gymnasien*, see, for example, *V. Jahresbericht über das k.-k. Staatsgymnasium in Wien, IV. Bezirk, für das Schuljahr 1889/90* (Vienna, 1890), pp. 46–48; *XXV. Jahresbericht über das k.-k. Elisabeth-Gymnasium in Wien für das Schuljahr 1909/10* (Vienna, 1910), pp. 27–30; *Jahresbericht des k.-k. Staatsgymnasiums im XIX. Bezirke für das Schuljahr 1895/96* (Vienna, 1896), pp. 51–55.

40. *Jahresbericht des Gymnasiums der k.-k. Theresianischen Akademie in Wien 1895/96* (Vienna, 1896), pp. 77–81.

41. *Jahresbericht des k.-k. Obergymnasiums zu den Schotten am Schlusse des Schuljahres 1911/12* (Vienna, 1912), p. 74; *Jahresbericht des k.-k. Obergymnasiums zu den Schotten in Wien am Schlusse des Schuljahres 1896* (Vienna, 1896), pp. 114–18.

42. *SJSW* (1910), p. 390.

43. *Vierter Jahresbericht des k.-k. Staatsgymnasiums im XIII. Bezirke in Wien, 1903/04* (Vienna, 1904), pp. 14–16.

44. *Zwölfter Jahresbericht des k.-k. Staatsgymnasiums in Hernals, 1885/86* (Vienna, 1886), pp. 47–49; *Zweiundzwanzigster Jahresbericht des k.-k. Staatsgymnasiums im XVII. Bezirke von Wien (Hernals), 1895/96* (Vienna, 1896), pp. 49–51.

45. *Achter Jahresbericht des k.-k. Staatsgymnasiums im XII. Bezirke von Wien (Unter-Meidling), 1890/91* (Vienna, 1891), pp. 39–43; *Achtundzwanzigster Jahresbericht des k.-k. Carl-Ludwig-Gymnasiums in Wien XII für das Schuljahr 1910/11* (Vienna, 1911), pp. 46–48.

46. *Öst. Stat.*, 28:4, pp. 80–99.

47. *SJSW* (1910), pp. 412–25; Monika Glettler, *Die Wiener Tschechen um 1900: Strukturanalyse einer nationalen Minderheit in der Grossstadt* (Munich and Vienna, 1972), pp. 65–66.

48. For 1890 see *Öst. Stat.*, 35:4, pp. 114–25.

49. Bolton, pp. 277–97; Russell, pp. 129–32.

50. *Jahresbericht des Mädchen-Lyzeums am Kohlmarkt in Wien der Frau Dr. Phil. Eugenie Schwarzwald . . . veröffentlicht am Schlusse des Schuljahres 1905/06* (Vienna, 1906), p. 16; *Jahresbericht des Cottage-Lyzeums XIX, 1912–13* (Vienna, 1913), p. 48.

51. For curricula, see, for example, *Jahresbericht des Mädchen-Lyzeums . . . Eugenie Schwarzwald . . . 1905/06*, p. 42; *Jahresbericht des Cottage-Lyzeums XIX, 1912/13*, p. 24; *Neunter Jahresbericht des öffentlichen Mädchen-Lyzeums im IX. Bezirke, 1914/15* (Vienna, 1915), p. 18. For Prussian *Mädchen-Lyzeen*, see Russell, p. 131, and Bolton, pp. 295–97.

52. Bolton, pp. 286, 292, 295–97, 187–263.

53. *Zehnter Jahresbericht der gymnasialen Mädchenschule des Vereines für erweiterte Frauenbildung am Schlusse des Schuljahres 1902* (Vienna, 1902), pp. 1–2; *19. Jahresbericht des Mädchen-Obergymnasiums . . . des Vereines für erweiterte Frauenbildung am Schlusse des Schuljahres 1910/11* (Vienna, 1911), p. 13; *I. Jahresbericht des Vereines für realgymnasialen Mädchenunterricht (Wien VIII), 1912/13* (Vienna, 1913), pp. 3–4.

54. *Oesterreichisches Städtebuch* (1897), VII, p. 89.

55. Records in *Hauptkatalog des öff. Mädchen-Lyzeums Eugenie Schwarzwald,* 1890/91 and 1910/11, Stadtschulrat der Stadt Wien. For sampling techniques, see Appendix I.

56. For a discussion of the role of secular education in distracting Jews from Jewish communal goals, see Cohen, p. 998.

57. Arthur Schnitzler, *My Youth in Vienna,* trans. Catherine Hutter (New York, 1970), p. 66.

58. Sigmund Mayer, *Ein jüdischer Kaufmann 1831 bis 1911: Lebenserinnerungen* (Leipzig, 1911), p. 101.

59. Zweig, p. 29.

60. Arnold Höllriegel, "Die Fahrt auf dem Katarakt" (unpublished memoir, Leo Baeck Institute, n.d.), p. 13.

61. Zweig, pp. 37–59.

62. Ibid., p. 41.

63. Schnitzler, p. 67.

64. For an interesting discussion of the Jewish recognition of the Christian character of Viennese schools, see "Der christliche Character der öffentlichen Schulen," *Neuzeit* 26, no. 2 (2 July 1886), pp. 251–52.

65. Schnitzler, p. 40.

66. Höllriegel, p. 14.

67. Ibid., p. 35, and *passim.*

68. Schnitzler, p. 63.

6. Intermarriage and Conversion

1. Marshall Sklare, *America's Jews* (New York, 1971), pp. 202–3; Fred Solomon Sherrow, "Patterns of Religious Intermarriage among American College Graduates" (Ph.D. Dissertation, Columbia University, 1971), p. 71.

2. Milton Gordon, *Assimilation in American Life: The Role of Race, Religion and National Origins* (New York, 1964), pp. 80–81. See also Arthur Ruppin, *The Jewish Fate and Future,* trans. E. W. Dickes (London, 1940), p. 114.

3. The only pre-nineteenth-century exception to this generalization were the Spanish laws of *limpieza de sangre,* purity of blood, enacted in the fifteenth and sixteenth centuries to prohibit descendants of Jewish converts from holding certain offices. See Yosef Hayim Yerushalmi, *From Spanish Court to Italian Ghetto: Isaac Cardoso, A Study in Seventeenth-Century Marranism and Jewish Apologetics* (New York, 1971), pp. 12, 14–16.

4. Leo Goldhammer, *Die Juden Wiens: Eine statistische Studie* (Vienna and Leipzig, 1927), p. 17; Arthur Ruppin, *The Jews of Today,* trans. Margery Bentwich (New York, 1913), p. 166; Jakob Thon, "Taufbewegung der Juden in Oesterreich," *ZDSJ* 4, no. 1 (January 1908), p. 7.

5. *SJSW* (1910), p. 50.

6. Gary B. Cohen, *The Politics of Ethnic Survival: Germans in Prague, 1861–1914* (Princeton, N. J., 1981), p. 80; and idem, "Jews in German Society: Prague, 1860–1914," *Central European History* 10 (1977), pp. 47–48. In Prague only one Jew married a non-Jew in 1881, and in 1911, only thirty did so. In Budapest, however, 11.8% of the Jewish men and 13.5% of the Jewish

women who married in 1900 married non-Jews. *Publications statistiques hongroises,* n.s. 7 (1900–02), pp. 30–31.

7. Arthur Ruppin, *Soziologie der Juden,* 2 vols. (Berlin, 1930), I, p. 211. On American Jewry, see Sherrow, p. 7; Steven Martin Cohen, "Patterns of Interethnic Marriage and Friendship in the United States" (Ph.D. Dissertation, Columbia University, 1974), pp. 51, 92, 177.

8. In his study of intermarriage in the U.S., Steven Martin Cohen also argued that "survivalist ideology," residential concentration, and institutional networks served as important brakes on interethnic and interreligious marriages (pp. 15–20, 292).

9. Sociologists have also found an absence of any strong correlation between higher social status and Jewish intermarriage in contemporary America. Sherrow, for example, found that the intermarriage rate of children of professionals and of workers was the same in a sample of 1961 Jewish college graduates (pp. 118–19). See also Steven Martin Cohen, pp. 172, 205–12.

10. Sklare, p. 201.

11. The IKG, in its role as registrar of all marriages involving Jews, also recorded the marriages of Jews and *konfessionslos* partners. Of the 894 marriages in the sample I took from those records, 24 (2.7%) consisted of Jewish brides and *konfessionslos* grooms, and 30 (3.4%) of Jewish grooms and *konfessionslos* brides, proportions which indicate that indeed the IKG recorded all intermarriages. Since the published statistics did not discuss the social background of intermarrying couples, the discussion here is based on these 54 men and women.

12. Goldhammer, p. 29. The Austrian *Staatsgrundgesetz* of 25 May 1868 allowed all those above age fourteen the free choice of religious confession. Children under seven automatically converted with their parents; children between seven and fourteen years old could not convert. See note in section "Konfessionsänderungen" in every *SJSW;* for example, 1896, p. 341.

13. Jakob Thon, *Die Juden in Oesterreich* (Berlin, 1908), p. 9.

14. Ibid., pp. 76, 78; Gary B. Cohen, *Politics of Ethnic Survival,* pp. 78, 80; idem, "Jews in German Society," p. 48. The fact that Jews were accepted as Jews and as equals in Prague German society probably accounts for the virtual absence of conversion in the Bohemian capital.

15. N. Samter, *Judentaufen im 19. Jahrhundert mit besonderer Berücksichtigung Preussens* (Berlin, 1906), pp. 77, 146–47.

16. Guido Kisch, *Judentaufen: Eine historisch-biographisch-psychologisch-soziologische Studie besonders für Berlin und Königsberg* (Berlin, 1973), pp. 22–24; Samter, pp. 78–79; Jakob Thon, "Taufbewegung," pp. 7–9; Goldhammer, pp. 31–32.

17. Jacob Katz, *Out of the Ghetto: The Social Background of Jewish Emancipation, 1770–1870* (Cambridge, Mass., 1973), pp. 106–7.

18. Ibid., p. 110.

19. Ibid., pp. 115–19; Michael A. Meyer, *The Origins of the Modern Jew: Jewish Identity and European Culture in Germany, 1749–1824* (Detroit, 1967), pp. 70–75.

20. On Marx's father see Saul K. Padover, "The Baptism of Marx's Family," *Midstream* 24, no. 6 (June/July 1978), pp. 36–44. Heine's conversion is discussed by Meyer, pp. 172–73.

21. A. Menes, "The Conversion Movement in Prussia during the First Half of the 19th Century," *YIVO Annual of Jewish Social Science* 6 (1951), pp. 187–205. Menes estimates (p. 191) that 3,171 Jews converted in Prussia between 1812 and 1846. No reliable statistics exist for the very early nineteenth century. Katz, pp. 121–22, quotes Friedlaender that in the 5–8 years before 1811, 50 Jews converted in Berlin out of a community of 450 families.

22. See especially Uriel Tal, *Christians and Jews in Germany: Religion, Politics, and Ideology in the Second Reich, 1870–1914*, trans. Noah Jonathan Jacobs (Ithaca, N.Y., and London, 1975), esp. p. 33; Samter, pp. 4–13; Kisch, pp. 21–37.

23. Sigmund Mayer, *Ein jüdischer Kaufmann 1831 bis 1911: Lebenserinnerungen* (Leipzig, 1911), p. 159.

24. Alma Mahler Werfel, *Gustav Mahler: Memories and Letters* (1946; reprint, New York, 1968), p. 44.

25. Ibid., p. 101. Oddly enough, Mahler's English biographers ignore Alma Mahler's testimony.

26. George Clare, *Last Waltz in Vienna: The Rise and Destruction of a Family, 1842–1942* (New York, 1982), pp. 21–22.

27. Mayer, pp. 158–59.

28. Julius Braunthal, *Victor und Friedrich Adler: Zwei Generationen Arbeiterbewegung* (Vienna, 1965), pp. 17–20.

29. As quoted in ibid., p. 20n.

30. Wilma Abeles Iggers, *Karl Kraus: A Viennese Critic of the Twentieth Century* (The Hague, 1967), pp. 179–80, 214–15; Frank Field, *The Last Days of Mankind: Karl Kraus and His Vienna* (New York, 1967), pp. 7, 23; Harry Zohn, *Karl Kraus* (New York, 1971), pp. 17, 23n; Robert Wistrich, "Karl Kraus: Jewish Prophet or Renegade," *European Judaism* (June 1975), pp. 32–38; Hans Kohn, *Karl Kraus, Arthur Schnitzler, Otto Weininger: Aus dem jüdischen Wien der Jahrhundertwende* (Tübingen, 1962), p. 12.

31. *OW* 19, no. 16 (18 April 1902), pp. 253–55 and no. 17 (25 April 1902), pp. 273–75.

32. For example, *Die Welt* 9, no. 19 (1905) contained a list of converts from Judaism from March to May 1905.

33. "Die Judentaufen in Wien und Galizien," *NNZ* (17 July 1908), pp. 5–6; "Los von Juda," *JV* (21 July 1905), pp. 1–2, are just two examples of this charge.

34. *JV* (31 October 1902), p. 1.

35. *JV* (24 October 1902), p. 1.

36. In Prussia in the early nineteenth century many lower-class Jews also accepted baptism (Menes, p. 190).

37. See squabble in *ZDSJ* in 1914 between Maximilian Paul-Schiff, "Die statistischen Ziffern für Austritte aus dem Judentum und Mischehen," *ZDSJ* 10, no. 3 (March 1914), pp. 46–48; and Horator, "Die statistischen Ziffern für Austritte aus dem Judentum und Mischehen," *ZDSJ* 10, no. 7/8 (July/August 1914), pp. 116–18.

38. See discussion below and note 49.

39. *SJSW* (1885), pp. 164–65; *SJSW* (1896), pp. 344–45; *SJSW* (1906), pp. 367–74.

40. Ibid. For example, 52% of the women who left Judaism in 1906 became Catholic in contrast to only 36.5% of the Jewish male converts in that year.

41. This sample was composed of two subsamples, one from the records of conversion kept by the IKG in 1890, 1900, and 1910, the other from nine selected Catholic parishes in the Leopoldstadt (II), the Inner City, and the Alsergrund (IX) in 1870, 1880, 1890, 1900, and 1910. For sampling techniques and the location of these parishes, see Appendix I. It was necessary to collect this sample because published statistics in most cases did not provide information on the social background of converts.

42. The sex of two of the converts could not be determined because their first names were illegible or not given.

43. These figures conform to those in the published statistics. See, for example, *SJSW* (1896), pp. 344–45 and *SJSW* (1906), pp. 367–74.

44. These figures accord well with those in the published statistics in ibid.

45. The only year in which *SJSW* provided occupational distribution for Jewish converts was 1906 (pp. 372–73), and its figures are somewhat different from my findings. Of the 364 Jewish men who converted in that year, 3% were civil servants, 18.7% professionals, 11% students, 11.5% merchants, 26.1% business employees, 3.6% artisans or industrialists, 12.4% workers, and 13.7% without occupation. Clearly more working-class converts appeared among those in the official statistics than in the records I consulted.

46. One 1910 convert, Sam Nuchim from Brody, Galicia, was a "Talmudist," a student of the Talmud. Either Nuchim was being sarcastic, or he converted out of genuine religious conviction.

47. See Marsha L. Rozenblit, "The Assertion of Identity—Jewish Student Nationalism at the University of Vienna before the First World War," *LBIYB* 27 (1982), pp. 171–86.

48. John Boyer, *Political Radicalism in Late Imperial Vienna: Origins of the Christian Social Movement 1848–1897* (Chicago and London, 1981), pp. 40–121.

49. Sample collected from IKG records of proselytes to Judaism in those years. This sample consisted of all converts to Judaism in the sample years.

50. Ruppin, *The Jews of Today*, pp. 186, 188. Ruppin went much too far, of course, in his charge that Vienna was a "metropolis of converts" (p. 186).

51. Addresses of converts traced in *Lehmann's Allgemeiner Wohnungs-Anzeiger nebst Handels- und Gewerbe-Adressbuch für die k.-k. Reichshaupt-und Residenzstadt Wien und Umgebung* for 1881, 1890, 1900, 1910. Name duplications rendered tracing very difficult.

52. Peter Gay, "Encounter with Modernism: German Jews in Wilhelmine Culture," in *Freud, Jews and Other Germans: Masters and Victims in Modernist Culture* (Oxford and New York, 1978), p. 78; and idem, "The Berlin Jewish Spirit: A Dogma in Search of Some Doubts," in ibid., p. 174.

53. On racial antisemitism, see George L. Mosse, *Toward the Final Solution: A History of European Racism* (New York, 1978); idem, *The Crisis of German Ideology: Intellectual Origins of the Third Reich* (New York, 1964); Tal, pp.

259–89; Geoffrey G. Field, *Evangelist of Race: The Germanic Vision of Houston Stewart Chamberlain* (New York, 1981). The classic statement of racial antisemitism was made by Houston Stewart Chamberlain, *The Foundations of the Nineteenth Century* (1899), trans. John Lees (New York, 1912).

54. Arthur Schnitzler, *The Road to the Open,* authorized trans. Horace Samuel (New York, 1923), p. 112.

55. Alma Mahler Werfel, p. 101; on Christmas, pp. 24–25.

56. As quoted in ibid., p. 109.

57. Arnold Schoenberg, *Letters,* ed. Erwin Stein, trans. Eithne Wilkins and Ernst Kaiser (New York, 1965), pp. 88–89.

58. Lucy Dawidowicz, "Arnold Schoenberg: A Search for Jewish Identity," in *The Jewish Presence: Essays on Identity and History* (New York, 1977), pp. 32–45.

59. See note 49.

7. Organizational Networks and Jewish Identity

1. See Salo W. Baron, *The Jewish Community,* 3 vols. (Philadelphia, 1942); Harriet Pass Freidenreich, *The Jews of Yugoslavia: A Quest for Community* (Philadelphia, 1979); or Paula Hyman, *From Dreyfus to Vichy: The Remaking of French Jewry, 1906–1939* (New York, 1979). Most ethnic groups form networks of voluntary organizations. In Vienna, the Czechs also established many organizations to meet their social and political needs. See Monika Glettler, *Die Wiener Tschechen um 1900: Strukturanalyse einer nationalen Minderheit in der Grossstadt* (Munich and Vienna, 1972).

2. Gustav Adolph Schimmer, *Statistik des Judenthums in den im Reichsrathe vertretenen Königreichen und Ländern* (Vienna, 1873), pp. 16–20; Israel Jeiteles, *Die Kultusgemeinde der Israeliten in Wien mit Benützung des statistischen Volkszählungsoperatus vom Jahre 1869* (Vienna, 1873), pp. 85–96; *Neuzeit* (25 April 1890), pp. 161–62; (2 May 1890), pp. 171–72.

3. N. M. Gelber, "The Sephardic Community in Vienna," *Jewish Social Studies* 10 (1948), pp. 359–96; Mordche Schlome Schleischer, "Geschichte der spaniolischen Juden in Wien" (Ph.D. Dissertation, University of Vienna [Philosophy], 1934?); M. Papo, "The Sephardi Community of Vienna," in Josef Fraenkel, ed., *The Jews of Austria: Essays on Their Life, History and Destruction* (London, 1967), pp. 327–46; Adolf von Zemlinszky, *Geschichte der türkisch-israelitischen Gemeinde zu Wien: von ihrer Gründung bis heute nach historischen Daten* (Vienna, 1888).

4. For example, see *Gemeinde* Boards in 1868, 1880, 1888, 1896, and 1904, in *Neuzeit* (13 December 1867), pp. 579–80; (10 January 1868), p. 16; (13 January 1888); "Wahlergebnisse 1896," CAHJP, AW 48/7; "Konstituierung des neuen Vorstandes, 1896," CAHJP, AW 48/10; "Konstituierung des neuen Vorstandes, 1904," CAHJP, AW 52/12; *OW* 13, no. 48 (27 November 1896), p. 956. The long tenure of IKG Board members is quite apparent from a comparison of the Board membership lists in those years. Gustav Kohn, for example, was elected to the Board in 1884 (*Neuzeit,* 5 December 1884), and was still on the *Gemeinde* Board in 1904. In most European Jewish *Gemeinden,*

the Board members were wealthy business men, industrialists, and lawyers. See, for example, Freidenreich, pp. 79–81.

5. "Unterstützungen und Subventionen, 1895," CAHJP, AW 901/1 0., "Unterstützungen und Subventionen, 1905," CAHJP, AW 901/11 0. For a complete list of Jewish charitable organizations in Vienna, see Appendix II. Statutes and yearly reports of these organizations in CAHJP, AW.

6. "Statuten des Vereines zur Beförderung der Handwerke unter den inländischen Israeliten in Wien, 1888," CAHJP, AW 2189/4; "Bericht des Vereines zur Beförderung der Handwerke unter den inländischen Israeliten, 1910," CAHJP, AW 2190/1; and 1880, 1890, and 1905 reports of this organization in AW 2191/30, 38, 50. On the founding of the *Allianz,* see Zosa Szajkowski, "Conflicts in the *Alliance israélite universelle,* and the Founding of the Anglo-Jewish Association, the Vienna *Allianz,* and the *Hilfsverein,*" *Jewish Social Studies* 19 (1957), pp. 29–50.

7. "Statuten der Israelitischen Allianz zu Wien, 1873," CAHJP, AW 2824, and yearly reports of the *Allianz* in AW 2828.

8. *OW* 4, no. 5 (4 February 1887), p. 71; *OW* 9, no. 23 (13 June 1892), p. 402; *OW* 8, no. 16 (17 April 1891); *Neuzeit* (18 August 1899), pp. 330–31; U.O.B.B., Humanitätsverein "Wien," *Festschrift zur Feier des fünfundzwanzigjährigen Bestandes, 1895–1920* (Vienna, 1920), p. 107.

9. "IX. Jahres-Bericht des Vereines zur Hebung der Gewerbe in Wien, 1899," CAHJP, AW 2882; *OW* 8, no. 21 (29 May 1891), p. 381; no. 47 (27 November 1891), p. 873; *Neuzeit* (28 April 1899), pp. 171–72. These two newspapers regularly reported the activities of all the Viennese Jewish charities.

10. U.O.B.B., Humanitätsverein "Wien," *Festschrift,* pp. 23–24, 29–30, 33; *Festschrift anlässlich des fünfundzwanzigjährigen Bestandes des israelitischen Humanitätsvereines "Eintracht" (B'nai B'rith) Wien, 1903–1928* (Vienna, 1928), pp. 11, 13; "Zwecke und Ziele der Vereinigungen B'nai B'rith," and "Was Wir Wollen," *Vierteljahres-Bericht für die Mitglieder der oesterreichisch-israelitischen Humanitätsvereine "B'nai B'rith"* 1, no. 1 (October 1897), pp. 1–2, 3–7; "Betrachtungen über den Stand der 'B'nai B'rith' am Ende des Jahrhunderts," *Vierteljahres-Bericht . . . "B'nai B'rith"* 2, no. 4 (December 1899), p. 139.

11. U.O.B.B., Humanitätsverein "Wien," *Festschrift,* pp. 80–85, 107; *Festschrift . . . des . . . Humanitätsvereines Eintracht (B'nai B'rith),* pp. 17–24; *Vierteljahres-Bericht . . . "B'nai B'rith"* 2, no. 4 (December 1899), pp. 155–57, 160–65; *Zweimonats-Bericht für die Mitglieder der oesterreich-israelitischen Humanitätsvereine "B'nai B'rith"* 14, no. 1 (January 1911), pp. 21–23, 31–34. For a discussion of the importance of the B'nai B'rith to Sigmund Freud, see Dennis B. Klein, *Jewish Origins of the Psychoanalytic Movement* (New York, 1981), pp. 69–102.

12. "Die Gründung des jüdischen Jugendbundes in Wien," *Zweimonats-Bericht . . . "B'nai B'rith"* 14, no. 3 (March 1911), pp. 146–47.

13. Statutes and yearly reports of most Viennese Jewish charitable organizations can be found in CAHJP, AW. The files of these two organizations are 2257, 2887, 2888. For a full list of Jewish charitable organizations in Vienna, see Appendix II.

14. Statutes and yearly reports of women's philanthropic organizations in CAHJP, AW 2216, 2232, 2235, 2236, 2253, 2267, 2297, 2361, etc. See also *OW* 18, no. 4 (27 January 1911), p. 63 for a description of some of the work of these organizations.

15. CAHJP, Vienna collection, contains the statutes of the *Landsmannschaften* from Austerlitz (AW 2331, 2332), Brody (AW 2294, 2295), Frauenkirchen (AW 2334, 2335), Eisenstadt (AW 2325, 2326), Holleschau (AW 2338, 2339, 2340), Lemberg (AW 2312), Mattersdorf (AW 2289, 2290), Schaffa (AW 2270), Tarnow (AW 2305, 2306), Trebitsch (AW 2337, 2338), and Triesch (AW 2345, 2346, 2347). For a discussion of the role of *Landsmannschaften* in the Parisian Jewish community, see Hyman, pp. 79–81.

16. In the early 1880s, one Jewish newspaper, the *Wiener Israelit,* was published in German written in Hebrew characters. The newspaper was not in Yiddish, however.

17. *JV* (26 May 1905); *OW* 22, no. 18 (5 May 1905), p. 284; *JZ* (7 February 1908), p. 7; (6 March 1908), p. 8. On vibrant Yiddish cultural life in New York, see Irving Howe, *World of Our Fathers* (New York and London, 1976), pp. 417–59.

18. The Yiddish theater advertised weekly in *JZ* and *OW.*

19. *OW* 9, no. 49 (2 December 1892), pp. 885–86; no. 47 (18 November 1892), p. 859; no. 7 (12 February 1892), p. 118; *Neuzeit* (18 December 1891), p. 493; *Statuten des israelitischen Synagogen-Vereines Beth Israel nach pölnisch-jüdischem Ritus in Wien, 1906,* CAHJP, AW 1421/1; *VIII. und IX. Jahresbericht des israelit. Bethhaus-Vereines Beth-Israel für die Jahre 1889 und 1890,* CAHJP, AW 1423/1.

20. *X. und XI. Jahresbericht des israelit. Bethhaus-Vereines Beth Israel für die Jahre 1891 und 1892,* CAHJP, AW 1423/1, pp. 1–7; *Neuzeit* (18 December 1891), pp. 492–93; *OW* 9, no. 7 (12 February 1892), p. 118; no. 45 (4 November 1892), p. 813; *OW* 10, no. 10 (10 March 1893), pp. 175–76; *Neuzeit* (10 March 1893), pp. 93–94; (8 September 1893), p. 359; (15 September 1893), pp. 368–70.

21. J. Grobtuch, "Eine Organisation der galizischen Juden in Wien," *OW* 25, no. 16 (17 April 1908), pp. 292–93.

22. Dr. K, "Zur Organisation der galizischen Juden in Wien," *NNZ* (29 May 1908), pp. 3–4.

23. *NNZ* (10 June 1910), pp. 1–2; (24 June 1910), p. 4.

24. *OW* 20, no. 46 (13 November 1903), p. 735; *Die Welt* (4 December 1903), p. 13; *NNZ* (3 May 1907), p. 10; (10 May 1907), p. 10; (26 July 1907), p. 10; *Statuten des Vereins Machsike Hadath in Wien, 1907,* CAHJP, AW 1424; *Encyclopedia Judaica* (1970), XI, 730–31.

25. Theodor Herzl, the founder of political Zionism, even had a Christmas tree in his home. See Amos Elon, *Herzl* (New York, 1975), p. 174. For an interesting example of how Zionists perceived their own assimilationist backgrounds, see Isidor Schalit, "Erinnerungen" of Kadimah (typescript), CZA, A 196/19, p. 14.

26. For a discussion of the integrationist posture of French and German Jewry, see Hyman, pp. 1–11; Michael R. Marrus, *The Politics of Assimilation: A Study of the French Jewish Community at the Time of the Dreyfus Affair*

(Oxford, 1971); and Ismar Schorsch, *Jewish Reactions to German Anti-Semitism, 1870–1914* (New York, 1972), pp. 1–13.

27. *Neuzeit* (22 August 1884), pp. 313–14.

28. *Neuzeit* (10 March 1893), p. 913.

29. *Neuzeit* (13 May 1870), pp. 209–11; see also *Neuzeit* (22 August 1884), pp. 313–14.

30. On the Jewish identity of the *Centralverein*, see Schorsch, pp. 117, 135–48.

31. Josef S. Bloch, *My Reminiscences* (Vienna and Berlin, 1923), pp. 61–125. All the standard histories of Viennese Jewry deal with the Bloch-Rohling Affair, e.g., Max Grunwald, *Vienna* (Philadelphia, 1936), pp. 430–37; Hans Tietze, *Die Juden Wiens: Geschichte-Wirtshaft-Kultur* (Leipzig and Vienna, 1933), pp. 243–45.

32. Bloch, p. 178. Bloch chose the title *Oesterreichische Wochenschrift* in conscious contradistinction to Heinrich Friedjung's newspaper *Deutsche Wochenschrift*, which, Bloch maintained, propagated German nationalism among Jews. Bloch argued that the Jews should declare themselves Austrian (p. 182). The newspaper changed names a few times, and after 1896 was frequently called *Dr. Bloch's Wochenschrift* or *Dr. Bloch's Oesterreichische Wochenschrift*.

33. Bloch, p. 182.

34. Ibid., p. 184; *OW* 1, no. 5 (21 November 1884), p. 1.

35. *OW* 1, no. 1 (15 October 1884), pp. 1–3; Bloch, p. 188.

36. *OW* 2, no. 14 (10 April 1885), p. 1; Bloch, pp. 188–89.

37. *OW* 3, no. 17 (30 April 1886), pp. 193–95.

38. *Statuten des Vereines Oesterreichisch-Israelitischer Union in Wien, 1886*, CAHJP, AW 2862; *OW* 3, no. 17 (30 April 1886), pp. 193–95; Bloch, pp. 192–93.

39. *OW* 3, no. 17 (30 April 1886), pp. 193–95.

40. Ibid.

41. *MITOIU* 1, no. 1 (October 1889), pp. 2–3; *MITOIU* 8, no. 81 (May 1896), p. 4.

42. *MITOIU* 6, no. 69 (March 1895), p. 2; *OW* 15, no. 17 (29 April 1898), pp. 322–24; *MITOIU* 10, no. 105 (May 1898), pp. 3–11. On the defense activities of the *Centralverein* in Germany, see Schorsch, pp. 123–35; and Jehuda Reinharz, *Fatherland or Promised Land: The Dilemma of the German Jew, 1893–1914* (Ann Arbor, Mich., 1975), pp. 59–89.

43. *MITOIU* 10, no. 105 (May 1898), p. 3.

44. *MONOIU* 13, no. 5/6 (May/June 1901), pp. 1–18; *MONOIU* 22, no. 2 (February 1910), pp. 1–3; *MONOIU* 15, no. 5 (May 1903), p. 6; *MONOIU* 17, no. 5 (May 1905), pp. 1–20; Sigmund Mayer, *Ein jüdischer Kaufmann 1831 bis 1911: Lebenserinnerungen* (Leipzig, 1911), ch. 8. The defense activities of the OIU were also regularly reported in *OW*.

45. Maximilian Paul-Schiff, "Die Aufgaben der Oesterreichisch-Israelitischen Union," *MONOIU* 13, no. 11 (November 1901), p. 3.

46. *MONOIU* 15, no. 2/3 (February/March 1903), pp. 9–10; CAHJP, AW 2863/2.

47. *MONOIU* 22, no. 2 (February 1910), pp. 1–3; *MONOIU* 22, no. 6/7 (June/July 1910), p. 9.

48. *MONOIU, Festschrift zur Feier des 25-jährigen Jubiläums der Oesterreich-Israelitischen Union, 17 April 1910,* pp. 3–6, 31; *MONOIU* 22, no. 5 (May 1910), pp. 5, 9–10.

49. *OW* 1, no. 4 (14 November 1884), p. 6.

50. *JZ* (29 April 1910), pp. 1–2.

51. *NNZ* (10 May 1907), pp. 7–8.

52. *NNZ* (15 December 1911).

53. *NNZ* (10 May 1907), p. 8.

54. Mayer, p. 289.

55. Ibid., pp. 308, 309–46, quotation on p. 342.

56. Schorsch, pp. 117, 135–48, 195–209.

57. On antisemitism at the university, see Peter G.J. Pulzer, *The Rise of Political Anti-Semitism in Germany and Austria* (New York, 1964), pp. 251–57; Andrew G. Whiteside, *The Socialism of Fools: Georg Ritter von Schönerer and Austrian Pan-Germanism* (Berkeley, Calif., 1975), pp. 43–63, 93, 99–101, and *passim.* The Jewish press regularly reported antisemitic violence at the university. See, for example, *JZ* (23 May 1912), pp. 1–2; (27 June 1913), pp. 2–3; (11 July 1913), p. 1.

58. See discussion of Jewish national and Zionist organizations below.

59. Letters of *Jüdisch-Akademischer Juristenverein* and *Akademischer Verein jüdischer Mediziner,* 1912, requesting support from IKG, CAHJP, AW 1536/5; *OW* 28, no. 46 (12 November 1911), pp. 759–60. Jewish students at the university also organized to build separate cafeterias and dormitories in order to escape antisemitic insults. See *Statuten des Vereines jüdischer Studentenheime in Wien, 1909,* CAHJP, AW 2340 (2341) and *JZ* (26 June 1912) and (28 March 1913).

60. William J. McGrath, *Dionysian Art and Populist Politics in Austria* (New Haven, 1974), pp. 33–82, 167–72, traces the growing German nationalism of this group. A glance at the membership lists of the *Leseverein der deutschen Studenten* reveals that while many members in the 1870s were Jewish, by 1909 none of the members of this club were Jewish. See *Jahresbericht des Lesevereines der deutschen Studenten Wien's über das Vereinsjahr 1871–72* (Vienna, 1872), pp. 13–14; *Jahresbericht des Lesevereines der deutschen Studenten . . . 1874–75* (Vienna, 1875), pp. 22–25; *Jahresbericht des Lesevereines der deutschen Studenten . . . 1877–78* (Vienna, 1878), pp. 17–20; *Jahresbericht des Lese- und Redevereines der deutschen Hochschüler in Wien "Germania" über das Studienjahr 1908/9* (Vienna, 1909), pp. 39–42.

61. *OW* 10, no. 11 (17 March 1893), p. 201; *Jahresbericht der Jüdisch-Akademischen Lesehalle in Wien für das Verwaltungsjahr 1894/95,* CAHJP, AW 1787; Schalit, "Erinnerungen" of Kadimah, p. 28 in CZA, A 196/19.

62. *Jahresbericht der Jüdisch-Akademischen Lesehalle . . . 1894/95,* CAHJP, AW 1787; *OW* 11, no. 39 (28 September 1894), p. 755; no. 46 (16 November 1894), pp. 884–85, 894; no. 49 (7 December 1894); *OW* 13, no. 29 (17 July 1896), p. 572.

63. *OW* 13, no. 6 (7 February 1896); no. 18 (1 May 1896), p. 360; no. 24 (12 June 1896), p. 482.

64. "Erteilung von Subventionen an Studenten-Vereinigungen 1907," CAHJP, AW 1536/1. For 1908, see AW 1536/2, for 1909, AW 1536/3, for 1911, AW 1536/4, and for 1912, AW 1536/5. In most of those years the reading club received 600 Kronen from the IKG.

65. *OW* 13, no. 45 (6 November 1896), pp. 895–96; no. 46 (13 November 1896); *OW* 15, no. 4 (28 January 1898), p. 72; *Jahresbericht der Lese- und Redehalle jüdischer Hochschüler in Wien über das Vereinsjahr 1900,* pp. 6, 8 in CAHJP, AW 1788/1; Schalit, "Erinnerungen" of Kadimah, pp. 29, 60 in CZA, A 196/19. Schalit claims a nationalist victory, but his account is too hazy to substantiate such a claim, and other evidence indicates that the *Lese- und Redehalle* remained aloof from nationalist politics.

66. For a discussion of the role of Zionism as a post-emancipation Jewish ideology, see Stephen M. Poppel, *Zionism in Germany, 1897–1933: The Shaping of a Jewish Identity* (Philadelphia, 1977).

67. Adolf Böhm, *Die zionistische Bewegung,* 2 vols., 2nd rev. ed. (Tel Aviv, 1935–37); Walter Laqueur, *A History of Zionism* (New York, 1972). On Herzl's life and work, see Elon, *Herzl;* Alex Bein, *Theodore Herzl: A Biography of the Founder of Modern Zionism* (1941; reprint, New York, 1970). Feuilletons were impressionistic articles placed "under the line" on the first page of the newspaper.

68. Statutes of Kadimah, January 1883, CZA, Z1/1; Schalit, "Erinnerungen" of Kadimah, p. 10, in CZA, A 196/19; Dr. Schnirer, "Stenographische Aufnahme der Festreden am Kommers zum Feier des 100. Semesters der Akademischen Verbindung Kadimah," pp. 7–11 in CZA, A 196/19. See also Böhm, I, pp. 135–37; Harriet Z. Pass (Freidenreich), "Kadimah: Jewish Nationalism in Vienna before Herzl," *Columbia University Essays in International Affairs: The Dean's Papers* (1969), pp. 122–25; Berthold Feiwel, "Die Universität," *Die Welt* (25 June 1897), pp. 4–6; and most recently Julius H. Schoeps, "Modern Heirs of the Maccabees—The Beginnings of the Vienna Kadimah, 1882–1897," *LBIYB* 27 (1982), pp. 155–70.

69. Schalit, "Erinnerungen" of Kadimah, pp. 14, 65–75, in CZA, A 196/19; Pass, pp. 128–31.

70. Schalit, "Erinnerungen" of Kadimah, p. 61, in CZA, A 196/19; Schnirer, "Stenographische Aufnahme der Festreden," p. 13 in CZA, A 196/19. On *Lovers of Zion,* see Laqueur, pp. 75–83.

71. On Birnbaum's "conversion" to Yiddishism and religious orthodoxy, see Emanuel S. Goldsmith, *Architects of Yiddishism at the Beginning of the Twentieth Century* (Rutherford, N. J., and London, 1976), pp. 99–119.

72. *SE* (1 February 1892), pp. 27–28.

73. Kadimah flyer, n.d., CZA, Z1/1; Schnirer, "Stenographische Aufnahme der Festreden," p. 20, in CZA, A 196/19, and throughout Kadimah propaganda.

74. *SE* (1 February 1885), second page (unnumbered).

75. Ibid.

76. *OW* 11, no. 46 (16 November 1894), p. 895.

77. *OW* 11, no. 42 (19 October 1894), p. 815; no. 44 (2 November 1894), p. 857; no. 45 (9 November 1894), p. 876.

78. Kadimah members established *Safah Berurah: Hebräischer Sprach- und Sprechverein* and *Morgenröthe* to promote the study of Hebrew language and Jewish history. See *SE* (30 November 1892), p. 211; (19 December 1892), p. 200; (15 September 1893), p. 7.

79. *Miriam* was founded in 1885 and *Moria* in 1892. See *OW* 2, no. 37 (29 September 1885), p. 6; *OW* 9, no. 8 (19 February 1892), p. 135; no. 11 (11 March 1892), pp. 187–88; *OW* 13, no. 3 (17 January 1896), p. 57; *SE* (1 February 1892), p. 33; (4 March 1892), p. 61; (4 April 1892), pp. 59–60.

80. *SE* (23 February 1892), pp. 39–41; (4 March 1892), pp. 52–54; (7 April 1892), pp. 57–58; Böhm, I, p. 137.

81. *SE* (15 May 1892), p. 93; (19 September 1892), p. 175; (7 June 1892); (30 November 1892), pp. 210–11; (19 December 1892); (1 June 1893), pp. 4–5; (1 October 1893), p. 6; *Neuzeit* (11 August 1893), p. 318; *Statuten des Zion: Verband der oesterreichischen Vereine für Colonisation Palästinas und Syriens, 1892,* in CAHJP, AW 2884.

82. Schalit, "Erinnerungen" of Kadimah, p. 80, in CZA, A 196/19.

83. "Aufruf des öst. Verbandes 'Zion' und der österreichischen Studentenverbindungen nach dem Erscheinen des *Judenstaat* sowie Adresse an Herzl, May 1896," CZA, Z1/7; Kadimah flyer, CZA, Z1/1.

84. Theodor Herzl, *Der Judenstaat* (Leipzig and Vienna, 1896).

85. On Herzl's diplomatic efforts, see Laqueur, pp. 96–135; Bein, chs. 7–14; Elon, chs. 9–19.

86. Adolf Böhm, "Verständigung" (n.d.), pp. 3–8, in CZA, A 141/18. In the mid-nineteenth century, Jewish integrationists who created the Reform Movement, which sought to strip Judaism of its national component, also argued that the Jews and Judaism worked for the salvation of mankind. See David Philipson, *The Reform Movement in Judaism,* rev. ed. (New York, 1931); and Max Wiener, *Jüdische Religion im Zeitalter der Emancipation* (Berlin, 1933).

87. *Die Welt* (29 September 1899), Supplement, p. 1; Böhm, I, pp. 222–23; CZA, Z1.

88. "Statistik des oesterreichischen Verbandes 'Zion,' 1901," CZA, Z1/6, and list of Zionist organizations in Vienna in CZA, Z1/375. See also *Zion* (20 June 1903), pp. 6–7.

89. Ibid. For a full list of Zionist organizations, see Appendix II.

90. Regular reports of all the Hebrew-speaking clubs, credit unions, and literary societies made in *Die Welt, JZ,* and *NNZ.*

91. *JZ* (2 May 1913), p. 5. Activities of the various sport clubs reported regularly in *JZ, Die Welt,* and *OW.* For a survey of Jewish sport clubs, see Eric Juhn, "The Jewish Sport Movement in Austria," in Fraenkel, pp. 161–64.

92. *JZ* (11 April 1913), p. 5; (2 May 1913), p. 5; *OW* 30, no. 17 (25 April 1913), p. 311. For a discussion of the influence of the Volkish ideology on the Jewish youth movement, see George L. Mosse, "The Influence of the Volkish Idea on German Jewry," in idem, *Germans and Jews: The Right, the Left, and the Search for a "Third Force" in pre-Nazi Germany* (New York, 1970), pp. 77–115.

93. *Zion* (20 June 1903), p. 6; "Statistik des oesterreichischen Verbandes Zion," CZA, Z1/6; "Erteilung von Subventionen an Studenten-Vereinigungen, 1907," CAHJP, AW 1536/1. For a full list of Zionist student organi-

zations, see Appendix II. Their activities were regularly reported in *Die Welt*, *JZ*, and *OW*.

94. *OW* 23, no. 44 (2 November 1906), p. 747; *OW* 27, no. 46 (18 November 1910), p. 762; *NZ* (23 March 1906), p. 6; *JZ* (25 February 1910); (28 March 1913); (27 May 1910).

95. "Erteilung von Subventionen an Studenten-Vereinigungen, 1907," CAHJP, AW 1536/6. Kadimah received more money than any other Zionist group. In 1907 it received 420 Kronen, while the other groups received between 100 and 250 Kronen.

96. *Die Welt* (19 October 1900), pp. 1–3; (7 December 1900), pp. 12–13; *Eine jüdische Toynbee-Halle in Wien* (Vienna, 1901), pp. 1–23. On the London Toynbee Hall, see Allen F. Davies, *Spearheads for Reform: The Social Settlements and the Progressive Movement, 1890–1914* (New York, 1967), pp. 3–8.

97. *Die Welt* (7 December 1900), p. 13.

98. Ibid. (22 February 1901), p. 13.

99. Ibid. (3 April 1901), pp. 28–30; (12 April 1901), pp. 10–12; (26 April 1901), p. 12; (20 February 1903), pp. 4–6; (27 February 1903), p. 9.

100. *Die Welt* (26 April 1901), p. 12; (1 July 1904), pp. 13–14; *Wahrheit* (10 November 1905), pp. 7–8.

101. *OW* 27, no. 7 (18 February 1910), pp. 131–32; "Die jüdische Toynbee-Halle in Wien im Jahre 1910," *Zweimonats-Bericht für die Mitglieder der österreichisch-israelitischen Humanitätsvereine "B'nai B'rith"* 14, no. 6 (November/December 1911), pp. 272–76.

102. Isidor Schalit, "Zur Geschichte der zionistischen Arbeiterbewegung: Aus meinen Erinnerungen" (Typescript), pp. 5–7, in CZA, A 196/23.

103. *Zion* (20 June 1903), p. 7; *Die Welt* (15 December 1899), p. 10; (17 August 1900), p. 8; (18 January 1901), p. 7; (15 February 1901), p. 12; (31 May 1901), p. 14; (15 August 1902), p. 9; (12 September 1902), p. 10; (1 January 1904), p. 17; (28 October 1904), p. 11; (4 November 1904), p. 12; (18 November 1904), p. 13; (13 October 1905), p. 11; (17 November 1905), p. 17; *JV* (6 February 1903), p. 4. For a full list, see Appendix II. On Ber Borochov and *Poale Zion*, see Laqueur, pp. 270–77.

104. *OW* 29, no. 50 (13 December 1912), p. 851; *OW* 31, no. 8 (20 February 1914), p. 122; *JZ* (3 January 1913).

105. *OW* 16, no. 27 (7 July 1899), p. 507.

106. "Jüdischer Kolonisationsverein, Konstituierende Versammlung . . . 1904," CAHJP, AW 2857; *Die Welt* (18 November 1904), p. 12; (25 November 1904), pp. 11–12; *OW* 21, no. 47 (18 November 1904), p. 757.

107. *Wahrheit* (21 December 1906), pp. 7–8; (8 February 1907), p. 7; *OW* 24, no. 7 (15 February 1907), pp. 118–19; *OW* 26, no. 7 (12 February 1909), p. 116; *OW* 30, no. 16 (18 April 1913); no. 25 (20 June 1913), pp. 456–57. On ITO in general, see Laqueur, p. 414.

108. Lists of shekel-payers are only available for 1899 and 1902. See "III. Zionistenkongress (1899); Schekelzahlerliste," CZA, Z1/440; "VI. Zionistenkongress (1902); Schekelzahlerliste," CZA, Z1/443. The following discussion of shekel-payers is based on the 1902 list. Before World War I the "shekel" was one German Mark or 1.20 Austrian Kronen (Böhm, I, p. 214).

109. "Ausweis über die Schekelbewegung im II. Congressjahre (1898)," CZA, Z1/375. Zionism found its greatest support in Eastern, not Western Europe. In 1898, Russian Zionists (52,789) contributed over 30,000 Gulden. Within Austria-Hungary, 60% of the affiliated Zionists lived in Galicia.

110. Despite the presence of important Zionist ideologues like Robert Weltsch and Hugo Bergmann, Zionism was never popular in Prague before World War I. See Gary B. Cohen, *The Politics of Ethnic Survival: Germans in Prague, 1861–1914* (Princeton, N. J., 1981), p. 227.

111. *Verzeichnis der im Wiener Gemeindegebiete wohnhaften Wähler für die Wahlen in den Cultusvorstand und der Vertrauensmänner im Jahre 1900,* CAHJP, AW 50/1. Voter eligibility lists were used to trace shekel-payers because IKG tax records were only extant for files Ko–Q. About 14% of the affiliated Zionists were women, and thus were untraceable on the voter lists.

112. Jeiteles, p. 95; "Wahlkundmachungen . . . 1902," CAHJP, AW 51/5.

113. Addresses of shekel-payers provided in CZA, Z1/440 and 443.

114. On the nationality conflict, see C. A. Macartney, *The Habsburg Empire 1790–1918* (New York, 1969); Oscar Jászi, *The Dissolution of the Habsburg Monarchy* (1929; reprint, Chicago and London, 1961); Arthur J. May, *The Hapsburg Monarchy 1867–1914* (1951; reprint, New York, 1968); A. J. P. Taylor, *The Habsburg Monarchy, 1809–1918: A History of the Austrian Empire and Austria-Hungary* (1948; reprint, Chicago and London, 1976); and Robert A. Kann, *The Multinational Empire: Nationalism and National Reform in the Habsburg Monarchy 1848–1918,* 2 vols. (1950; reprint, New York, 1964).

115. See works on antisemitism cited in ch. 1, n. 17.

116. Werner J. Cahnmann, "Adolf Fischhof and His Jewish Followers," *LBIYB* 4 (1959), p. 116; see also Robert Kann, "German-Speaking Jewry during Austria-Hungary's Constitutional Era (1867–1918)," *Jewish Social Studies* 10 (1948), pp. 239–56; P. G. J. Pulzer, "The Austrian Liberals and the Jewish Question, 1867–1914," *Journal of Central European Affairs* 23 (1963), pp. 131–42; Walter B. Simon, "The Jewish Vote in Austria," *LBIYB* 16 (1971), pp. 97–121; William A. Jenks, "The Jews in the Hapsburg Empire, 1879–1918," *LBIYB* 16 (1971), pp. 155–62.

117. On Jewish nationalism in Austria, see Kurt Stillschweig, "Die nationalitätenrechtliche Stellung der Juden im alten Oesterreich," *Monatsschrift für Geschichte und Wissenschaft des Judentums* 81 (1937), pp. 321–40; idem, "Zur neueren Geschichte der jüdischen Autonomie," ibid., 83 (1939), pp. 509–32; idem, "Nationalism and Autonomy among Eastern European Jewry," *Historia Judaica* 6 (1944), pp. 27–68.

118. Stillschweig, "Nationalism and Autonomy," pp. 35–40; Böhm, I, pp. 320–49.

119. *JV* (14 March 1902), pp. 3–4; Hermann Kadisch, *Jung-Juden und Jung-Oesterreich* (Vienna, 1912), pp. 5–6.

120. *JV* (10 January 1902), p. 1; *OW* 19, no. 3 (17 January 1902), p. 42.

121. Richard Rappaport, "Was Wollen Wir," *JV* (10 April 1903), pp. 1–2.

122. *OW* 24, no. 27 (5 July 1907), pp. 440–41.

123. *JV* (10 January 1902), pp. 2–3; *Neuzeit* (19 November 1897), p. 476.

124. "Die Notwendigkeit einer jüdischen Volkspolitik," *JV* (28 April 1905), pp. 2–3; Kadisch, p. 12.

125. "Programm der Jüdischen Volkspartei," *JV* (10 January 1902), p. 1; *OW* 19, no. 3 (17 January 1902), p. 42; *Statuten der Jüdischen Volksverein*, CAHJP, AW 2883.

126. Kadisch, pp. 10, 18–20, 27–28.

127. Ibid., pp. 20–25, 28–31.

128. On Karl Renner, see Kann, *The Multi-national Empire*, II, pp. 155–67; Karl Renner, *Der Kampf der oesterreichischen Nationen um den Staat* (Leipzig and Vienna, 1902); Böhm, I, pp. 334–47; Robert S. Wistrich, "Marxism and Jewish Nationalism: The Theoretical Roots of Confrontation," *Jewish Journal of Sociology* 17 (1975), pp. 43–54; and idem, *Socialism and the Jews: The Dilemmas of Assimilation in Germany and Austria-Hungary* (Rutherford, N. J., and London and East Brunswick, N. J., 1982), pp. 298–348, esp. 302–5.

129. Simon Dubnow, *Nationalism and History: Essays on Old and New Judaism* (Philadelphia, 1958).

130. See arguments in *JV* (10 January 1902), p. 1.

131. *JV* (13 February 1903), pp. 1–2; (28 April 1905), pp. 2–3; Kadisch, p. 13.

8. The Struggle

1. *Die Welt* (8 December 1905), pp. 1–2; (15 December 1905), p. 8.

2. *JV* (15 December 1905), pp. 4–5.

3. *NZ* (19 January 1906), pp. 1–3; "Programm der zionistischen Partei der Juden in Oesterreich" (n.d.), CZA, Z2/433; "Programm der zionistischen Partei in Oesterreich" (n.d.), CZA, A 196/17; "An Oesterreichs Judenschaft," CZA, Z2/433; Adolf Böhm, *Die zionistische Bewegung*, 2 vols., 2nd rev. ed. (Tel Aviv, 1935–37), I, pp. 331–32.

4. *Die Welt* (19 January 1906), p. 16; (26 January 1906), pp. 10–11; *NZ* (9 January 1906), p. 1; (16 January 1906), p. 1; (19 January 1906), pp. 1–3.

5. *NZ* (20 February 1906); *Wahrheit* (23 February 1906), p. 3; *Neue Freie Presse* (18 February 1906), p. 6, clipping in Schalit papers, CZA, A 196/17.

6. *JZ* (10 May 1907), p. 2; "Thesen der Krakauer Partei-Congress, 1 Juli 1906," CZA, A 141/19I; "Stenographisches Protokoll des Zionistentages am 1. Juli 1906 in Krakau," CZA, A 141/19I.

7. *JZ* (10 May 1907), p. 2; Böhm, I, pp. 342–43.

8. For example, see Adolf Böhm, "Zionismus und Nationalpolitik in Oesterreich," *Selbstwehr* (Prague) (21 April 1911), clipping in CZA, A 14/18.

9. Letter of Schalit to Wolffssohn, March 1907, CZA, Z2/433. When Schalit asked for financial support for the electoral campaign, Wolffssohn refused because he considered it too much of a drain on Zionist financial resources (Letter of Wolffssohn to Schalit, n.d., but after Schalit to Wolffssohn, 15 April 1907, CZA, Z2/433).

10. *JZ* (10 May 1910), p. 3.

11. *JZ* (10 May 1910), pp. 4–5.

12. *NNZ* (19 April 1907), pp. 1–2; (26 April 1907), pp. 1–2, quotation, p. 2. Landau had been an early follower of Herzl and editor of the Zionist weekly *Die Welt,* but had split from the political Zionists for personal and political reasons in 1898. See Saul Raphael Landau, *Sturm und Drang in Zionismus; Rückblicke eines Zionisten vor, mit und um-Theodor Herzl* (Vienna, 1937).

13. *Öst. Stat.,* 84:2, p. 2.

14. *JZ* (5 June 1907), pp. 2, 4.

15. *JZ* (20 June 1907); Böhm, I, pp. 343–44.

16. *NNZ* (14 June 1907), pp. 1–2; (21 June 1907), pp. 4–6.

17. *JZ* (12 April 1912), pp. 2–3; *NNZ* (30 June 1911). There were eighteen Jews in the 1911 Parliament: Straucher (Jewish National), Kuranda and Ofner (Liberals), seven in the Polish Club, and eight Social Democrats. See *OW* 28, no. 25 (23 June 1911), p. 413.

18. *JZ* (22 September 1911), p. 1; (29 September 1911), pp. 2–4; (6 October 1911), p. 1; (20 October 1911); (3 November 1911); (17 November 1911); (1 December 1911), pp. 3–4.

19. "Der mährische Ausgleich und die Juden," *MONOIU* 17, no. 12 (December 1905), p. 3.

20. "Die Agitation für die jüdische Kurie," *MONOIU* 18, no. 1 (January 1906), pp. 1–2.

21. Ibid., p. 2; "Der mährische Ausgleich," *MONOIU* 17, no. 12 (December 1905), pp. 1–2.

22. "Die Agitation," *MONOIU* 18, no. 1 (January 1906), pp. 2–3; *Wahrheit* (23 February 1906), p. 3; Sigmund Mayer, *Ein jüdischer Kaufmann 1831 bis 1911: Lebenserinnerungen* (Leipzig, 1911), pp. 348–50.

23. Walter Simon, "The Jewish Vote in Austria," *LBIYB* 16 (1971), pp. 103–6, 112–13; Peter G. J. Pulzer, *The Rise of Political Anti-Semitism in Germany and Austria* (New York, 1964), pp. 199–218.

24. *Neuzeit* (3 June 1870), pp. 345–47; (30 December 1870), pp. 605–7. The affirmation of loyalty to the Liberals was a constant refrain in *Neuzeit* articles.

25. *Neuzeit* (1 July 1870), pp. 291–93; (3 June 1870), pp. 345–47.

26. *Neuzeit* (14 February 1890), p. 62.

27. *Neuzeit* (13 February 1891), pp. 62–63; (8 May 1891), p. 186; (23 October 1891), pp. 412–13; (6 November 1891), pp. 431–32.

28. *MITOIU* 3, no. 10 (February 1891), pp. 10–11.

29. *OW* 9, no. 28 (8 July 1892), pp. 477–78; no. 32 (5 August 1892), pp. 585–86.

30. *OW* 9, no. 41 (7 October 1892), pp. 735–36.

31. *MITOIU* 9, no. 94 (March 1897), pp. 1–2; *OW* 14, no. 12 (19 March 1897), pp. 242–43; no. 42 (15 October 1897), p. 847; *Neuzeit* (19 March 1897).

32. "Die Juden und das allgemeine Wahlrecht," *MONOIU* 18, no. 12 (December 1906), p. 1.

33. Ibid., p. 2.

34. Ibid. See also "Die Vertretung der Juden im neuen Parlament," *MONOIU* 19, no. 1 (January 1907), pp. 1–4; and Dr. Alexander Mintz, "Die politische Lage der Juden," *MONOIU* 18, no. 11 (November 1906), pp. 1–11.

35. "Jüdische Reichsratskandidaturen in Wien," *MONOIU* 19, no. 2 (February 1907), pp. 1–4.

36. Ibid., p. 4; *OW* 24, no. 9 (1 March 1907), pp. 140–44.

37. *OW* 24, no. 7 (15 February 1907), p. 105; no. 8 (22 February 1907), pp. 121–27; no. 11 (15 March 1907), pp. 181–82; no. 13 (29 March 1907), pp. 213–17; no. 14 (5 April 1907), pp. 229–30; no. 15 (12 April 1907), p. 245.

38. *OW* 24, no. 16 (19 April 1907), pp. 261–62; no. 17 (26 April 1907), pp. 277–78; no. 18 (3 May 1907), pp. 293–95.

39. *OW* 24, no. 17 (26 April 1907), pp. 277–78; "Die jüdischen Reichsratskandidaturen in Wien," *MONOIU* 19, no. 4 (April 1907), pp. 1–3.

40. *Wahrheit* (22 March 1907), pp. 3–4; (19 April 1907).

41. *Wahrheit* (10 May 1907), pp. 3–4.

42. *Wahrheit* (26 April 1907), pp. 2–3; (3 May 1907), pp. 3–4.

43. *MONOIU* 19, no. 5 (May 1907), p. 15. In his memoirs Mayer makes no mention of the debate over OIU support for Ofner, but does note that he was pleased with *Union* support for Kamillo Kuranda (Inner City), because "seine Stellung zur Judenfrage ist mir persönlich gewiss sympathisch; er ist ein Assimilant alten Schlages" (p. 353).

44. *MONOIU* 19, no. 5 (May 1907), pp. 1–2, 15–19.

45. *OW* 24, no. 19 (10 May 1907), pp. 310–12.

46. *Wahrheit* (10 May 1907), pp. 3–4.

47. *MONOIU* 19, no. 5 (May 1907), p. 22; "Die Oesterreichisch-Israelitische Union an die jüdische Wählerschaft," *MONOIU* 19, no. 6/7 (June/July 1907), pp. 1–13.

48. *OW* 24, no. 20 (17 May 1907), pp. 326–27.

49. *OW* 24, no. 25 (21 June 1907), pp. 405–6; *Wahrheit* (15 November 1907), pp. 3–6.

50. Böhm, I, p. 201.

51. The 1914 elections were cancelled because of the outbreak of World War I that fall.

52. *Die Welt* (16 November 1900), p. 2.

53. *JZ* (27 November 1908), pp. 2–3.

54. *Die Welt* (30 November 1900), p. 1; (7 December 1900), pp. 2–4.

55. *Die Welt* (4 November 1904), pp. 6–7; (21 October 1904), p. 7. See also *Die Welt* (16 November 1900), pp. 2–4; *NNZ* (18 September 1908), p. 5.

56. *NZ* (9 October 1906), pp. 1–2.

57. "Wahlkundmachungen . . . 1900," CAHJP, AW 50/3; "Wahlkundmachungen . . . 1902," CAHJP, AW 51/5.

58. *JZ* (12 June 1908), pp. 1–2; see also *JZ* (17 September 1908); (20 November 1908).

59. *JZ* (27 November 1908), pp. 2–3.

60. *Die Welt* (9 November 1900), p. 6; (16 November 1900), pp. 2–4; (28 October 1898), pp. 10–11; (2 December 1898), pp. 2–3; (1 June 1900), pp. 6–7; *NZ* (27 April 1906), p. 6; (11 May 1906); (3 August 1906).

61. *Die Welt* (28 October 1898), pp. 10–11; (25 November 1898), p. 9; (2 December 1898), pp. 2–3; (10 October 1902), pp. 5–7; (21 October 1904), p. 7; (4 November 1904), pp. 6–7; *JZ* (30 October 1908), pp. 1–2; (18 November 1910), pp. 1–3; (25 November 1910), p. 2; (11 October 1912), pp. 1–2; *JV* (14 November 1902), p. 1; *NZ* (27 April 1906), p. 6; (11 May 1906), pp. 1–2.

62. "An die jüdischen Wähler in die israelitische Cultusgemeinde," flyer, 1902, in CAHJP, AW 51/7.

63. *JZ* (30 October 1908), pp. 1–2; (18 November 1910), pp. 1–3; (25 November 1910), p. 2; (11 October 1912), pp. 1–2; *Die Welt* (9 November 1900), p. 6; (16 November 1900), pp. 2–4; (10 October 1902), pp. 5–7; *JV* (14 November 1902), p. 1; (21 November 1902).

64. *Die Welt* (23 November 1900), pp. 1–3; (10 October 1902), pp. 5–6; *JZ* (30 October 1908), pp. 1–2; (11 October 1912), pp. 1–2; *JV* (14 November 1902), p. 1.

65. *NNZ* (18 September 1908), p. 5; (30 October 1908), p. 3; (20 November 1908), pp. 1–4; (27 November 1908), pp. 7–8.

66. For lists of candidates, see *Die Welt* (23 November 1900); *OW* 17, no. 48 (30 November 1900), pp. 853–54; *Die Welt* (21 November 1902); *JV* (21 November 1902), p. 1; *JZ* (23 October 1908); (22 November 1910); (25 November 1910), p. 1; (15 November 1912), p. 2.

67. "Wahlprotokolle 1900," CAHJP, AW 50/8; "Wahlprotokolle 1902," CAHJP, AW 51/9; "Wahlprotokolle 1904," CAHJP, AW 52/9; "Wahlprotokolle 1906," CAHJP, AW 53/10; "Wahlprotokolle 1908," CAHJP, AW 54/12; "Wahlprotokolle 1910," CAHJP, AW 55/8; and reports in *Die Welt* (30 November 1900), pp. 1–2; (7 December 1900), p. 2; (28 November 1902), pp. 4–7.

68. "Wahlprotokolle 1900," CAHJP, AW 50/8; *Die Welt* (30 November 1900), p. 2; (7 December 1900), p. 2.

69. "Wahlprotokolle 1906," CAHJP, AW 53/10.

70. Letter of S. Krenberger to Zionist Actions Committee, 23 November 1904, CZA, Z1/256. It seems that Marmorek entered the official list on his own, not with the party's blessings. See also *Die Welt* (2 December 1904), p. 9.

71. *JZ* (15 November 1912), p. 2; *OW* 29, no. 46 (15 November 1912), p. 770; *Wahrheit* (15 November 1912), front page (unnumbered). The Jewish nationalist Saul Raphael Landau regarded this compromise agreement as treasonous. See *NNZ* (8 November 1912), pp. 1–2; (22 November 1912), p. 3; and (20 December 1912), pp. 3–6.

72. "Wahlprotokolle 1902," CAHJP, AW 51/9; "Wahlprotokolle 1906," CAHJP, AW 53/10; "Wahlprotokolle 1910," CAHJP, AW 55/8; *Die Welt* (28 November 1902), pp. 4–7; *JZ* (2 December 1910).

73. "Wahlprotokolle 1902," CAHJP, AW 51/9.

74. "Wahlprotokolle 1906," CAHJP, AW 53/10.

75. "Wahlprotokolle 1908," CAHJP, AW 54/12; "Wahlprotokolle 1910," CAHJP, AW 55/8.

76. For example, in 1870, 559 *Gemeinde* members voted; in 1880, 633; and in 1890, 876; see "Wahlprotokolle 1870," CAHJP, AW °47; "Wahlprotokolle 1880," CAHJP, AW 3086; "Wahlprotokolle 1890," CAHJP, AW 3096.

77. *OW* 6, no. 45 (22 November 1889); no. 46 (29 November 1889), pp. 842–43; *OW* 3, no. 33 (26 November 1886), pp. 549–52; *OW* 9, no. 2 (8 January 1892), p. 28; *OW* 14, no. 9 (26 February 1897), pp. 173–74; *OW* 21, no. 2 (8 January 1904), p. 17; no. 16 (15 April 1904), pp. 249–50.

78. *OW* 17, no. 48 (30 November 1900), pp. 853–54; no. 50 (14 December 1900), p. 890. The connection between the tone of the Zionists and that of the Viennese antisemites has been made brilliantly by Carl E. Schorske, "Politics in a New Key: An Austrian Triptych," *Journal of Modern History* 39 (1967), pp. 343–86.

79. *MONOIU* 14, no. 12 (December 1902), pp. 1–3.

80. *OW* 19, no. 45 (7 November 1902), pp. 723–26.

81. *OW* 25, no. 40 (2 October 1908), pp. 697–98; no. 47 (20 November 1908), pp. 813–14; no. 48 (27 November 1908), pp. 838–39; *Wahrheit* (27 November 1908), p. 5.

82. *Neuzeit* (28 November 1884), pp. 451–52.

83. *MITOIU* 10, no. 106 (October 1898), p. 3.

84. *Neuzeit* (24 January 1902).

85. *OW* 23, no. 50 (14 December 1906), pp. 856–57; *OW* 24, no. 2 (11 January 1907), p. 22; *OW* 25, no. 47 (20 November 1908), pp. 813–14; *MONOIU* 18, no. 11 (November 1906), p. 15; *Wahrheit* (30 November 1906), pp. 4–5.

86. *OW* 25, no. 47 (20 November 1908), pp. 813–14.

87. *OW* 19, no. 47 (21 November 1902), p. 759; *OW* 23, no. 50 (14 December 1906), pp. 856–57; *OW* 24, no. 2 (11 January 1907), p. 22; *MONOIU* 18, no. 11 (November 1906), p. 14; *Wahrheit* (30 November 1906), pp. 4–5.

88. *OW* 10, no. 42 (20 October 1893), pp. 826–28.

89. "Vereinigte Wahlkomité; Programm," CAHJP, AW 52/4; *Wahrheit* (25 November 1904), pp. 3–5.

90. *OW* 25, no. 47 (20 November 1908), pp. 816–17; *Wahrheit* (20 November 1908), p. 5; "Kandidaten-Aufstellung; Zentral-Komité für die Kultusvorstands-Wahlen 1910," CAHJP, AW 55/2. The OIU did not participate in the Central Electoral Committee that year, but presented its own, similar, program in *MONOIU* 20, no. 11 (November 1908), pp. 3–6.

91. *OW* 13, no. 39 (25 September 1896), pp. 765–69; *OW* 15, no. 43 (4 November 1898), p. 798. See also *OW* 16, no. 18 (5 May 1899), pp. 341–43; *OW* 17, no. 21 (25 May 1900), pp. 386–88; *OW* 18, no. 20 (17 May 1901), pp. 337–40.

92. "Wahlprogramm der OIU, 1896," CAHJP, AW 48/3; *OW* 13, no. 42 (16 October 1896), p. 826.

93. *OW* 13, no. 47 (20 November 1896), p. 926; *MITOIU* 10, no. 108 (November 1898), pp. 1–2.

94. *OW* 24, no. 47 (20 November 1908), pp. 813–14, 814–17; *Wahrheit* (20 November 1908).

95. *OW* 17, no. 50 (14 December 1900), p. 890.

96. *OW* 27, no. 48 (2 December 1910), pp. 797–98.

97. "Vereinigte Wahlcomité, 1904," CAHJP, AW 52/4; *OW* 21, no. 48 (25 November 1904), pp. 764–65; *Wahrheit* (25 November 1904), pp. 3–5.

98. *OW* 25, no. 47 (20 November 1908), pp. 816–17; *Wahrheit* (20 November 1908), p. 5; 1908 flyer in "Kandidatenaufstellung, 1910," CAHJP, AW 55/2.

99. *OW* 17, no. 48 (30 November 1900), pp. 853–54; *OW* 23, no. 50 (14 December 1906), pp. 856–57; *OW* 29, no. 46 (15 November 1912), p. 770; *Wahrheit* (15 November 1912), front page (unnumbered).

100. Dr. Oswald Byk, "Glossen zum Kompromiss mit den Zionisten anlässlich der Kultuswahlen 1912," *OW* 29, no. 46 (15 November 1912), pp. 770–71.

101. *OW* 29, no. 47 (22 November 1912), pp. 796–97 and 789–90.

Conclusion

1. Leo Goldhammer, *Die Juden Wiens: Eine statistische Studie* (Vienna and Leipzig, 1927), p. 7.

2. For a moving description of interwar antisemitism in Austria, see George Clare, *Last Waltz in Vienna: The Rise and Destruction of a Family, 1842–1942* (New York, 1982).

Bibliography

Primary Sources

1) *Archival Material*

Central Archives for the History of the Jewish People, Jerusalem
AW—Archiv der Israelitischen Kultusgemeinde, Wien
Central Zionist Archives, Jerusalem
Z1—Central Zionist Office, Vienna, 1897–1905
Z2—Central Zionist Office, Cologne, 1905–11
F1—Austria, 1898–1915
Private Archives:
A 30—Zevi Peretz Chajes
A 80—Wilhelm Stiassny
A 141—Adolf Böhm
A 196—Isidor Schalit
Israelitische Kultusgemeinde, Vienna
Trauungsbücher, 1870, 1880, 1890, 1900, 1910
Geburtsbücher, 1870, 1880, 1890, 1900, 1910
Austrittsbücher, 1890, 1900, 1910
Proselytenbücher, 1870, 1880, 1890, 1900, 1910
Bundesgymnasium, I, Stubenbastei 6–8 (formerly Franz-Joseph-Gymnasium, I, Hegelgasse 3), Vienna
Hauptkatalogen, 1890/91 and 1910/11
Bundesgymnasium, II, Wohlmutgasse 3 (formerly Erzherzog-Rainer-Gymnasium, II, Kleine Sperlgasse), Vienna
Hauptkatalogen, 1890/91 and 1910/11
Bundesgymnasium, IX, Wasagasse 10 (formerly Maximilian-Gymnasium), Vienna
Hauptkatalogen, 1890/91 and 1910/11
Stadtschulrat der Stadt Wien, Vienna
Hauptkatalogen des öff. . . . Mädchen-Lyzeums Eugenie Schwarzwald, 1890/91 and 1910/11
Dompfarramt St. Stephan, I, Stephansplatz, Vienna
Matrikel, 1870, 1880, 1890, 1900, 1910
Kirche St. Michael, I, Habsburgergasse 12, Vienna
Matrikel, 1870, 1880, 1890, 1900, 1910
Kirche St. Peter, I, Petersplatz, Vienna

Matrikel, 1870, 1880, 1890, 1900, 1910
Pfarramt u.l. Frau zu den Schotten, I, Freyung 6, Vienna
Matrikel, 1870, 1880, 1890, 1900, 1910
Kirche St. Johann von Nepomuk, II, Nepomukgasse 1, Vienna
Matrikel, 1870, 1880, 1890, 1900, 1910
Kirche St. Josef, II, Karmelitergasse 10, Vienna
Matrikel, 1870, 1880, 1890, 1900, 1910
Kirche St. Leopold, II, Alexander-Poch-Platz, Vienna
Matrikel, 1870, 1880, 1890, 1900, 1910
Propsteipfarre zum göttl. Heiland (Votivkirche), IX, Rooseveltplatz, Vienna
Matrikel, 1870, 1880, 1890, 1900, and 1910
Kirche Rossau (Maria Verkündigung), IX, Servitengasse 9
Matrikel, 1870, 1880, 1890, 1910

2) *Unpublished Memoirs,* Leo Baeck Institute, New York

Berliner, Gertrude. "From My Family, Fiction and Truth." New York, 1958.

Cassirer, Toni. "Aus meinem Leben mit Ernst Cassirer." New York, 1949–50.

Eisner, Bruno. "Gedenken und Gedanken aus dem Leben eines Musikers." New York, 1959.

Friedländer-Prechtl, Robert. "Oppeln aus einem Lebensrückblick." Starnberg, 1950.

Güdemann, Moritz. "Aus meinem Leben." N.p., n.d.

Hindls, Arnold. "Erinnerungen aus meinem Leben." Brünn, 1966.

Höllriegel, Arnold (Richard Arnold Bermann). "Die Fahrt auf dem Katarakt (Autobiographie ohne einen Helden)." N.p., n.d.

Müller, Ernst. "Wiener Universitätsjahre." N.p., n.d.

Müller, Ernst. "Geistige Spuren in Lebenserinnerungen." N.p., n.d.

3) *Newspapers*

Freies Blatt: Organ zur Abwehr des Antisemitismus (1892–1896).

Jerusalem: Zeitschrift für die Interessen des Judentums (Antizionistischer Tendenz) (1907).

Jüdisches Volksblatt (after 1905: *Nationalzeitung*) (1902–1905).

Jüdische Volkszeitung (formerly *Selbstemancipation*) (1894–1895) (superseded by *Zion* [Berlin]).

Jüdische Zeitung: National-jüdisches Organ (1907–1913).

Kalendar für Israeliten (1892–1893).

Mittheilungen der Oesterreichisch-Israelitischen Union (1889–1900) (superseded by *Monatsschrift der OIU*).

Monatsschrift der Oesterreichisch-Israelitischen Union (formerly *Mittheilungen der OIU*) (1901–1914).

Nationalzeitung: Organ für die gesamten Interessen des jüdischen Volkes (formerly *Jüdisches Volksblatt*) (1906–1907) (superseded by *Neue National-Zeitung*).

Neue National-Zeitung: Jüdisch-politische Wochenschrift (formerly *Nationalzeitung*) (1907–1914).

Die Neuzeit: Wochenschrift für politische, religiöse, und Cultur-Interessen (1867–1903).

Oesterreichische Wochenschrift (also: *Doktor Bloch's Wochenschrift; Blochs Oesterreichische Wochenschrift*): *Central-Organ für die gesammten Interessen des Judentums* (1884–1914).

Selbstemancipation: Organ der Jüdisch-Nationalen (1885–1893) (superseded by *Jüdische Volkszeitung*).

Unsere Hoffnung: Monatsschrift für die reifere jüdische Jugend (1904).

Vierteljahres-Bericht für die Mitglieder der oesterreichisch-israelitschen Humanitätsvereine "B'nai B'rith" (later *Zweimonatsbericht*) (1897–1913).

Die Wahrheit: Unabhängige Zeitschrift für jüdische Interessen (1903–1914).

Die Welt: Zentralorgan der zionistischen Bewegung (1897–1905).

Wiener Israelit (1883–1897).

Zion: Mitteilungen des "Zion," des Verbandes oesterreichischer Vereine für Kolonisation Palästinas und Syriens (1903–1904).

4) Published Statistical Collections

Austria. K.-k. Statistische Central-Commission. *Bevölkerung und Viehstand von Böhmen, Bukowina, Dalmatien, etc. nach der Zählung vom 31. October 1857.* Vienna: k.-k. Hof- und Staatsdruckerei, 1859.

Austria. K.-k. Statistische Central-Commission. *Bevölkerung und Viehstand von Böhmen etc. nach der Zählung vom 31. Dezember 1869.* Vienna: k.-k. Hof- und Staatsdruckerei, 1871.

Austria. K.-k. Statistische Central-Commission. *Oesterreichisches Städtebuch; Statistische Berichte von grösseren oesterreichischen Städten.* 15 volumes. Vienna: k.-k. Hof- und Staatsdruckerei, 1887–1918.

Austria. K.-k. Statistische Central-Commission. *Oesterreichische Statistik.* 93 volumes. Vienna: k.-k. Hof- und Staatsdruckerei, 1882–1916.

Austria. K.-k. Statistische Central-Commission. *Oesterreichische Statistik, Neue Folge.* 18 volumes. Vienna: k.-k. Hof- und Staatsdruckerei, 1916–1918.

Austria. K.-k. Statistische Central-Commission. *Statistisches Handbuch für die im Reichsrathe vertretenen Königreiche und Länder.* Vienna: Alfred Hölder, 1883, 1884.

Austria. K.-k. Statistische Central-Commission. *Statistisches Jahrbuch der oesterreichischen Monarchie.* 19 volumes. Vienna: k.-k. Hof- und Staatsdruckerei, 1864–1884.

Austria. K.-k. Statistische Central-Commission. *Oesterreichisches Städtebuch.* 2 volumes. Vienna: Hollineck, 1868.

Austria. K.-k. Statistische Central-Commission. *Bevölkerung der Gemeinden mit mehr als 2000 Einwohnern in den im Reichsrathe vertretenen Königreichen und Ländern nach der Zählung vom 31. December 1880.* Vienna: k.-k. Hof- und Staatsdruckerei, 1881.

Austria. K.-k. Statistische Central-Commission. *Allgemeines Ortschaften-Verzeichniss der im Reichsrathe vertretenen Königreiche und Länder nach den Ergebnissen der Volkszählung vom 31. December 1900 nebst vollständigem alphabetischem Namensregister.* Vienna: Alfred Hölder, 1902.

Austria. K.-k. Statistische Central-Commission. *Gemeinde-Lexikon der im Reichsrathe vertretenen Königreiche und Länder bearbeitet auf Grund der Ergebnisse der Volkszählung vom 31. December 1900.* 14 volumes. Vienna: A. Hölder, 1903–1908.

Austria. K.-k. Ministerium des Innern. *Statistische Übersichten über die Bevölkerung und den Viehstand von Oesterreich nach der Zählung vom 31. Oktober 1857.* Vienna: k.-k. Hof- und Staatsdruckerei, 1859.

Austria. K.-k. Finanzministerium. *Beiträge zur Statistik der Personaleinkommensteuer in den Jahren 1898 bis 1902.* Vienna: k.-k. Hof- und Staatsdruckerei, 1903.

Hungary. Magyar Kir Központi statisztikai hivatal. *Publications statistiques hongroises, nouvelle série.* Budapest: Athenaeum, 1902–1918.

Hungary. Központi Statisztikai hivatal. *Magyar statisztikai évkönyv = Ungarisches statistisches Jahrbuch.* 20 volumes. Neue Folge, 22 volumes. Budapest: Athenaeum, 1873–1914.

Lehmann's Allgemeiner Wohnungs-Anzeiger nebst Handels- und Gewerbe-Adressbuch für die k.-k. Reichshaupt- und Residenzstadt Wien und Umgebung. Vienna: Alfred Hölder, 1881–1914.

Vienna. Statistischer Departement des Wiener Magistrates. *Statistisches Jahrbuch der Stadt Wien.* 32 volumes. Vienna: Verlag des Wiener Magistrates, 1883–1914.

Vienna. Praesidium des Gemeinderathes und Magistrates der k.-k. Reichshaupt- und Residenzstadt Wien. *Statistik der Stadt Wien,* 2. Vienna: k.-k. Hof- und Staatsdruckerei, 1861.

5) *Published Memoirs*

Baum, Vicki. *Es war alles ganz anders: Erinnerungen.* Berlin, Frankfurt, Vienna: Ullstein, 1962.

Benedikt, Moritz. *Aus meinem Leben: Erinnerungen und Erörterungen.* Vienna: Verlagsbuchhandlung Carl Konegen, 1906.

Bloch, Josef S. *My Reminiscences.* Vienna and Berlin: R. Löwit, 1923.

Canetti, Elias. *The Tongue Set Free: Remembrance of a European Childhood.* Translated by Joachim Neugroschel. New York: The Seabury Press, 1979.

Clare, George. *Last Waltz in Vienna: The Rise and Destruction of a Family, 1842–1942.* New York: Holt, Rinehart and Winston, 1982.

Mayer, Sigmund. *Ein jüdischer Kaufmann 1831 bis 1911: Lebenserinnerungen.* Leipzig: v. Drucker und Humblot, 1911.

Schnitzler, Arthur. *My Youth in Vienna.* Translated by Catherine Hutter. New York: Holt, Rinehart and Winston, 1970.

Schoenberg, Arnold. *Letters.* Edited by Erwin Stein, and translated by Eithne Wilkins and Ernst Kaiser. New York: St. Martin's Press, 1965.

Szeps, Berta. *My Life and History.* New York: Alfred A. Knopf, 1939.

Wassermann, Jakob. *My Life as German and Jew.* Translated by S. N. Brainin. New York: Coward-McCann, 1933.

Wechsberg, Joseph. *The Vienna I Knew: Memories of a European Childhood.* Garden City, N. Y.: Doubleday, 1979.

Werfel, Alma Mahler. *Gustav Mahler: Memories and Letters.* 1946. Reprint. New York: Viking Press, 1968.
Zweig, Stefan. *The World of Yesterday.* New York: Viking Press, 1943.

6) Other Published Primary Sources

Ascher, Richard. *Die Creditnoth des jüdischen Handwerkers und Kleingewerbetreibenden.* Vienna: *Jüdisches Volksblatt,* 1900.
Bauer, Otto. *Die Nationalitätenfrage und die Sozialdemokratie.* 2nd ed. Vienna: Verlag der Wiener Volksbuchhandlung, 1924.
Birnbaum, Nathan. *Die nationale Wiedergeburt des jüdischen Volkes in seinem Lande als Mittel zur Lösung der Judenfrage.* Vienna, 1893.
Bloch, Josef S. *Gegen die Antisemiten.* Vienna: D. Löwy, 1882.
———. *Der nationale Zwist und die Juden in Oesterreich.* Vienna: M. Gottlieb, 1886.
———. *Talmud und Judenthum in der oesterreichischen Volksvertretung: Dr. Blochs Parlamentsreden.* Vienna, 1900.
Dubnow, Simon. *Nationalism and History: Essays on Old and New Judaism.* Philadelphia: Jewish Publication Society, 1958.
Festschrift anlässlich des fünfundzwanzigjährigen Bestandes des israelitischen Humanitätsvereines "Eintracht" (B'nai B'rith), Wien, 1903–1928. Vienna: Selbstverlag, 1928.
Festschrift zur Feier des 50-Jährigen Bestandes der Union Oesterreichischer Juden. Vienna: Selbstverlag, 1937.
Festschrift zur Feier des 100. Semesters der akademischen Verbindung Kadimah (1883–1933). Ludwig Rosenhek, editor. Vienna: Mödling, 1933.
Güdemann, M. *Nationaljudentum.* Leipzig and Vienna: Breitenstein, 1897.
Herzl, Theodor. *Diaries.* Edited and translated by Marvin Lowenthal. New York: Dial Press, 1956.
———. *Der Judenstaat.* Leipzig and Vienna: Breitenstein, 1896.
———. *The Jewish State.* Translated by Harry Zohn. New York: Herzl Press, 1970.
Jahresbericht der Israelitischen Allianz zu Wien. Vienna: Selbstverlag, 1904, 1908, 1911.
Jahresbericht der deutschen Lesehalle an der technischen Hochschule zu Wien, XIII. Vereinsjahr 1884–85. Vienna: Selbstverlag, 1885.
Jahresbericht des Lesevereines der deutschen Studenten Wien's. Vienna: Selbstverlag, 1872–1878.
Jahresbericht des Lese- und Redevereines der deutschen Hochschüler in Wien "Germania" über das Studienjahr 1908/9. Vienna: Selbstverlag, 1909.
Jahresbericht der Lese- und Redehalle jüdischer Hochschüler in Wien, 1906/7. Vienna: Selbstverlag, 1907.
Jahresbericht über das k.-k. Franz-Joseph-Gymnasium in Wien (I). Vienna: Gistel, 1873–1919.
Jahresbericht des k.-k. Staatsgymnasiums im II. Bezirke von Wien. (After 1900 *Sophiengymnasium.*) Vienna: Selbstverlag, 1878–1918.
Jahresbericht der zweiten k.-k. Staatsrealschule im II. Wiener Gemeindebezirke. Vienna: Selbstverlag, 1904–1933.

Jahresbericht des Leopoldstädter Communal-Realgymnasiums. (After 1898 k.-k. II. Staatsgymnasium im II. Bezirke; after 1901 k.-k. Erzherzog-Rainer-Gymnasium.) Vienna: Selbstverlag, 1865–1918.

Jahresbericht über die Wiener Kommunal-Oberrealschule in der Vorstadt Wieden (IV). Vienna: Selbstverlag, 1859–1918.

Jahresbericht über das k.-k. Staatsgymnasium in Wien IV. (After 1901 Elisabeth-Gymnasium.) Vienna: Selbstverlag, 1886–1919.

Jahresbericht des öffentlichen Unterrealgymnasiums in der Josefstadt in Wien. Vienna: Selbstverlag, 1910–1915.

Jahresbericht der k.-k. Staatsrealschule im VIII. Wiener Gemeindebezirk. Vienna: Gerold, 1906–1919.

Jahresbericht der Staats-Realschule und des Staats-Reformrealgymnasiums im VIII. Wiener Gemeindebezirke. Vienna, 1913.

Jahresbericht der Haupt-, Unterreal-, und Oberrealschule in der Josefstadt (Wien VIII). Vienna: Gerold, 1871–1919.

Jahresbericht der k.-k. Staats-Realschule und des k.-k. Staats-Reformrealgymnasiums im VIII. Wiener Gemeindebezirke. Vienna, 1911.

Jahresbericht über die k.-k. Staatsrealschule im IX. Wiener Gemeindebezirke. Vienna: Selbstverlag, 1905–1919.

Jahresbericht über die k.-k. Staatsrealschule im X. Bezirke in Wien. Vienna: Selbstverlag, 1903–1919.

Jahresbericht des öffentlichen Communal-Gymnasiums in Unter-Meidling bei Wien (XII). (After 1897 k.-k. Karl-Ludwig-Gymnasium.) Vienna: Selbstverlag, 1883–1917.

Jahresbericht der Vereinsrealschule des Vereines zur Gründung einer Kaiser-Jubiläums Realschule im XII. Wiener Gemeindebezirke. Vienna: Selbstverlag, 1911–1919.

Jahresbericht des k.-k. Staatsgymnasiums im XIII. Bezirke in Wien. Vienna: Selbstverlag, 1901–1916.

Jahresbericht der k.-k. Staatsrealschule in Wien XIII. Vienna: Selbstverlag, 1907–1917.

Jahresbericht der k.-k. Realschule im Berzirke Sechshaus bei Wien (XV). Vienna: Seidel, 1873–1917.

Jahresbericht der Staats-Oberrealschule im XV. Bezirke von Wien (XV). Vienna: Moessmer, 1900.

Jahresbericht des Vereins-Gymnasiums im XVI. Wiener Gemeindebezirke. Vienna: Holzwarth, 1907–1918.

Jahresbericht der Vereinsrealschule, Otttakring. Vienna: Nekham, 1900–1905, N.F. 1906–1919.

Jahresbericht des k.-k. Staats-Realgymnasiums in Hernals (XVII). Vienna: Selbstverlag, 1873–1914.

Jahresbericht des k.-k. Staatsgymnasiums im XVIII. Bezirke von Wien. Vienna: Hofmann, 1908–1917.

Jahresbericht des Vereines-Realgymnasiums im XVIII. Bezirke von Wien. Vienna: Selbstverlag, 1915–1920.

Jahresbericht des öffentlichen Communal-Gymnasiums in Ober-Döbling bei Wien (Wien XIX). (Later k.-k. Staatsgymnasium im XIX. Bezirke.) Vienna: Selbstverlag, 1886–1919.

Jahresbericht der Vereins-Realschule im XIX. Wiener Gemeindebezirke. Vienna: Schöler, 1908–1919.

Jahresbericht über das k.-k. Staatsgymnasium in Floridsdorf (Wien XXI). Floridsdorf: Selbstverlag, 1901–1921.

Jahresbericht über das Gymnasium an der k.-k. Theresianischen Akademie (Wien IV). Vienna: Theresianische Akademie, 1851–1918.

Jahresbericht des Gymnasiums zu den Schotten in Wien (I). Vienna: Selbstverlag, 1853–1921.

Jahresbericht des Privat-Mädchen-Lyzeums Luithlen (Wien I). Vienna: Selbstverlag, 1902–1916.

Jahresbericht des Privat-Mädchen-Lyzeums der Frau Eugenie Schwarzwald (Wien I). Vienna: Selbstverlag, 1902–1913.

Jahresbericht des Mädchen-Obergymnasiums des Vereines für erweiterte Frauenbildung (I). Vienna: Selbstverlag, 1902–1919.

Jahresbericht des öffentlichen Mädchen-Lyzeums Hilda von Gunesch, Wien, I. Vienna: Selbstverlag, 1912–1916.

Jahresbericht des öffentlichen Reform-Realgymnasiums für Mädchen. (Öffentliches Mädchenlyzeum im II. Bezirke in Wien). Vienna: Selbstverlag, 1915–1918.

Jahresbericht des öffentlichen Wiedener Mädchen-Lyzeums und der damit verbundenen reformrealgymnasialen Oberklassen der Christlichen Verein zur Förderung der Frauenbildung, Wien, IV. Vienna, 1914–1916.

Jahresbericht des "öffentlichen" Mädchen-Lyzeums auf der Wieden (Wien IV). Vienna: Selbstverlag, 1909.

Jahresbericht des öffentlichen Mädchen-Lyzeums Liste, V. Vienna: Selbstverlag, 1910–1918.

Jahresbericht der höheren Bildungsschule (Mittelschule) für Mädchen, am Wiener Frauenerwerbverein, Wien, VI. Vienna: Wallishausser, 1881–1916.

Jahresbericht des Vereines für realgymnasialen Mädchenunterricht, Wien, VIII. Vienna: Selbstverlag, 1913–1919.

Jahresbericht des öffentlichen Mädchen-Lyzeums im IX. Bezirke. Vienna: Selbstverlag, 1915–1917.

Jahresbericht des öffentlichen Mädchen-Lyzeums . . . Wien, XIII. Vienna: Selbstverlag, 1915.

Jahresbericht des Cottage-Lyzeums, XIX. Vienna: Selbstverlag, 1913–1916.

Jüdische Toynbee-Halle, Wien. *Eine jüdische Toynbee-Halle in Wien.* Vienna: Selbstverlag, 1901.

Jüdischer Almanach 5670; Herausgegeben aus Anlass des 25. semestrigen Jubiläums von der Vereinigung jüdischer Hochschüler aus Galizien, Bar Kochba, in Wien. Vienna: Selbstverlag, 1910.

Kadisch, Hermann. *Die Juden und die oesterreichische Verfassungsreform.* Vienna, 1918.

———. *Jung-Juden und Jung-Oesterreich.* Vienna: Adria, 1912.

———. "Die Juden und die Nationalitätenfrage," *Hickl's jüd. Volkskalendar für das Jahr 5687 (1926–27)*, pp. 96–100.

Landau, Saul Raphael. *Fort mit Hausjuden: Grundlinien jüdischer Volkspolitik.* Vienna, 1907.

———. *Der Polenklub und seine Hausjuden.* Vienna: C. W. Stern, n.d.

________. *Sturm und Drang in Zionismus; Rückblicke eines Zionisten vor, mit und um-Theodor Herzl.* Vienna: Neue National-Zeitung, 1937.

________. *Unter jüdischen Proletarien.* Vienna: L. Rosner, 1898.

Renner, Karl. *Der Kampf der oesterreichischen Nationen um den Staat.* Leipzig and Vienna: F. Deuticke, 1902.

Rosenfeld, Max. *Nationale Autonomie der Juden in Oesterreich.* Czernowitz: Buchdruckerei Gutenberg, 1912.

________. *Die polnische Judenfrage: Problem und Lösung.* Vienna, 1918.

Rosenmann,Moritz. *Jüdische Realpolitik in Oesterreich.* Vienna: R. Löwit, 1900.

Schnitzler, Arthur. *Professor Bernhardi.* Translated by Hetty Landstone. New York: Simon and Schuster, 1928.

________. *The Road to the Open.* Translated by Horace Samuel. New York: Alfred A. Knopf, 1923.

Stricker, Robert. "Rede in der Leopoldstadt am 30. September 1910." In *Aufsätze und Reden.* Vienna and Leipzig, 1929.

U.O.B.B., Humanitätsverein "Wien." *Festschrift zur Feier des fünfundzwanzigjährigen Bestandes, 1895–1920.* Vienna: Selbstverlag, 1920.

Secondary Sources

Andree, Richard. *Andrees allgemeiner Handatlas.* 4th ed. Bielefeld and Leipzig: Verlag von Velhagen und Klasig, 1904.

Aron, Willy. "Notes on Sigmund Freud's Ancestry and Jewish Contacts." *YIVO Annual for Jewish Social Science* 11 (1956/57), pp. 286–95.

Baer, Alwyn. "Occupational and Geographic Mobility in San Antonio, 1870–1900." *Social Science Quarterly* 51 (1970), pp. 396–403.

Bakan, David. *Sigmund Freud and the Jewish Mystical Tradition.* Princeton, N.J.: Van Nostrand, 1958.

Baltzarek, Franz, Alfred Hoffmann, and Hannes Stekl. *Wirtschaft und Gesellschaft der Wiener Stadterweiterung.* Vol. V of *Die Wiener Ringstrasse: Bild einer Epoche,* edited by Renate Wagner-Rieger. Wiesbaden: Franz Steiner, 1975.

Barany, George. "Magyar Jew or Jewish Magyar? (To the Question of Jewish Assimilation in Hungary)." *Canadian-American Slavic Studies* 8 (1974), pp. 1–44.

Baron, Salo W. *The Jewish Community.* 3 vols. Philadelphia: Jewish Publication Society, 1942.

Barton, Josef J. *Peasants and Strangers: Italians, Rumanians, and Slovaks in an American City, 1890–1950.* Cambridge, Mass.: Harvard University Press, 1975.

Bato, Ludwig. *Die Juden im alten Wien.* Vienna: Phaidon, 1928.

Bein, Alex. *Theodore Herzl: A Biography of the Founder of Modern Zionism.* Translated by Maurice Samuel. 1941. Reprint. New York: Atheneum, 1970.

Bendix, R., and S.M. Lipset, eds. *Class, Status and Power: Social Stratification in Comparative Perspective* 2nd ed. New York: Free Press, 1966.

Benedikt, Heinrich. *Die wirtschaftliche Entwicklung in der Franz-Joseph-Zeit.* Vienna: Herold, 1958.

Berend, Iván T., and György Ránki. *Economic Development in East-Central Europe in the Nineteenth and Twentieth Centuries.* New York: Columbia University Press, 1974.

Berrol, Selma C. "Education and Economic Mobility: The Jewish Experience in New York City, 1880–1920." *American Jewish Historical Quarterly* 65 (1975/76), pp. 257–71.

Bihl, Wolfdieter. *Bibliographie der Dissertationen über Judentum und jüdische Persönlichkeiten die 1872–1962 an österreichischen Hochschulen (Wien, Graz, Innsbruck) approbiert wurden.* Vienna: Notring der wissenschaftlichen Verbände Oesterreichs, 1965.

———. "Die Juden in der Habsburgermonarchie 1848–1918." *Studia Judaica Austriaca* 8 (1980), pp. 5–73.

Blau, Bruno. "Sociology and Statistics of the Jews." *Historia Judaica* 9 (1949), pp. 145–62.

Blau, Peter M., and Otis D. Duncan. *The American Occupational Structure.* New York: Wiley, 1967.

Bobek, Hans, and Elisabeth Lichtenberger. *Wien: Bauliche Gestalt und Entwicklung seit der Mitte des 19. Jahrhunderts.* Graz: Verlag Hermann Bohlaus Nachf., 1966.

Böhm, Adolf. *Die zionistische Bewegung.* 2 vols. 2nd rev. ed. Tel Aviv: Hozaah Ivrith, 1935–37.

Bogue, Donald J. *Population Growth in Standard Metropolitan Areas, 1900–1950.* Washington, D.C.: Housing and Home Finance Agency, 1953.

———. *Principles of Demography.* New York: Wiley, 1969.

———. "Internal Migration." In *The Study of Population,* edited by P.M. Hauser and O.D. Duncan, pp. 486–509. Chicago: University of Chicago Press, 1959.

Bolton, Frederich Elmer. *The Secondary School System of Germany.* International Education Series 47. N.p., n.d.

Boyer, John. *Political Radicalism in Late Imperial Vienna: Origins of the Christian Social Movement 1848–1897.* Chicago and London: University of Chicago Press, 1981.

Braham, Randolph, ed. *Hungarian-Jewish Studies.* New York: World Federation of Hungarian Jews, 1966.

Braunthal, Julius. *Victor und Friedrich Adler: Zwei Generationen Arbeiterbewegung.* Vienna: Verlag der Wiener Volksbuchhandlung, 1965.

Briggs, Asa. *Victorian Cities.* London: Odhams, 1963.

Broch, Hermann. *Hofmannsthal und seine Zeit; Eine Studie.* Munich: R. Piper, 1964.

Burgess, Ernest W. "Residential Segregation in American Cities." *Annals of the American Academy of Political and Social Science* 140 (1928), pp. 105–15.

Cahan, Abraham. *The Rise of David Levinsky.* New York and London: Harper and Bros., 1917.

Cahnmann, Werner J. "Adolf Fischhof and His Jewish Followers." *LBIYB* 4 (1959), pp. 111–39.

———. "The Fighting Kadimah." *Chicago Jewish Forum* 17, no. 1 (Fall 1958), pp. 24–27.

Cardona, Heinrich R. *Die Armenpflege der Israeliten mit besonderer Rücksicht auf die israelitischen Cultusgemeinden in Oesterreich und die israelitischen Vereine in Galizien.* Graz, 189?

Chamberlain, Houston Stewart. *Foundations of the Nineteenth Century.* 1899. Translated by John Lees. New York: John Lane, 1912.

Charmatz, Richard. *Deutsch-oesterreichische Politik; Studien über den Liberalismus und über die auswärtige Politik Österreichs.* Leipzig: Duncker and Humblot, 1907.

———. *Oesterreichs innere Geschichte von 1848 bis 1907.* 2nd ed. Leipzig: B.G. Teubner, 1911–12.

Chudacoff, Howard. *Mobile Americans: Residential and Social Mobility in Omaha, 1880–1920.* New York: Oxford University Press, 1972.

Cohen, Carl. "The Road to Conversion." *LBIYB* 6 (1961), pp. 259–79.

Cohen, Gary B. *The Politics of Ethnic Survival: Germans in Prague, 1861–1914.* Princeton, N.J.: Princeton University Press, 1981.

———. "Jews in German Society: Prague, 1860–1914." *Central European History* 10 (1977), pp. 28–54.

Cohen, Steven Martin. "Patterns of Interethnic Marriage and Friendship in the United States." Ph.D. Dissertation, Columbia University, 1974.

———. "Socioeconomic Determinants of Interethnic Marriage and Friendship." *Social Forces* 55 (1977), pp. 997–1010.

Cressey, Paul Frederick. "Population Succession in Chicago, 1898–1930." *American Journal of Sociology* 44 (1938), pp. 59–69.

Crew, David F. *Town in the Ruhr: A Social History of Bochum, 1860–1914.* New York: Columbia University Press, 1979.

Cuddihy, John Murray. *The Ordeal of Civility: Freud, Marx, Levi-Strauss, and the Jewish Struggle with Modernity.* New York: Basic Books, 1974.

Czeike, Felix, and Walter Lugsch. *Studien zur Sozialgeschichte von Ottakring und Hernals.* Vienna: Verlag für Jugend und Volk, 1955.

Czoernig, Karl von Czernhausen. *Ethnographie der oesterreichischen Monarchie.* Vienna: k.-k. Hof- und Staatsdruckerei, 1857.

Darroch, A. Gordon, and Wilfred G. Marston. "The Social Bases of Ethnic Residential Segregation: The Canadian Case." *American Journal of Sociology* 77 (1971), pp. 491–510.

Davey, Ian, and Michael Dancet. "The Social Geography of a Commercial City ca. 1853." Appendix I in *The People of Hamilton, Canada West,* by Michael B. Katz, pp. 319–42. Cambridge, Mass.: Harvard University Press, 1975.

Davies, Allen F. *Spearheads for Reform: The Social Settlements and the Progressive Movement, 1890–1914.* New York: Oxford University Press, 1967.

Dawidowicz, Lucy S. "Arnold Schoenberg: A Search for Jewish Identity." In *The Jewish Presence: Essays on Identity and History,* pp. 32–45. New York: Holt, Rinehart and Winston, 1977.

———. *The Golden Tradition: Jewish Life and Thought in Eastern Europe.* New York: Holt, Rinehart and Winston, 1967.

Deák, István. *Weimar Germany's Left-Wing Intellectuals: A Political History of the Weltbühne and Its Circle.* Berkeley, Calif.: University of California Press, 1968.

DeYoung, Peter Y., Milton J. Brawer, and Stanley S. Rubin. "Patterns of Female Inter-generational Occupational Mobility." *American Sociological Review* 36 (1971), pp. 1033–42.

Dollar, Charles M., and Richard J. Jensen. *Historian's Guide to Statistics: Quantitative Analysis and Historical Research.* New York: Holt, Rinehart and Winston, 1971.

Dohm, Christian Wilhelm von. *Über die bürgerliche Verbesserung der Juden.* Berlin and Stettin, 1781–83.

Drabek, Anna, Wolfgang Häusler, Kurt Schubert, Karl Stuhlpfarrer, and Nikolaus Vielmetti. *Das österreichische Judentum: Voraussetzungen und Geschichte.* Vienna and Munich: Jugend und Volk, 1974.

Drage, Geoffrey. *Austria-Hungary.* London: John Murray, 1909.

Dubnow, Simon. *History of the Jews in Russia and Poland from the Earliest Times to the Present Day.* 3 vols. Translated by I. Friedlaender. Philadelphia: Jewish Publication Society, 1916–20.

Duncan, Otis D. and Beverly Duncan. "A Methodological Analysis of Segregation Indexes." *American Sociological Review* 20 (1955), pp. 210–17.

Duncan, Otis D. and Stanley Lieberson. "Ethnic Segregation and Assimilation." *American Journal of Sociology* 24 (1959), pp. 364–74.

Edwards, Alba. "A Social-Economic Grouping of the Gainful Workers of the United States." *Journal of the American Statistical Association* 28 (1933), pp. 377–87.

Elon, Amos. *Herzl.* New York: Holt, Rinehart and Winston, 1975.

Engelmann, R. "Oesterreichs städtische Wohnplätze mit mehr als 25,000 Einwohnern Ende 1910, ihr Wachstum seit 1869 und die konfessionelle und sprachliche Zusammensetzung ihrer Bevölkerung 1880–1910." *Statistische Monatsschrift* (Vienna) 40 (1914), pp. 413–510.

Fall, Gustav Heinrich. *Die rechtliche Stellung der Juden in Oesterreich.* Vienna: Verlag des Vereines zur Abwehr des Antisemitismus, 1892.

Feldbauer, Peter. *Stadtwachstum und Wohnungsnot: Determinanten unzureichnender Wohnungsversorgung in Wien 1848-1914.* Vienna: Verlag für Geschichte und Politik, 1977.

Field, Frank. *The Last Days of Mankind: Karl Kraus and His Vienna.* New York: St. Martins, 1967.

Field, Geoffrey G. *Evangelist of Race: The Germanic Vision of Houston Stewart Chamberlain.* New York: Columbia University Press, 1981.

Fleischer, Siegfried. "Enquête über die Lage der jüdischen Bevölkerung Galiziens." In *Jüdische Statistik,* edited by Alfred Nossig. Berlin: Jüdischer Verlag, 1903.

Fraenkel, Josef, ed. *The Jews of Austria: Essays on Their Life, History and Destruction.* London: Vallentine, Mitchell, 1967.

———. ed. *Robert Stricker.* London, n.p., 1950.

———. "Moritz Güdemann and Theodor Herzl." *LBIYB* 11 (1966), pp. 67–82.

Frankenberger, Max. "Die Vitalität und die Morbidität der Wiener Juden." Ph.D. Dissertation, University of Vienna, 1943.

Frei, Bruno. *Jüdisches Elend in Wien.* Vienna and Berlin: R. Löwit, 1920.

Freund, Arthur. "Um Gemeinde und Organisation: Zur Haltung der Juden in Oesterreich." *Bulletin des Leo Baeck Instituts* (1960) no. 10, pp. 81–100.

Freud, Martin. *Sigmund Freud: Man and Father.* New York: Vanguard Press, 1958.

Freidenreich, Harriet Pass. *The Jews of Yugoslavia: A Quest for Community.* Philadelphia: Jewish Publication Society, 1979.

Friedländer, Otto. *Letzer Glanz der Märchenstadt: Bilder aus dem Wiener Leben um die Jahrhundertwende, 1890–1914.* Vienna: Ring-Verlag, 1948.

Friedman, Isaiah. "The Austro-Hungarian Government and Zionism, 1897–1918." *Jewish Social Studies* 27 (1965), pp. 147–67 and 236–49.

Friedmann, Philipp. "Die galizischen Juden in den Jahren 1848–1868." Ph.D. Dissertation, University of Vienna, 1925.

Fuchs, Albert. *Geistige Strömungen in Oesterreich 1867–1918.* Vienna: Globus Verlag, 1949.

Gans, Herbert J. *The Urban Villagers: Group and Class in the Life of Italian Americans.* New York: Free Press, 1962.

Gay, Peter. *Freud, Jews and Other Germans: Masters and Victims in Modernist Culture.* Oxford and New York: Oxford University Press, 1978.

Gelber, N. M. "The Sephardic Community in Vienna." *Jewish Social Studies* 10 (1948), pp. 359–96.

Glass, David V., ed. *Social Mobility in Britain.* London: Routledge and Kegan Paul, 1954.

Glass, D.V., and D.E.C. Eversley, eds. *Population in History: Essays in Historical Demography.* London: E. Arnold, 1965.

Glazer, Nathan, and Daniel P. Moynihan. *Beyond the Melting Pot: The Negroes, Puerto Ricans, Jews, Italians and Irish of New York City.* Cambridge, Mass.: Massachusetts Institute of Technology Press, 1963.

Glettler, Monika. *Die Wiener Tschechen um 1900: Strukturanalyse einer nationalen Minderheit in der Grossstadt.* Munich and Vienna: R. Oldenbourg Verlag, 1972.

Gold, Hugo. *Geschichte der Juden in Wien: Ein Gedenkbuch.* Tel Aviv: Olamenu, 1966.

———, ed. *Die Juden und die Judengemeinde Bratislava in Vergangenheit und Gegenwart.* Brünn: Jüdischer Buchverlag, 1932.

———, ed. *Die Juden und Judengemeinden Mährens in Vergangenheit und Gegenwart.* Brünn: Jüdischer Buch- und Kunst Verlag, 1929.

Goldemund, Heinrich. *Die Wiener Wohnungs-Verhältnisse und Vorschläge zur Verbesserung derselben.* Vienna, 1910.

Goldhammer, Leo. *Die Juden Wiens: Eine statistische Studie.* Vienna and Leipzig: R. Löwit, 1927.

Goldsmith, Emanuel S. *Architects of Yiddishism at the Beginning of the Twentieth Century.* Rutherford, N.J.: Fairleigh Dickinson University Press and London: Associated University Presses, 1976.

Goldstein, Sidney. *Patterns of Mobility, 1910–1950: The Norristown Study.* Philadelphia: University of Pennsylvania Press, 1958.

Gordon, Milton M. *Assimilation in American Life: The Role of Race, Religion and National Origins.* New York: Oxford University Press, 1964.

Grunfeld, Frederic V. *Prophets without Honour: A Background to Freud, Kafka, Einstein and Their World.* New York: Holt, Rinehart and Winston, 1979.

Grunwald, Max. *90 Jahre israelitische Kinderbewahranstalt (Wien 1843–1933).* Vienna: Wilhartitz, 1933.

———. *Vienna.* Philadelphia: Jewish Publication Society, 1936.

Guest, Avery M., and James A. Weed. "Ethnic Residential Segregation: Patterns of Change." *American Journal of Sociology* 81 (1976), pp. 1088–1111.

Gurock, Jeffrey S. *When Harlem Was Jewish 1870–1930.* New York: Columbia University Press, 1979.

Haas, Theodor. *Die Juden in Mähren: Darstellung der Rechtsgeschichte und Statistik unter besonderer Berücksichtigung des 19. Jahrhunderts.* Brünn: Jüdischer Buch- und Kunstverlag, M. Hickl, 1908.

Habas, Braha. *Vina* (Vienna). Tel-Aviv, 1934 (in Hebrew).

Handlin, Oscar. *Boston's Immigrants, 1790–1880: A Study in Acculturation.* Rev. ed. Cambridge, Mass.: Harvard University Press, 1959.

Handlin, Oscar, and John Burchard, eds. *The Historian and the City.* Cambridge, Mass.: M.I.T. and Harvard University Presses, 1963.

Hannak, Jacques. *Karl Renner und seine Zeit.* Vienna: Europa Verlag, 1965.

Hanák, Péter. *Magyarország története, 1890–1918* (History of Hungary). 2 vols. Budapest, 1978.

Hantsch, Hugo. *Die Nationalitätenfrage im alten Oesterreich.* Vienna: Herold, 1953.

Hardy, Charles. *The Housing Problem of the City of Vienna.* Washington, D.C.: The Brookings Institute, 1934.

Häusler, Wolfgang. "Der Weg des Wiener Judentums von der Toleranz bis zur Emancipation." *Jahrbuch des Vereines für Geschichte der Stadt Wien* 30–31 (1974–75), pp. 84–124.

Hecke, Wilhelm. "Die Methode und Technik der oesterreichischen Volkszählungen." *Statistische Monatsschrift* (Vienna) 38 (1912), pp. 466–74.

———. "Die Städte Oesterreichs nach der Volkszählung vom 31. December 1910." *Statistische Monatsschrift* (Vienna) 39 (1913), pp. 179–221.

———. *Die Verschiedenheit der deutschen und slawischen Volksvermehrung in Oesterreich.* Stuttgart: Verlag von Ferdinand Enke, 1916.

———. *Volksvermehrung, Binnenwanderung und Umgangssprache in Oesterreich.* Brünn: Friedrich Irrgang, 1914.

———. *Wachstum und Berufsgliederung der Bevölkerung; Wirtschaftsgeographische Karten und Abhandlungen zur Wirtschaftskunde der Länder der ehemaligen oesterreichisch-ungarischen Monarchie.* Vienna: Handelsmuseum, in Kommission bei E. Hölzel, 1919.

Heer, Friedrich. "Judentum und 'Oesterreichischer Genius.'" In *Land im Strom der Zeit: Oesterreich gestern, heute, morgen,* pp. 293–314. Vienna: Herold, 1958.

Herrmann, Leo. *Nathan Birnbaum: Sein Werk und seine Wandlung.* Berlin: Jüdischer Verlag, 1914.

Hertzberg, Steven. *Strangers within the Gate City: The Jews of Atlanta 1845–1915.* Philadelphia: Jewish Publication Society, 1978.

Hickmann, Anton Leo. *Historisch-statistische Tafeln aus den wichtigsten Gebieten der geistigen und materiellen Entwicklung der k.-k. Reichshaupt- und Residenzstadt Wien im neunzehnten Jahrhundert.* Vienna: Alfred Hölder, 1903.

Hopkins, Richard. "Occupational and Geographical Mobility in Atlanta, 1870–1890." *Journal of Southern History* 34 (1968), pp. 200–213.

Howe, Irving. *World of Our Fathers.* New York and London: Harcourt, Brace, Jovanovitch, 1976.

Hubbard, William. "A Social History of Graz, Austria, 1861–1914." Ph.D. Dissertation, Columbia University, 1973.

________. "Der Wachstumsprozess in den oesterreichischen Grossstädten, 1869–1910; eine historisch-demographische Untersuchung." *Kölner Zeitschrift für Soziologie und Sozialpsychologie* 16 (1973), pp. 386–418.

Hutchinson, E. P. *Immigrants and Their Children, 1850–1950.* New York: Wiley, 1956.

Hyman, Paula. *From Dreyfus to Vichy: The Remaking of French Jewry, 1906–1939.* New York: Columbia University Press, 1979.

Ianni, Francis A. J. "Residential and Occupational Mobility as Indices to the Acculturation of an Ethnic Group." *Social Forces* 36 (1957/58), pp. 65–72.

Iggers, Wilma Abeles. *Karl Kraus: A Viennese Critic of the Twentieth Century.* The Hague: Martinus Nijhoff, 1967.

Inama-Sternegg, K. Th. von. *Die persönlichen Verhältnisse der Wiener Armen.* Vienna: Verein gegen Verarmung und Bettelei in Wien, 1892.

Janik, Allan, and Stephen Toulmin. *Wittgenstein's Vienna.* New York: Simon and Schuster, 1973.

Jansen, C. J., ed. *Readings in the Sociology of Migration.* Oxford and New York: Pergamon Press, 1970.

Jászi, Oscar. *The Dissolution of the Habsburg Monarchy.* 1929. Reprint. Chicago and London: University of Chicago Press, 1961.

Jeiteles, Israel. *Die Kultusgemeinde der Israeliten in Wien mit Benützung des statistischen Volkszählungsoperatus vom Jahre 1869.* Vienna: L. Rosner, 1873.

Jenks, William A. "The Jews in the Hapsburg Empire, 1879–1918." *LBIYB* 16 (1971), pp. 155–62.

________. *Vienna and the Young Hitler.* New York: Columbia University Press, 1960.

"The Jewish Background of Victor and Friedrich Adler: Selected Biographical Notes." *LBIYB* 10 (1965), pp. 266–76.

Johnston, William M. *The Austrian Mind: An Intellectual and Social History 1848–1938.* Berkeley, Calif.: University of California Press, 1972.

Jones, Ernest. *The Life and Work of Sigmund Freud.* Edited and abridged by Lionel Trilling and Steven Marcus. Harmondsworth, Eng.: Penguin Books, 1961.

Joseph, Samuel. *Jewish Immigration to the United States from 1881 to 1910.* Columbia University Studies in History, Economics, and Public Law 59, no. 4 (New York, 1914).

Kaiser, Franz. "Siedlungs-, Bevölkerungs- und Industrieentwicklung der Brigittenau seit der Donauregulierung in historisch-topographischer Sicht." Ph.D. Dissertation, University of Vienna, 1966.

Kann, Robert A. "German-Speaking Jewry during Austria-Hungary's Constitutional Era (1867–1918)." *Jewish Social Studies* 10 (1948), pp. 239–56.

———. *A History of the Habsburg Empire, 1526–1918.* Berkeley, Calif.: University of California Press, 1974.

———. *The Multinational Empire: Nationalism and National Reform in the Habsburg Monarchy 1848–1918.* 2 vols. 1950. Reprint. New York: Octagon Press, 1964.

Kantrowitz, Nathan. *Ethnic and Racial Segregation in the New York Metropolis: Residential Patterns among White Ethnic Groups, Blacks, and Puerto Ricans.* New York: Praeger, 1973.

Kaplun-Kogan, Wladimir W. *Die jüdische Wanderbewegung in der neuesten Zeit (1880–1914).* Bonn: A. Marcus und E. Weber, 1919.

Karbach, Oscar. "The Founder of Political Antisemitism: Georg von Schönerer." *Jewish Social Studies* 7 (1945), pp. 3–30.

Katz, Jacob. *Out of the Ghetto: The Social Background of Jewish Emancipation, 1770–1870.* Cambridge, Mass.: Harvard University Press, 1973.

Katz, Michael B. "Occupational Classification in History." *Journal of Interdisciplinary History* 3 (1972), pp. 63–88.

———. *The People of Hamilton, Canada West: Family and Class in a Mid-Nineteenth-Century City.* Cambridge, Mass.: Harvard University Press, 1975.

Kellner, Leon. "Eine jüdische Toynbee-Halle in Wien." *Ost und West* 1 (1901), pp. 291–98.

Kessner, Thomas. *The Golden Door: Italian and Jewish Immigrant Mobility in New York City 1880–1915.* New York: Oxford University Press, 1977.

Kestenberg-Gladstein, Ruth. "The Jews between Czechs and Germans in the Historic Lands, 1848–1918." In *The Jews of Czechoslovakia.* 2 vols. I, pp. 21–71. Philadelphia: Jewish Publication Society, 1968.

Kisch, Guido. *Judentaufen: Eine historisch-biographisch-psychologisch-soziologische Studie besonders für Berlin und Königsberg.* Berlin: Colloquial Verlag, 1973.

Klaar, Adalbert. *Die Siedlungsformen Wiens.* Vienna: Paul Zsolnay Verlag, 1971.

Klein, Dennis B. *Jewish Origins of the Psychoanalytic Movement.* New York: Praeger, 1981.

Knights, Peter. "Population Turnover, Persistence and Residential Mobility in Boston." In *Nineteenth-Century Cities: Essays in the New Urban History,* edited by Stephan Thernstrom and Richard Sennett, pp. 258–74. New Haven: Yale University Press, 1969.

———. *The Plain People of Boston, 1830–1860: A Study in City Growth.* New York: Oxford University Press, 1971.

Knodel, John. *The Decline of Fertility in Germany, 1871–1939.* Princeton, N.J.: Princeton University Press, 1974.

Knöpfmacher, Wilhelm. *Entstehungsgeschichte und Chronik der Vereinigung "Wien," 1895–1935.* Vienna: n.p., 1935.

Kohn, Hans. "Before 1918 in the Historic Lands." In *The Jews of Czechoslovakia.* 2 vols. I, pp. 12–20. Philadelphia: Jewish Publication Society, 1968.

———. "Eros and Sorrow (Notes on Arthur Schnitzler and Otto Weininger)." *LBIYB* 6 (1961), pp. 152–69.

———. *Karl Kraus, Arthur Schnitzler, Otto Weininger: Aus dem jüdischen Wien der Jahrhundertwende.* Tübingen: J. C. B. Mohr, 1962.

———. *Martin Buber: Sein Werk und seine Zeit.* Cologne: Joseph Melzer, 1961.

Köllmann, Wolfgang. "The Population of Barmen before and during the Period of Industrialization." In *Population in History,* edited by D. V. Glass and E. D. Eversely. London: E. Arnold, 1965.

———. "The Process of Urbanization in Germany at the Height of the Industrialization Period." *Journal of Contemporary History* 4 (1969), pp. 59–76.

———. *Sozialgeschichte der Stadt Barmen im neunzehnten Jahrhundert.* Tübingen: J. C. B. Mohr, 1960.

———. "Zur Bevölkerungsentwicklung ausgewählter deutscher Grossstädte in der Hochindustrialisierungsperiode." *Jahrbuch für Sozialwissenschaft* 18 (1967), pp. 129–44.

Korkis, A. "Zur Bewegung der jüdischen Bevölkerung in Galizien." In *Jüdische Statistik,* edited by Alfred Nossig, pp. 311–15. Berlin: Jüdischer Verlag, 1903.

Körösi, Josef. *Die Hauptstadt Budapest im Jahre 1881; Resultate der Volksbeschreibung und Volkszählung vom 1. Januar 1881.* 3 vols. Berlin: Puttkammer und Mühlbrecht, 1881–83.

———, and Gustav Thirring. *Die Hauptstadt Budapest im Jahre 1891; Resultate der Volksbeschreibung und Volkszählung.* 3 vols. Berlin: Puttkammer und Mühlbrecht, 1894–98.

Krauss, Samuel. *Geschichte der Isr. Armenanstalt in Wien aus Anlass ihrer Jahrhundertfeier aus Archivalien zusammengestellt.* Vienna: Armenanstalt der Isr. Kultusgemeinde, 1922.

Laqueur, Walter. *A History of Zionism.* New York: Holt, Rinehart and Winston, 1972.

Leftwich, Josef. "Stefan Zweig and the World of Yesterday." *LBIYB* 3 (1958), pp. 81–100.

Leser, Norbert. "Austro-Marxism: A Reappraisal." *Journal of Contemporary History* 11 (1976), pp. 133–48.

Lestschinsky, Jacob. "Die jüdische Wanderung, ihre Ursachen und ihre Regelung." *Archiv für Wanderungswesen* 1 (1928/29), pp. 127–31, 168–72; 2 (1929/30), pp. 20–25.

———. *Jewish Migration for the Past Hundred Years.* New York: YIVO, 1944.

———. "The Jews in the Cities of the Republic of Poland." *YIVO Annual of Jewish Social Science* 1 (1946), pp. 156–77.

Liang, Hsi-Huey. "Lower-Class Immigrants in Wilhelmine Berlin." *Central European History* 3 (1970), pp. 94–111.

Lieberson, Stanley. *Ethnic Patterns in American Cities.* New York: The Free Press of Glencoe, 1963.

Lipset, S. M., and Reinhard Bendix. *Social Mobility in Industrial Society.* Berkeley, Calif.: University of California Press, 1959.

Liptzin, Solomon. *Arthur Schnitzler.* New York: Prentice Hall, 1932.

———. *Germany's Stepchildren.* Philadelphia: Jewish Publication Society, 1944.

———. *Richard Beer-Hofmann.* New York: Bloch Publishing Company, 1936.

Löw, Akos. "Die soziale Zusammensetzung der Wiener Juden nach den Trauungs- und Geburtsmatrikeln, 1784–1848." Ph.D. Dissertation, University of Vienna, 1952.

Löwy, Wilhelm. *Das Unterrichtswesen in Wien.* Vol. II, *Mittel- und Hochschulen.* Vienna: k.-k. Hof- und Staatsdruckerei, 1891.

Macartney, C. A. *The Habsburg Empire 1790–1918.* New York: The MacMillan Company, 1969.

McCagg, William O., Jr. *Jewish Nobles and Geniuses in Modern Hungary.* Boulder, Colo.: East European Quarterly, 1972.

McGrath, William J. *Dionysian Art and Populist Politics in Austria.* New Haven: Yale University Press, 1974.

———. "Student Radicalism in Vienna." *Journal of Contemporary History* 2 (1967), pp. 183–201.

Mahler, Raphael. "The Economic Background of Jewish Emigration from Galicia to the United States." *YIVO Annual of Jewish Social Science* 7 (1952), pp. 255–67.

———. *A History of Modern Jewry 1780–1815.* New York: Schocken Books, 1971.

Marrus, Michael R. *The Politics of Assimilation: A Study of the French Jewish Community at the Time of the Dreyfus Affair.* Oxford: Clarendon Press, 1971.

März, Eduard. *Oesterreichische Industrie- und Bankpolitik in der Zeit Franz Josephs I.* Vienna: Europa Verlag, 1968.

Matis, Herbert. *Oesterreichs Wirtschaft 1848–1913: Konjunkturelle Dynamik und gesellschaftlicher Wandel im Zeitalter Franz Josephs I.* Berlin: Duncker und Humblot, 1972.

May, Arthur J. *Vienna in the Age of Franz Joseph.* Norman, Okla.: University of Oklahoma Press, 1966.

———. *The Hapsburg Monarchy 1867–1914.* 1951. Reprint. New York: W. W. Norton and Co., 1968.

Mayer, Arnold F. "Über eine historische Ethnographie Wiens: Das Ziel und der Weg." *Wiener städt. Jahrbuch* (1889), pp. 295–301.

Mayer, Hans, ed. *Hundert Jahre oesterreichischer Wirtschaftsentwicklung, 1848–1948.* Vienna: Springer Verlag, 1949.

Mayer, Sigmund. *Die Wiener Juden 1700–1900: Kommerz, Kultur, Politik.* Vienna and Berlin: R. Löwit Verlag, 1917.

Menes, A. "The Conversion Movement in Prussia during the First Half of the 19th Century." *YIVO Annual of Jewish Social Science* 6 (1951), pp. 187–205.

Messerklinger, Walter. "Die Fruchtbarkeit der Wiener jüdischen Ehen im Verlauf des letzten Jahrhunderts." Ph.D. Dissertation, University of Vienna (Medicine), 1942.

Meyer, Michael A. *The Origins of the Modern Jew: Jewish Identity and European Culture in Germany, 1749–1824.* Detroit: Wayne State University Press, 1967.

Mitchell, Donald. *Gustav Mahler: The Early Years.* London: Rockliff, 1958.

Molisch, Paul. *Geschichte der deutschnationalen Bewegung in Oesterreich von ihren Anfängen bis zum Zerfall der Monarchie.* Jena: G. Fischer, 1926.

———. *Die deutschen Hochschulen in Oesterreich und die politisch-nationale Entwicklung nach dem Jahre 1848.* Munich: Drei Masken, 1922.

Moore, Deborah Dash. *At Home in America: Second Generation New York Jews.* New York: Columbia University Press, 1981.

Moser, Jonny. "Von der Emanzipation zur antisemitischen Bewegung." Ph.D. Dissertation, University of Vienna, 1962.

Moses, Leopold. *Die Juden in Niederoesterreich.* Vienna: Glanz, 1935.

Mosse, George L. *The Crisis of German Ideology: Intellectual Origins of the Third Reich.* New York: Grosset and Dunlop, 1964.

———. *Germans and Jews: The Right, the Left, and the Search for a "Third Force" in Pre-Nazi Germany.* New York: H. Fertig, 1970.

———. *Toward the Final Solution: A History of European Racism.* New York: H. Fertig, 1978.

Mumford, Lewis. *The City in History: Its Origins, Its Transformation, and Its Prospects.* New York: Harcourt, Brace and World, 1961.

Nelli, Humbert S. *Italians in Chicago, 1880–1930: A Study in Ethnic Mobility.* New York: Oxford University Press, 1970.

Newlin, Dika. *Bruckner, Mahler, Schoenberg.* Rev. ed. New York: W. W. Norton, 1978.

Nie, Norman, et al. *Statistical Package for the Social Sciences.* 2nd ed. New York: McGraw-Hill, 1970, 1975.

Nossig, Alfred, ed. *Jüdische Statistik.* Berlin: Jüdischer Verlag, 1903.

———, ed. *Materialien zur Statistik des jüdischen Stammes.* Vienna: Carl Konegin, 1887.

Oehler, I. "Geschichte des 'Leopoldstädter Tempels,' in Wien." *Zeitschrift für die Geschichte der Juden* 1, no. 1 (1964), pp. 22–27.

Oesterreichischer Ingenieur und Architekten Verein. *Wien am Anfang des XX. Jahrhunderts.* 2 vols. Vienna: Gerlach und Wiedling, 1905.

Padover, Saul K. "The Baptism of Marx's Family." *Midstream* 24, no. 6 (June/July 1978), pp. 36–44.

Park, Robert E. "The Urban Community as a Spatial Pattern and a Moral Order." In *On Social Control and Collective Behavior.* Chicago: University of Chicago Press, 1967.

Park, Robert E., Ernest W. Burgess, and Roderick D. McKenzie. *The City.* Chicago: University of Chicago Press, 1925.

Pass, Harriet Z. (Freidenreich). "Kadimah: Jewish Nationalism in Vienna before Herzl." *Columbia University Essays in International Affairs: The Dean's Papers* (1969), pp. 119–36.

Paulsen, Friedrich. *Geschichte des gelehrten Unterrichts auf den deutschen Schulen und Universitäten vom Ausgang des Mittelalters bis zur Gegenwart.* 2nd rev. ed. Leipzig: Veit & Co., 1896–97.

Petermann, Reinhard E. *Wien im Zeitalter Kaiser Franz Josephs I.* Vienna: R. Lechner, 1908.

Philippovich von Philippsberg, Eugen von. *Wiener Wohnungsverhältnisse.* Berlin: Carl Heymann, 1894.

Poppel, Stephen M. *Zionism in Germany, 1897-1933: The Shaping of a Jewish Identity.* Philadelphia: Jewish Publication Society, 1977.

Pulzer, P. G. J. "The Austrian Liberals and the Jewish Question, 1867–1914." *Journal of Central European Affairs* 23 (1963), pp. 131–42.

———. Pulzer, Peter G. J. *The Rise of Political Anti-Semitism in Germany and Austria.* New York: John Wiley and Sons, 1964.

Pounds, Norman J. G. "The Urbanization of East-Central and Southeast Europe: An Historical Perspective." In *Eastern Europe: Essays on Geographical Problems,* edited by George W. Hoffmann. New York: Praeger, 1971.

Rabinbach, Anson G. "The Migration of Galician Jews to Vienna, 1857–1880." *Austrian History Yearbook* 11 (1975), pp. 44–54.

Rainey, Reuben M. "Freud As Student of Religion: Perspectives on the Background and Development of His Thought." Ph.D. Dissertation, Columbia University, 1971.

Rauchberg, Heinrich. *Die Bevölkerung Oesterreichs auf Grund der Ergebnisse der Volkszählung vom 31. December 1890.* Vienna: Alfred Hölder, 1895.

———. "Die Heimatsverhältnisse der Bevölkerung Oesterreichs nach den Ergebnissen der Volkszählung vom 31. December 1890." *Statistische Monatsschrift* (Vienna) 18 (1892), pp. 345–401.

———. "Der Zug nach der Stadt." *Statistiche Monatsschrift* (Vienna) 19 (1893), pp. 125–200.

Ravenstein, E. G. "The Laws of Migration." *Journal of the Royal Statistical Society* 48 (1885), pp. 167–227; 52 (1889), pp. 241–301.

Redford, Arthur. *Labour Migration in England, 1800–1850.* 2nd ed. Manchester, Eng.: Manchester University Press, 1964.

Reinharz, Jehuda. *Fatherland or Promised Land: The Dilemma of the German Jew, 1893–1914.* Ann Arbor: University of Michigan Press, 1975.

Richarz, Monika. *Der Eintritt der Juden in die akademischen Berufe: Jüdische Studenten und Akademiker in Deutschland.* Tübingen: J. C. B. Mohr, 1974.

Rischin, Moses. *The Promised City: New York's Jews 1870–1914.* 1962. Reprint. New York: Harper Torchbooks, 1970.

Robert, Marthe. *From Oedipus to Moses: Freud's Jewish Identity.* Translated by Ralph Manheim. Garden City, N.Y.: Anchor Books, 1976.

Rogoff, Natalie S. *Recent Trends in Occupational Mobility.* Glencoe, Ill.: Free Press, 1953.

Roof, Wade Clark, Thomas L. Van Valey, and Daphne Spain. "Residential Segregation in Southern Cities: 1970." *Social Forces* 55, no. 1 (September 1976), pp. 59–71.

Roof, W. Clark, and Thomas L. Van Valey. "Residential Segregation and Social Differentiation in Urban Areas." *Social Forces* 51, no. 1 (September 1972), pp. 87–91.

Rosen, Charles. *Schoenberg.* London: Marion Bayers, 1975.

Rosenberg, Terry J., and Robert W. Lake. "Toward a Revised Model of Residential Segregation and Succession: Puerto Ricans in New York, 1960–1970." *American Journal of Sociology* 81 (1976), pp. 1142–50.

Rosenfeld, Julius. *Die Matrikelführung der Israeliten in Oesterreich nach den bestehenden staatlichen Vorschriften.* Vienna: R. Löwit, 1913.

Rosenfeld, M. *Der jüdische Religionsunterricht.* Vienna: R. Löwit, 1920.

Rosenmann, Moses. *Dr. Adolf Jellinek; Sein Leben und Schaffen.* Vienna: J. Schlesinger, 1931.

Rothkirchen, Livia. "Slovakia: I. 1848–1918." In *The Jews of Czechoslovakia.* 2 vols. I, pp. 72–84. Philadelphia: Jewish Publication Society, 1968.

Rotter, Hans, and Adolf Schmieger. *Das Ghetto in der Wiener Leopoldstadt.* Vienna: Burgverlag, 1926.

Rozenblit, Marsha L. "The Assertion of Identity—Jewish Student Nationalism at the University of Vienna before the First World War." *LBIYB* 27 (1982), pp. 171–86.

Rudolph, Richard L. *Banking and Industrialization in Austria-Hungary: The Role of Banks in the Industrialization of the Czech Crownlands, 1873–1914.* Cambridge and New York: Cambridge University Press, 1976.

Ruppin, Arthur. *The Jewish Fate and Future.* Translated by E. W. Dickes. London: MacMillan and Co., 1940.

———. *The Jews of Today.* Translated by Margery Bentwich. New York: Henry Holt & Co., 1913.

———. *Soziologie der Juden.* 2 vols. Berlin: Jüdischer Verlag, 1930.

Russell, James E. *German Higher Schools: Their History, Organization and Methods of Secondary Education in Germany.* New York: Longmans, Green, 1899.

Samter, N. *Judentaufen im 19. Jahrhundert mit besonderer Berücksichtigung Preussens.* Berlin: Poppelauer, 1906.

Schimmer, Gustav Adolph. *Die Bevölkerung von Wien und seinen Umgebungen nach dem Beruf und der Beschäftigung.* Vienna, 1874.

———. *Die Juden in Oesterreich nach der Zählung vom 31. December 1880.* Vienna: Hölder, 1881.

———. *Statistik des Judenthums in den im Reichsrathe vertretenen Königreichen und Ländern.* Vienna: k.-k. Hof- und Staatsdruckerei, 1873.

Schleischer, Mordche Schlome. "Geschichte der spaniolischen Juden in Wien." Ph.D. Dissertation, University of Vienna, 1934?

Schmidtbauer, Peter. "Zur sozialen Situation der Wiener Juden im Jahre 1857." *Studia Judaica Austriaca* 6 (1978), pp. 57–89.

Schnitzler, Henry. "Gay Vienna: Myth and Reality." *Journal of the History of Ideas* 15 (1954), pp. 94–118.

Schoeps, Julius H. "Modern Heirs of the Maccabees—The Beginnings of the Vienna Kadimah, 1882–1897." *LBIYB* 27 (1982), pp. 155–70.

Schorsch, Ismar. "Moritz Güdemann—Rabbi, Historian and Apologist." *LBIYB* 11 (1966), pp. 42–66.

———. *Jewish Reactions to German Anti-Semitism, 1870–1914.* New York: Columbia University Press, 1972.

Schorske, Carl E. *Fin-de-Siècle Vienna: Politics and Culture.* New York: Alfred A. Knopf, 1980.

———. "Politics and the Psyche in *fin-de-siècle* Vienna: Schnitzler and Hofmannsthal." *American Historical Review* 66, no. 4 (1961), pp. 930–46.

———. "Politics and Patricide in Freud's Interpretation of Dreams." *American Historical Review* 78 (1973), pp. 328–47.

———. "Politics in a New Key: An Austrian Triptych." *Journal of Modern History* 39 (1967), pp. 343–86.

Sedlaczek, Stephan. *Die definitiven Ergebnisse der Volkszählung vom 31. December 1890 in der k.-k. Reichshaupt- und Residenzstadt Wien.* Vienna: Alfred Hölder, 1891.

________. *Die k.-k. Reichshaupt- und Residenzstadt Wien: Ergebnisse der Volkszählung vom 31. December 1880.* Vienna: Verlag des Wiener Magistrates, 1887.

________. *Die Wohnverhältnisse in Wien; Ergebnisse der Volkszählung vom 31. December 1890.* Vienna: Verlag des Wiener Magistrates, 1893.

Sherrow, Fred Solomon. "Patterns of Religious Intermarriage among American College Graduates." Ph.D. Dissertation, Columbia University, 1971.

Shorter, Edward. *The Historian and the Computer: A Practical Guide.* Englewood, N. J.: Prentice-Hall, 1971.

Silberner, Edmund. "Austrian Social Democracy and the Jewish Problem." *Historia Judaica* 8, no. 2 (October 1951), pp. 121–40.

Simon, Ernst. "Sigmund Freud, the Jew." *LBIYB* 2 (1957), pp. 270–305.

Simon, Walter B. "The Jewish Vote in Austria." *LBIYB* 16 (1971), pp. 97–121.

Skalnik, Kurt. *Dr. Karl Lueger: Der Mann zwischen den Zeiten.* Vienna and Munich: Herold, 1954.

Sklare, Marshall. *America's Jews.* New York: Random House, 1971.

Sole, Aryeh. "Subcarpathian Ruthenia: 1918–1938." In *The Jews of Czechoslovakia.* 2 vols. I, pp. 125–54. Philadelphia: Jewish Publication Society, 1968.

Spiegel, L. "Das Heimatrecht und die Gemeinden." *Schriften des Vereines für Sozialpolitik* 112 (1907), pp. 7–49.

Spigl, Elisabeth. "Das Wiener Judentum der achtziger Jahre in Literatur und Presse." Ph.D. Dissertation, University of Vienna, 1943.

Springer, Ernst. "Das Mittelschulwesen." In *100 Jahre Unterrichts-Ministerium 1848–1948; Festschrift des Bundesministeriums für Unterricht in Wien,* pp. 114–38. Vienna: Oesterreichischer Bundesverlag, 1948.

Statistique concernant la Galacie et la Bukovine. Paris: Impr. Slave, n.d.

Stillschweig, Kurt. *Die Juden Osteuropas in den Minderheitenverträgen.* Berlin: J. Jastrow, 1936.

________. "Die nationalitätenrechtliche Stellung der Juden im alten Oesterreich." *Monatsschrift für Geschichte und Wissenschaft des Judentums* 81 (1937), pp. 321–40.

________. "Nationalism and Autonomy among Eastern European Jewry." *Historia Judaica* 6, no. 1 (April 1944), pp. 27–68.

________. "Zur neueren Geschichte der jüdischen Autonomie." *Monatsschrift für Geschichte und Wissenschaft des Judentums* 83 (1939), pp. 509–32.

Stouffer, Samuel A. "Intervening Opportunities: A Theory Relating Mobility and Distance." *American Sociological Review* 5 (1940), pp. 845–67.

Szajkowski, Zosa. "Conflicts in the *Alliance israélite universelle* and the Founding of the Anglo-Jewish Association, the Vienna *Allianz* and the *Hilfsverein.*" *Jewish Social Studies* 19 (1957), pp. 29–50.

Taeuber, Karl E., and Alma F. Taeuber. *Negroes in Cities: Residential Segregation and Neighborhood Change.* Chicago: Aldine Publishing, 1965.

———. "The Negro as an Immigrant Group: Recent Trends in Racial and Ethnic Segregation in Chicago." *American Journal of Sociology* 69 (1964), pp. 347–82.

Tal, Uriel. *Christians and Jews in Germany: Religion, Politics, and Ideology in the Second Reich, 1870–1914*. Translated by Noah Jonathan Jacobs. Ithaca, N. Y. and London: Cornell University Press, 1975.

Taylor, A. J. P. *The Habsburg Monarchy, 1809–1918: A History of the Austrian Empire and Austria-Hungary*. 1948. Reprint. Chicago and London: University of Chicago Press, 1976.

Thon, Jakob. *Die Juden in Oesterreich*. Berlin: Bureau für Statistik der Juden, 1908.

Thernstrom, Stephan. *The Other Bostonians: Poverty and Progress in the American Metropolis, 1880–1970*. Cambridge, Mass.: Harvard University Press, 1973.

———. *Poverty and Progress: Social Mobility in a Nineteenth Century City*. Cambridge, Mass.: Harvard University Press, 1964.

———. "Reflections on the New Urban History." In *Historical Studies Today*, edited by Felix Gilbert and Stephen Graubard, pp. 320–36. New York: W. W. Norton, 1972.

———. "Urbanization, Migration, and Social Mobility in Late-Nineteenth-Century America." In *Towards a New Past: Dissenting Essays in American History*, edited by Barton J. Bernstein, pp. 158–75. New York: Pantheon, 1968.

———. "Working Class Social Mobility in Industrial America." In *Essays in Theory and History: An Approach to the Social Sciences*, edited by Melvin Richter, pp. 221–38. Cambridge, Mass.: Harvard University Press, 1970.

Thernstrom, Stephan, and Peter Knights. "Men in Motion: Some Data and Speculations about Urban Population Mobility in Nineteenth-Century America." *Journal of Interdisciplinary History* 1 (1970/71), pp. 7–35.

Thernstrom, Stephan, and Richard Sennett, eds. *Nineteenth-Century Cities: Essays in the New Urban History*. New Haven: Yale University Press, 1969.

Tietze, Hans. *Die Juden Wiens: Geschichte-Wirtschaft-Kultur*. Leipzig and Vienna: E. P. Tal, 1933.

Till, Rudolf. "Geschichte der spanischen Juden in Wien." *Jahrbuch Wien* 6–7 (1946/47), pp. 108–23.

———. "Zur Herkunft der Wiener Bevölkerung im 19. Jahrhundert." *Vierteljahrsschrift für Sozial- und Wirtschaftsgeschichte* 34 (1941), pp. 16–37.

van Arkel, Dirk. "Antisemitism in Austria." Ph.D. Dissertation, University of Leiden, 1966.

Vienna. Stadtbauamt. *Festschrift herausgegeben anlässlich der Hundertjahrfeier des Wiener Stadtbauamtes am 12. Mai 1935 von der Technikerschaft des Wiener Stadtbauamtes und der grossen technischen Unternehmungen der Stadt Wien*, edited by Rudolf Tillman. Vienna: Deutscher Verlag für Jugend und Volk, 1935.

Vienna. Verein für Geschichte der Stadt Wien. *Wien in der liberalen Ära*. Forschungen und Beiträge zur Wiener Stadt-Geschichte. Vol. I. Vienna: Verein für Geschichte der Stadt Wien, 1978.

Wagner-Rieger, Renate, ed. *Die Wiener Ringstrasse: Bild einer Epoche; Die Erweiterung der inneren Stadt Wien unter Kaiser Franz Joseph.* 5 vols. Vienna: H. Böhlaus Nachf., 1969–.

Walter, Bruno. *Gustav Mahler.* Translated by James Galston. 1941. Reprint. New York: Vienna House, 1973.

Wandruszka, Adam. *Geschichte einer Zeitung: Das Schicksal der "Presse" und der "Neuen Freien Presse" von 1848 zur zweiten Republik.* Vienna: Neue Wiener Presse, 1958.

Wandycz, Piotr S. *The Lands of Partitioned Poland, 1795–1918.* Seattle and London: University of Washington Press, 1974.

Warner, Sam B., Jr. *Streetcar Suburbs: The Process of Growth in Boston, 1870–1900.* 1962. Reprint. New York: Atheneum, 1973.

Weber, Adna Ferrin. *The Growth of Cities in the Nineteenth Century: A Study in Statistics.* New York: MacMillan, 1899. Reprint. Ithaca, N. Y.: Cornell University Press, 1963.

Wechsberg, Joseph. *Sounds of Vienna.* London: Weidenfeld and Nicolson, 1968.

Weinzierl, Erika. "Die Stellung der Juden in Oesterreich seit dem Staatsgrundgesetz von 1867." *Zeitschrift für die Geschichte der Juden* 5, no. 2/3 (1968), pp. 89–96.

Werner, Siegmund. "Die jüdischen Studentenverbindungen in Oesterreich." *Ost und West* 1, no. 6 (June 1901), pp. 415–22.

Wertheimer, Jack L. "German Policy and Jewish Politics: The Absorption of East European Jews in Germany (1868–1914)." Ph.D. Dissertation, Columbia University, 1978.

Whiteside, Andrew G. *The Socialism of Fools: Georg Ritter von Schönerer and Austrian Pan-Germanism.* Berkeley, Calif.: University of California Press, 1975.

Wien: Eine Auswahl von Stadtbildern. 5th rev. ed. Vienna: Gemeinde Wien, n.d.

Windt, B. "Die Juden an der Mittel- und Hochschulen Oesterreichs seit 1850." *Statistische Monatsschrift* (Vienna) 7 (1881), pp. 442–57.

Wirth, Louis. *The Ghetto.* Chicago and London: University of Chicago Press, 1928, 1956.

Wischnitzer, Mark. *To Dwell in Safety: The Story of Jewish Migration Since 1880.* Philadelphia: Jewish Publication Society, 1948.

Wistrich, Robert S. "Karl Kraus: Jewish Prophet or Renegade." *European Judaism* (June 1975), pp. 32–38.

———. "Marxism and Jewish Nationalism: The Theoretical Roots of Confrontation." *Jewish Journal of Sociology* 17, no. 1 (June 1975), pp. 43–54.

———. *Socialism and the Jews: The Dilemmas of Assimilation in Germany and Austria-Hungary.* Rutherford, N.J.: Farleigh Dickinson University Press, and London and East Brunswick, N.J.: Associated University Presses, 1982.

Wolf, Gerson. *Geschichte der Juden in Wien (1156–1876).* 1876. Reprint. Vienna: Geyer-Edition, 1974.

———. *Die Juden.* Vienna: Prohaska, 1883.

———. *Judentaufen in Oesterreich.* Vienna: Herzfeld und Bauer, 1863.

———. *Vom ersten bis zum zweiten Tempel: Geschichte der Israelitischen Cultusgemeinde in Wien (1820–1860).* Vienna: Wilhelm Braumüller, 1861.

Wrigley, E. A. *Population and History.* New York: McGraw-Hill, 1969.

Zehavi-Goldhammer, A. "Vina." In *Arim v'Imahot b'Yisroel,* I, pp. 176–289 (Hebrew). Jerusalem: Mosad ha-Rav Kook, 1946.

Zeitschrift für Demographie und Statistik der Juden. Berlin: Bureau für Statistik der Juden, 1905–1922?

Zemlinszky, Adolf von. *Geschichte der türkish-israelitischen Gemeinde zu Wien: von ihrer Gründung bis heute nach historischen Daten.* Vienna: Knopfelmacher, 1888.

Zohn, Harry. *Karl Kraus.* New York: Twayne Publishers, 1971.

———. *Wiener Juden in der deutschen Literatur.* Tel Aviv: Olamenu, 1964.

———. *Oesterreichische Juden in der Literatur; ein bio-bibliographisches Lexikon.* Tel Aviv: Olamenu, 1969.

———. "A Crown for Zion: Karl Kraus and the Jews." *Wiener Library Bulletin* 24, no. 2 (1970), pp. 22–25.

Index